Doughboys, the Great War,
and the
Remaking of America

War/Society/Culture EDITED BY MICHAEL FELLMAN

Doughboys, the Great War, and the Remaking of America

JENNIFER D. KEENE

THE JOHNS HOPKINS UNIVERSITY PRESS
BALTIMORE AND LONDON

© 2001 The Johns Hopkins University Press
All rights reserved. Published 2001
Printed in the United States of America on acid-free paper
9 8 7 6 5 4 3 2 1

The Johns Hopkins University Press
2715 North Charles Street
Baltimore, Maryland 21218-4363
www.press.jhu.edu

LIBRARY OF CONGRESS CATALOGING-IN-PUBLICATION DATA
Keene, Jennifer D., 1962–
  Doughboys, the Great War, and the remaking of America /
  Jennifer D. Keene.
      p.   cm. — (War, society, culture)
  Includes bibliographical references and index.
  ISBN 0-8018-6592-1 (acid-free paper)
    1. World War, 1914-1918—United States.   2. United States.
  Army—History—World War, 1914-1918.   3. Draft—United
  States—History—20th century.   4. United States—History—
  1913-1921.   I. Title.   II. Series.
  D570.1 .K38   2001
  355'.00973'09041—dc21   00-010273

A catalog record for this book is available from the British Library.

CONTENTS

List of Maps and Illustrations   vii

Preface   ix

Acknowledgments   xi

Introduction   1

1. A Force to Call Our Own: Establishing a National Army   8

2. Americans as Warriors   35

3. The Meaning of Obedience   62

4. The Politics of Race: Racial Violence and Harmony in the Wartime Army   82

5. Forging Their Own Alliances: American Soldiers' Relations with the French and the Germans   105

6. The Legacy of the War for the Army   132

7. War Memories: Reexamining the Social Contract   161

8. "The Yanks Are Starving Everywhere": The Bonus March   179

Epilogue. The Great War's Final Legacy to the Country: The GI Bill   205

Notes   215

Sources   275

Index   287

MAPS AND ILLUSTRATIONS

Maps

1 The American Expeditionary Forces, 1918   45
2 The Occupation of the Rhineland after the Armistice   119
3 American Forces in Northern Russia, September 4, 1918–
  August 5, 1919   146

Illustrations follow p. 104

Citizen-soldiers entering a training camp
Illustration of the similarity between boxing and bayonet fighting
A training camp boxing class in progress
Friendship between an American and a French soldier
A helmet saves a soldier's life on the Western Front
A ruined French church
Collecting souvenirs on the Western Front
Black soldiers haul an artillery piece
Engineers at work
Black American soldiers help a French civilian rebuild his home
An American officer and a German officer shake hands after the
    Armistice
American soldiers sightseeing in Paris
Veterans lobby Congress during the 1932 Bonus March
Camp Marks in the summer of 1932

PREFACE

Doughboys, Yanks, Pershing's Crusaders: these were common nicknames for the American men who marched off to fight in the Great War. I often joked during the research and writing of this book about having undertaken a crusade of my own to restore to our historical memory an appreciation of the importance of World War I in American history. The public and historians eagerly study the Civil War, World War II, and the Vietnam War, but World War I has received scant attention recently. Compared to those other great conflicts, it is seen as a brief, mostly dissatisfying, experience, with little transcendent significance.

Some complain that the American effort in World War I lacked a key, pivotal battle that defined the war's purpose, strategy, and suffering. The other great wars had their horrific days, such as Antietam and the D-Day landings, which represent the horror of combat and the immensity of the struggle in stark, dramatic terms. Because American battle deaths in the Great War (50,280) pale in comparison to those of France (1.3 million), Britain (900,000), Germany (1.6 million), and Russia (1.7 million), the United States is often portrayed as having been "barely bloodied" by it. But what of the Meuse-Argonne offensive in the fall of 1918, a historically unique great battle? Combat in this densely forested and well-defended area lasted forty-seven days and involved nearly 1.2 million American soldiers, more than the entire Confederate Army during the Civil War. Casualty rates averaged 2,550 a day, with 6,000 Americans dying each week. With no distinct beginning and end to the fighting, as in previous great battles, the psychological and physical horror was analogous to the continuous struggles waged by platoons of men during the jungle campaigns of World War II and the Vietnam War. Day after day, the numbers of dead and dying rose steadily. Once the terrifying reality of this momentous battle begins to take form, it becomes harder to argue there was no defining battlefield experience for the Americans.

This book looks beyond the battlefield, however, to seek the true importance of the Great War in American history. Here again, the domestic impact of the war seemingly pales when compared to other key conflicts. The Civil War ended slavery, and World War II established the United States as a nuclear and economic superpower. How did World War I change America? In the pages that follow, I argue that it was a pivotal experience because the Great War generation shaped the contours of the modern American military and was responsible for the most sweeping piece of social welfare legislation in American history, the GI Bill. World War I transformed the federal Army into a strong, national institution, and these soldiers played a critical role in shaping it. As a result, they determined what mass military service would mean for the millions of American men who served throughout the rest of the twentieth century. This generation left its mark on domestic society as well. Conscription set in motion a contentious twenty-year relationship between these veterans and the U.S. government, one that threatened to become violent during the Great Depression when veteran Bonus Marchers descended on Washington, D.C.

Vowing not to let the government repeat the mistakes of the past, World War I veterans wrote the GI Bill and maneuvered it through Congress during World War II. Through their political activism, drawing on their experiences in the Great War, these Doughboys remade the economic and social landscape of America. This is their story.

ACKNOWLEDGMENTS

I have many friends, colleagues, mentors, funding organizations, and editors to thank for their unwavering support while I completed this book.

At Carnegie-Mellon University, I discovered intellectual kinship with a wonderful group of unique and talented individuals. John Hinshaw, Madi Goodman, and Steve Hoffman helped make those years in Pittsburgh very special ones. In my dissertation committee, no graduate student could have asked for a brighter, more enthusiastic group of scholars to direct one's research program. John Modell, Lizabeth Cohen, and Lynn Eden pushed me when I needed to be pushed, encouraged independent thinking when my ideas took me into uncharted territory, and, most important, read absolutely everything I sent them quickly and critically. An R. K. Mellon Fellowship and other in-house funding eased the financial burden of my graduate student years. I also owe much to Peter Stearns, Joe Trotter, and Susan Ambrose.

The bulk of my dissertation research took place in the U.S. Army Military History Institute in Carlisle, Pennsylvania, and the National Archives in Washington, D.C. In Carlisle, Richard Sommers, David Keogh, John J. Slonaker, and Louise Arnold-Friend provided key guidance, and a Research Associate Grant helped defray the costs of traveling. After many months of shadowing each other in our journeys through World War I records, Nancy Gentile Ford and I finally met and became fast friends. I am beholden to Tim Nenninger of the National Archives for alerting me to the existence of the Thomas Files, a series of World War II–era studies of World War I personnel policies, and to John Taylor for suggesting that I consult intelligence files. Michael Knapp was always willing to take a walk with me into the stacks to locate an obscure reference, and Mitchell Yockelson went beyond the call of duty too many times to count.

Once I began the onerous process of turning the dissertation into a book, my real travel adventures began. Thanks to travel funds provided by a Perrine Fellowship, I traveled to West Branch, Iowa, to the Herbert Hoover Presidential Library. There, Dwight Miller provided invaluable help using Hoover's private and public correspondence and introduced me to the best pie in town. During this trip, Doug Craig from Australian National University shared what nightlife West Branch had to offer in midwinter to two lone researchers, and I thank him profusely for the later insights he offered into my project during an AHA lunch (it is about conscription, Jennifer), which revolutionized my thinking.

Bill Wallach and Nancy Barlett made my trip to the Bentley Historical Library at the University of Michigan, funded by a Bordin-Gillette Travel Fellowship, profitable and fun. I shall always remember sitting in a near empty gym with Bill watching the women's basketball team play, although I can no longer recall whether they won or lost that night. A Kaiser Research Support Grant made possible a visit to the Archives of Labor and Urban Affairs at Wayne State University. Later that spring, after having received a Beeke-Levy Research Fellowship, I spent a month working in the Franklin D. Roosevelt Presidential Library in Hyde Park, New York, where the staff, especially Raymond Teichman, were terrific.

As much traveling as I completed in the United States for this project, the real adventure began when I accepted a Ministère des Affaires étrangères *bourse post-doctorale* from the French government to spend a year in France to work in the French military archives. Living in a foreign city for the first time with only my high school French to support me, I was terrified. Words cannot express my gratitude to Marianne Debouzy, who took me under her wing from the moment I arrived and carefully shepherded me through the new world of French academia. As a mentor, she listened carefully to what I had to say before steering me in a better, more productive direction. As a friend, she no doubt never knew how her warm embrace gave me the confidence to strike out on my own and take the risk of stumbling along the way. In the second part of that year, after she returned from the United States, Catherine Collomp became a dear colleague. Her support for my grant application had brought me to France, and her energy and enthusiasm for maintaining cross-Atlantic collaborations continue to enrich my intellectual life. Naomi Wulf provided wonderful intellectual exchanges throughout the year, and best of all became a lifelong friend. Annick Foucrier alone deserves the credit for my eventual mastery of French, and for pushing me to give talks on my project while in Paris. Because I was desperate to fit a lifetime of experiences into one year, Annick's enthusiasm and companionship considerably enriched my tour of the culinary and theatrical sites of Paris.

To be able to go to France, I took a one-year leave from my two-year National Research Council Postdoctoral Research Fellowship at the Army Research Institute for Behavioral and Social Sciences. At ARI, I was the only historian among a group of psychologists and sociologists conducting research on personnel polices in the modern Army. Once again, I was fortunate to receive support and guidance from an outstanding mentor. Paul Gade introduced me to life-course research, a field that significantly shaped the second part of the book. Given his unfaltering support for this project, Paul is undoubtedly pleased to see it finally in print.

For their encouragement and support along the way, I would also like to thank Harlow Sheidley at the University of Colorado in Colorado Springs, Ed Angel, Jim Horton, and Ron Spector at George Washington University, Margaret Darrow at Dartmouth College, and Kathy Ogren and Jim Sandos at the University of Redlands. Bob Brugger, my editor at the Johns Hopkins University Press, maintained steady enthusiasm and interest in this project over the years it took to turn the dissertation into a book, and I thank him for his patience and helpful guidance. Michael Fellman at Simon Fraser University, the editor for the War/Society/Culture series, offered many fine and important suggestions that helped to shorten and tighten the book's argument. Stuart McConnell of Pitzer College did a meticulous job in reviewing the original manuscript and provided a detailed critique that reflected an extraordinary recognition of the importance of his role as an outside reviewer. Peter Dreyer, my copy editor, read the book thoughtfully as well, and he has my thanks for improving the clarity and lucidity of the prose.

Finally, my family has my love. If my parents Lucille Keene and Michael Keene, my stepmother Pat, my siblings Emily, Neil, and Sam, my mother- and father-in-law Caroline and Howard Wilkins, and my sister-in-law Caroline Wilkins ever doubted that some day there would be a book that they could put on their shelves, they never let me know. I must at last thank the one person who often knows me better than I know myself, my husband, Paul Wilkins. Our life together has been one of adventure and purpose. Paul's steadfast faith in my abilities, both athletic and intellectual, provided me with the strength to persevere when the future looked uncertain, and his admonition to enjoy the moment was always good, if usually ignored, advice. He is my true soul mate, and I dedicate this book to him.

Doughboys, the Great War,
and the
Remaking of America

INTRODUCTION

During World War I, conscription filled the ranks of the U.S. military and set in motion a volatile relationship that shaped American society for the next twenty-five years. Both the federal government and its citizen-soldiers emerged from their joint wartime undertaking indelibly changed. Citizen-soldiers entered an army whose contours and characteristics remained undefined, and they soon seized the opportunity to make their mark on this powerful state institution.[1] The army had similar designs on transforming the attitudes, opinions, and behavior of its citizen-soldier population. Army officials envisioned obedient soldiers fighting bravely on the battlefield and politically active veterans avidly supporting expanded defense budgets. They never imagined these politicized servicemen viewing conscription as a social contract whose terms they could negotiate both during and after the war.

The classic works on the American experience in World War I view the war as a moral crusade, filled with broad ideological pronouncements by American civil and military leaders and a quest for adventure by citizen-soldiers. The reality of trench warfare and the failure of the war to become the "war to end all wars" caused this high-mindedness and youthful spirit to devolve into modernist disillusion, even as soldiers came home with their basic faith in their military leaders and democratic values intact. In this study, I offer a different interpretation of the Great War experience. Instead of focusing on ideological questions or military strategy, I discuss citizen-soldiers' experiences with training, combat, discipline, race relations, the French, and their return home, among other things. After scrutinizing the actual behavior and attitudes of citizen-soldiers, it becomes clear that the war experience bore little resemblance to the great crusade or innocent adventure other historical accounts describe. The problems with discipline, racial violence, fraternization, and disaffected veterans created near constant conflict between citizen-soldiers and army authorities. This book recounts these struggles and their resolutions, thus offering a dramatically different paradigm for understanding the American experience in the Great War.

When the United States entered World War I in 1917, the federal government broke with tradition and conscripted the majority of the required wartime force. With this one decision, the meaning of U.S. military service changed significantly. Most citizen-soldiers who fought in the Civil War and the Spanish-American War were volunteers who wore the uniforms of their individual states. During the Civil War, the federal government used conscription mainly to encourage increasingly reluctant men to either volunteer or reenlist and avoid the stigma of being conscripts. The Union Army ultimately only drafted 8 percent of its wartime force. The Confederacy used conscription to prevent enlistees from leaving the army and to build its force, and raised a greater proportion of its troops (estimates range between 10 and 21 percent) with the draft. Both sides turned to conscription in desperation and considered conscripts unpatriotic and untrustworthy on the battlefield. In the Great War, however, the country immediately embraced the draft as an honorable, efficient, and equitable way to raise an army. The World War I generation served in the country's first national mass army, of which 72 percent was conscripted. Within eighteen months, federal army forces grew from roughly 127,588 regular army active-duty troops and 164,292 National Guard reserves to nearly 3.9 million soldiers.[2] Rapid growth, along with the logistical difficulties of instructing, transporting, and commanding a massive force overseas, made organizing the wartime army an unprecedented and difficult task. This turbulent situation also provided citizen-soldiers with an unparalleled opportunity to affect what kind of institution the modern American army would become.

On the eve of America's entry into the war, far in arrears of armies in European nations, the federal army created a General Staff and secured more authority over the National Guard. Gaining exclusive control of the nation's manpower resources through conscription complemented these earlier efforts to centralize command in the modern U.S. military establishment. Individual communities selected men for the draft, but once they had donned their federal uniforms, their state governments had little influence over where they fought or who commanded them. Instead, it became up to individual soldiers, drawing when possible on help from members of Congress or their families, to manage their own fates in the U.S. Army.

The American public affectionately referred to these soldiers as *doughboys*, a nickname for infantrymen since the nineteenth century. Some historians trace the name's origins to 1854, when infantrymen along the Texas border cleaned their belts with a "dough-like" pipe clay and lived in adobe buildings. A competing account claims that the name doughboy came from the large brass buttons that the infantry wore in the Civil War. Although their nickname tied them to the traditions of America's past armies, this generation of doughboys would share little else with their predecessors.

Army officials aspired to monopolize the army-building process, but they soon faced immediate obstacles from the very citizen-soldiers they sought to control. In the end, battles between army officials and citizen-soldiers shaped the modern organization every bit as much as the conflict roaring along the Western Front. At first glance, the coercive power the army employed to control troops would seem to have eliminated the possibility of citizen-soldiers exerting any independent influence on official policy or organizational behavior. Instead, over time, conscripted civilians transformed the way the army ran itself and fought the war. All areas of military life—training, leadership, combat, discipline, race relations—became battlegrounds where citizen-soldiers and army officials vied for the upper hand. Nearly any concession to citizen-soldiers amounted to a loss or modification of the army's goal of retaining the desired unilateral authority to direct its wartime force. This study explores why citizen-soldiers gained substantial ability at this particular historical moment to affect policy decisions and organizational habits and investigates how citizen-soldiers wielded their power.

The draft gave citizen-soldiers the opportunity and motivation to shape the modern military. This generation accepted conscription as an equitable and efficient way to raise an army. Draft riots and widespread desertion had plagued Abraham Lincoln's and Jefferson Davis's experimental conscription efforts during the Civil War, but in 1917, Americans overwhelmingly embraced compulsory national service as a way for men to fulfill their obligation to defend their country in a time of crisis.[3] When Congress first declared war on the Central Powers in April, President Woodrow Wilson expected to send a small, representative expeditionary force to France and to offer mostly economic support to the Allied nations. It soon became apparent, however, that the Allies needed fresh troops as well as matériel. By May, the United States had agreed to send a substantial number of troops to Europe. Wilson promised the nation a selective service system that equalized the risk of serving and guaranteed the smooth functioning of the wartime economy.[4] Beyond its ideological and economic appeal, the political expediency of a draft also attracted Wilson, who wanted to direct the war in a politically neutral manner and therefore needed to establish a wartime coalition of his political opponents and allies. Theodore Roosevelt's announcement that he intended to sail immediately to France with his own independently raised band of volunteers posed a serious political threat to Wilson's wartime leadership. This declaration by the enormously popular former president had the inadvertent effect of resolving Wilson's doubts about conscription in March 1917, even before he seriously considered sending a large mass army overseas.[5] In eliminating the possibility that Roosevelt might use a military campaign to revive his flagging political career, Wilson also determined how the nation would raise its largest military force to date in its history.

Unlike their political and military leaders, however, citizen-soldiers saw conscription as other than a politically desirable and economically efficient method of filling the ranks. In their eyes, conscription established a social contract between citizen-soldiers and the federal government for the lifetime of the wartime generation. As soldiers, these men focused on defining the limits of the army's legitimate authority to control their lives. As veterans, they turned to inducing the federal government to meet its responsibility to distribute the burdens of fighting a total war evenly throughout the population. Conflicting interpretations of how conscription changed the relationship between citizen-soldiers and the federal government endured for nearly thirty years, affecting both the functioning of the federal government and millions of private lives.

The questions that dominated this prolonged power struggle between soldiers and the state emerged from the unique circumstances of World War I. The need to allocate manpower resources wisely in time of total war provided a crucial justification for conscription. Fighting the heavily industrialized war raging in France required a new kind of military organization, one with a voracious appetite for industrial goods, and heavily dependent on service and support troops to maintain units in the field. The structure of this army bore little resemblance to previous American armies, when being a soldier practically guaranteed time at the front. In the Civil War, only 10 percent of troops on either side served as noncombatants, but by World War I, this had climbed to 60 percent.[6] The changing nature of military service and the importance of continued industrial production generated fundamental questions about the social contract that conscription established between the state and citizen-soldiers. Citizen-soldiers questioned whether the government had the right to conscript men as laborers, essentially putting a shovel rather than a gun in their hands for the duration of the war. Training men to fight and leading them on the battlefield remained the army's key concern, but given the size and importance of its noncombatant element, the army could not ignore their demands. Citizen-soldiers also came to wonder about the justice of requiring soldiers to work and fight for a mere thirty dollars a month while war profiteering ran rampant at home. The postwar government found it impossible to escape the wrath of veterans who eventually demanded their fair share of the wealth generated by the Great War.

Civilians came into the military from all walks of life, and they brought a tremendous range of civilian attitudes and behaviors with them. With gusto, army trainers assaulted recruits with the new, uniform norms that would now regulate their lives, and focused especially on teaching them to obey orders unquestioningly. But critical gaps soon appeared in the army's ability to dictate what constituted a legitimate order. Racial prejudices shared by the military and civilian worlds meant that most black American soldiers served in subservient laboring roles, but lobbying by black organizations and manpower shortages combined to force the army to place some blacks in positions of authority, both as officers and as camp guards. When white soldiers disobeyed them and avoided punishment, they successfully redefined discipline as a relative, rather than absolute, concept. Similarly, army officials discovered that punitive action did not deter citizen-soldiers from committing hosts of other infractions. The emerging repertoire of accommodative and persuasive techniques to command these troops further illustrated the army's diluted ability to dictate the terms of obedience.

The political needs of the military and the emerging popularity of modern management theories also influenced the army's responses to its new conscripted population. During World War I, a vocal core of reformers in the General Staff believed that soldiers needed to understand their cause to fight well. Rather than relying exclusively on coercion to maintain discipline, they preferred manipulating troop behavior and attitudes. Those who argued that citizen-soldiers' opinions mattered did so because they expected to mold those views to advance the army's goals both on the battlefield and in Congress. They did not envision their surveys of the troops' opinions becoming a way for citizen-soldiers to gain an independent voice in internal policy making. The army's own investigations indicated widespread dissatisfaction among the troops, however, which army officials then had the choice of either ignoring or placating. Throughout the war, the army consistently treated citizen-soldiers as future voters, who were expected to support a large and well-funded peacetime army. Encouraged to think about the ultimate purpose of the war and the role of the military in American society, soldiers stationed in France, Russia, and Germany came to their own conclusions about the ultimate meaning of their crusade for democracy. Their interpretations often differed from those of army officials, who worried that citizen-soldiers were emerging as a renegade force steering international relations and domestic politics in uncharted, and sometimes unwanted, directions.

When peace arrived in 1918, demobilization proved as big a challenge as mobilization. Persuading returned servicemen to put the war behind them replaced the earlier task of turning civilians into soldiers. In the war's immediate aftermath, the question of how it had changed these men dominated the national political agenda. One outcome became immediately apparent. World War I veterans were determined to have a voice in the public arena. While Congress and the army courted veterans' votes, the Wilson administration hoped to make a clean break with the men it had used conscription to lure or force into the wartime military. The army's worst nightmares came true in 1919, when veterans focused their energies on denouncing the authoritarian practices of the regular army. Congressional investigations abounded, but veterans quickly lost interest in democratizing the military establishment. Now the White House had reason to lament the changing direction of veteran political activism. Veterans increasingly perceived the answer to their financial and personal problems in the decisive exercise of state power. In their eyes, if the state had the power to draft men, it also had the ability and responsibility to prevent the war from ruining the lives of those it conscripted.

This generation ultimately settled on adjusted compensation as its prime postwar cause. Securing government compensation for the civilian wages lost during the war required an effective lobbying organization, a role the American Legion assumed with gusto from 1922 to 1924 once its members made their wishes known. During the Depression, however, the collective will of Great War veterans found other avenues of political expression when the Legion refused to press for immediate payment of the adjusted compensation bonds secured in 1924 but not due in full until 1945. In 1932, 40,000 veterans formed the Bonus March and descended on Washington, D.C., to lobby Congress personally. Intended as a second phase of reckoning with the war's social contract, the Bonus March instead served as a transition from societal debate about the long-term consequences of conscription to public discussion of the government's responsibility to help needy citizens. The public hailed the Bonus Marchers as representatives of the common man illustrating the dire consequences of President Herbert Hoover's refusal to grant direct relief. After the army brutally evicted them from the city, veterans enjoyed enormous popularity, until a more astute politician, Franklin D. Roosevelt, entered the White House and accused them of demanding special privileges at the expense of others. They finally received the full amount of their adjusted compensation certificates in 1936, once the New Deal had embraced the ethos of federal responsibility for the deserving poor.

The ability of World War I veterans to shape the federal government's response to total war appeared over by the mid 1930s, even though the army continued to study their experience to improve its handling of the next generation of conscripts. World War II, however, provided one last chance for Great War veterans to make a substantial mark on American society. They took it, and some of them authored the most extensive piece of social welfare legislation in U.S. history, the 1944 GI Bill of Rights. Thanks to World War I veteran activism, the state would become a positive, transforming force in the lives of millions of Americans.

Why is World War I important in American history? Quite simply, the Great War generation played a critical role in constructing the modern U.S. Army, turning World War II soldiers into the most privileged veteran generation in American history and determining what mass military service would mean for millions of American men throughout the twentieth century. No one anticipated in 1917 how influential this generation of citizen-soldiers would become. Only by reconstructing their experiences during and after World War I can we fully understand why and how these citizen-soldiers gained the ability to affect twentieth-century American society so dramatically.

1

A FORCE TO CALL OUR OWN

ESTABLISHING A NATIONAL ARMY

President Woodrow Wilson's decision in 1917 to form a national conscripted army touched the lives of practically all Americans. In retrospect, the federal government's preoccupation with the potential for dissension and draft evasion seems to have been misplaced, given how readily Americans responded to the call to arms. Yet the decision to go to war had been difficult for both the president and the country. Both had stood by for nearly three years while the troops of the Allied and Central powers slaughtered one another on various fronts throughout the world, uncertain as to whether this was really America's war to fight. When faced with the threat of increased German aggression toward the United States, both on the high seas and potentially along the Mexican border, Wilson and the majority of Americans decided for war, but without mass enthusiasm.

With the number of volunteers sparse, men who had never planned to become soldiers suddenly found themselves drafted into the army by members of their own communities, who faced the dilemma of deciding whose sons and brothers would serve and whose would not. Within the army, officials harbored a host of doubts about the conscripted civilians pouring into domestic training camps. Having spent the decades since the Civil War disparaging the usefulness of citizen-soldiers in the age of modern warfare, regular army officers now had to accomplish exactly what they had claimed could not be done. Within a matter of months, the army had to prepare civilians who had no previous military training for battle and then transport and support them overseas. Amazingly enough, given the length of time that had elapsed since the Civil War, the General Staff used their institution's dismal encounter with conscripts in that conflict to predict the problems they might soon face. Expecting to encounter a hostile rank and file in the training camps, the army planned to resolve any lingering doubts citizen-soldiers might have about conscription with a forceful display of its power to control every aspect of their lives.

The army interacted with a variety of civilian groups to mobilize the citizen army. The provost marshal delegated the responsibility for selecting men to local draft boards, which imposed their own agendas on the recruitment process. Local boards weighed the army's need for the most able men against their members' own desires to preserve the social, economic, and political order of civilian society. The army also accepted help from a host of civilian experts in scientific management, psychology, and business to help make induction more efficient.

Military professionals shared with draft boards and civilian experts an overriding concern for how citizen-soldiers would react to forced military service. Any hint of hesitancy on the part of these troops would make their induction and training more difficult. Military officials waited, therefore, with nervous anticipation as equally anxious citizen-soldiers boarded the trains that would carry them to their new military lives.

The Initial Encounter

Once Congress had formally approved national conscription legislation, the General Staff immediately began reviewing all possible reactions to compulsory military service. In the short term, the army hoped for volunteers, because all Class I registrants, those men local examining boards classified as eligible to serve immediately, could enlist in the army until December 15, 1917.[1] At the beginning of the war, the regular army contained roughly 127,588 officers and men. Approximately 80,446 National Guard officers and men were in federal service along the Mexican border, with an equal number serving in the states. The army anticipated filling the divisions reserved for National Guard and regular army troops with volunteers in the summer of 1917, but the expected numbers failed to materialize. Army officials soon realized that they would have to use draftees to bring these volunteer-oriented divisions up to combat strength and also funnel conscripts into the national army units reserved exclusively for draftees. For the first time in American military history, draftees formed the majority of the citizen-soldier population. By November 11, 1918, federal army forces had grown to almost 3.9 million men, 72 percent of them conscripts.[2]

The turmoil that had surrounded the Civil War draft and the pre-war controversy over universal military training gave army administrators ample reason to doubt the willingness of Americans to submit to a federal draft peacefully. General Staff officers reexamined the Civil War draft riots, which had broken out most violently in New York City's ethnic neighborhoods and those of midwestern cities, to prepare for a hostile public reaction to registration. But army officials did not have to go back to their history books to find opposition to required military service. Since the 1890s, universal military training had been one of the most hotly contested legislative struggles of the period.

Civilian proponents of military preparedness had cultivated some public support with the claim that universal military training would create politically loyal citizens out of America's increasingly diverse urban populations. Democrats and isolationists from southern and midwestern states opposed the universal military training idea, suspecting that a desire to expand overseas markets fueled industrialists' sudden interest in a stronger army. Labor organizations expressed similar doubts, convinced that industrialists wanted to use military training to pacify or break an increasingly militant workforce. Immigrants who had abandoned their respective countries to avoid compulsory military service also opposed mandatory peacetime military training. With the declaration of war, support and dissent fell along the same political lines when Congress debated the initial selective service legislation.

Given this controversy, Provost Marshal General Enoch H. Crowder, who headed the Selective Service system throughout the war, decided early on that the best way to ensure cooperation was to avoid using federal agents to register and to induct men. To appease fears of an intrusive federal government interfering in the lives of individuals, he licensed local communities to take responsibility for meeting draft quotas. Local officials serving on the 4,647 local draft boards thus filled the draft quotas assigned to their regions by the War Department.

Public perceptions of the draft, Crowder realized, would also influence reactions to registration. To counter views that the draft infringed on individual freedom, government officials declared it a citizen's public and patriotic duty to comply with the draft law. The War Department turned the first registration day, June 5, 1917, into a national patriotic celebration, with local communities sponsoring pageants and festivals to honor men registering with their local boards. When Secretary of War Newton E. Baker drew the first eligible registration number out of a huge fishbowl on July 20, 1917, local boards had recorded the names of 10 million men between the ages of 21 and 30. By the end of the war, approximately 24 million men had registered.

Although most men registered without resistance, they failed to volunteer in sufficient numbers for the units reserved for them. Registering had an advantage over volunteering: one could appear patriotic and loyal, but still hope never to receive an induction notice. Most local communities turned registration drives into public pageants to honor and identify registrants in the community, which undoubtedly encouraged men who wished to avoid ostracism to register. To further stimulate compliance, the federal government threatened to publish the names of men who did not register and round them up for public trials as "slackers." When Henry Charles Ward gambled and lost, he showed his induction notice to his father, a follower of the American socialist Eugene Debs, who offered to help him avoid military service. After contemplating this offer, Ward decided to enter the army, because he realized that he had few appealing options. "If I went I would lose control of my life and be thrown into that great mass of puppets . . . if I did not go I would lose control of my life hiding and dodging," he wrote in his memoirs. "If caught I would go to prison, at best I could never hold my head up again."[3]

Despite the success of registration drives, the General Staff officers responsible for devising and implementing a uniform training program continued to harbor doubts about the willingness of American men to serve involuntarily in the army. Opponents of universal military service had long argued that the coercive nature of military life clashed dramatically with the democratic values championed in civilian society. Now the army wondered if civilians with strong democratic values could accept its authoritarian customs.

It is easy to overstate the differences between civilian and military values. Indeed, in many areas, especially race relations, the similarity between civilian and military worlds remained striking. During the war, many officers became increasingly enamored with the possibility that Progressive ideas on scientific management, assimilating immigrants, and worker motivation might help officers handle the influx of recruits more efficiently. Despite these overlapping values, however, critical differences persisted between civilian and military life. The most important of these remained the military's insistence on unquestioning obedience from subordinates.

Army trainers had ample experience handling recruits who initially resented the protocol separating officers and enlisted men or had trouble learning military regulations. But the army's inexperience with mass mobilization and the accelerated pace of wartime organization building magnified the importance of draftee compliance. Men who enlisted in the regular army made a voluntary decision to join. The peacetime military had absorbed only a small number of recruits each year and had followed a leisurely schedule of instruction, which took up to two years to complete. If recruits proved unsuitable, the army had discharged them, a luxury it no longer had.

Division commanders and the War Plans Division (the part of the General Staff responsible for the training program) increasingly focused their fears about conscripted soldiers on a single issue—the expectation that citizen-soldiers would purposely commit military crimes in order to obtain dishonorable discharges.[4] Throughout the country, many commanders reported alarming increases in such deliberate crimes among citizen-soldiers. The judge advocate general responded by prohibiting sentences of dishonorable discharge for the duration of the war, because of "the resulting tendency to encourage some men, especially among those drafted into the military service, to commit offenses in order to escape such service."[5] The War Department rejected suggestions that the army be allowed to execute all deserters or to put the expected mass of convicted criminals in disciplinary battalions that stayed stateside. Instead, offenders had to serve their sentences of hard labor in their units, where their humiliation would deter other potential military offenders.[6]

The fear that many citizen-soldiers wanted to avoid overseas duty overshadowed the alternative explanations offered by National Guard commanders, who had more experience with citizen-soldiers. Their ignorance of army regulations caused citizen-soldiers to commit a seemingly large number of military infractions during the first few months of training, the commander of the 27th Division argued. "These young men are wholly unaccustomed to the exactions, restrictions and discipline of camp and field life," he told the director of the War Plans Division; "during the early months of training, they will commit many offenses against military law, such as desertion, absence without leave, disobedience of orders, sleeping on post, various disorders and neglects and other offenses which are peculiar to the military establishment."[7] He unsuccessfully urged the judge advocate to suspend the sentences of all wartime offenders who had not had time to adjust to the peculiarities of military life.[8]

Regular army officials refused to wait for a voluntary demonstration, which might never materialize, of citizen-soldiers' willingness to put themselves under army control. Instead, they deemed it crucial to confront citizen-soldiers immediately with the unambiguous force of military authority.[9] Multitudes of untrained conscripted men might quickly become unmanageable unless army authorities immediately diffused any potential resistance these hordes might offer to their induction. Besides quashing any thoughts of rebellion dormant in the minds of recruits, this immediate authoritarianism would force men to abandon their civilian orientations quickly.

Corporal Paul Murphy revealed in a memoir how it felt to be on the receiving end of this policy: "Soldiering meant a complete new life for all of us and it was pretty hard to become adjusted to taking orders and having your whole life regulated by authority other than your own," he recalled.[10] Many recruits quickly became disoriented upon entering the alien army environment. A group of draftees arrived in Camp Meade, Maryland, with some men laughing and joking, according to one observant officer, while "others (many, many of them) were sullen, subdued, sad—and I saw a good many of them who were having a hard time (and not always successfully) in keeping the tears back." The bewildering schedule of examinations, waiting in lines for supplies, meeting hordes of strangers, and encountering military authority for the first time caused nearly every recruit, one neurologist at Camp Upton, New York, observed, to exhibit symptoms of anxiety neurosis during the first few days in camp.[11]

When confronted with forceful commands from military authorities, these men obeyed. Oscar Carl Heig saw his first officer after gathering his uniform from the supply tent with some other new recruits, who "were green and dumb and only stared at him admiring his well pressed uniform and polished boots and did not salute," until they received a tirade from the well-groomed officer.[12] Officers in Camp Dodge, Iowa, berated Henry L. Henderson's group, burning "our ears with hard boiled language" when some recruits hesitated or answered too slowly to their first roll call.[13] Encounters with harsh army officers made home and the civilian world appear distant and remote. Soldiers interviewed toward the end of the war recalled feeling "humiliated by swearing, punished for an unknown offense" by " 'hard-boiled' non-commissioned officers" in Camp Grant, Illinois. If they had realized during these first few days that enlisted men had rights, some said, they would have learned to adapt to army life more quickly.[14] But during those first few weeks, the army only intended to inform new recruits of their obligation to obey all orders unquestioningly.

As the mobilization effort entered its second year, the success of the first year helped erase some, but not all, of the army's fears about the willingness of citizen-soldiers to serve. The new agencies the army created to handle management problems provided insight into the mind-set of citizen-soldiers. The Military Intelligence Department sent agents to stateside training camps and overseas to monitor citizen-soldiers who appeared discontented or unpatriotic. Halfway through the war, the Morale Division, which had begun as a subsection of the Intelligence Department, became another important investigative agency. Infused with Progressive ideas on modern management techniques and the new science of psychology, this newly organized bureau began to lobby toward the end of the war for a gentler training process, arguing that the old methods ruined the enthusiasm of civilian recruits. One Morale Division officer, after observing officers taking away flags given to the men as part of their hometown send-off, wondered, "[W]hy couldn't the newly arrived draftees be given a reception at the depot which contains at least some element of cordiality and welcome?"[15] Thus began an important division within army leadership circles over how to handle citizen-soldiers. Hard-liners battled reformers in 1918 to influence the direction of army personnel policies decided by the chief of staff, Secretary of War Baker, and General John J. Pershing, commander of the American Expeditionary Forces (AEF).

Their lack of resistance to conscription was only one of the surprises citizen-soldiers gave army officials. Volunteers might not like military life any more than the average conscript, but regular army officers believed that their decision to enlist demonstrated their dedication to winning the war, and that this commitment would make them enthusiastic soldiers. When camp commanders began scrutinizing their enlisted population, many of their presuppositions about the superiority of volunteer troops began to evaporate. Few soldiers who enlisted did so because of interest in winning a "war for democracy." As one volunteer officer candidate observed, "the possibility of what the future might hold in store for the individual was discussed a great deal more among the candidates than the intricacies of the international situation" in after-hours conversations.[16] The attraction of the war as a great adventure motivated many volunteers, but other motivations also appear in the letters and memoirs of citizen-soldiers who enlisted. Faced with the likelihood of conscription, some volunteered in order to be able to control their own fates in the wartime army. "You remember what Phil said about being two jumps ahead of the draft, that also has a very practical value which you do not seem to realize," Greager

Clover, an American who had driven an ambulance for the French Army, explained to his father. "You can pick any branch you want *now*, later they pick you."[17] Clover's observation of the life of French infantrymen caused him to enlist in the American Air Service. Most enlistees did not have Clover's firsthand experience, but they knew enough about army life to prefer to enter the service as officers rather than as privates. Specialist units attracted others who wanted to avoid the harsh life of infantry troops.[18]

Soon the mixed motivations of enlistees so annoyed induction officers that they began to feel affection for the "stoic" drafted man, who willingly served wherever the country needed him. Commanders' diminished regard for volunteers, coupled with their early success in subduing conscripts, quickly caused them to abandon their initial distinctions between volunteers and conscripts. Civilians who enlisted continued to claim that a higher sense of purpose made them deserving of special recognition, but the army now refused to recognize this. When Robinson Shepard arrived at Camp Devens, Massachusetts, after enlisting in the Signal Corps, he and his comrades whitewashed stones in front of their company barracks to distinguish themselves as volunteers. "Some of the artillery, having been drafted, came by and got sore. . . . [T]hey wrote to the *Boston Herald* and they printed it that while we enlisted we did it to escape the draft and so we could choose the Signal Corps, the least dangerous branch," Shepard recalled.[19] Shepard's group wrote their own letter refuting this charge, but camp officials still made them remove the white stones around their barracks. A popular poem, "Only a Volunteer," reflected how insufficiently appreciated volunteers soon felt:

> Why didn't I wait to be drafted?
> And led to the train by a band?
> And put in a claim for exemption?
> Oh why did I hold up my hand?
> Why didn't I wait for the banquet?
> Why didn't I wait to be cheered?
> For the drafted men get the credit,
> while I merely volunteered.[20]

Volunteers therefore failed to become a distinctive faction within the mass army, except perhaps in specialist units. Low enlistment rates, repeated personnel transfers among divisions, and the use of conscripted replacement troops soon erased the relevance of distinctions between National Guard and national army divisions. In April 1918, these distinctions were formally eliminated, and all regular army, National Guard, and national army divisions became units of the United States Army.

Besides the huge obstacles that the army faced in absorbing hundreds of thousands of recruits, army officials also had to determine what criteria they would use to select officer candidates from the thousands of men applying for slots in officer training camps. There were approximately 18,000 regular army and National Guard officers available when the war began, and the army would train nearly 182,000 civilian officers in the next year and a half.[21] The army obviously sought intelligent, able men capable of mastering military skills quickly, but the political reliability of potential officer candidates also interested those in authority. White, college-educated young men answered to both criteria and did, in fact, provide most new officers. Small town civic and business leaders who had officered local National Guard units and factory foremen often presented themselves as viable officer material, but army leaders hoped to prevent men with these backgrounds from becoming officers, despite their demonstrated expertise or potential in managing men. Although they might perhaps help defeat the Germans, such men were thought unlikely to support maintaining a strong, full-time professional military establishment in the postwar era, and the army intended to use the war to create a corps of strong civilian advocates to that end.

Trade union officials peppered the War Department with requests to open up officer training camps to their constituents in the early months of the war. Why didn't experience as a shop foreman qualify one to attend, Samuel Gompers, president of the American Federation of Labor (AFL), asked Baker in June 1917. These experienced supervisors knew how to work hard. The army so far had chosen "monied" rather than "working" men, Gompers asserted, men too unpopular to lead common soldiers effectively. "The system of placing greatest stress on the additional pages of textbooks studied by boys after the age of fourteen or sixteen at which apprentices enter industrial life shuts the door of opportunity to the masses of the workers," Gompers noted. "It seems a distinction of class as against mass."[22] When Baker referred this request to General Tasker H. Bliss, then acting chief of staff, Bliss flatly refused to consider commissioning labor supervisors. He reminded Baker that when the army had proposed a universal military training program in 1916, organized labor had rallied to defeat the legislation, and that labor leaders therefore deserved some blame for the army's present unprepared state. The army wanted officers whose primary institutional loyalty lay with the federally controlled military establishment. Besides rejecting the compulsory military training program, labor leaders had also spurned opportunities to receive voluntary training in the prewar Plattsburg camps, which college-educated men had voluntarily attended, Bliss noted. Workers could not catch up, he claimed, but he failed to explain why the army accepted college-educated officer candidates regardless of their lack of previous military experience.[23]

During the war, the army also tried to replace as many National Guard officers as possible with officers whose primary allegiance was to Washington. The regular army's political campaign to either professionalize, control, or eliminate the National Guard had dominated army politics since the turn of the century, although the roots of the conflict extended back to the Civil War. By 1900, the ideas of Emory Upton dominated the regular army. Upton blamed the carnage of the Civil War on poorly trained citizen-soldiers and politically appointed state militia officers. The regular army wrangled continuously with the National Guard over funding from the federal government, training methods, and officer appointments. In the years leading up to the war, the political tide turned in favor of the regular army. Congress tied the National Guard's federal funding to increased supervision by the regular army, and the National Defense Act of 1916 gave the regular army responsibility for coordinating the nation's military resources. This peacetime control laid the foundation for the supervisory power the regular army assumed during the war.[24]

For many regular army officers, the war provided a chance to destroy the credibility of the National Guard once and for all. Although National Guard and national army commanders faced strikingly similar disciplinary problems, inspectors visiting National Guard units inevitably attributed poor discipline to deficiencies intrinsic to the National Guard and its politically appointed officers. Observers considered familiarity between officers and enlisted men a National Guard trademark. "Most of the orders I heard given were in a more or less apologetic and familiar manner . . . the officers accompanying me practically asked the enlisted men to stand at attention and salute the Inspector," Lieutenant Colonel R. G. Peck reported after touring the 35th Division in France. He then went on to recommend that these "National Guard types" be sent back to officer training school or removed altogether.[25]

The regular army had the authority to select officers, but the power to choose enlisted men lay with local draft boards. Because the army relied so heavily on conscripts, the predilections of local draft boards heavily influenced the character of the nation's wartime force. Crowder initially charged local boards simply with carrying out the mandates of the Washington-based General Staff. Preoccupied with the problem of organizing the wartime army, when local boards began modifying the official selection criteria, the General Staff made few objections to the preferred choices of civilian communities. Selective service regulations were designed to ensure the smooth functioning of the civilian economy, but local communities used more than economic criteria to decide who went to war. Draft boards also ensured that mobilization did not unduly disturb racial, ethnic, or familial relations in American communities.

American Communities Select the Wartime Army

When large numbers of men applied for exemptions, the local boards who sifted through these requests secured the power to form a wartime army out of their preferred choices. Having assumed primary responsibility for selecting wartime troops, civilian communities soon began to pressure the army to acquiesce to some of the reservations they had about how the army planned to employ these conscripts. Public attention now focused on many manpower decisions the General Staff would rather have made privately, and consequently public pressure and opinion played a role in shaping official policy.

Rather than disrupting the family as they raised an army, local draft boards tended to use conscription to reaffirm it.[26] The greatest numbers of deferments, 43 percent of all registrants, went to married men with dependents to support. The government undoubtedly wanted to avoid the burden of supporting multitudes of wives and children. Local boards protected more than the economic welfare of American families with such exemptions. "As a New York City board put it," the provost marshal reported, " 'All American life is built around the marriage status, and great effort should be made not to dissolve the home ties.' " [27] Some local boards actually bragged that they had forced wayward husbands to fulfill their domestic responsibilities by threatening to take away their draft exemptions. The country's commitment to exempting husbands and fathers from military service never wavered. When the War Department faced manpower shortages in 1918, for instance, Congress extended the age limits of the draft from 21–30 to 18–45 rather than draft married men. The army accepted these exemptions and never made any substantial inquiry into the skills the organization lost by wholesale exemptions for husbands and fathers. Only exemptions granted for marriages that men contracted after the declaration of war to avoid the draft aroused controversy. An amendment to the Selective Service regulations returned these men to Class I status.

Unmarried men eligible for industrial and agricultural deferments had less success gaining exemptions from service. While the army did not challenge exemptions for married men, it fought any further drain on available manpower. Refused blanket exemptions for their workers, coal-mining companies and railroads accused the government of paralyzing industries needed to win the war. Low exemption rates also spurred outcries from powerful farm lobbies, who pressured Congress to secure more deferments for agricultural workers and to furlough soldiers to farm communities that needed help with their harvests. These pressures worked: in 1918, industrial deferments jumped from 43 percent to 53 percent of all requests granted, and agricultural deferments increased from 36 percent to 52 percent. Congress authorized short agricultural and industrial furloughs for men from industries experiencing severe labor shortages, but army officials only reluctantly furloughed men back to civilian work.[28]

While the general public remained rather indifferent about whether or not workers or farmers received exemptions, public sentiment rose to hysterical levels on the subject of "alien slackers." Reports, for example, that Italian men in New York were boasting that they had "robbed three years of life" from the United States by avoiding military service in the Italian Army antagonized public opinion.[29] Selective Service regulations only required immigrants who had declared their intention of becoming citizens of the United States to serve. Foreign embassies repeatedly emphasized this point when protesting the induction of nondeclarant alien residents. Unfortunately, nondeclarant aliens did not automatically receive exemptions from their draft boards, but instead had to apply for them. Consequently, many aliens who either did not understand the law or English found themselves inducted into the army. Those who fought their induction from the training camps faced an uphill battle persuading army officers, who knew how emphatically the public wanted immigrants to serve, to release them. The army typically viewed intransigent aliens with as much contempt as did the American public. After investigating the case of Private Mitrieg Kogut, a Russian immigrant who claimed he should not have to serve because he intended to remain a noncitizen, a Camp MacArthur intelligence officer deduced that "the man is afraid to fight, is a slacker and should be watched."[30] This sentiment reflected both the public and army's general opinion on the issue of alien exemptions. Prevailing views about different ethnic groups described Italians as readily swayed by patriotic and emotional appeals to fight, Irish as willing to fight but not as British allies, and Russian Jews as despondent and uncooperative.[31]

Civilian interest in the alien soldier did not end once it became clear that many aliens would not avoid performing military service, and in fact, like blacks, they would be slightly overdrafted. Officials estimated that 18 percent of enlisted men were foreign-born and 13 percent black, although these groups only made up 14.5 percent and 10 percent of the total population respectively. Approximately 100,000 of the half million foreign-born troops serving in the military could not speak English. The political loyalties of ethnic soldiers remained suspect. K. W. Strzelec, an undercover agent in Camp Grant, Illinois, investigated his fellow Poles to learn whether alien soldiers understood what they were fighting for, and whether they had been exposed to enemy propaganda. AEF Intelligence reports listed the names of alien soldiers who expressed disloyal thoughts, those with relatives in the opposing army, and men who did not want to fight. German-speaking operatives often tried to entice German-speaking soldiers into expressing sympathy for Germany. American intelligence officers viewed first- and second-generation ethnic soldiers with suspicion, but German intelligence officers reported with amazement that American prisoners of war "of German, Dutch and Italian parentage, . . . semi-Americans almost all of whom were born in America and never have been in Europe, fully feel themselves to be true-born sons of their country."[32]

By the second year of the war, reform-minded officers in policy-making circles began pushing for a more lenient, Progressive approach to handling alien soldiers. The military, they argued, could endear itself to the general public by Americanizing these non-English-speaking soldiers. This group of General Staff officers saw a politically attractive opportunity for the army to align itself with civilian groups that might support an expanded peacetime army if the organization could successfully administer this educational scheme during the war. Development battalions composed of ethnically specific companies were formed in the spring of 1918 and eventually absorbed 25,000 non-English-speaking soldiers.[33]

Some aliens who were willing to serve encountered obstacles because they came from ethnic groups officially considered part of the Austro-Hungarian Empire. Proponents claimed that the strong motivation of men from oppressed Austro-Hungarian minority groups to fight the Germans would be a significant boost to the Allied cause, even though they were fighting more for their own people than for the United States. The army opposed efforts to attach ethnic appendages to the American national army, but these ethnic groups lobbied effectively and won permission to recruit both Polish and Slavic legions.[34]

Civilian opinion on the importance of alien participation in the war clearly affected the composition of the U.S. Army. Harsh 100 percent Americanism—the view, held by many civilians at the time, that an immigrant must shed all Old World attributes—in many ways fitted perfectly with a military training regime that required all civilians to adopt an entirely new soldier identity, but over time the army chose the more moderate, Progressive approach, which accepted the dual identity of immigrant soldiers.[35] By the second year of the war, Progressive social reformers and civilian ethnic organizations were volunteering to help army trainers instruct immigrant troops in their duty toward their new country by translating official pamphlets and giving lectures in foreign languages on war-related topics. These reformers also convinced army trainers that allowing immigrant troops to retain their cultural traditions improved morale. Consequently, Polish priests heard confession, Greek soldiers received furloughs for the feast of St. Nicholas, and the War Department eventually agreed to mark Jewish soldiers' graves with the Star of David.

Civilian ideals also influenced the way the army used black soldiers. Unlike the idea of ethnic-specific units, which took time to form, the segregation of blacks in race-specific units was a foregone conclusion. Serving in a segregated unit did not mean the same thing for an immigrant as it did for a black soldier. Army officials, ethnic community leaders, and citizen-soldiers all agreed that development battalions should prepare immigrant soldiers for assignment in regular army units. The army embraced racial separation as a permanent arrangement to allow the black and white races to live in peace, however, not as a stepping-stone to eventual social equality. Army officials could mix white native-born soldiers with ethnic soldiers, including Native Americans, without second thoughts about the overall effect on discipline, because most white native-born soldiers did not object to serving alongside them.[36] Even if they disliked specific nationalities, native-born white soldiers could hardly expect to find much civilian support for contradicting the prevailing ethos of the melting pot and demanding the permanent segregation of ethnic minorities. Racially distinct units, however, complemented the Jim Crow values that communities in the South recently had turned into law and many northern and western areas had adopted as a de facto way to regulate race relations.

The General Staff shared the civilian belief that segregation preserved racial peace and never considered racially integrating individual units. These planners did, however, expect many black recruits to man trenches along the Western Front. Army officials, both publicly and privately, credited black infantrymen (led by white officers) with competent service in the Civil War, Indian wars, the Spanish-American War, and along the Mexican border. Consequently, when the United States declared war in 1917, the army prepared, as it had in previous wars, to train black combat troops. Black regular and National Guard companies quickly filled their enlistment quotas as the General Staff made plans to organize the black draft. The first mobilization plan accepted by the General Staff, on July 31, 1917, suggested training the majority of black draftees for combat. This plan would have placed an equal number of black troops in each camp across the nation and created company grade positions for the black candidates currently attending the Fort Des Moines Colored Officers' Training Camp.[37] It assigned the remaining men, a minority of the draft, to service units.[38]

A month later, however, political pressure to maintain the status quo of civilian race relations beyond simply segregating black and white troops began to affect General Staff views on how to make use of blacks. The army's pressing need for infantry troops no longer dominated discussions on mobilizing black troops. The opposition of many communities, especially those surrounding southern camps, to arming so many black men soon caused the chief of staff to reconsider the approved plan.[39] After his review, General Bliss agreed with those civilians who claimed it was too dangerous. "In some of the cantonments there would be as many as 14,000 colored troops alongside of not more than 18,000 white troops," Bliss told Baker. "If either or both get out of hand . . . nothing short of a national calamity would be the result."[40] Bliss also rejected proposals to place black infantry units in segregated camps a mile away from the white cantonments or to concentrate all black troops in two mobilization camps. While these options might have appeased Bliss's apprehensions about racial violence in the camps, he rejected them because he now fully appreciated southern fears about giving black men substantial training in handling firearms. "It is not so much that they fear that the Negro will strike if he gets a chance, but rather that they assume with curious unanimity that he has *reason* to strike, that any other persons in his circumstances or treated as he is would rebel," W. E. B. Du Bois commented caustically after the war on this wartime preoccupation of the white South with the domestic consequences of training black men to fire rifles.[41]

Bliss consequently advised Baker to approve a more politically viable plan that suspended the organization of any more black combat units and assigned black draftees to the Quartermaster and Engineer Corps, which provided most of the army's menial, unskilled labor. He supported this solution, Bliss told the secretary of war on August 21, 1917, because "the regiments organized for the service mentioned in this plan . . . [need] the minimum of training *under arms*."[42] When black regular army soldiers rioted and killed white civilians in Houston after a clash with white police on August 25, 1917, southern civilian opposition to training additional black troops for combat solidified.[43] Rather than manning the front lines, therefore, the majority of black troops would serve in assorted labor battalions, pioneer infantry units, salvage companies, and stevedore organizations. Given their pressing need for infantry troops, army officials had a broader appreciation of the sacrifices involved in agreeing to assign blacks primarily to noncombatant positions than did civilian communities interested primarily in preserving the racial status quo. Still, the General Staff did not find it difficult, given their own racial prejudices, to accede to the wishes of civilians on this subject.[44]

White citizens were not, however, the only ones who had vocal representatives pleading their case to the government as the army decided the fate of black conscripts. Leaders of national black organizations had lobbied hard for the black officers' training camp at Fort Des Moines and now began a national petition drive to win clemency for the Houston rioters. To quiet accusations of discrimination from these leaders, the War Department formed one national army division (four infantry regiments rather than the sixteen initially proposed) out of black draftees and scattered these regiments among various northern training camps.[45] The other black combat unit, the provisional 93rd Division, which contained three National Guard and one drafted regiment, would eventually serve with the French Army. Regular army black units spent the war guarding the Mexican border and island territories.

Ironically, these manpower decisions often delayed the induction of black troops, because the army emphasized filling infantry units in the first draft call. Congressmen from southern states with large black populations protested about these delays because white civilians then became primarily responsible for meeting each state's 1917 draft quota. By the winter of 1918, the new cry in the South, like this one from Kentucky Congressman R. Y. Thomas, claimed "that the negroes are permitted to stay at home and hang around the towns and steal, while the white boys are taken from the farms and sent into the army."[46] Once again, the army found itself under pressure to tailor its absorption of black draftees to satisfy the demands of white southern civilians. This time, Wilson told the army to create laboring units whether or not the war effort required them. The Provost Marshal General's Office consequently "assured the Governors of several of those [southern] states that, before any more white men are drafted, the remainder of the negroes [selected for the first draft call] will be taken. I am informed by the General Staff that we can make good on this promise."[47] The army finally began large-scale induction of black troops in the spring of 1918, but the restrictions placed on its use of black troops made absorbing these men a slow process. By July, the War Plans Division anticipated a severe manpower shortage if it could not bring in more white men. The department solved this problem by reorganizing sixteen white pioneer infantry units as infantry brigades, filling the original pioneer infantry units with black troops and creating enough service units "to enable the remaining 27,190 colored men to be called, thus making available in all states, the white registrants, Class I, 1918."[48]

The public did not stop with its successes in curbing the army's initial plan to train numerous black combatants, in preventing the "alien slacker" from evading service, and in keeping married men at home. Many communities also voiced concern that army life would rob men of this generation of their moral imperative by exposing them to the contaminating influences often associated with army life. Rather than concentrating on the immorality of the war's catastrophic violence, Americans focused on monitoring the aspects of army life over which they could exercise some control. Progressive reformers, who had avidly campaigned to eliminate drinking and prostitution from civilian society before the war, now undertook a crusade against vice in the wartime army.

Wilson and Baker, Progressive reformers themselves, sympathized, but the army had no time to tackle the issue of vice. Wilson therefore resolved this problem in the same way that he managed other predicaments that his overtaxed administrators could not handle. Throughout the federal government, Wilson had appointed civilian "dollar a year" men to head bureaus within strained federal agencies. To meet the challenge of coordinating a campaign for moral uplift and clean living in domestic training camps, he now created the Commission on Training Camp Activities (CTCA) and appointed Raymond Fosdick, a civilian reformer, to head it. The CTCA enforced sections 12 and 13 of the Selective Service Act, which forbade the sale of liquor to men in uniform and enabled the president to outlaw prostitution in broad zones around each camp. Building on its Progressive foundation, the CTCA launched a massive sex education campaign that vividly introduced soldiers to the horrors of venereal disease and the availability of a reasonably effective chemical prophylaxis treatment. To further deter soldiers from engaging in illicit sex, the CTCA organized athletic and educational activities within the training camps to consume soldiers' free time and pent-up sexual energy. The CTCA's sexual education campaign served an important military purpose, because it helped keep venereal disease at an all-time low in the wartime army. Pershing refused to let soldiers infected with venereal disease serve in the overseas army, mostly because he did not want any potentially infirm troops to care for in France. The CTCA also supervised the various welfare agencies, including the Young Men's Christian Association, Jewish Welfare League, and Knights of Columbus, which set up huts in each training camp and worked with the War Camp Community Service to encourage communities to provide wholesome diversions to troops on leave.[49] By the end of the war, owing in large part to the work of the CTCA, the army was able to claim to parents that their son returned "to you a better man."[50]

Shared ideas among top level administrators thus became a third tie the army developed with civilians during the war, in addition to those developed with men inducted into the organization and with civilians serving on local draft boards. The army delegated other critical tasks of its own choosing to civilian elites during the war. In the opening phases of mobilization, army administrators struggled to develop a personnel system capable of placing the thousands of men entering the organization every day. The army created the Psychological Division of the Surgeon General's Office and the Committee for the Classification of Personnel, and recruited civilian experts to head them. Seeking the "right man for the right job," these civilian experts forced army officials to examine their own beliefs about the qualities they desired in civilian recruits.

Civilian Experts Join the Army

As it had traditionally done, the army initially defined the qualities it sought in citizen-soldiers primarily in physical terms. "The fighting man has to meet special ideals of physical fitness corresponding to the special service he has to perform," a report summarizing the physical defects in drafted men asserted. "The military man must, therefore, have sound feet and a body capable of standing great mechanical stress and one in which the sense organs, the central nervous system, and organs of emotional control are as active as possible."[51] Many civilians who entered the army during the war fell far below this standard. A postwar Medical Department study revealed that northern middle- and upper-middle-class men from suburban areas formed the healthiest potential army population. Indoor work and a higher standard of living had kept these men free from disease and injury, but it had not done much for their physical fitness. "It is quite apparent," one medical officer observed at the induction of drafted troops at Camp Funston, Kansas, "that the physical condition of the men as they file past, stripped, is poor. Many have been office workers or indoor salesmen, and their pale skins and flabby tissues bespeak lack of tone, and indicate the absence of any kind of exercise."[52] Laborers, on the other hand, suffered the widespread physical problems associated with poor working conditions. "Straining the body by heavy work induces hernia; millwork in the South and lumbering in the North causes loss of upper extremities," the authors of this postwar Medical Department study observed. "[L]umbering and saw-mill operations cause loss of fingers and arms, and railroading causes loss of legs." Obviously, the army could not induct men missing arms and legs; nor did it take most men suffering from epilepsy, tuberculosis, heart disease, or defective hearing. But it did accept men with venereal disease, goiters, hemorrhoids, hernias, and tonsillitis. One study estimated that local boards had to examine 3,082,949 men to secure the first million men for the army.[53]

Rejection rates varied among local boards and training camps, much to the chagrin of the surgeon general. Revealing once again the vulnerability of the army to the standards set by local boards, the surgeon general complained that low rejection rates did not reflect substantially healthier regional populations but only more lenient examination practices.[54] Other reasons, besides an examiner's personal whims, accounted for these varying acceptance rates. "December [1917]," the surgeon general reported, "was characterized by the greatest proportion of men accepted despite defects and the smallest proportion rejected. This month marks the acme of our purpose of securing an army even by making use of more or less defective men."[55] The demand for troops became so acute that some men who had been rejected as physically unfit when trying to enlist found themselves accepted by local draft boards six months later.

Meeting manpower quotas by lowering physical standards created new problems for those who had to find a role for soldiers with physical deficiencies within the organization. "Organization Commanders of every description, on the average," Colonel Lutz Wahl, chairman of the Operations Branch noted, "when they are ordered to transfer men, do select the men that they regard as least desirable . . . to purify their organizations of poor soldiers, and men of deficient intelligence and physical stamina."[56] Eventually, the War Department created convalescent units in depot brigades for unfit men, and the provost marshal developed a "limited service" category for men who could perform noncombatant work.

The psychological examiners sent to test men by the newly formed Psychological Division soon raised new concerns for army trainers. Robert M. Yerkes, president of the American Psychological Association, won approval from the surgeon general for intelligence testing early in the war. Commissioned civilian psychologists claimed that mental deficiencies, like physical flaws, limited the usefulness of many recruits to the army. Confused army commanders initially thought the tests measured mental disease. While mental disease clearly disqualified a man for service, considerable debate emerged over the importance to the army of a recruit's intelligence. The new intelligence tests assigned each man a mental age as a score, and civilian psychologists wanted to establish a minimum mental age for all types and levels of service.[57] Many officers resented these outside intrusions into placement decisions traditionally made by company officers. Psychologists tried to allay this anger by producing numerous studies showing that test results overwhelmingly supported rather than contradicted officers' estimations of the same group of men. Assigning men by test results, they argued, provided a quicker and more efficient way to mobilize a mass army. Some advocates even claimed they would help officers distinguish between slow learners and men who simply were not trying.

Besides friction over turf, Army officers also questioned whether intelligent men made the best soldiers, and whether low-scoring men should be grouped in separate training organizations. Colonel R. J. Burt, who conducted a study on intelligence testing for the chief of staff, was "not convinced that the stupid man, with proper training and leading, is necessarily going to give way in the trenches." One company commander told Burt that intelligence testers had rated "one of my cooks as 'D' and brand[ed] him as 'illiterate.' . . . It would be a difficult matter to find as good a cook; he is worth his weight in gold to the military service and it doesn't matter a whit whether he has any 'intelligence' or not."[58] Although they failed to provide an effective, modern method for assigning men (compiling the test results took too long for them to have a significant impact on personnel assignments), these psychologists succeeded in establishing intelligence as a distinct trait, which officers increasingly noticed and evaluated in their men.[59] Lieutenant Edwin Spies, for example, complained to the surgeon general that men of inferior mental capacity assigned to hospital units could not learn how to apply simple splints, and that consequently many troops returned from the front with broken limbs improperly splinted.[60]

The discovery that large numbers of men could not take the alpha intelligence test designed for literate recruits convinced many officers that illiteracy, not intelligence, was the more important problem. Intelligence testers, who had designed a special pictorial exam for illiterates, estimated that the illiteracy rate hovered around 21.5 percent of all white troops and 50.6 percent of all black troops.[61] Sample testing classified 49.5 percent of South Carolina men as illiterate, compared to 16.6 percent of New York men (despite large numbers of alien soldiers in the region) and 14.2 percent of men from Minnesota. "Such a percentage of illiteracy as is found among the men from South Carolina is startling," wrote an officer at Camp Wadsworth, South Carolina. "Among Virginia negroes reporting at Camp Lee, Va., in the fall of 1917, the percentage of illiteracy was 40.0 percent. The conclusion is that the problem of illiteracy among South Carolina men drafted is a most serious one." At Camp Jackson, South Carolina, 36.5 percent of white southern recruits were classified as illiterate, compared to only 7.9 percent of northern white recruits.[62]

Why did literacy become so important during this war? After all, other wars had been successfully fought with illiterate recruits. Many officers reported that uneducated men responded quite slowly to the training regime and especially to army discipline.[63] Men without a formal education often did not exhibit the patience needed to learn in a structured setting, attitudes the army did not have time to teach. Without basic reading and writing skills, these soldiers could not communicate within an increasingly complex bureaucratic organization. They could not fill out forms, such as the basic induction questionnaire and classification cards, read passes, if assigned to guard duty, or direction signs, if carrying messages through the trenches. They were more isolated from their families than soldiers who could write letters home and more insulated from camp morale workers, who used camp newspapers to distribute wartime propaganda among citizen-soldiers.[64] The emphasis in public schools on heroic military accomplishments and the duties of American citizenship, army analysts later concluded, gave educated young men a "will to fight."[65] The General Staff estimated that large percentages of uneducated men did not respond to their draft notices or became conscientious objectors. In Texas, two uneducated men deserted immediately from training camp and killed a ranger trying to capture them. Baker urged the president to commute their sentences from death to life imprisonment. "My strong feeling," Baker wrote, "is that the society which left them illiterate might well exact less than the extreme penalty." [66] Baker offered a similar explanation for conscientious objection. [67]

A basic education now emerged as a minimum requirement for common soldiering in the national army, which also developed an insatiable demand for skilled men to work as engineers, railroad men, and truck drivers. Civilian experts, working through the Committee on the Classification of Personnel, designed a program to help army trainers identify skilled men among the incoming masses of farmers and laborers. [68] The army welcomed this help, in part because of unexpected problems such as finding enough men with clerical skills to staff division headquarters. When Clarence Bertler was training at Camp Grant, for instance, he found it hard to believe that only he and one other man out of hundreds of recruits knew how to operate a typewriter. [69] Walter D. Scott, a psychologist, who had perfected "scientific personnel procedures" as director of the Bureau of Salesmanship Research at the Carnegie Institute of Technology, founded the committee. He proposed that its staff filter out among the camps to fill out cards detailing the skills of each recruit. It took interviewers weeks to complete these cards for each group of recruits, but officers had to assign men in the first few days. Committee members also realized halfway through the war that men who hoped to receive a better assignment in the army exaggerated their skills. The committee then proposed that its staff not only interview incoming men but give them trade tests to ascertain their real skills. This proposal was simply too elaborate for an already overtaxed army bureaucracy. In practice, induction officers assigned most men to fill whatever available positions existed at the time of their induction. Even men who had graduated from government-sponsored specialist training programs at universities in civilian life found it difficult to get army assignments in the work they had voluntarily studied. [70] It often, therefore, fell to local commanders to devise their own schemes for absorbing incoming recruits. Rather than test scores, officers of the 89th Division used their knowledge of regional industries to assign men. Lieutenant Milton Bernet described how recruits arriving at Camp Funston had to

march over and align themselves in front of signs which designate the states from which they came . . . now the peculiar thing about it is that all the men from the Western states such as Colorado and New Mexico are being assigned to the artillery on the assumption that they are good horsemen for that is one of the essentials of that branch of service. The infantry is coming mostly from Kansas and Missouri while the engineering regiment is being supplied from certain particular counties in all the states, counties in which the inhabitants are supposed to have certain practical engineering experience such as the lead mining and river districts of Missouri and the mining counties of Colorado and New Mexico.[71]

The approach of the 89th Division also accommodated the desire of many citizen-soldiers to serve with men from the same area. Army officials recognized the importance of regional cohesion and initially intended to retain the local integrity of its wartime units to recreate the esprit de corps of the state militia. But the army gradually abandoned this principle by filling National Guard units with conscripts, transferring white and black troops between regions to maintain a racial balance in all training camps, constantly pilfering skilled men from already formed divisions, hastily transferring men to bring divisions about to depart to France up to strength, and, ultimately, culling replacement troops for all divisions from one collective pool of reserves. Soldiers might begin their service with men from the same state, but most units quickly lost their regional affiliations.

The ability to assign and transfer citizen-soldiers freely from one unit to the other without considering their regional backgrounds illustrated the enormous administrative power that the federal army had acquired to create a national wartime organization. This disregard for regional affiliation violated the principle that the National Guard dedicated itself to preserving in peacetime. Entering the wartime army now meant serving side by side with Americans from all walks of life, rather than with men from one's community. This break with tradition helped create a mass army that was truly national in character, not just in administration.

Finally, the army relied on the expertise of former businessmen to help supply and arm the men that it was busy evaluating and assigning. These professionals both worked as civilian employees for army supply bureaus and donned uniforms to serve as military bureaucrats. The bureaus found themselves inundated with citizen-officers who advocated replacing a system based on tradition and personal relationship with the latest fads of factory management. Many regular army supply officers, often already angered at having to serve out the war in Washington, D.C., defended their professional turf jealously against these civilian interlopers who brashly claimed to have the expertise needed to make the supply bureaus function efficiently. Civilian management styles influenced some army supply functions, especially in bureaus such as the Ordnance and Quartermaster Corps, where the regular army officers in charge had become enamored with the possibilities of scientific management theories.[72] Civilian officers and employees uniformly found themselves frustrated by army red tape, which in the end curbed the ability of civilian businessmen to take over the supply bureaus completely. Civilian officers, however, correctly diagnosed key administrative problems, such as the failures that prompted a winter congressional investigation in 1918 after reports of soldiers shivering in their training camp tents and marching around with wooden sticks.[73] The War Department reorganized its supply functions in 1918, and General George W. Goethals appointed the presidents of prominent corporations to help the General Staff replace the old bureau system with a centralized supply system. Yet civilian businessmen in uniform often faltered in promoting efficient solutions even when accepted by regular army officers. Rather than offering one new way of organizing supply, a regular army critic charged after the war, "a multitude of systems crept in depending largely upon the prior training of the individual as to whether it was a Sears Robuck [sic] or a Montgomery Ward system."[74]

Meeting Fellow Americans in the Wartime Army

Enlisted men shivering in the training camps certainly bore the brunt of these supply failures. Looking around at one another, citizen-soldiers focused less on physical or mental differences and more on class, regional, and ethnic disparities. With no firm identity as soldiers yet created, many sought out men with similar civilian backgrounds. Milton Bernet joyfully compared going to officers' training camp to attending a college reunion. Meeting men who had played the same college sports or belonged to the same college fraternity gave him an immediate sense of belonging.[75] Henry Warren Jones did not make many friends in his training camp and noted: "I think it is the roughest bunch ever collected at one place. Many cannot read or write and nearly all are but eighth grade or less. Some have high school education. I don't know of any other man in this company besides myself who is a college graduate."[76] Not until Jones was on his way to France would he meet some other college-educated men and end his self-imposed isolation.

Citizen-soldiers brought regional tensions into the organization, which most often occurred between men from the South and the North and between city and country men. Mixing men from different regions, many soldiers vehemently complained, disrupted their efforts to maintain shared customs, traditions, and beliefs. When recruits from the Lower East Side of New York City joined a company of Texan soldiers in the 90th Division, "they changed the whole tone of battery life," Henry Ward recalled in his memoirs. "At Camp Travis, in spite of some friction and clashing of personalities it had been all for one and one for all. We had similar backgrounds and moral codes . . . we were sitting ducks for the new recruits. Socks, handkerchiefs, razors, shoes, anything—if you laid it down and looked away it was gone. Not only were they unkempt and untrained, they were lazy and rebelled against discipline."[77] Men from different regions also disturbed the protocol of race relations accepted among men from the same region. Southern white troops resented the familiarity northern officers sometimes exhibited toward black troops, while northerners viewed southerners as often fanatical in their fear of black aggressiveness.[78]

Friction also emerged among southern and northern black soldiers placed in the same units. It is difficult to gain a firsthand account of how black soldiers viewed one another in these units, because evidence of this tension comes from the observations of white intelligence officers. Some observers feared that northern blacks might persuade their southern brothers to fight for social equality. "It's like mixing rotten apples with good ones," an intelligence officer from Camp Jackson exclaimed. Others felt that educated black soldiers, who exhibited better discipline and work habits, set a good example for southern blacks.[79] Differences in educational and regional background often strained intra-company relations. "I knew one company in which negroes from Tennessee were mixed with negroes from Philadelphia. They did not get along well together, each group keeping separate, and there was considerable bad blood," observed an intelligence officer from Camp Logan, Texas. "The Philadelphia negroes asserted a superiority over the Tennessee negroes, which the latter resented."[80] These tensions in some respects resembled the tensions among whites from different regions, but black soldiers never forgot their unique position in the army. Illiterate black soldiers who saw educated black men placed in the same labor battalions as themselves became demoralized, realizing that black men, no matter how educated, were destined to become laborers in the army. "Strange to say that even the colored soldiers from the south take notice of this state of affairs and several of them mentioned the matter to me," noted Major W. H. Loving, a black officer, after inspecting conditions at Camp Humphreys, Virginia, for the War Department, "saying that the educated colored man was not given a chance."[81]

As already noted, soldiers of various European ethnicities formed another distinct group within the wartime army. Development units received enormous publicity during the war, but most ethnic soldiers received the bulk of their Americanization training from their American peers in national army units.[82] Unprepared by their civilian backgrounds to accept ethnic soldiers as their racial and cultural equals, "old stock" Americans attached derogatory labels to various ethnic groups, calling them "wops," "dagoes," "hunkies," or "guineas." In the second year of the war, morale officials waged an unsuccessful battle to eliminate ethnic slurs from the vocabulary of citizen-soldiers.

Ethnic soldiers often voluntarily separated themselves during their off-duty hours to avoid verbal or physical abuse, to speak their own languages, and to retain their own customs. Occasionally, ethnic soldiers took matters into their own hands, using the pugilist skills many urban ethnic youths had acquired. "The whole trouble started at mealtime when Joe called Merrick a wop and that was more than Merrick could stand, although he was an Italian," a soldier in the 91st Division recounted in his memoirs. The slur incited Merrick to kick the offending soldier in the throat while he was sleeping. The soldier awoke, grabbed Merrick by the throat, and "would have choked him to death if my brother Ralph had not talked him into stopping before it was too late."[83]

Soldiers of German descent formed another distinct ethnic group within the army. Large numbers of Germans had emigrated to the United States since the early nineteenth century, and the descendants of these immigrants constituted a substantial part of the eligible draft population. In the 90th Division, men from Texan German-speaking communities formed small cliques who "used extensive German language in the barracks, etc. The rest of us did not question their patriotism . . . however there must have been some qualms from some quarter as they were all apparently investigated . . . and one or two were transferred out," a veteran of the division recalled.[84] Edward Schafer, the son of German immigrants, enlisted in the 26th Division against the wishes of his widowed mother, who reminded him that his father had left Germany to avoid compulsory military service. Schafer understood his unique position in the wartime army when he balked at serving men what he suspected was spoiled meat. As he told a medical officer, "I am of German descent and if I serve them food I feel I shouldn't I am in trouble if a whole company of 250 men are made sick."[85]

An array of civilians, therefore, came into direct contact with the army during the war, either to help it select, entertain, and induct citizen-soldiers or as the men recruited to perform the key task of winning the war. As these exchanges and relationships multiplied, so did the impact of civilian attitudes on the emerging wartime army. During the mobilization process, the army agreed with civilian decisions and attitudes more often than it disagreed. This was fortunate, because dependence on public support to mobilize a civilian-based army would have made it difficult for officials to resist conditions imposed by civilian society over who served and how they served.

Army officials quelled their doubts about conscripted troops by inculcating the principle of unquestioning obedience immediately among recruits, but new questions of how the army should command citizen-soldiers soon appeared. It would now be up to citizen-soldiers to determine the scope of the army's wartime authority. Army officials had only just begun to appreciate how vast a challenge it would be to mold their recruits, who had ideas of their own, into a compliant mass army.

2

AMERICANS AS WARRIORS

War had always created new challenges for American armies, but military officials set unique goals during the Great War, even for wartime. In an important modification of previous wartime policies, the federal army for the first time established a uniform training program. During the Civil War, the majority of men had entered local volunteer regiments, which state governments had equipped, trained, and provided with officers. Citizen-soldiers' experience during World War I differed dramatically. The federal army wanted to do more than train soldiers well enough to avoid catastrophic battle casualties, or even use a standardized training program to solidify its supervisory control of the nation's war effort and thereby diminish the National Guard's importance. Army officials also intended to create a relatively closed institutional environment in which common values and behavior would help distance citizen-soldiers from their previous lives and foster a sense of common purpose among them.

Unsurprisingly, the army did not develop its training program with the help of civilians but depended on its own experts in turning civilians into soldiers. At times the wartime army appeared quite like other government agencies charged with mobilizing the civilian population for war, and the challenge of assimilating and disciplining citizen-soldiers bore a remarkable resemblance to the problems that industrialists in civilian society faced controlling a workforce with a mind of its own. These analogies help pinpoint key characteristics of the changing American military establishment, revealing its evolution into both a powerful state agency and a giant bureaucratic enterprise. Yet, at the same time, the distinctively violent purpose for which the army existed separated it dramatically from the federal agencies and corporations it resembled.

Life within the army revolved around the unique wartime mission that citizen-soldiers now shared with federal army officials. Through its formal training program and contrived recreational activities, the army fostered a culture of aggressiveness acceptable only within the confines of the military. As all citizen-soldiers, regardless of their eventual destination within this military "corporation," embraced their distinct wartime mission, a unifying spirit gradually emerged among them.

Yet in many ways the army would become a victim of its own success in fostering the notion that a courageous performance on the battlefield served as the truest test of manhood and patriotism, for many men in the wartime army were not headed for the battlefield. Ironically, as the overall destructive capabilities of the nation's military multiplied, the percentage of men who actually faced imminent death on the battlefield decreased. An assignment behind the lines belied everything that citizen-soldiers' preconceived expectations and training camp experiences had prepared them to confront during their military service. The contradiction between the belligerent posture the army enticed all recruits to embrace and what military service actually entailed for noncombatants precipitated an unforeseen crisis of identity for noncombatants in the wartime army. Even combatants had trouble relating the reality of combat to the romanticized ideal they brought to France.

Turning Civilians into Soldiers

In keeping with their intention to create a coherent federal organization, rather than a loose confederation of local military divisions, the General Staff developed a standard training program. An important departure from the country's wartime traditions, this decision also undermined the customary freedom of regular army commanders to train their peacetime units as they saw fit. Many regular army wartime commanders initially objected to this sudden curtailment of their command autonomy. The War Plans Division, however, refused to compromise on the principle that primary authority to define the wartime army's training lay with Pershing, who had already established his headquarters in France.[1]

The ambition to translate Pershing's dictums into a uniform domestic training program was imperfectly realized during the war. At first, for example, the War Plans Division prepared a comprehensive course in trench warfare, which divisional commanders undertook with the help of British and French instructors. This program continued unabated until Pershing reiterated to the General Staff in no uncertain terms that he wanted stateside training to emphasize marksmanship. The War Plans Division initially required each commander to send a weekly training schedule, then switched to a system of sending out field inspectors when it became clear that divisions were not following the professed schedules commanders were sending to Washington.

Report after report from these inspectors detailed the state of confusion in the camps. A commander's willingness to follow the War Plans Division's program became almost irrelevant, because men trickled into the camps unevenly for months, making it impossible for even the most dedicated commander to adhere completely to these schedules. Induction centers efficiently sent men to the camps, but shortages of supplies and barracks forced the War Department to stagger new camp arrivals. The 84th Division, one inspector reported in the spring, had 5,755 men with less than two weeks' training, 9,389 with less than four weeks' training, and 10,062 with less than two months' training.[2] Many recruits arrived at camps still under construction, and consequently they spent many early days building their own training trenches and rifle ranges. These kinds of conditions kept men at Camp Greene, North Carolina, busy "trying to keep comfortable, . . . cutting and hauling wood, digging ditches, [and] building up company streets" during their first few weeks in camp, reported a division inspector. Transferring trained men out of already formed units to fill specialist units or to bring divisions about to depart for France up to strength, and then replacing them with raw recruits, exacerbated training discrepancies within divisions.[3]

Despite problems establishing a coherent training regime in the camps, the designated program did define the skills and attitudes that the War Plans Division and Pershing expected men to acquire before the process of transforming them from civilians to soldiers was complete. Army trainers in the camps agreed with their General Staff colleagues that constant close order drill during the first few weeks of camp taught recruits to obey orders unquestioningly. Some trainers went to enormous lengths to emphasize this point. The officer drilling William Graf's company marched the men straight to a steep embankment, waiting until the last moment before ordering them to halt. If he had not given the order to stop, he warned them, their only option would have been to march over the edge. Some recruits, however, interpreted this drilling as aimless wandering around a field, and, like Captain Roy Meyers, itched to get on to the "real" task of learning to kill Germans. Like many, Sergeant Charles R. Blatt viewed drills as "tiresome, and an appalling waste of time."[4]

Pershing expected citizen-soldiers to perfect their marksmanship during their stateside training, a view recruits shared. Most regular and citizen-soldiers agreed with the sentiment, expressed by one inspector general, that "one cannot become a thoroughly trained soldier without first becoming a good shot."[5] Pershing's training principles established the rifle and bayonet as the principal weapons of the combat soldier. Besides the obvious advantages in combat of knowing how to fire a rifle effectively, the army wanted soldiers who trusted their weapons and their own ability to use them. Yet equipment shortages seriously hampered the adequacy of this training. "I thought we ought to be getting acquainted with the rifle but we only had the wooden type play guns," Sergeant Richard McBride recalled.[6]

Aggressiveness accompanied discipline and individual marksmanship as key training goals. Pershing derived this principle from his own reading of what had gone wrong for the Allies on the Western Front. Trench warfare, the AEF commander concluded, had weakened the aggressive spirit of the Allied Forces, and now their troops fought ineffectively when forced out of the trenches and into the open battlefield. Pershing's strategy to win the war focused on open warfare. Although it was never clearly defined as a tactical strategy, for training purposes, open warfare meant teaching men personal combat skills so that they would be willing to fight without trench or artillery protection. To underscore how differently Pershing expected his troops to fight, trainers in the camps emphasized to recruits that Americans' innate individualism and aggressiveness made them naturally superior to French, British, and German soldiers.[7] Senior officers, who predicted the war would last another two years, believed that unless American soldiers maintained an aggressive determination to win, they would be unable to fight for that long. Each man "must be made to feel he cannot be beaten," Major General Charles Summerall concluded. "They must be placed in an exalted mental state in which they resolve to die rather than dishonor themselves or their country by retreating or surrendering."[8] Changes in the Infantry Drill regulations also reflected the new expectations of what the soldier would face on the battlefield. The 1917 version simply required a soldier to memorize the answers to questions asked during inspections. By May 1918, however, lessons from the limited fighting experiences of the AEF came trickling back to the United States, and now Infantry Drill regulations cautioned soldiers that during inspections they would have to learn to think for themselves when asked hypothetical questions about tactical situations, and to give the solution that "advances the line farthest with the least loss of men, time, and control."[9]

An army that barely managed to teach its frontline troops how to fire a rifle had no time to give noncombatants much military training in the aggressive ideal. Engineers, the largest noncombatant technical service, found themselves detailed immediately to construction projects after a minimum of specialized training. "We weren't really trained," Private Jack Ninneman recalled, "we were an engineering unit and were expected to be expert in maintaining or rebuilding roads and bridges, . . . [we were] trained in trucks and shovels."[10] Signal and Transportation Corps soldiers, who needed skills less common in civilian industry, attended specialist schools before beginning their work. Service units, however, received neither military nor specialist training. Most labor battalions, many of them black, were "simply filled up—uniformed and shipped," noted an investigator from Camp Greene.[11]

Noncombatants constituted a significant portion of the army's workforce. The technological sophistication of modern warfare, combined with the increased bureaucratic and logistical needs of a mass army, had created numerous new noncombatant positions. For the first time, more soldiers served as skilled technicians and supply, transportation, and service troops than as combat soldiers. In the Civil War, combatants had formed over 90 percent of the army, but by World War I, this had dropped to 40 percent. Approximately 33 percent of the army consisted of skilled noncombatants, including 13.5 percent who were craftsmen, 7.4 percent mechanics or repairmen, 6.8 percent technicians, and 5.3 percent administrative or clerical staff. The remaining 27 percent of the army performed unskilled or semi-skilled labor.[12] These unskilled support troops typically worked on construction projects, at road repair, or as stevedores.

The reactions of noncombatant troops to their brief, or nonexistent, military training in part reflected their initial impressions of the status of their noncombatant work. Skilled men, who had often enlisted in specialist units to avoid the draft, expected to evade all types of infantry duties. These engineers, loggers, machinists, railroad workers, and miners considered their skills more valuable than more easily learned infantry skills and resented any drilling. Colonel P. S. Bond thought that the 107th Engineer Regiment had excellent construction skills, but noticed that the unit's officers were having a hard time drilling these men. "An organization of intelligent men such as this one very rapidly reaches a certain indifferent military standard with which they appear to be content," Bond noted.[13]

Black soldiers, relegated to low-status assignments as unskilled labor-ers, reacted with dismay to minimal training opportunities.[14] "I didn't come to the army to learn how to work, I came to learn how to fight," la-mented Private Arthur Daniels, but complaints like his fell on deaf ears.[15] Nervous about how civilians would react to the black soldiers they sta-tioned permanently in the South, the General Staff decided not to issue these labor units uniforms. "Each southern state has negroes in blue over-alls working throughout the state with a pick and shovel," Colonel E. D. Anderson observed. He recommended that the image and demeanor of army labor units resemble these civilian work groups as much as possible.[16] Intent on assuring the public that these men were not really soldiers, the army not surprisingly convinced them of the same thing. Many recognized their status as conscripted laborers, a War Department investigator dis-covered. One man he interviewed "expressed this attitude by saying that their manpower was wanted but not their manhood."[17]

These diverse training experiences indicate that no period of stan-dard military instruction existed to unify wartime troops. Nonetheless, as combatants and noncombatants prepared for their respective assignments, they realized that in many respects, they were sharing a unique lifetime experience. One official documented the appearance of this encompassing perspective among citizen-soldiers when he noted that after a few months, "morale improves but it is seemingly by means of an increasing gang spirit in which the higher ideals are not predominant."[18] Common concerns, fears, frustrations, and expectations permeated the training camp experi-ence. The exams, shots, baths, abusive noncommissioned officers, inept supply officers, quarantine, terrible food, ill-fitting uniforms, repetitious drills, long marches, and slow mail delivery provided ample material for shared complaints and criticisms. An army folklore soon emerged, includ-ing horror stories about "the bullpen" in which soldiers waited like cattle on their first day, veteran recruits who razzed new men about foot-long needles, and constant rumors of immediate departure for France.

These universal attributes of the training camp experience only partly developed the communal spirit that soon prevailed stateside, for the army also sought to promote a common army esprit de corps based on a cult of aggressiveness. This was true even of the CTCA, the agency primarily responsible for providing recreational and entertainment activities for sol-diers. To make their efforts at wholesome moral uplift more palatable to army officials, CTCA reformers designed their recreational programs to reinforce the aggressive ideals stressed in more formal military instruction. This won the CTCA's camp programs avid official cooperation, especially the boxing program, which soon became its most popular offering.

A mania for boxing swept through the camps when the CTCA hired professional prizefighters to teach soldiers the finer points of the manly art. From the CTCA's standpoint, boxing provided a healthy diversion that kept participants and spectators away from bootleggers and prostitutes, but superior officers became enamored with the CTCA's effort to mimic the motions essential to successful bayonet fighting in its boxing lessons. Because these programs dominated the recreational life of the camp, they also inadvertently reinforced the distinctive mission of the wartime soldier to noncombatants as well. Through the camp boxing program, most soldiers, regardless of their eventual destination within the army, participated in the prevailing cult of aggressiveness.

The army had clear reasons for sponsoring massive boxing programs, and citizen-soldiers responded enthusiastically to boxing, especially to the prizefighters who organized camp bouts. As one division commander noted, the former prizefighter in his camp was "just the kind that enlisted men love to follow and so successful in his instruction that he gets excellent results."[19] Why, however, did enlisted men "love to follow" their boxing instructors? The answer perhaps can be found by reexamining some of the common expectations these men had of military service. Many citizen-soldiers believed that they would face the ultimate test of their manhood on the battlefields in France. In many respects boxing instructors epitomized the masculine ideal most soldiers subscribed to when they entered the army. "After a man has boxed a few rounds he knows what this means and he stands up and takes what is coming to him if he is any kind of man," the boxing instructor at Camp Custer, Michigan, told his classes.[20] Boxing instructors provided living illustrations of the courage, virility, self-reliance, and self-control that recruits imagined, and officers and noncommissioned officers told them, successful soldiers possessed. The military community's obsession with physical expressions of masculinity encouraged many soldiers to accept the challenge to prove their soldierly merit in the camp boxing ring. Within the camps, however, boxing also helped sustain harsh and, at times, brutal customs that served soldiers' own distinctive purposes. "When I went into the service with 200 other men in my company, our captain told us we should be able to leave our money or valuables on our beds safely," Mortimer Myers recalled. "If it was stolen do not complain to him, we should know how to handle it. We did."[21] Soldiers boxed to settle grudges, gain prestige, and earn money or privileges by participating in tournaments. Successful boxers became renowned within their respective units. When Kenneth Jones's company lined up one morning during his first few weeks in Camp Lewis, Washington, "a slender guy elbowed his way ahead of me and I asked him who he thought he was, but he only grinned. The next day I mentioned it to one of our fellows and asked who could this man be? . . . He told me that it was Billy Nelson, the lightweight champion of Camp Lewis, and I replied well I am glad I didn't say any more to Nelson, and he laughed."[22]

Fighting Overseas

In France, it soon became apparent that the focus on individual aggressiveness and marksmanship had been at the expense of other skills needed to turn the trench stalemate into a war of movement. Pershing's strategy of open warfare required effective coordination between artillery and infantry units, but these units rarely completed the joint training exercises needed to perfect their battlefield maneuvers. AEF planners had further hampered their army's mobility by rejecting light howitzers in favor of heavy French 75-mm and 155-mm guns, which improved the firepower of artillery units but limited their ability to keep up with the advancing infantry.[23] Coordination between the two branches also suffered when unreliable communications made it difficult for frontline scouts to redirect artillery fire in response to developments on the field.

American soldiers' battlefield behavior indicated that training doctrine, especially one imperfectly taught and learned, was a poor predictor of how troops would fight. Stateside training had emphasized the importance of marksmanship, but inspectors quickly discovered that many troops resisted advancing without artillery support and stopped when their big guns got mired in mud or fog. "The officers of infantry battalions that were fortunate enough to have their accompanying guns or infantry batteries keep up with them," reported the AEF inspector general, "stated that their fire was very 'comforting' to the men and greatly increased their determination to advance upon the various strong points that started to hold up the line."[24] Without enough artillery firepower to cover them on the opening days of the Meuse-Argonne offensive in late September 1918, slow-moving tanks drew such heavy enemy artillery fire that American soldiers refused to advance near them and abandoned them to enemy troops, who dropped grenades through portholes.[25] In October, wounded American soldiers told investigators that they felt safer with French artillery support, which they rated as more dependable than the American.[26]

The other major criticism of citizen-soldiers' combat behavior seems to contradict the assessment that American soldiers hesitated to advance without their artillery. "In the front line trenches awaiting the orders that would send them into the jaws of certain death, let's go was the phrase that was impatiently circulated down the trenches, [and] as they charged over the top with their buddies falling about them, it was still let's go, let's go against German machine fire," recalled a chaplain who went into battle with the 80th Division.[27] Commanders claimed that they could not stop men who understood the desirability of aggressiveness from rushing straight into machine-gun fire. They had, one soldier explained, been told repeatedly that "the sole idea of the American Army was to attack, to push forward."[28] When the AEF inspector general evaluated the army's performance from September to November 11, 1918, he noted that when enemy machine guns held up attacking lines, reserve lines would surge forward into the front line rather than wait. Despite repeated orders, he claimed, "the rear lines could not be made to see that their crowding forward did not help the attack but merely fed the men to the machine guns."[29] This was not solely the fault of the men. Officers leading their men into battle, Colonel George Marshall acknowledged after the war, abandoned tactical maneuvering in favor of "steamroller operations" that forced men to keep going until exhaustion stopped them, because "morale suffered from delays under fire."[30]

Anticipating the importance of sheer numbers on the Western Front, the AEF had assembled divisions much larger than European ones. Pershing reasoned, in part, that larger divisions would be able to stay in the field longer, but instead they soon proved unwieldy and difficult to maneuver in battle. Rather than improving the staying power of troops in the line, large divisions filled with poorly trained troops only raised casualty rates.

In one breath, army commanders lambasted reserve troops for rushing forward, and in the next, they complained that troops hung back waiting for their artillery units to catch up with them. These seemingly contradictory battle responses both indicate, however, that citizen-soldiers did not want to expose themselves individually on the battlefield. Soldiers tried instead to create some relative combat safety by advancing in groups or with artillery protection. Precise and detailed battle plans also undermined training camp lessons in individual initiative. With circumstances forcing him to send many troops into battle before they had completed their training program, Pershing understandably tried to predetermine the objectives and motions of his army. Prescribed orders contradicted the importance he attributed to initiative in battle, however, and in the St. Mihiel offensive (September 12–15, 1918) and the Meuse-Argonne campaign (September 26–November 11, 1918), some divisions reached their preset objectives easily and then halted, thereby giving the Germans time to regroup and counterattack (see map 1).[31]

AEF commanders' lack of confidence in their imperfectly trained troops mirrored citizen-soldiers' realization that the army had not prepared them adequately for combat. Soldiers training in Camp Meade, Maryland, when the war ended, who never went overseas, rated their combat readiness as high. Most respondents had had at least six months' training and claimed that they had received between 75 percent to 100 percent of the training they would desire before risking their lives in battle.[32] Combat veterans tended to respond quite differently to questions about their training. "I am afraid that we had too many who were like me to fight a well trained army, and it cost us dearly," one veteran sadly concluded.[33] When asked if his training had prepared him adequately for overseas service, Sergeant Fred Ross replied, "No! Our training was for camp routine, how to use a rifle, etc., not much for active war conduct."[34] Others questioned why army trainers emphasized marksmanship when hand grenades served as much more effective trench weapons. Learning Infantry Drill Regulations wasted valuable training time for combat-bound soldiers, another veteran asserted. What infantrymen really needed to know, according to Private T. P. Wilson, was "do what you are told, and exercise common sense, and in so far as possible, do not make a target of yourself while doing it."[35]

What the official training program failed to provide, citizen-soldiers sometimes could cull from other sources in the field. Battlefield conditions—whether in the trenches or on the open battlefield—created numerous opportunities for individual soldiers to manipulate operational and training doctrine. By passing along tips, customs, and trench protocol, Allied soldiers and veteran American troops assumed the responsibility of training newcomers to survive their deadly contest with the German Army. This "in the field" education was often more substantial and important than anything citizen-soldiers received in the training camps. Citizen-soldiers conducted their "classes" for one another far away from the supervisory authority of senior officers.

Allied soldiers with whom they initially trained were the first independent source of information that American soldiers encountered in France.

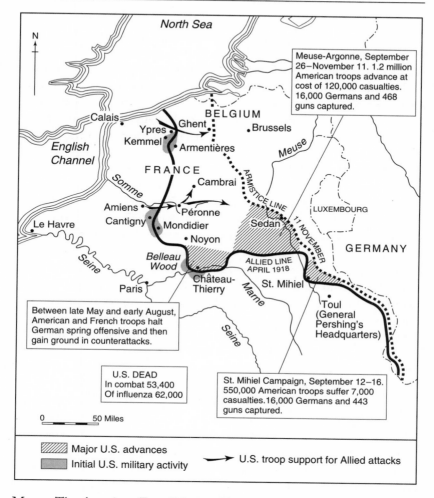

Map 1. The American Expeditionary Forces, 1918. *Source:* Martin Gilbert, *Atlas of the First World War* (London: Orion Publishing Group, 1994), p. 112.

Sometimes, recently arrived U.S. troops solicited advice immediately from Allied troops about what to expect in the trenches, but most often they waited until after their initial turn in the front line. Allied General Staffs had developed a trench warfare doctrine in 1915 that required entrenched troops to harass the enemy constantly. It prescribed minimum daily goals for snipers, raiding parties, and heavy artillery units. Allied commanders had hoped these aggressions would keep the war active and unpredictable. In the trenches, however, Allied soldiers cultivated defensive skills to protect themselves against the reciprocal assaults provoked by such constant belligerence. One tactic ritualized these required offensive actions. Artillery and sniper attacks began and ended at the same time every day, with gunners aiming shells into no-man's-land rather than at the opposite trench. Patrols who silently avoided each other at night also helped troops keep their unspoken truces.[36] This "live-and-let-live" mentality particularly pervaded troops who occupied relatively quiet sectors of the Western Front.

Green American soldiers, lectured in camp on Allied defeatism, tended to view such trench rituals as evidence of Allied soldiers' cowardice. Edward Schafer recalled that during his unit's first tour of duty with French troops, they stared out at no-man's-land until "our barbed wire posts seemed to be moving, causing many of the men believing [sic] they actually saw the enemy's men at the wire." This, he noted, "started uncalled for machine gun, rifle fire, and at times artillery fire . . . until someone not so fatigued would calm this whole action down."[37] Their initial eagerness to engage the Germans angered the French troops supervising them. The French complained that their constant sniping disturbed the unspoken agreement between French and German troops to limit shelling along this quiet sector of the front. The Germans would respond to these disruptions with equally unpredictable shell attacks, these tired French troops claimed, and soon life in the trenches would become unbearable.

Despite their initial disdain, Americans eventually learned to mimic the behavior of the Allied soldiers. Corporal Elmer Roden learned the importance of forecasting imminent danger; "in combat we named the different shells by their sounds, they were whizz-bangs, 75s and the large ones from heavy artillery we called GI cans," he recalled.[38] Private Ernie Hilton "had heard of the fellows dodging bullets and now I am learning how to do this myself, with great speed whenever the warning is given," he assured his family. Hilton responded to every passing shell by falling flat on his face and waiting for it to pass, but the noise it made through the air indicated to him how much danger existed. "Whenever the sound is as if crying the danger is slight, as the shell will pass over your head. There's just two sounds, a scream or a cry," he noted in his letter home.[39] "When you are under fire a shovel is as important as your rifle," another soldier noted. "I had to get a shovel off the first dead German I found."[40] Members of the 42nd Division, sequestered with British troops during the winter, went so far as to help these Allied troops maintain established shelling rituals. American soldiers in this division could then move freely about, except between two and four o'clock in the afternoon, when the Germans shot off their required rounds of ammunition.[41] In another sector, British soldiers with a less benevolent view of their enemies captivated American soldiers with vivid stories of German dirty tricks. They told how Germans had once got hold of some British grenades and replaced the safety fuse with instantaneous fuse. The Germans then threw these rigged grenades with the pins still in place into the British trenches, where British soldiers, thinking the Germans didn't know enough to pull the pin, would themselves pull the pin and immediately be killed. American soldiers learned "that this was common practice for the Germans and that it wasn't safe to pick up anything that they left behind. They even booby trapped such things as cameras, field glasses and their cases and most anything you might be tempted to pick up as a souvenir."[42]

The flaws American trench veterans noted in replacement troops revealed how much they themselves had learned during their time on the line and from Allied soldiers. By October 1918, AEF combat divisions faced serious troop shortages of almost 80,000 men.[43] Pershing broke up seven newly organized divisions when they arrived in France and funneled these recruits directly into veteran units. With neither the stateside camps nor the AEF taking time to train them, many untrained men found themselves headed for the front. Milton Sweningsen "was on the firing range once" before finding himself "at the bottom of a hill, in a pit of fog, and on the attack."[44] Individual initiative took on a new meaning when it referred to the lack of unit cohesion caused by replacement policies that sent strangers marching into battle together.

Division commanders complained bitterly about these men, feeling, as one inspector general put it, that sending untrained men into battle was "little short of murder. How we have escaped a catastrophe is a clear demonstration of the German demoralization."[45] Although aware of their poor preparation, few untrained replacement troops refused to fight. Instead, "when issued rifles they asked to be shown 'how to work this thing so that they could go up and get a boche,'" exclaimed the inspector general.[46] Private Michael Byrne, who wrote an account of his combat experience while recuperating from wounds in an army hospital, began his army career as a truck driver in the Quartermaster Corps. After accepting a transfer into the infantry to "see a little excitement," Byrne entered the trenches without any rifle training. There he had a few shaky days getting used to the constant sound of shell explosions before entering the line.

"This was my first time to go on the lines and [I] knew the fellows would all be looking to see how I would act," Byrne recalled. As he advanced and saw the first casualties hit the ground, he felt his "teeth come a little tighter together" and his lips "grow into a wild but silent smile . . . the feeling that I had wanted was now on me." Byrne happily had mustered up what he considered an appropriately aggressive demeanor in his first battle, the kind he expected veteran soldiers would be looking for in him. Veteran soldiers probably took more notice of the fact that, like many untrained men who did not know how to protect themselves at the front, Byrne was wounded almost immediately.[47]

Veteran troops had to contend with more than green enlisted men during critical moments in the fighting. Not only was the casualty rate among line officers high, but promising officers were sent to AEF training courses, exacerbating soldiers' fears that they were going into battle without the leadership they needed. When a new captain sent up to join the 111th Infantry of the 28th Division had a company redecorate the bare stretch of ground in front of their trench with scrub pines, "this should have been like waving a red flag at a bull or putting up a sign that said shell here," complained one veteran of the area.[48] The Germans must have suspected a trick, he surmised, so the men did not have to pay the ultimate price for this officer's foolishness. When asked about the quality of leadership at the front, former Private Gus M. Kantrud echoed the views of many when he replied, "the leadership at the top, I think was good but at the front it changed so often it was hard to tell."[49]

For late-arriving troops, combat veterans became the primary source of information about how to conduct themselves in the front lines. The numerous mistakes replacement troops made during their first trench tour included throwing rifles away when they jammed and forgetting passwords when returning from a patrol. Men who repeated the instructions they had received in training camp on "how to take a bath at the front" amused combat veterans who felt lucky having enough water to drink in their canteens. Few could hope to prepare for the reality of life along the Western Front, where soldiers adjusted to living with mud, rats, debris, and the stench of decomposing bodies. Fear, dirty water, and spoiled food made diarrhea a common ailment of the troops. "A sergeant of ours tore his pants open and squatted whenever he felt the need," Private Arthur Nelson recalled.[50] The shock of this degradation caused bewilderment among many replacements. These new men also disrupted the routine earlier men had established, and veterans voiced complaints similar to the ones French soldiers had made about them. Sleepless nights for all increased during the false gas alarms and wild shooting that accompanied the arrival of new troops.[51] Combat veterans often took the time to teach these new men proper trench protocol to minimize these dangers. Veterans' advice, their religious beliefs, and the superstitions and rumors that circulated among the troops all helped combatants cope with the physical, psychological, and emotional strain of combat.[52]

Few combatants squarely confronted the irrationality of their situation, in which men died indiscriminately every day. Many remained adamant in believing that order could be discerned in the chaos of frontline life. Soldiers often contended, for instance, that only one deadly shell had a man's name or number on it. Fate, rather than the Germans, targeted this shell expressly at him. Bernard Eubanks revealed in his wartime recollections how obsessed he personally became with this idea. One night, "I had a strange dream or nightmare really. My company number was 84. During an intense bombardment I saw a huge missile coming my way with my number, 84, on it . . . but it passed over and never touched me." His temperament changed dramatically after this dream, because it "seemed to give me a sense of immunity that stayed with me for quite a while. I lost my jittery feeling."[53] Just as Eubanks's positive vision gave him comfort, others believed that poorly chosen thoughts or conversations jinxed them. Corporal Ernie Hilton recalled the time he and his buddies overcame their reluctance to discuss the future, a subject they usually considered taboo, and had a long conversation about what they planned to do after the war. The next day, thirty-four of the forty men in the trench were wounded or killed during a shell attack. "From then on I never spoke of the future," Hilton said.[54] Others turned to more traditional sources for resolve. "My prayer book gave me courage and comfort when under fire," Sergeant Stephen Morray recalled.[55]

Besides seeking comfort and protection in their cultural customs, citizen-soldiers monitored the habits of their German opponents. An array of rumors helped soldiers create tangible images of their unseen enemy. Thirsty for information about the enemy who sometimes resided only a few hundred yards away from them, these "soldier's tales," as army authorities termed them, described extraordinary German cleverness and brutality. In a favorite ruse, according to company storytellers, German soldiers wore French uniforms or Red Cross brassards, pretended they were wounded, and lay on the battlefield to lure Allied soldiers in direct range of German machine guns. Another German trick began with a group of German machine gunners pretending to surrender by yelling "Comrade" in order to draw the troops who came to collect the prisoners into the open. Equally gory stories of the bloodthirsty revenge American soldiers exacted for such crimes countered these lavish tales of barbaric treachery. Soldiers repeatedly spoke of companies who captured snipers, gave them shovels, forced them to dig their own graves, then shot them.

A particularly popular rumor told of a "man found crucified upside down and therefore we won't take any prisoners." According to this legend, U.S. troops had retaliated for the crucifixion of an American soldier by castrating German prisoners before killing them. An investigator sent to discover the truth behind these tales of American atrocities observed that "each division seems to have a tough regiment upon which these tales were pinned in each area [along the front.]" This investigator concluded that U.S. troops had not actually committed these acts, but had simply adopted stories also popular among British, Canadian, and French troops. "Our soldiers appear to delight in telling how fierce they are, and any good tale in circulation is quickly appropriated," he concluded.[56] This provides striking evidence that soldiers used their combat experiences to reinforce, rather than reject, the aggressive ideal given to them in their training camp days.

However, some men at least temporarily rejected or withdrew from the prevailing cult of aggression. After-battle accounts all include some mention of soldiers breaking down under the strain of the hours-long artillery bombardments that opened attacks, seeing bodies blown to bits, wearing tight, hot gas masks for hours, or sheer exhaustion.[57] After morning-to-night bombardments during the three straight weeks the 78th Division spent along the front lines in the Meuse-Argonne campaign, some soldiers "went into shock or coma from which they could not be aroused . . . these shell-shock victims fell down as if they had been hit but actually they hadn't been touched," Corporal Paul Murphy recalled in 1963; "they were completely helpless, mumbling and trembling at each new explosion."[58] Most soldiers who suffered from shell shock, battle exhaustion, or gas hysteria (a malady in which soldiers described physical symptoms associated with gas but had no actual injuries) voluntarily returned to the front after a few days' rest in a field hospital. In the 28th Division, for example, once the tremors had stopped and speech and memory returned, field psychiatrists emphasized to men that their comrades needed them and that the glory of victory would be lost to them forever if they failed to return to the front. In case they doubted the cause, Dr. Edward A. Strecker pointed to the columns of German prisoners often streaming past the hospitals in the Meuse-Argonne theater. During a time when, as one chaplain noted, "the abnormal was normal," doctors considered returning to face combat once again a rational and sane decision for these men to make.[59] Men returned to the front after these appeals to their honor, masculinity, duty, and ambition, but whether this rest cured soldiers remains in dispute, because veterans suffering from shell shock filled three out of every five beds in government hospitals in the interwar period.[60] Shell-shocked men did not receive wound chevrons to mark them as suffering from a legitimate war injury. According to the chief surgeon of the Medical Department, "the so-called 'shell-shock' patients are no more entitled to a 'wound' chevron than are soldiers who are seized with an acute medical complaint due to exposure in battle, to the elements or to bad water or indigestible food."[61]

The constant presence of danger and fear in combatants' lives underscored the emotional and physical distance between combatant and noncombatant wartime experiences. Yet behind the lines, noncombatants also faced distinctive challenges that forced them to ask how well the army had prepared them for the lives they were leading overseas. Whether assigned to menial or skilled positions, noncombatants all confronted the same basic dilemma: noncombatant work simply did not inspire them to act and feel like soldiers. The aggressive ideal haunted noncombatants, and many wondered whether the government could legitimately conscript them to work, rather than fight, in the wartime army.

Working in the Wartime Army

Both at home and overseas, the army now asked many wartime soldiers to perform tasks normally reserved for civilian laborers. American wartime armies had always needed a huge labor force to provide logistical support. In previous wars, however, the army had relied primarily on civilian contractors to perform this work. A severe shortage of civilian workers at home and in France, along with prohibitively high civilian wages, precluded the army from hiring or transporting workers overseas. Liaison officers sent overseas in the summer of 1917 realized immediately that the AEF would not be able to hire French laborers. "One sees nothing," Major General James Harbord noted during his initial overseas visit, "but old men, sad-eyed women and children in little towns and on the farms."[62] Consequently, the army decided to secure the bulk of the labor it needed from the twenty-four million men available through the Selective Service system. Pershing could not maintain an independent army in France without also bringing over sizable numbers of support troops, and he eventually secured enough shipping space to bring approximately 670,000 nondivisional service troops to France.[63] Developing a large internal noncombatant population became a significant step in the army's institutional development, because the self-sufficiency that resulted enhanced its ability to pursue the war autonomously. It also meant, however, that a significant number of soldiers would spend the war working, rather than fighting, for their country.

Some noncombatants spent the entire war in the United States working side by side with civilian workers, and for them military service primarily meant losing discretion over where they labored. Army authorities occasionally sent men to districts experiencing severe labor shortages during a harvest or to work in civilian industries.[64] A picric acid plant in Brunswick, Georgia, for example, received furloughed black soldiers for three months.[65] After a series of strikes threatened to paralyze the lumbering industry in the Pacific Northwest, the army dispersed 30,000 soldiers through 234 camps in Oregon and Washington.[66] Uniformed soldiers also served on domestic road crews. Working side by side with civilians who received five dollars a day, as compared to their one dollar, incensed these noncombatant troops.[67] Despite their complaints about the legitimacy of these work assignments, these soldiers remained stuck on these crews for the duration of the war. Congress did not question this practice until the postwar winter of 1919, when legislators scrutinized every aspect of the war effort. Congress then legislated, a bit too late, that the army could not send soldiers to work on the roads unless they had volunteered for this work and were compensated with civilian-scale wages.[68]

In France, having successfully brought over the labor his army needed, Pershing turned his attention to his combatant divisions and delegated support responsibilities to a new department, the Service of Supply (SOS).[69] The SOS was an umbrella organization that coordinated the work of previously independent bureaus, whose functions had often overlapped. Within the SOS, engineer troops served primarily in construction and railroad units, signal corps troops manned telegraph and telephone lines, and quartermaster units organized and transported supplies, while the medical corps operated army hospitals. The SOS not only purchased and transported supplies to combatant units but also commanded replacement troops until they joined organized combat divisions. Not all men who performed noncombatant tasks, however, belonged to the SOS. Noncombatant positions within combat units existed in the headquarters staff, supply and ambulance trains, and in attached engineer and signal corps units. Twenty percent of the troops in each division were assigned to non-combatant duties.[70] The SOS was only officially part of the AEF organization, but "SOS" became the common designation for all noncombatant army work both at home and overseas.

The army recognized its dependence on the combatants' willingness to persevere on the battlefield, and the same principle held behind the lines as well. With too few officers to supervise all noncombatants directly, supporting their morale by other means became critical. Numerous signs soon appeared, however, that noncombatants had little motivation to perform the tedious tasks assigned to them unless under the threat of army authority. It was a common sight, for example, to see squads of enlisted men loafing on the side of the road and taking advantage of their freedom to drink and meet Frenchwomen.[71] When the venereal disease rate began rising among unsupervised black road crews, General Harbord concluded that the sexual freedom they gained "no doubt accounts in part for the willingness of colored troops to be employed on this road work."[72] That bands of men AWOL from combat units in the Second Army could successfully elude military authorities by claiming that they belonged to such road crews further attested to the road crews' relative independence.[73] When Private Henry Stewart went to work on the roads behind no-man's-land, he and some friends turned an abandoned German dugout into a private residence. Stewart built a stove, nailed up a door, and found a lamp to make the dugout "more homelike." He and his friends filled their dugout with food they had pilfered for late-night snacks. The energy they expended fixing up their new home differed distinctly from their attitude to their official job. "[T]hey have been pushing us so hard that we just naturally slow up," Stewart recorded in his diary on October 18, 1918.[74] With no tangible rewards for those who worked harder, many unsupervised soldiers worked slowly.[75]

Noncombatants were becoming an increasingly alienated faction within the wartime army. Even those who chose an assignment in the rear had anticipated that going to France would be an exciting, dangerous adventure, and the actual monotony of life in the rear thus took these troops by surprise. "Our work here was to assemble motor cycles, trucks and automobiles" arriving off ships from the United States, Melvin Wroolie recalled of one work assignment. Despite the obvious importance of these motor vehicles, Wroolie and his comrades remained indifferent to their contribution to the war effort. "Most of us had no idea where the parts belonged, but put them where they seemed to fit best. In some cases the machines would go backwards when started up. This work was very tedious and the Y was a very popular place especially when hot chocolate was served during work time," he recalled.[76]

By deliberately working slowly, or refusing to work outside direct supervision, increasingly alienated noncombatants essentially contested the army's right to delegate them to work rather than fight. Skilled troops tended to view themselves as privileged soldiers who made important contributions to battle preparation and progression. Many discovered, however, that as far as the army was concerned, they were noncombatants first and skilled technicians second. Army authorities did not hesitate to use them as common laborers, arousing indignation among those who resented such assignments. Private Vincent Everett, a skilled map drawer, noted in his diary that he was "back on detail today loading 600 boxes. Some job for a so-called 'intelligence regiment.' Not so hard work though, unless you choose to 'make it so.' "[77] An even more damning indictment came from engineers who claimed that the army was treating them like black laborers. One soldier recalled that when his engineer company was ordered to unload ships for an indefinite period, they all feared that "we were destined to share the lot of negro stevedores that were permanently detailed to Brest for dock work."[78]

Although the greatest challenge for many noncombatants remained overcoming the boredom of life in rear areas, some noncombatants found their lives endangered by their work. Engineer, signal, supply, and ambulance work all exposed noncombatants to artillery shelling and battlefield carnage. In the St. Mihiel offensive, pioneer troops and engineers entered the field first after the artillery barrage stopped to cut holes for the infantry in the barbed wire.[79] Even salvage troops were wounded by shrapnel as they picked up trash discarded by combat units.[80] In an ironic twist of fate, noncombatants and stateside recruits became likely candidates for death when the Spanish Influenza pandemic infected rear area and stateside units in the fall of 1918. Between September 1, 1918, and the Armistice on November 11, 1918, approximately 9,000 AEF soldiers and 23,000 stateside soldiers died of influenza. During this same period, nearly the same number of U.S. soldiers (35,000) died of combat wounds.[81] In Private Joseph Kern's camp, the overtaxed medical authorities did not even have the time to make sure a man had died before arranging his funeral. Kern recalled that the doctors had put one soldier out on a screened porch and told his father to come to claim the body. When the father arrived, he discovered that his son was still alive. "They died faster than they could pick them up," another recruit remembered. "Handed them on trucks like cord wood." As draining as this experience might have been, however, the military community still recognized only physical hardships on the battlefield as meaningful.[82]

Even when exposed to legitimate danger, noncombatants still failed to receive the recognition reserved exclusively for combatants. Consequently, despite the enormous differences in the type of work they performed, all noncombatants shared the problem of defining their status within the wartime army. Civilian-type work kept them emotionally distant from the life-and-death struggle that preoccupied those at the front. In many respects, the importance of the logistical tasks they fulfilled revealed that the aggressive ideal fostered in the training camps was becoming increasingly obsolete in the modern army. Yet, rather than abandoning that ideal, noncombatants instead enumerated the various ways in which their experiences fitted the mold it provided. Seeking to reintegrate themselves into the military mainstream, they encountered combatants and army officials who jealously guarded the integrity of the warrior model. The ensuing struggle revealed, not just how fractionalized the rank and file had become, but how soldiers and officials determined status and legitimacy in the wartime army.

Status and Legitimacy in the Army

Army commanders, with a bird's-eye view of the war effort, recognized the pressing need for support troops. Official rewards still went primarily to combat soldiers, however, who, like traditional warriors, risked their lives on the battlefield. According to one army investigator, combat troops displayed contemptuous indifference and open hostility to noncombatant soldiers, whom they viewed as purposely evading the really arduous work of subduing the Germans.[83] Noncombatant troops refused to accept the lowly status designated for them because they had been forced to assume untraditional wartime roles. Instead, they sought an esteemed place for themselves within the military by emphasizing the hazardous nature of their work. Engineers spoke of working in no-man's-land at night as "going over the top," the expression combat soldiers used to describe charging the enemy line.[84] Veterans of these units noted how they commonly laid barbed wire and sandbagged trenches amid intermittent shelling. Ambulance drivers for the 90th Division believed they risked their lives more often than combat soldiers and felt, their commanding officer noted, that "the Lord takes care of medical officers, ambulance drivers, and litter bearers because they have no way of taking care of themselves."[85]

Noncombatants did not demand equal recognition because their work contributed invaluably to the progression of important battles, but rather because they, like combat soldiers, had been under fire. Wagoner Charles McKinney experienced terror firsthand when an exploding shell knocked him off a bridge as he delivered rations to men in the 80th Division. He survived this fall unhurt because he luckily landed on a bloated horse floating in the water.[86] Private Elmer Goodrick put a piece of the shell that had exploded near him as he was driving supplies up to the front in his pocket to show his family when he returned home.[87] In his next letter home, Goodrick emphasized other dangers facing truck drivers, who had to drive at night without lights on muddy roads with steep embankments. On one such night, the car he was driving slid off the road and turned over in a ditch, a common hazard of motor transport work.

Noncombatants had more than one audience whom they wanted to impress by casting their own wartime experiences in terms usually reserved for battlefield encounters. Beyond their peers, noncombatants also sought to persuade the brass to improve their official status within the wartime army and in the eyes of civilians at home. Army authorities proved no more willing than combatants, however, to view hardships encountered behind the lines as equivalent to those experienced in battle. SOS soldiers, 17,000 of whom lived in Brest, the main U.S. Army embarkation and debarkation port, at one point complained publicly to camp officials about eating in the rain and sleeping on wet, muddy tent floors. Investigators chastised them for complaining about camp "inconveniences" when they had successfully avoided serving in the trenches.[88]

Even though army officials did not appreciate the strain of living behind the lines, they did have to react to the serious morale problems that plagued noncombatant units. At home, most intelligence officers stationed in stateside training camps agreed that the army should relent and give black service units some cursory military training before sending them overseas. These officers felt that if these troops believed it was possible for them to improve their position within the organization, they would work harder and obey military regulations.[89] Toward the end of the war, the chief of staff consequently agreed to honor an earlier promise to form one training company within each black labor battalion stationed in stateside camps. The General Staff had no intention of increasing the number of black combatant troops, but by giving blacks a basic course in military training, it gave them an opportunity to view themselves as soldiers, not just laborers in uniform.[90]

Pershing and Harbord, however, hesitated to offer AEF noncombatants even the slightest hope that they might become combatants to ease their malaise. Pershing instead made a limited effort to commend noncombatants for their accomplishments. Having fought strenuously with Allied commanders to bring these troops to France, Pershing understood their importance to AEF victories and purposefully included noncombatant units in his inspection rounds. A few days after he had delivered a motivational speech to 3,000 black stevedores working in an army warehouse, Pershing visited an engineering unit repairing railroad lines. "These men are skilled railroad men," Pershing noted in his diary, but they were "now doing common track labor and I consider that they need some recognition of the splendid spirit they have shown."[91] Individual commanders who followed Pershing's example and explained the importance of noncombatant work to their units found a receptive audience. When Colonel John Sewell published a memorandum for his engineer company outlining the significance of their work, the men responded by submitting "a request that they be assembled and given a little talk upon the real meaning of the work they are now doing and its relation to the success of our forces in the war. I shall, of course, comply with this request at the earliest possible moment."[92]

Improving the status of noncombatant work, however, required more than rousing speeches to individual units. The title of Private Paul Maxwell's memoir, "The Diary of a Dud," sums up the conclusion many noncombatants reached about their military careers.[93] After working as a clerk in the 80th Division's Headquarters company, Corporal Robert Harbison told his family that his standing within the enlisted community ranked him "with the quartermaster fellows as one that stayed away from the sound of the guns."[94] Men commonly justified their noncombatant role, as Private Everett Taylor did, with the assertion that "it was not my fault I was behind the line." Taylor emphasized to his family that he had in fact seen many atrocities during his tenure in France, and that although they would not see his name in the paper for winning any medals, he had served honorably.[95]

In his letter, Taylor noted that the army would not officially recognize his contribution with the same rewards it offered combatant troops. For despite the encouraging speeches commanders made, the army refused to consider noncombatants eligible for medals awarded for exceptional service. The War Department created two new medals to reward acts of extraordinary service during the war, but they were intended to stimulate aggressiveness on the battlefield, not hard work behind the lines.[96] Soldiers could receive either the Distinguished Service Cross for acts of extraordinary heroism on the battlefield or the Distinguished Service Medal, which recognized exceptionally meritorious service to the government in a position of great responsibility or during military operations. As Harbord noted, until military authorities willingly recognized that enlisted men sometimes informally assumed roles of responsibility, they had no hope of receiving the Distinguished Service Medal. "The man at the front has a chance, if he desires to risk his life, to win perhaps the Medal of Honor or the Distinguished Service Cross," Harbord complained. "The fellow in the SOS has to win the Distinguished Service Medal or nothing. The way it has been construed it makes it look like nothing."[97]

During the war, the army also adopted war service and wound chevrons, and the reluctance of AEF commanders to award them to SOS soldiers further revealed the low status of noncombatants. The army modeled the war service chevron on a badge the French Army awarded to its troops for six months of service within the Army Zone. The only problem with the French badge, AEF staff officers concluded, was that the Army Zone extended fifty miles behind the front, and many soldiers working behind the lines therefore received it. AEF officials decided to award American chevrons only to those who had served in a more narrowly defined "Zone of the Advance," so as to guarantee that the American chevron remained a symbol of dangerous service at the front, rather than simply an acknowledgment of honorable overseas service.[98]

The first challenge to this restrictive policy came from commanders of combat divisions who had some regiments training in the appropriate zone, who received the chevron after six months, and others training a few miles behind, who did not. SOS officials also disputed this decision, arguing that all shared the hardships of living overseas, and that many noncombatant units performed hazardous duties outside the Zone of the Advance, for which they received no recognition.[99] AEF Headquarters finally gave in to these objections in July 1918, and from that point on, a gold service chevron signified six months of service in the "Theater of Operations," now defined as all the territory under Pershing's command. Noncombatants applauded this change. According to one clerk in the 90th Division, "it was worth a gold stripe to go through a Port of Embarkation, make a seasick voyage, debark at a rest camp (so-called) and take a boxcar train ride to 'somewhere in France.' "[100]

After the war, the War Department awarded silver chevrons for each six months of army service in the United States.[101] The silver chevron, intended to recognize honorable stateside service, became instead a badge of shame to those who wore it, and awarding all overseas soldiers the gold chevron did not end internal debates over the value of noncombatant work either. "Those who are entitled to wear only the silver chevron feel that some of those who wear the overseas chevron have done no more, and perhaps less, than those who remained at home . . . and this is true enough," editorialized the *Army and Navy Register.*[102]

Yet, rather than relying exclusively on army officials to document the value of their work, many noncombatants took the matter of associating themselves with the danger and belligerence fundamental to popular notions about soldiering into their own hands. All American soldiers became compulsive collectors of artifacts, because souvenirs from the front offered concrete evidence that a soldier had actually been near the enemy. Combatant and noncombatant soldiers lusted after German military equipment. Few saw a shovel or typewriter, although perhaps more reflective of how they had spent the war, as acceptable symbols of their military service. Legitimate souvenirs associated the owner with the peril of the overseas military expedition. German bayonets, helmets, and uniform buttons evoked the romance and brutality of a personal encounter with enemy soldiers on the battlefield. These keepsakes honored the traditional image of soldiering. The occupational structure of the army was changing, but the appeal of the warrior remained constant.

Despite numerous attempts, military authorities could not stop enterprising soldiers from souvenir hunting and profiteering. A healthy trade in German contraband evolved among American soldiers during the war. "That morning the call became too strong so a party of us, including three privates and our interpreter started out for souvenirs," Private Emmett Riggin recorded about one such escapade in his wartime diary. "I can truthfully say that we got what we went after, as I returned with a couple of helmets, bugle, a rifle, a bayonet, a belt and a set of steel glasses. The others brought in even more than I and to see us from the rear we looked more like walking junk shops than anything else."[103] Noncombatant salvage crews, scouring abandoned German dugouts as the line moved forward, often collected more marketable merchandise than combat soldiers.

Soldiers did not consider it stealing to "roll over" dead German soldiers or "frisk" German prisoners for pistols, shoulder straps, belt buckles, or watches. Once an American soldier claimed possession of German equipment, moreover, it belonged to him until he sold it. Wounded soldiers unconditionally viewed SOS hospital and transport workers who took souvenirs from their bags as thieves.

By collecting similar keepsakes and emphasizing the same hazardous aspects of their work, noncombatants incorporated parts of the combatants' identity into their own army personas. Within their own spheres, both combatants and noncombatants recognized that an enormous disparity existed between the official military model of the warrior and the roles they had actually assumed in the AEF. The defensive posture that combatants adopted to stay alive conflicted with the aggressive stance military officials encouraged, although there is no evidence to suggest that combatants ever acknowledged this contradiction outright. Instead, combatants' disdainful view of noncombatants shows that the ever-present threat of death that hung over them and the quick successes they enjoyed against the retreating German army convinced fighting men that they were the only real soldiers in the wartime army.

Noncombatant soldiers admitted the glaring disjunction between the aggressive ideal and their actual work assignments more openly, and the resulting disaffection created serious morale and disciplinary problems in noncombatant units. In their more alienated moments, noncombatants appeared to be questioning the army's right to designate them as laborers, rather than warriors, for the duration of the war. The revolutionary potential inherent in this particular line of questioning to curb the wartime power of the state never matured, however, because noncombatants remained invested in the hegemonic model of soldiering fostered by army officials.

Aware of the temporary nature of their military careers, noncombatants remained acutely interested in validating their military roles to civilians at home. The public endorsed the belligerent wartime mission of citizen-soldiers as heartily as did the army. The fact that both citizen-soldiers and civilians subscribed to the same ideal of soldiering kept an important bond with civilian society intact for these wartime troops during their time in uniform. Disaffection with the traditional warrior ideal, therefore, remained minimal in the wartime army in part because challenging it would have entailed confronting not only outdated military notions but strong civilian predilections as well. Army officials and citizen-soldiers shared the warrior ideal, yet this was but one facet of their wartime association. Issues completely divorced from those actually involved in fighting the war, such as defining disciplinary and racial policies, became in some ways more important in determining the character of the wartime relationship that army officials and citizen-soldiers developed.

3

THE MEANING OF OBEDIENCE

Before the war, the U.S. Army had relied on a slow indoctrination process, coupled with harsh disciplinary tactics, to maintain order. The sheer number of infractions that inexperienced citizen-soldiers committed made it impossible to punish each one, but coercive tactics still remained the bedrock of disciplinary policy. Citizen-soldiers' responses to army life created an array of new disciplinary problems, however, which responded poorly to punitive measures. Keeping citizen-soldiers' attention on the war rather than on their own particular predicaments presented a serious disciplinary challenge for wartime army commanders. Both in Washington, D.C., and in the AEF, many favored a hard-line approach to curb infractions of military regulations, but the magnitude of unrest prompted others to devise innovative solutions that incorporated accommodative and persuasive techniques into the army's disciplinary repertoire.

Simply training soldiers to obey direct orders proved insufficient to sustain the nation's massive war campaign. Army officials gradually realized that to achieve victory, they needed troops who would cooperate voluntarily with military leaders. To meet these new demands, hard-liners grudgingly changed some restrictive policies, while a vanguard of new reformers lobbied for morale programs that would motivate citizen-soldiers and educate them politically. Coercive and persuasive policies thus coexisted uneasily within an army that was struggling to maintain the integrity of the chain of command while fighting the war with citizen-soldiers. Internal surveillance of suspected subversives by army intelligence officials provided valuable insights into the political attitudes of the AEF's citizen-soldiers. Army officials intended to use this information to manipulate their attitudes and behavior more effectively. The mere premise that citizen-soldiers' political opinions mattered enough for the army to take systematic steps to manipulate them, however, represented a dramatic shift in the army's attitude.

The AEF's citizen-soldiers liberated the army from its parochial status as unwanted stepchild of the American people and hastened its evolution into an organization of national stature. As it became increasingly apparent during the course of the war that citizen-soldiers were responsible for changing public perceptions of the military, the army began to seek not only the obedience but the allegiance of its men. The first step in this process, however, was confronting the meaning of discipline, obedience, allegiance, and loyalty in the wartime army.

Punitive Discipline in the Wartime Army

When General Pershing outlined the AEF's general training principles, he emphatically demanded that civilian recruits meet the same disciplinary criteria required at West Point. To him, there was no question of negotiating discipline. Instead, "rigid attention, upright bearing, attention to detail, [and] uncomplaining obedience to instructions" encapsulated what he expected from his troops as commander of the AEF.[1] Pershing believed that every infraction that a citizen-soldier knowingly committed called into question how well he would perform on the battlefield, when unquestioning obedience mattered most. By examining the development of battlefield disciplinary policies more closely, the suppositions that encouraged many army officials to condone coercive disciplinary measures throughout the entire military community become clearer.

When army officials began to contemplate discipline, they once again thought of the Civil War. "We need only refer to the history of our Civil War to show that the American is not above desertion," declared Brigadier General Lytle Brown, director of the War Plans Division. During the Civil War, the desertion rate in the Union Army had jumped from 13.7 percent in 1861 to 45 percent by 1865, in part, World War I military leaders believed, because officers had not handed out stringent punishments to the first offenders. The precedent set in the South during the Civil War particularly worried the governor of North Carolina. Deserters from the Confederate Army had rarely been punished. Men who lived in the mountain regions of North Carolina now believed that if they could successfully hide until the war ended, the government would give up trying to find them, the governor contended. The army must, he claimed, convince citizen-soldiers that the government would never give up trying to track them down. To General Brown, the Civil War experience simply illustrated that "when we become really engaged in the fighting in France with half a million to a million men on the firing line and the consequent heavy casualty losses begin to be learned," the desertion rate would rise drastically.[2]

Although all army policymakers agreed on the need to punish deserters severely, they clashed over the best policy to pursue. Some argued in favor of sentencing those who fled the front line to hard labor in the combat zone. At Camp Sheridan, Alabama, the commanding officer wanted permission to execute eighty-eight soldiers who had deserted from his camp.[3] Others proposed penitentiary sentences that extended well beyond the projected end of the war. Since desertion never became a widespread problem, discussions about the merits of each proposal remained hypothetical. They were, however, the earliest and most comprehensive discussions among army officials about effective disciplinary policy in a mass army, and army officials relied on them for guidance when a new and unanticipated array of disciplinary problems arose on the battlefield.

Few American soldiers deserted in a foreign country, but frontline commanders soon experienced severe problems with soldiers who refused to move forward and engage German troops. Men in the 305th Infantry knew, one soldier noted, that officers sent malingerers up "to the front for punishment, not to the rear."[4] AEF officials feared that a penitentiary sentence only rewarded combat shirkers by helping them avoid danger, so until these soldiers redeemed themselves through exemplary conduct, they remained at hard labor along the front.[5] The 102nd Infantry Regiment received a group of twenty-four prisoners from the 28th Infantry Regiment, who arrived without their weapons just as the 102nd took over the front line in the Toul sector. The Germans attacked a few nights later, and "these men were also caught in the battle and fought with shovels and whatever they could," recalled Corporal Fred Anson Tyrell.[6] The nine who survived were subsequently considered redeemed and returned to their original unit. Witnessing unarmed men fighting for their lives no doubt illustrated the hazards of bucking army regulations more vividly to Tyrell than the extra labor he had previously watched the prisoners perform.

Although hard labor in the front lines remained the preferred punishment, Pershing gave his officers formal authority to execute shirkers on the spot if they refused an order to return to the front. The legality of this policy seems questionable, because Pershing did not have the authority to execute men sentenced to death by a court-martial for "misbehavior in the face of the enemy" until the president and War Department had reviewed the case. Pershing wanted unilateral power to carry out all court-martial sentences, but acting on the recommendation of Secretary of War Newton E. Baker, President Wilson ruled that the power Pershing had to execute soldiers sentenced to death for rape, murder, mutiny, desertion, or espionage was all the American public would accept. Civilians rejected the idea of executing citizen-soldiers for misconduct, especially if inexperience or ignorance created extenuating circumstances. On Baker's recommendation, Wilson reduced numerous death sentences to long penitentiary terms when the offenses broke only military regulations. Baker understood the potential political crisis that widespread military executions could cause. While considering the cases of two young volunteers who had fallen asleep while on sentry duty and two others who had refused to drill because they had not received adequate time to rest after standing guard all night, Baker received an astounding number of letters from concerned citizens. "Many of them are from mothers of soldiers whose general anxiety for the welfare of their sons is increased by apprehension lest exhaustion or thoughtlessness may lead their boys to weaknesses like those involved in these cases which the newspapers describe as trivial and involving no moral guilt," Baker told Wilson.[7] Wilson heeded the public's message and pardoned these soldiers. Baker therefore successfully prevented the army from executing soldiers who had broken only military regulations. The twenty-five soldiers executed by the army in the United States and ten soldiers hanged in France had all been found guilty of murder and rape, crimes in both military and civilian society.

Neither President Wilson nor Secretary of War Baker dissuaded Pershing from his basic faith in coercive discipline, however, especially on the battlefield. Wilson refused to give Pershing unilateral power to approve formal sentences of execution, but Pershing nonetheless advised his division commanders that "when men run away in front of the enemy, officers should take summary action to stop it, even to the point of shooting men down who are caught in such disgraceful conduct."[8] By communicating this message in a personal letter to each commander, Pershing successfully avoided the stateside scrutiny this statement inevitably would have received if he had published it as a general order. Brigadier General W. A. Bethel, the AEF judge advocate general, argued that in the heat of battle, commanders could execute fleeing soldiers legally without first court-martialing them. Every officer had the duty, he noted, to maintain order in his command, especially if the refusal of a few men to go forward and fight threatened to incite a more general mutiny. Bethel concluded that the officer was "not only justified in taking human life when necessary, but it is his duty to do so if orders can not otherwise be enforced."[9] Within these carefully established boundaries, designed to supersede the legal, documented channels of the military justice system, army commanders could use executions to maintain battlefield order, Bethel felt, and although there is no evidence to indicate whether or not any commanders ever shot down soldiers who hid while their comrades attacked, the likelihood is that some did.

This decision reflected the general power commanders had to punish soldiers they deemed guilty without resorting to time-consuming courts-martial.[10] In principle, executions were a last resort for field commanders unable to control their troops in any other way. Military police more commonly followed the advancing line of troops to urge stragglers forward, checking among the "walking wounded" for malingerers. When a suspicious MP stopped the wounded Corporal Paul Murphy and another soldier, he let Murphy pass after examining the tag on his coat that identified him as wounded, but "held the other fellow and sent him back. I guess he thought he could get back to the rear by walking among the wounded. But he didn't make it and I sort of felt sorry for him," Murphy recalled.[11] Being wounded did not, however, exempt one from scrutiny. Hospital workers put all men they suspected of self-inflicted wounds in a ward with a large sign reading SIW.[12] "The hardest work that I did or saw done by others in France was the holding of our men to duty and service in battle," Major General Robert Lee Bullard later recalled. During the Meuse-Argonne offensive, he wrote in his memoirs, military police had "to be augmented in every possible way. An unbroken line of them now followed our attacks."[13] By mid-October, General Hunter Liggett estimated there were close to 100,000 stragglers in the American First Army.

If a soldier successfully fled the front lines, he might stumble across gatherings of absentee soldiers who collected on the fringes of the front lines and army encampments. The commanders of the 1st and 2nd Divisions claimed that their patrols routinely discovered bands of stragglers near their lines. The Château-Thierry district became a rendezvous for AWOL (absent without leave) troops who banded together to steal provisions from French villages between Épernay and La Ferté-sous-Jouarre. In the fall of 1918, MPs arrested fifteen to twenty stragglers each week around Château-Thierry, but this meager effort made no discernible dent in this community's vitality because a steady influx of new delinquents continually replenished it.[14] Further east, to reinforce the line during the Meuse-Argonne campaign, General Liggett "sent out officers with patrols to search the woods and dugouts, and thousands of strays and hideaways poured in."[15]

Soldiers had numerous alibis for absenting themselves temporarily from the battlefield. Often four men would serve as litter-bearers to help carry back one wounded man, and consequently "one wound inflicted by a German reduces our effectives [troops] by five, whereas one bullet which causes death reduces our effectives by one," the AEF inspector general noted.[16] Company commanders who grew impatient waiting for rolling kitchens or ammunition supply trains to catch up with them and sent men back to collect these only added to the stream headed for the rear. Many soldiers inadvertently lost contact with their units on the way to the front after they stopped either to rest or to recover from gas inhalation. Occasionally, non-English-speaking soldiers failed to understand directions to the eventual rallying points of their units. Other soldiers became disoriented in the "fog of war" during assaults as they tried to maneuver along ravines and depressions to avoid enemy fire, or panicked during shell attacks and hid in abandoned dugouts. Terrified soldiers who ran toward the rear spreading rumors of massive casualties at the front posed a much greater threat, AEF officials concluded, than soldiers who quietly skulked away, because the stories they told reduced the resolve of others to press on.[17]

It is impossible to determine how many soldiers deliberately decided to straggle and how many became overwhelmed by the physical obstacles that hampered their progress forward. The horrible sights soldiers encountered on the way to the front could shake the resolve of even the most steadfast. Harry Logsdon, a member of the 359th Ambulance Company, believed the route reinforcements were following toward Montfaucon in the fall of 1918 was "certainly bad for the morale of the troops being brought up for service on this front. Dead bodies were everywhere on both sides of the road. Both men and animals, and friends and enemy, and were said to have been there for five days or a week which was probably true as they were swollen badly and the odor and stench was awful."[18] In general, the army tried to bury dead American soldiers quickly to avoid demoralizing others. But, one soldier noted, "the graves scattered here and there [still] told the story."[19]

Throughout the war, army officials used the threats of frontline hard labor, harassment by military police, public humiliation, and court-martialing to discourage straggling and malingering. Taking their cue from the demands of the battlefield, army officials condoned similarly punitive methods behind the lines, because they felt that the battlefield experience epitomized the standard, rather than extraordinary, obedience required from citizen-soldiers in time of war. Consequently, in the rear, officers sentenced citizen-soldiers to hard labor, long penitentiary sentences, public humiliation, and even death (although these death sentences were commuted by the president) for much lesser crimes than refusing to engage the enemy.

Such punitive measures, however, soon proved inappropriate in circumstances where the disciplinary challenge was keeping soldiers' attention on the war, rather than advancing on the battlefield. When AWOL soldiers went on drunken binges despite knowing that they would receive harsh punishments if caught, the General Staff began to focus on rooting out the reasons why so many soldiers refused to obey. The solutions that they subsequently developed to manipulate troop behavior departed dramatically from the forthright deterrents that they had previously judged sufficient to discipline a mass army. Slowly, citizen-soldiers were forcing the army to develop other tactics to elicit obedience from wartime troops.

Soldiers Redefine the Meaning of Obedience

On the battlefield, citizen-soldiers felt the full force of the army's coercive powers. Behind the lines, however, the army was discovering citizen-soldiers' own unyielding strength. The failed attempts to coerce noncombatants to work hard behind the lines, to stop men going AWOL, and to get them to salute officers reveal that citizen-soldiers often used their own discretion in deciding when, and when not, to be obedient. To protect their credibility, army officials began either accommodating behavior that the troops themselves refused to modify or abandoning policies deemed unenforceable. Prompting such policy changes, however, was just one of the ways in which citizen-soldiers weakened the basis of coercive discipline. Officials also began to search for ways to persuade, rather than force, citizen-soldiers to comply with customs that the army deemed essential, such as saluting. As the army adopted more persuasive and manipulative techniques, the essence of citizen-soldiers' relationship with it changed. Although the army's coercive prerogative still remained an important part of its wartime authority, citizen-soldiers succeeded in redefining obedience as negotiable, rather than enforced.

The most glaring failure of the army's battle-tested punishments to handle disciplinary problems behind the lines came when rear area commanders tried to send intransigent noncombatants to work along the front lines. Service of Supply (SOS) officials complained about the impossibility of punishing black troops effectively behind the lines, because they considered jail time a vacation rather than a stigma. The only thing these troops wanted to avoid, these rear base officials claimed, was an arduous labor detail near the front. Officials futilely hoped that the sight of disciplinary detachments heading off to work in quarries or on roads near the front lines would improve discipline in the rear areas.[20] When the commanders of black stevedore units began sending their troublemakers to frontline engineer units in the summer of 1918, the inappropriateness of such a punishment became evident. The fifty black quartermaster troops attached to the 508th Engineer Regiment, for example, immediately created havoc in their frontline sector. These troops were soon brawling with white noncombatants and refusing to keep up the required work pace. "The ordinary duties of this company are of course hard labor, and the only punishment that can be given as discipline to these attached men is the same regular duties required of this company," Captain F. J. Fitzpatrick noted in a complaint he filed with his battalion commander.[21] The infractions committed by these men were only part of the problem Fitzpatrick faced. White engineers in his regiment realized that the work they performed on a daily basis was being used to punish others. After these black troublemakers had "redeemed" themselves, they would return to the rear, but, as the demoralized white engineers understood, they would have to do this work indefinitely. Using frontline labor as a punishment therefore tended to reinforce the low regard most soldiers already had for it.[22] Fitzpatrick's letter, which traveled up military channels, persuaded ambivalent officers at General Headquarters (GHQ) that the experiment of sending unruly black quartermaster troops to the front had failed.[23]

In this case, army officials simply abandoned an ineffective punitive policy. More often, however, commanders opted to modify disciplinary policies, hoping to preserve at least the pretense of authority in the face of widespread insubordination. Many soldiers in domestic training camps, for example, repeatedly went AWOL to visit their families, or to enjoy a binge in a nearby town, with little fear of drastic punishment. "With warm weather inside rumors that we were ready to go overseas kept us unsettled," Sergeant Henry Ward explained. "Many asked for furloughs home, all were refused. Several of the more daring privates went AWOL. Each sent back a telegram that he was at home and would return in ten days," which was how long they had until they were listed as deserters.[24] As long as soldiers maintained an unspoken rotation among themselves that minimized the gaps in each company, company officers tended to punish these rule infractions with only a few extra days of fatigue duty. Citizen-officers often sympathized with soldiers who went AWOL. Most of the men who went AWOL from his company over Christmas were "just homesick and wanted to be with their families" over the holidays, Lieutenant John Maginnis noted.[25]

General Staff officials criticized citizen-officers for failing to enforce military rules unwaveringly, but these same officials reacted similarly when faced with unenforceable policy. When the number of individual soldiers going AWOL in New York from units about to depart for overseas reached epidemic proportions, the General Staff demanded that embarkation camp officials use the condoned coercive tactics at their disposal to enforce the prohibition on leaves. Because these troops had passed their final venereal disease inspection, camp officials refused to give them a few days to explore New York City. Pershing had complained when some troops with venereal disease arrived in France, urging Washington to improve security around Hoboken. Camp officials' refusal to issue any passes did little, however, to deter citizen-soldiers intent on seeing New York City before they left for France from simply leaving the embarkation camp.

The moratorium on passes created a full-blown crisis when camp officials began reporting the abnormally high AWOL rate to Washington. Going AWOL while one's company was waiting to depart from Camp Merritt, New Jersey, or Camp Upton, New York, could easily look like an attempt to desert, especially to army officials who in general doubted the dependability of their conscripted population. Despite orders from the War Department requiring officers to outline the serious penalties for taking unauthorized leaves from the embarkation camps, by February 1918, divisional commanders and the director of the port of embarkation advised the War Plans Division that these punitive measures were failing miserably. Unless the army installed a high barbed-wire fence with lighted sentry posts, and in effect made a prison out of the embarkation camp, few officials could any longer see a way to keep men from taking leaves.[26] Heeding this advice, the General Staff revised its earlier decision and instructed camp officials to issue a limited number of passes to embarking troops.

The trepidation Sergeant Richard J. McBride felt while watching his company filter out of Camp Upton with 36-hour passes in their pockets illustrated the tendency of embarking troops to abuse even the new pass policy. "Somehow I could not dismiss the feeling that a new crisis would develop on Monday morning," McBride recalled, when all soldiers from the 328th Infantry Regiment, 82nd Division, were scheduled to return. Thirty-six hours did not give men with families in the area enough time both to travel and to visit them, or for soldiers visiting the city to exhaust their physical or monetary resources. At reveille on Monday morning, each company commander reported fifteen to twenty men missing. By issuing 36-hour passes, camp officials had reduced the AWOL problem to manageable proportions, but it still festered. After a trip to regimental headquarters for a tongue-lashing, the commanding officer of McBride's company gathered his officers and noncommissioned officers together to figure out how to round up absentees. The unit had just received its shipping date and would have to sail without these men unless they turned up soon. Then, "First Sergeant Highland had an idea," according to McBride. "He told the Captain he knew where to look for a few of the absentees and suggested that he be allowed to go to New York to round them up."

"There is no appreciable change in the list of AWOLs," McBride wrote in his diary the next day, "but more disturbing is the fact that Sergeant Highland is also among the missing after volunteering to search for the absentees." With time running out, McBride distributed the delinquents' rifles and packs among his troops, who no doubt cursed their comrades for the added weight they now had to carry. Company E wasted no more time wondering about their missing comrades, because the next day they sailed to "somewhere in France." About a month later, after the company had forgotten all about them, their wayward companions finally rejoined their unit, "among them our old First Sergeant who had been reduced in rank in the meantime (he got his job back later)," McBride recalled. These men had spent a few weeks in the port of embarkation stockade and then were shipped to France as a casual detachment. A few had been reassigned to noncombatant units in Le Havre, but most were returned to their original company.[27] They thus paid only a small price for their escapade. By this point, army officials seem to have given up on following through with their threat to reassign all AWOL offenders to replacement companies; instead, they were satisfied when such men at least made it overseas. Future warnings of "strict punishments" probably did not deter those in the 328th Infantry hankering for a Parisian adventure. But as some unlucky souls discovered, the Paris-area military police outdid all others in the abuse they handed out to absentee soldiers. Their brutality would lead to a congressional investigation and cause the General Staff to publicly condemn the very harshness they themselves believed necessary to maintain discipline.

The army had similar trouble enforcing the extremely strict prohibition on alcohol consumption by troops during the war, but in this case, officials took a different tack to ensure that citizen-soldiers behaved. Rather than abandoning or modifying this policy, they developed more manipulative tactics to stop soldiers from drinking. At home, citizen-soldiers astutely thwarted liquor regulations. The Selective Service Act contained a clause that prohibited selling alcohol to men in uniform near army camps, but soldiers had little trouble procuring liquor from illegal sources. A healthy bootlegging trade thrived around domestic army camps, and soldiers could solicit liquor directly from these merchants or hire a messenger to bring it to them. Looser regulations existed in France, because the French government refused to prohibit its civilians from selling liquor to American soldiers. G. W. Reed slipped out into a nearby village one afternoon with his friends and discovered "crowds of soldiers and sailors representing at least four nations at war" jammed into every available cafe and wine shop. His tour through the village convinced him that the short hours these shops kept did not stop the majority of soldiers from getting drunk when they visited the town.[28] American soldiers could buy wine whenever they wanted, because Frenchwomen filled soldiers' canteens with wine as they marched through French villages and sold wine on the fringes of most army encampments.

Drunkenness worried army officials for a number of reasons. Besides appeasing prohibition crusaders, numerous crime studies initiated during the war also pointed to drunkenness as a contributory factor in many military crimes.[29] The unruliness of drunken American soldiers in French villages created other headaches for the army. "General Pershing is already having his troubles in connection with the drinking of wine by the men," Lieutenant Colonel W. A. Castle, a member of the General Staff, reported. "While a Frenchman drinks a little cheap wine at meals, mixing it well with water, and is very sparing in his use of expensive and stronger wine, we are all of us well aware of the manner in which the American soldier is likely to comport himself when flush with money."[30]

American soldiers, General Staff officers pointed out, could easily procure wine, because they almost always had cash in their pockets. Privates in the U.S. Army received thirty dollars a month if stationed in the United States, and thirty-three dollars overseas. This enormous sum, compared to the paltry pay French soldiers received, gave American soldiers tremendous spending power in the depressed French wartime economy. American soldiers had little respect for the poverty the French endured, fumed the Reverend Alfred W. Wishart, after he personally witnessed an American soldier standing among a group of French civilians who, "to show his contempt of torn and dirty French money, . . . tore a five franc note into bits, threw it into the air, and said 'To hell with French money.'"[31] But French merchants quickly adjusted their prices to profit from American soldiers' spending habits.[32]

In view of the growing strain between French civilians and U.S. soldiers, and the large sums the latter spent on liquor, the General Staff decided to reduce overseas soldiers' pay. This was a turning point in disciplinary policy, because army leaders now resolved to manipulate, rather than dictate, troops' behavior to compel compliance with their otherwise unenforceable regulations. Some soldiers had already voluntarily reduced their net monthly pay by subscribing to liberty loan campaigns or life insurance policies. Soldiers with dependents were required to send half their pay home, but unless a soldier told the army that he had dependents, no allotment check was sent. When the General Staff decided to reduce overseas pay, half the pay that soldiers without dependents received was deposited in interest-bearing savings accounts, which soldiers could redeem at the end of the war. "The fact that the commanding general of the American Expeditionary Forces believes that receipt of full pay is subversive of discipline is the strongest possible argument in favor of compulsory deposit of at least part of the soldier's pay," concluded Colonel P. D. Lochridge, acting chief of the War College Division.[33]

The innovative solution army officials adopted to curb drunken, disorderly conduct in France epitomized the manipulative disciplinary methods they learned to use. The army's response to yet another annoying discipline problem, the consistent refusal of citizen-soldiers to salute their officers, capped the disciplinary revolution under way in the wartime army. For besides abandoning unenforceable policies, modifying others, and manipulating soldiers' lives to create a façade of compliance, army officials also tried to persuade citizen-soldiers to comply with some key military customs.

Inspectors repeatedly criticized citizen-officers for timidly enforcing military regulations. "When violations of such orders were brought to the attention of the junior line officers they would answer, 'Well I gave the order to stop it,'" the AEF inspector general concluded at the end of the war.[34] The tendency of citizen-officers to plead for lenient sentences when serving on court-martial panels further revealed their unwillingness to use the full range of their disciplinary powers.[35] Inspectors also repeatedly criticized citizen-officers for their failure to force their troops to salute them. Superior officers understood the distaste citizen-soldiers had for the salute, but they nonetheless felt it essential for discipline. Soldiers who did not recognize military authority with a salute could not, the army believed, be counted on to obey orders in battle. Yet, ironically, army officials devalued the salute as a symbol of obedience themselves when they commenced a campaign to persuade, rather than compel, citizen-soldiers to perform the gesture. By the last few months of the war, AEF officials were earnestly trying to popularize the salute as a simple exchange of military courtesies—not as a symbol of subservience but as a way for officers and enlisted men to greet one another.[36] Yet army officials fought a losing battle in trying to persuade citizen-soldiers that no caste system existed in the wartime army. Numerous officer privileges conveyed exactly the opposite message.[37]

These confrontations between army officials and citizen-soldiers, whether over saluting, unauthorized leaves, drinking, or loafing, all revolved around the same dilemma. Army officials and citizen-soldiers each had dramatically different ideas of what constituted obedience, and their debates over its meaning gradually revolutionized the way the army achieved discipline. Especially on the battlefield, citizen-soldiers faced the full force of the army's ability to coerce unquestioning obedience. While they learned to appreciate the scope of the army's punitive authority, they simultaneously compelled army officials to realize that these forceful measures could not alone ensure obedience. Instead, army officials had to accommodate some troop preferences and manipulate or persuade troops into complying with unpopular military regulations.

A vanguard of reform-oriented officers rising in prominence in the military advocated going even further, arguing that the army should make a deliberate attempt to mold citizen-soldiers' opinions, rather than ignore them as insignificant. Responding to the general lack of ideological purpose exhibited by citizen-soldiers, these officers encouraged the army to monitor soldiers' opinions more directly. In the closing months of the war, new surveillance agencies briefed the chief of staff and General Pershing on the state of morale and unrest among their wartime troops in a way unimaginable in the first few months of the crisis. The information that reform-minded officers provided created a dilemma among hard-liners, however, because they would have rather continued with their punitive approach. Once the army had been alerted to the dissatisfactions and desires of the citizen-soldier population, it became increasingly difficult to ignore them.

Creating Morale

The vanguard of reformers who eventually became influential within the upper echelon of the wartime army urged the General Staff to consider building morale systematically, rather than presuming that it would spontaneously appear as a by-product of good leadership in the field. These efforts paralleled similar endeavors by civilian Progressive reformers to use education and propaganda to improve the country's moral character and gain public support for their reform agenda. Illustrating once again how general political currents in American society seeped into the military, army Progressives shared with their civilian counterparts the belief that informed dedication to a cause was necessary for it to succeed.

During the war, Progressive reformers took over a number of key wartime agencies. Muckrakers—journalists who had previously used factually based, emotional stories and photographs to spearhead legislative reforms in child labor, trust-busting, compulsory education, and workingmen's compensation—now created the posters, speeches, and films that the Committee on Public Information (CPI) used to encourage Americans to do their bit for an initially unpopular war.[38] Progressives also worked through the Commission on Training Camp Activities to further middle-class principles of clean living by purging alcoholic and sexual vices from communities near training camps. As they took over the social life of civilian communities, CTCA officials appeared intoxicated with the power of the federal government now at their disposal. In defiance of local customs, the CTCA closed locally regulated red-light districts, organized Sunday entertainment for soldiers in violation of local statutes, and ignored Catholics' concerns about the explicit sex education films distributed by the agency.[39]

Within military circles, reform-minded officers' initial appreciation of the importance of political idealism came from observing the morale problems and outbreaks of pacifist sentiment that plagued Allied armies.[40]

French and British advisors recommended that the Americans learn from their mistakes and use systematic political education to enhance morale before matters got out of hand. Major General J. F. Morrison, director of training in the War Plans Division, and Colonel E. L. Munson of the Medical Corps lobbied for a formal morale program throughout the winter of 1918. Morrison based his plan on captured documents detailing the German Army's extensive morale and educational program. Officials in the Chief of Staff's Office, however, rejected Morrison's suggestion that the U.S. Army simply mimic the German system. Rather than abandon the idea, Morrison joined forces with Munson, who was independently lobbying for a broad morale program, and with Intelligence Division officials who already were monitoring citizen-soldier opinion. In the spring, these officials held an "Informal Conference on Morale" and included Assistant Secretary of War Frederick Keppel and Committee on Public Information officials on their guest list. "Two-thirds of the French and British will say that they are fighting that 'this thing shall never be again,'" Will Irwin noted, pointing out that such aroused passion rarely surfaced among American troops.[41] Such declarations swayed Keppel, and his support proved crucial. He immediately ordered the War Plans Division to examine morale programs within the Allied armies. At the end of this comprehensive study, in May 1918, the War Plans Division created the Morale Division, which became an independent bureau in the fall of 1918.

"The citizen-soldier of a democracy is entitled to understand the cause in which he fights, and the reasons and principles underlying the policy of the government," Munson told his field-workers, because "unless he both understands and believes in them he is always potentially dangerous."[42] Officially charged with detecting any disloyal or pacifist sentiments among troops, intelligence and morale investigators freely scrutinized citizen-soldiers' political views. At the Le Mans Classification Camp, Captain Charles D. Gentsch collected and forwarded to AEF Headquarters reports from camp operatives who routinely questioned soldiers returning from the front and army hospitals on their feelings about the war and Allied soldiers.[43] Interviews with recuperated soldiers uncovered diverse feelings about their imminent return to the front. Some wanted to go back because "they have personal scores to settle with the Germans now that they have been wounded or gassed, while others want to go back on general principles and still others because they feel they have greater liberty and more privileges at the front than they have enjoyed behind the lines," a field observer reported.[44]

These interviews revealed that, as Irwin had suggested, the nation's war goals remained remote to many soldiers. Rather than striving to further the cause, Private Henry Van Landingham wrote somewhat sheepishly to his family, he spent most of his time worrying about himself. Paradoxically, a letter he received from a friend a few days later helped him refocus his attention on the war's mission to spread democratic values. He had, he confessed, lost sight of the larger point of war "in the days' petty worries [and] . . . the reminder that one is serving his country such as you mentioned in your message to me is refreshing . . . many thanks to you for it."[45] Officers censoring soldiers' letters wished that more soldiers would undergo a similar metamorphosis. Officers continually lamented the absence of ideological convictions in the letters soldiers sent home. Soldiers instead concentrated on their health, discomforts, and family gossip. "Do you think this business is being brought home as strongly as possible to our people?" Second Lieutenant Donald Dinsome pondered in one letter home. "I know that nine out of every ten of our enlisted men do not know what they are fighting for, the idea is simply to kill the Boche."[46]

Yet it was inaccurate to claim, as many intelligence and morale observers did in their most alarmist moments, that citizen-soldiers had no idea what they were fighting for, because many had arrived at their own conclusions about the purpose of the war: to win, to kill as many German soldiers as possible, to help France in her hour of need, to avenge dead comrades, or simply to fulfill a civic duty. The army's dilemma was reconciling these personal ideas with national war aims, especially if doing so would enhance its combat might.

As officials became more and more convinced that citizen-soldiers' political views mattered, the War Department initiated a concentrated propaganda and education campaign in its domestic training camps. There, morale officers disseminated propaganda through camp newspapers, prepared officer lectures, camp song sessions, movies, plays, and religious services. The network of morale workers never crossed the Atlantic, however. The General Staff organized a domestic morale program too late for Pershing to consider adding one to the AEF, even if he had wanted to, because he had no officers to spare. Although he rejected the idea of assigning morale workers to cultivate political conviction among his troops, Pershing agreed to let Brigadier General D. E. Nolan, who headed the AEF's Intelligence Bureau, circulate a soldier's newspaper that accomplished the same task, perhaps more effectively. The *Stars and Stripes* began publishing a weekly issue in February 1918. GHQ expected the paper to keep morale high in the AEF by giving men the news they wanted from home, providing information about what soldiers themselves were doing, and, finally, interpreting "the spirit of a great Democracy at war for a just cause, in the encouragement of individuality of expression consistent with tolerance and sanity of view." [47] To accomplish these heady goals, the sergeant, three privates (one of whom, Private Harold Ross, went on to become the founder and legendary editor of the *New Yorker*), and occasional officer who headed the paper's editorial board had official approval to promote the notion that the paper belonged to citizen-soldiers themselves. The paper's editors urged soldiers to write with contributions and comments, although the editors placed any serious complaints in its censored file and printed only humorous, patriotic letters.

Citizen-soldiers learned to trust a publication that reflected their own ideas expressed in their daily vernacular. An official Board of Control perused every issue and received orders to print some items from GHQ, but an enormous amount of the paper's material came from soldiers themselves. Only once did an Intelligence Department official consider ordering the editors to stop publishing soldiers' minor criticisms of the AEF. Captain Mark Watson, the editor, successfully insisted that as soon as the paper stopped printing the "humorous, harmless grouches of the soldiers, just at that time will *The Stars and Stripes* be regarded as a GHQ organization, or more serious, as a J.J.P. [John Joseph Pershing] organ, and when that time comes there is one man who will suffer and that is the commander-in-chief." [48]

These civilian and military political education campaigns clearly had an effect upon citizen-soldiers in the wartime army. German intelligence officers who had interrogated American prisoners of war noted that they looked at the war "from the point of view of the 'Big Brother,' who comes to help his hard oppressed brethren." [49] A psychologist working in Camp Grant, Illinois, interviewed soldiers toward the end of the war about their wartime experiences and concluded that these men had an unusually astute understanding of the war. Without prompting, they explained that they had fought to "save ourselves from [the] fate of Belgium," and that the country was fighting both to redress "wrongs committed against us" and to preserve the "world from German domain." [50] Civil and military propaganda also conveyed the important message that the United States had a higher set of war ideals, which in many ways set America apart from the Allies. Unlike the French or British, U.S. soldiers fought for more than self-interest; they had dedicated themselves to seeing democracy triumph over autocracy and to creating a harmonious postwar world out of the ashes the war had wrought.

Pershing, however, still harbored doubts that soldiers' convictions mattered as much as obedience on the battlefield. Hard-liners in the AEF and General Staff shared his belief that traditional training instilled sufficient collaborative spirit to ensure battlefield success. Although army officials debated whether citizen-soldiers' opinions had any significant bearing on how the organization functioned, few doubted that citizen-soldiers could sway political sentiments at home in their favor. Most high-ranking army officials, including Pershing, could contemplate at least a few ways in which citizen-soldiers could provide potential support for the army in civilian society. Some, like Captain W. K. Wallace, believed that if soldiers felt that they and the army shared the same wartime goals, the army would be able to count on returning soldiers "to weld public opinion along lines of sane patriotism during the difficult period of reconstruction after the war."[51] Other officials, however, thought that the test of citizen-soldiers' allegiance to the wartime state would come sooner. "It is not unlikely that the time may come when our soldiers in the field, in the aggregate, may be able to see more clearly what the necessities of the situation require more than do the voters at home," Colonel D. W. Ketcham, the acting chief of the War College Division, cautioned in February 1918. "In such an event, they should not be deprived of their right of suffrage, not only because it is their right, but because their deprivation, at such a time, might seriously endanger the interests of the nation."[52] The issue of the soldiers' vote elicited a similarly strong reaction from civilian communities. Untroubled by the fact that, in peacetime, most U.S. states disenfranchised regular army soldiers by prohibiting absentee ballots or by defining soldiers as transients, the American public became as anxious as the army to ensure that citizen-soldiers did not lose their vote.[53]

The nationalization of the army during World War I and the extensive deployment of these troops along an active battle line created problems collecting soldiers' votes that had not existed in previous American conflicts. In both the Civil War and the Spanish-American War, army units had retained their local integrity, and state election officials had simply instructed state-appointed officers to collect votes from their troops. Tracking down and recording the votes of residents whom the army had dispersed throughout the country and in France proved difficult. The army's deliberate campaign to replace or reassign state-appointed National Guard officers, who had previously collected soldiers' votes for the states, further complicated the issue. To collect soldiers' votes successfully in the new national army, states consequently needed help from the War Department.[54]

The ensuing discussion among army officials over exactly what kind of help to give shows their growing sense of the potential importance of soldiers' votes both then and in the future. The main problem was formulating a viable polling procedure that did not interfere with pursuing the war. Yet few solutions met this criterion. New York sent election commissioners to France in the fall of 1917 to collect votes from local troops training in rear areas. New York officials considered the endeavor successful because they registered the votes of approximately 27,000 soldiers.[55] They estimated that military votes had elected mayors in two towns and claimed that 17,139 soldiers had voted for women's suffrage and 8,753 against. Army officials expressed less satisfaction. General Staff officers concluded that they had underestimated how much work it would be to supply these commissions with updated address rosters, shipping space, and land transportation. Consequently, the AEF refused to let any more state commissions come to France, although other state commissions followed a similar procedure to collect votes in domestic training camps.

Soon proposals to let soldiers vote through the mail appeared, but AEF officials refused to suspend censorship regulations to preserve the sanctity of the secret ballot. Army officials also worried about the large amount of mail these ballots would generate for the Army Postal Service. These objections should have made it easy for the War Department to resolve the issue by only letting states collect votes in domestic training camps, but the army continued to try to devise a viable way to collect votes overseas.[56] "It is not believed necessary or even desirable that a professional army should have the right of suffrage," Ketcham noted as he prepared yet another plan to facilitate elections abroad. "At present however, the case is very different. The Army is now composed for the most part of citizens of the United States, . . . who represent every community and almost every family in the country, and who in risking their lives for the United States have certainly a high degree of interest in maintaining its best ideals."[57] Pershing urged the War Department to simplify the issue by only polling overseas troops in national elections. Believing that national military service had diluted soldiers' interest in local affairs, AEF Judge Advocate General Bethel argued that they would not mind ballots limited to electing Congress and the president.[58] By September, the logistical difficulties of sustaining the overseas campaign forced the army to abandon negotiations with state officials.[59]

Views aired during these discussions about the wartime soldiers' vote foreshadowed the army's postwar efforts to mold returning citizen-soldiers into a loyal political constituency. The Morale Division would mature into an invaluable agency when army officials began to lobby for veterans' votes during the demobilization period.[60] During the war itself, however, the organized effort to collect information on the political views of soldiers, to shape those opinions with patriotic educational programs, to manipulate morale, and to facilitate overseas voting all denoted growing recognition that citizen-soldiers' political opinions mattered in a mass army. The emergence of a reform-minded group of army officers who wanted to entice citizen-soldiers into voluntarily bolstering the army's strength on the battlefield and in civilian society paralleled a soldier-inspired transformation of the meaning of obedience in the wartime army. Although these changes originated from different sources, they each reinforced the potent position of authority that citizen-soldiers now confidently held in the wartime army. Army officials no longer simply commanded obedience: they negotiated it. Nothing illustrated this change in disciplinary policy more starkly than how the army handled racial violence within its own ranks.

4

THE POLITICS OF RACE

RACIAL VIOLENCE AND HARMONY
IN THE WARTIME ARMY

That World War I citizen-soldiers truly were civilians in uniform became apparent whenever racial tensions emerged: both white and black soldiers brought racial agendas into the army that made race relations unpredictable and volatile. From the army's perspective, citizen-soldiers' pursuit of their respective goals had little to do with the overall military mission of defeating Germany. Conflicts between white southern soldiers' desire to minimize the visibility of blacks and black soldiers' hopes to improve their societal status by serving as combatants had great potential to sidetrack soldiers into waging their own internal civil war. Soldiers never saw their racial clashes as detrimental to the nation's international crusade, but army officials did. They had little faith that whites would control themselves in racially motivated situations or that blacks would willingly subordinate their own campaign for equality to winning the war.

As might have been expected at such a dreadful period in American race relations, most army commanders (with few notable exceptions) concurred with white soldiers on the need for segregation, but the demands of the war sometimes forced the army to place black soldiers in close proximity to whites and even in positions of minor authority. Whenever white soldiers protested these arrangements, army commanders accommodated their demands. This pacification bore consequences that transcended the parameters of this particular debate. For in acquiescing to these demands, the army compromised its own unilateral authority to set internal military policy and direct the behavior of all troops regardless of their preferences. What was at issue was how much power army commanders would have to forfeit in tackling the unprecedented challenge of turning millions of citizen-soldiers into a viable mass army. Citizen-soldiers' ability to dilute the principle of unquestioning obedience offers a compellingly vivid illustration of the powerful role these troops played in shaping the wartime army.

The Army's Dilemma

Early on, the General Staff decided both to use most black troops in noncombatant capacities and to maintain white majorities at all training camps. While for the most part quelling the apprehensions of white civilians that military service might create black terrorist bands, these decisions neither eliminated racial conflict in the army nor sealed the fate of black U.S. soldiers. These policies chiefly clarified where recruiters should send black draftees and how they should assign them, but absorbing black recruits in an uncontentious and expeditious manner became an uphill struggle. Consequently, General Staff officials and division commanders continued to discuss possible revisions to their initial mobilization decisions throughout the war.

These unending policy discussions strikingly portray how racial instability preyed on the minds of army officials, especially when they realized the consequences if they faltered in containing it. In the summer of 1917, newly overwhelmed with a large number of black recruits whom they could not absorb easily, General Staff policymakers considered assigning black drafted troops as cooks and assistant cooks in white combatant units. This scheme would help the army immediately absorb at least 35,000 of the 75,000 black troops anticipated from the first draft, advocates argued. As important, these assignments would relieve white combat troops of fatigue duties, thus increasing the number of hours they could spend training each day.

General Staff policymakers rejected this proposition several times, however, even though it complemented their decision to use drafted black troops primarily as laborers. Assigning black and white troops to the same units might, they believed, push racial tempers to the breaking point. Brigadier General C. H. Barth, commander of the 81st Division, training in Camp Jackson, South Carolina, tried to allay this concern, telling the General Staff that southern officers with whom he had spoken felt that "there would be no friction between races in consequence of such assignments . . . [because] no colored man would be in position to give orders to any white man."[1] Members of the War Plans Division remained unswayed, however. Even if white soldiers accepted the proximity of blacks, they noted, such an arrangement had the potential to damage army discipline even more severely than outright racial rioting. Few soldiers enjoyed general fatigue duties, and reserving it for black troops would only confirm the lowly status of this work. White soldiers might subsequently refuse such assignments, thereby creating a mutinous situation. "There is at present wide-spread objection in the service to the performance of duties of a menial nature, but to admit their menial quality by assigning such duties exclusively to an inferior race would make it well nigh impossible to persuade white men to ever again resume these duties," Lieutenant Colonel J. W. Barker concluded in the General Staff's third review of the plan.[2] If white soldiers refused to work in the kitchen, who would substitute when black kitchen workers became ill? Officers used kitchen police duty as a common company punishment for rule infractions, but army authorities knew they did not have the power to punish white soldiers by detailing them to work with black soldiers. To prevent these limitations in their power over white troops from becoming explicit, General Staff officers rejected this suggestion. The gain in training time did not outweigh the potential damage such assignments could inflict on army authority.

War Plans Division officials also remained leery of black advancement organizations, which they suspected would immediately protest these assignments unless they made black men eligible for all positions in white units. Among themselves, these officials frankly admitted the desire to avoid antagonizing black organizations by sponsoring such a blatant policy of inequality. Implicit in their concern not to "unnecessarily emphasize the inferiority of the colored race" lay an apprehension that such a policy would dishearten black soldiers as well as their civilian leaders. So while the assignment of black labor units to training camps exempted white troops from general maintenance duties, white troops remained responsible for fatigue duties within their units. This two-year exchange highlights an important goal of army racial policy—to maintain disciplinary control by segregating black and white troops as systematically as possible. It also underscores how the army tried to juggle the competing concerns both of white and black civilians and of white and black citizen-soldiers when formulating racial policy.

Army planners believed that they could formulate distinct personnel plans for white and black soldiers, but because racially motivated mobilization policies influenced the structure of the wartime army, they affected all members of the organization, white and black, in some way. White racial prejudices directly affected the military experience of black soldiers by limiting their combat opportunities. Decisions made about the treatment of black soldiers also, however, influenced the fate of white soldiers. Maintaining a white majority in each mobilization camp undermined the initial intention to form regional units in the national army. Army planners originally adopted a plan to preserve the local integrity of individual units after considering the prohibitive cost of transporting troops to training camps far from their homes. Men might be happier and easier to discipline, army planners reasoned, if they entered the army with men from the same region. Yet because some sections had higher concentrations of blacks than others, the army could not automatically send men to the camp closest to their home and still keep an acceptable racial balance. Instead, the army sent black men from Alabama, Florida, Mississippi, North Carolina, Oklahoma, and Tennessee to train and to work in the North. When the draft in southern states did not provide enough white men to fill up the divisions organizing in southern camps, the army had to ship white draftees from northern and western states to train in Camp Gordon, Georgia, and Camp Pike, Arkansas.[3] Subsequent replacement and classification procedures further diluted the local integrity of most units, but racial policies provided the critical first push to abandon this principle.

Yet the army, like American society, remained an imperfectly segregated institution. Placing black and white soldiers in the same camp (the General Staff had rejected a plan to concentrate black soldiers in two mobilization camps), in the same ships, and the same French towns guaranteed contact, and conflict, between the two races. Black and white soldiers may not have served in the same units, but it proved impossible to isolate members of the same army working together toward a common war goal. Army officials believed that they had settled the most pertinent racial questions by assigning blacks to noncombatant positions, giving them little military training, and keeping a white majority in every camp. But camp commanders discovered that citizen-soldiers, white and black alike, did not hesitate to enlist the aid of their respective civilian supporters to bolster their stand against an official decision they deemed unacceptable.

The court-martial of Captain C. Rowan, who refused to allow his white troops to stand in a formation that included a black unit in Camp Pike, Arkansas, on March 25, 1918, revealed both the impossibility of complete segregation and the importance of outside political pressure. The first series of complaints from Rowan, which the governor of Mississippi tele-grammed to President Wilson, included charges that the brigade com-mander, Colonel F. B. Shaw, was "forcing white privates to cook for negro soldiers."[4] By the time of his court-martial, investigators dismissed most of his accusations except the one charging that white and black units had stood next to one another in formation. Rowan called this formation order illegal because racial "intermingling" violated the self-respect of white sol-diers. "They are all Southerners and it would have been a direct violation of the customs they had abided by all during their lives," Rowan's coun-sel argued during his court-martial for willful disobedience of orders.[5] On the surface, his conviction reaffirmed the principle of unquestioning obe-dience to orders, but concerned citizens and congressmen descended on Camp Pike to ensure that the camp commander was not giving orders that, in their view, white men could justifiably disobey.[6] Rowan was dis-missed from the army, but Major General Samuel D. Sturgis, the camp commander, thereafter forbade brigade commanders to place black and white units in the same formation. Secretary of War Baker also assured the president that the commanding general of the camp was offending "neither Southern nor Northern sensibilities" with his racial policies.[7] In this camp, therefore, the commander carefully censored orders to avoid another confrontation with white troops and civilians.

Black soldiers also had advocates to whom they could appeal, although often with less satisfactory results. The black press publicized incidents of discrimination against black soldiers, and the War Department found itself investigating rumors that black soldiers were being "exposed in places of special danger in order to save the lives of white soldiers."[8] Emmett J. Scott, Charles Williams, and Major William H. Loving were three black men who provided the bulk of official information, supple-mented by the observations of white intelligence officers, to army officials and to black advancement organizations about black troops.[9] Scott, secre-tary of the Tuskegee Institute and an associate of the late Booker T. Wash-ington, began advising the secretary of war on racial matters in October 1917, but he had minimal power to remedy army racial problems. He re-ceived a steady stream of complaints from black soldiers throughout the war, which he could only pass on to the Intelligence Division to investi-gate. Although he occasionally visited the camps, Scott concentrated on persuading War Department officials to open more skilled and commis-sioned positions to educated blacks. He noted with pride after the war that whereas blacks had previously only served in cavalry and infantry units, during this war, blacks had served in every technical branch of the organization.[10] Charles Williams began surveying camp conditions in March 1918 for the Federal Council of Churches, but filed all his reports and recommendations with the War Department. His background as a welfare worker made him especially curious about the harmful recreational habits of black soldiers. The Intelligence Division sent Major William Loving, a retired black army officer, to investigate the morale of black troops. His postwar report, which severely criticized army treatment of black soldiers, carried a good bit of weight with Brigadier General Marlborough Churchill, director of the Military Intelligence Division, because he had always regarded Loving as "a white man's negro." The situation must indeed be serious, Churchill concluded, if Loving criticized it.[11] Although each investigator had a somewhat different agenda, each tried, at one point or another, to persuade policymakers to abandon strict segregation. The peaceful interracial relationships cropping up in some camps across the country, they argued, suggested that a strong commander could enforce an official effort to promote equality in the army.[12]

Civilian allies helped white and black soldiers articulate their grievances to high-ranking army officials, but citizen-soldiers also manipulated the racial tempo of army life themselves. Because most white army officials shared the racial beliefs of white soldiers, the potential for conflict with white soldiers over racial matters appeared slim. Yet in the camps, commanders often unintentionally set up situations in which they could not express their sympathy or support for white soldiers' racial preferences without diluting their own (and the institution's) insistence on unquestioning obedience.

Simply walking through the camp gates brought black and white troops into contact with members of the other race whom the army had invested with some official authority. In an effort to minimize the hours white troops lost from training, black noncombatants were assigned to share the task of guard duty with white military police (MPs), although they did not serve in guard units together. Black sentries rarely carried guns, but they nonetheless checked passes and admitted visitors to the camp. Camp officials faced a dilemma when white soldiers refused to recognize black guards as legitimate representatives of army authority. Black skin in their eyes gave them license to disobey, and they could often find junior officers who supported their actions. A company officer's reaction when a white stevedore in his unit complained to him that a black sentry had stopped him from leaving Camp Hill, Virginia, without a pass aptly illustrated this dynamic. Rather than disciplining the soldier for his unauthorized attempt to leave camp, the lieutenant armed himself and twelve of his men and confronted the black guard. When the sentry explained that he only was obeying his orders to turn back every man who did not have a pass, the lieutenant, an investigator noted, said: "Damn the order! My men must not be stopped!" When the officer of the day arrived at the gate and asked the lieutenant to clarify exactly what he had meant by the words "Damn the order!" the lieutenant made it clear he would not allow a black guard to stop his men. Convinced that his guards could not enforce an order white troops deemed inappropriate, the officer of the day did nothing to punish the white troops for disobeying it.[13]

White troops also invoked their own definition of appropriate military authority to justify their disobedience of black officers.[14] At Camp Pike, Arkansas, the assignment of black officers to the Central Officers' Training School prompted a rash of disciplinary problems among the white troops stationed in the camp. "There is ever present a great danger of infraction of the rules of discipline as regards proper saluting and recognizing the authority of the colored officer by virtue of his commission over the white soldier," Colonel C. Miller complained to General Staff officials. An overwhelming number of men refused to salute black officers, and Miller claimed that he could not force them to do so. Unless the adjutant general removed the black officers from the camp, Miller feared, white troops would soon lose all respect for army authority.[15] White officer candidates also disliked saluting black officers, but because their commissions depended upon their exemplary conduct as students, Miller expected less immediate trouble from them. Even when white soldiers agreed to recognize the superior rank of a black officer, they often found a way to make their true feelings clear. Mississippi troops, for example, saluted the black officers from Camp Zachary Taylor, Kentucky, they met in Camp Merritt, New Jersey, but added "Damn you!" under their breath.[16] Black officers fared better in Camp Hancock, Georgia, because they did not "look for salutes" from white soldiers, a demeanor army officials encouraged all black officers to adopt.[17]

Refusals to arrest white soldiers who physically assaulted black soldiers accompanied the tendency to rescind unpopular racial orders and to discourage black officers from demanding salutes from white soldiers. Sergeant David Myers returned to Camp Gordon, Georgia, with two black eyes and a bruised face after a group of white MPs, who were corporals, beat him for wearing sidearms through town. Ignoring his rank, one corporal demanded that he remove his sidearms. When Myers responded too slowly, the corporal warned: "Hey dar nigger, why so smart bout taken off dem side-arms [sic], don't you know that you is down in Georgia?" before the group jumped on him.[18] The camp authorities refused to prosecute the white corporals; instead, they concentrated on persuading Myers to drop his complaint against them.

Black troops proved no more willing than whites to obey authority figures of the other race, however, if they saw a means of preserving their racial dignity. Subjected to continuous abuse from whites, black soldiers counterattacked whenever possible.[19] In August 1918, two white MPs arrived in the black troop housing area in Camp Funston, Kansas, to disperse a group whose loud yelling outside an open air theater was disrupting the show inside. When the MPs ordered the men to disperse, only a few complied. The others, MP Leman B. Johnson reported, jeered at them, "telling him that he couldn't do anything, and also telling him to 'About Face' and 'Squads Right' and laughing at him and telling him that he couldn't make any arrest." Determined to enforce their order, the MPs decided to arrest one particularly belligerent soldier. As the MPs approached him, he fled into a ditch, picked up a rock, and stood poised ready to hurl it at the two white men. "I then pulled my pistol," Corporal Leon Michaelis, the other MP, testified later, "and told him if he threw the rock I would shoot him. The other colored soldiers had been throwing rocks and near-beer bottles and other missiles during this time." When the man turned and ran toward the barracks, Johnson raised his pistol and shot him in the shoulder. Within minutes an angry crowd encircled the two white men. Two black noncommissioned officers hurriedly advised them to hide in the barracks across the street and wait for the guard. The guard, a group of unarmed black soldiers, successfully dispersed the crowd while the two white men waited under cover. Johnson was not arrested for shooting the black soldier.[20]

For black soldiers, obeying white officers became synonymous with accepting the demeaning position that military authorities in general had imposed upon them: challenging white officers therefore became a viable way for them to reassert racial dignity. Lieutenant Corbett witnessed the gestation of this sort of race consciousness when a black troop train in France stopped near him and he ordered the black combat soldiers to come down off the boxcar roofs and find places inside the boxcars. One soldier refused to obey his order, and the sight of this lone black man defying a symbol of white authority prompted his comrades to support his actions vocally. "I was told by one man that he was no dog, I presume meaning the man I was ordering down, and this was followed by several outcries . . . one in particular I do recall was 'we'll take no orders from no white man.' "[21] Soldiers began pouring off the train to join the group of agitated soldiers until a black corporal appeared and succeeded in coaxing the men inside the troop coaches. The black officers in charge, however, made no motion to protect the white officer, whom they no doubt knew was receiving the kind of treatment they endured so often from white troops. Racial violence was an undisputed fact of army life, Corporal Lloyd Blair, a member of the black 92nd Division, noted years later, because "we couldn't get along with the white to [sic] much."[22]

To army officials the dissolution of the principle of unquestioning obedience to orders emerged as the most vexing aspect of citizen-soldiers' tendency to reject racially offensive directives or to ignore rank and justify disobedience in terms of the skin color of the man wearing the uniform. White soldiers usually won immediate concessions from army officials, who, when faced with their insubordination, revised offensive policies and abandoned the black soldiers charged with enforcing them. Occasionally, however, army officials stuck by their policy decisions if no potential disciplinary problem existed. Ill black and white soldiers, for instance, sometimes found themselves assigned beds in the same army hospital wards. When Private Roy Chesebro fell ill from his inoculations, he landed in the hospital for thirty days, "the only white soldier in the ward."[23] Army officials ignored the objections white troops raised. "While the negro soldiers are segregated in the army, they are not separated from whites in hospitals," Colonel D. W. Ketcham of the War Plans Division explained to the chief of staff. "[I]n hospitals, patients have to be classified by diseases rather than with reference to other considerations and, moreover, while men are sick in bed there is scarcely any opportunity for friction due to race troubles."[24] The surgeon general, however, advised the Red Cross to segregate its convalescent houses for soldiers. Although ill white troops could not act on their racial prejudices, white doctors could and did. Black army observers noted that many white doctors refused to treat blacks. Loving, for example, reported from Camp Zachary Taylor that black soldiers suffering from venereal disease went untreated, because white doctors "must actually handle the privates of colored men in order to get results," and they refused to do so.[25]

Racial relationships within the army proved extremely complex, and even more important, unpredictable. In some areas, full-blown racial riots broke out among soldiers. In others, white and black soldiers coexisted peacefully, even harmoniously. Black advancement officials argued that the constructive relationships found in some camps offered another viable alternative for the army besides always siding with white racists. Given the divided white opinion on appropriate racial practices, these black advancement advocates claimed that the army could have the deciding vote by forcing white soldiers to conform to mandated egalitarian policies.[26] Given their own conservative views on race, few army officials agreed with the principle of integration or the idea that they possessed the power to force troops to comply with such a radical notion. They had no interest in making either the wartime or the professional army a place for social experimentation. Traditionally, the army stationed its four black regiments far away from white soldiers and civilians, in garrison posts along the Mexican border, in Hawaii, and in the Philippines. Race relations in the professional army had deteriorated significantly since the 1906 Brownsville riot shattered a forty-year lull in racial violence between black soldiers and white civilians, and the 1917 Houston riot seemingly gave the General Staff evidence that this dangerous new trend might continue. Their wartime experiences only reinforced professional officers' commitment to using segregation to maintain racial peace. But the suggestion that the army take an activist role in enforcing civil rights was not as far-fetched as it may have sounded at the time, although it required civilian, not military, leadership to succeed. Thirty years later, the military used its authoritarian power to force troop acceptance of President Harry Truman's 1948 decision to desegregate the armed forces, even though civilian society continued to embrace Jim Crow practices.

The Search for Predictability

Entering the army with distinct racial ambitions, white and back soldiers found many reasons to disagree during their service. But white and black soldiers also discovered grounds for cooperation. Two riots, one in Charleston, South Carolina, and one in Camp Merritt, New Jersey, illuminate how citizen-soldiers responded to these competing forces in the wartime army.[27] Significantly, race relationships between soldiers did not simply mirror the prevalent racial tensions of civilian society but also evolved in response to pressures specific to the military environment.

The U.S. Army uniform, which most citizen-soldiers wore proudly during the national emergency, had perhaps the greatest potential to create a bond between black and white soldiers. It was a badge of honor that unified otherwise dissimilar men, not only symbolizing faithful service and their status as defenders of the nation, but distinguishing them both from civilians and from members of other armies. The General Staff recognized the symbolic importance of the uniform by advising commanders not to issue the uniform white soldiers wore to black noncombatant troops. But like many army policies, this one was haphazardly enforced, and in many camps black and white soldiers wore some similar version of the national uniform.

The civilian police in Charleston, South Carolina, dramatically underestimated the strength of the uniform as a rallying point for American soldiers when they arrested a drunk black soldier they found wandering down a street one night. Their brutal treatment of the soldier corresponded with regional racial custom, and conceivably MPs arrested black soldiers in the same brutal way. But this harassment quickly lost its racial legitimacy when the arrest evolved into a confrontation between civilians and soldiers, rather than between white and black men.

On December 8, 1918, a crowd of about thirteen soldiers and sailors gathered on a street corner in Charleston to watch a white policeman arrest Private Colis Sylvester, a black soldier who had consumed a pint of whiskey. Private Fred Carrier, a white soldier and military guard, walked up to the policeman and told him that he knew Sylvester. Carrier offered to take him back to camp and turn him over to the military police. As he reached for Sylvester's arm, the policeman raised his club and struck his prisoner on the head. The crowd witnessing this assault stood by shocked, and "one of the sailors passed the remark '[R]emember, you are hitting a United States Uniform,'" Carrier testified. To which the policeman responded, "Fuck the uniform!"[28] He had meant, the policeman later claimed, that "'these God damn sons of bitches have no business in the uniform,' referring to the colored soldiers."[29] Clearly, the civilian policeman expected support from the white soldiers and sailors in the crowd. Instead, he turned their initial curiosity about the arrest into a defense of the uniform they all wore. "As he hit the stevedore someone yelled 'beat him up,'" Carrier recalled, and the military members of the crowd responded by pulling Sylvester away from the policeman and carrying him away from town toward camp.

A few blocks later, the crowd met an assembled block of police reserves, who, with drawn pistols, rearrested Sylvester and another black soldier. The police claimed they made this additional arrest after "they were cursed violently by the soldiers and sailors and attacked by them."[30] The servicemen later denied assaulting the policemen, alleging that they only asked where the police were taking Sylvester. By this point the original crowd of thirteen men had swelled. "After the police had arrested the soldiers . . . a crowd of several hundred people, composed of both white and colored, soldiers, sailors and citizens, started to the police station," the investigating officer noted in his report.[31] The soldiers and sailors in the crowd demanded that the police release the prisoners and arrest the policeman who had cursed the uniform. The police, fearing a riot, began dragging the soldiers they identified as the ringleaders, including Carrier, into the jail and called the U.S. Guards to come and "quell the riot." When the Guards arrived, they discovered a large gathering standing patiently outside the jail waiting for a response to their demands, and no evidence that the crowd had tried to break into the jail. By midnight, the Guards had cleared the streets by ordering all soldiers back to their quarters.

Despite the participation of both black and white troops in the disturbance, civilian authorities continued to depict it as a race riot. They pursued their crusade against black soldiers by choosing to free the white soldier they had arrested while prosecuting all black prisoners. The town courts convicted every black soldier arrested that night and imposed fines or sentences of up to thirty days' hard labor, which they were powerless to enforce. Military authorities, however, rejected the racial overtones that the civilian authorities interjected into their interpretation of the incident. Major General Henry G. Sharpe, the commander of the Southeastern Department, refused to censure or to quarantine black troops near Charleston, negating racial friction as the reason for the clash. Instead, he told the mayor, the enlisted men were reacting to the unnecessary brutality used while arresting "a member of their command . . . and that a member of your Police Force had cast reflections on the uniform of the United States Army, and the men wearing it."[32] To avoid future clashes, Sharpe urged civilian authorities to turn all men in uniform over to the army for prosecution in military courts.

This incident is striking in part because it occurred in the South, where civilian communities had been particularly successful in imposing their racial customs on both army officials and black soldiers. Clashes between white civilians and black soldiers commonly occurred, and clearly the Charleston police at first viewed their arrest of Sylvester as just another trophy they could claim in their campaign to keep black soldiers "in their place." Yet, the police did not appreciate that in the reordered worldview of white soldiers and even, it appears, among some white civilians, protecting the uniform came before punishing a disorderly black soldier.[33] However, if white soldiers had agreed with the police interpretation of events, the camp commander would likely have punished black troops under his command. White soldiers always retained the power to sanction some racial behavior as legitimate and to judge other actions as contentious.

Ironically, however, peaceful coexistence between black and white soldiers and the decision of some civilian recreational officials to integrate their facilities often troubled army officials as much as outbursts of racial violence. In some camps, white and black soldiers negotiated racial truces that enabled them to share recreational facilities; in others, the camp commander required it. Black and white soldiers at one time or another contentedly shared facilities in Camp Devens, Camp Funston, Camp Lee, Camp Meade, Camp Merritt, Camp Travis, and Camp Upton.[34] In these cooperative situations, white and black troops played games together, watched movies and shows, or wrote letters for each other. A white lieutenant in Camp Shelby, Mississippi, went as far as to organize a series of baseball games between his black labor outfit and a unit of white engineers. The YMCA provided general recreation to troops in the camps, and the willingness of YMCA secretaries and white troops to accept black soldiers in camp YMCA huts varied tremendously.[35] In some camps, the Y established separate huts for black soldiers, while in others black soldiers frequented all existing facilities. Other organizations, including the Knights of Columbus and the Jewish Welfare Board, established integrated huts in the larger camps. "In all camps the K. of C. [Knights of Columbus] displayed the word 'WELCOME,' which meant all that the word implied," an investigator concluded in his survey of camp conditions. "There was absolutely no discrimination practiced by this organization."[36]

Such racial reconciliation worried army officials, who feared that this tranquility could not last, and that violence was bound to explode at some point. The shared access policies pursued by some camp welfare secretaries and a few northern commanders created further problems by inspiring black advancement organizations to continue pressing army officials to guarantee equal treatment throughout the military.

The race riot at Camp Merritt, New Jersey, the port of embarkation, on August 18, 1918, sent a strong message throughout the army about the inevitable consequences of social integration. Black and white troops at Camp Merritt lived in close quarters and shared all recreational facilities for a short period of time while they waited to embark for France. The fragility of racial truces resembled the "live-and-let-live" pacts that emerged along the Western Front. Informal racial and enemy truces both could end suddenly when the range of behavior one group of men accepted proved intolerable to the next occupants of a camp or trench. Just as newly assigned troops often turned a quiet sector into an active one, the arrival of new troops in camp could terminate established racial agreements abruptly. Embarkation camp officials bore the burden of disciplining a completely transient population, whose officers had often already sailed for France. These circumstances magnified the problems associated with maintaining stable race relations. "There have been outbursts of friction before," William Lloyd Imes, a black YMCA secretary in Camp Merritt acknowledged. "Whenever Southerners are also in camp and near the hut used by the men [black and white] in common, there are many insults passed and threats."[37] Nonetheless, YMCA secretaries had without incident ignored requests from embarking white troops that they bar black troops from recreational facilities.

When the 155th Infantry, a unit filled with recruits from Mississippi, arrived in Camp Merritt, they, like many groups of southern soldiers who had entered the camp before them, demanded that the YMCA segregate the facilities near their quarters. As he had done many times before, the white secretary in charge of Hut # 2 refused. A note he discovered by the stamp counter the next afternoon indicated that this time a tenacious stance might not work. If the Y secretary did not meet their demands, these troops planned to rectify this offensive racial situation themselves. The note read:

> You Y.M.C.A. men are paying entirely too much attention to the niggers, and white men are neglected. Because of this, if it is not corrected by sundown, we are coming to clean this place out. (Signed),
> Southern Volunteers[38]

Tension grew throughout the day as isolated scuffles broke out between white and black soldiers, but no encounter evolved into a mêlée. Finally, at 6:30, twenty-five "Southern Volunteers" marched into the YMCA and confronted the five black soldiers they found there writing letters. The white troops threw these black soldiers onto the street. The YMCA secretary followed the men out of the building, stood at the entrance, and closed the building to all soldiers until white soldiers agreed to accept the presence of black soldiers. As accounts of the incident spread back to the barracks from those who had witnessed it, alarm swept the camp. Black troops gathered outside their barracks to prepare for an anticipated attack, while the "Southern Volunteers" searched other public buildings. They soon discovered a black soldier playing the piano in the main auditorium and rushed up to him. The soldier immediately rose, pulled out his knife and successfully defended himself by cutting one of the white assailants on the neck. "By this time the military police had come, so that no further trouble occurred in this building," Imes recalled. "The barracks trouble [however] was now very much aflame, and two shots were heard. No one seemed able, up to this time, to state who fired these shots or where they were fired, but the alarm had been given." Confused soldiers milled about trying to locate the origin of the shots when thirteen guards from the 50th Infantry ran up and positioned themselves directly in front of the black soldiers' barracks. Within minutes the nervous white guards fired into the crowd, wounding three men inside the barracks and killing Private Edward Frye. The guards had fired without orders, misinterpreting the agitated black troops standing outside their barracks as instigators of the riot. "Greatest credit must be given the colored officers of a contingent of men from Camp Sherman, who were just across the road from the Camp Taylor men, into whom the guards had fired and who held their men in restraint from attacking the guards from the rear," Imes noted. The potential for further violence quickly dissipated when the authorities moved white troops to the opposite side of camp and quarantined all black troops until they left for France a few days later.

The General Staff Intelligence Division, fearful that a racial war might engulf the entire camp, immediately launched an investigation. The Camp Merritt riot underscored to the General Staff the value of strict segregation as the most effective way to control race relations. Camp YMCA officials and the investigating intelligence officer, Major L. B. Dunham, recommended a different course, however, in the days immediately following the riot. Dunham urged officials to support the secretaries' effort to integrate camp facilities. "If it is impossible for the white Southern troops to get along with negro troops, it is conceivable that the Government could make arrangements whereby the entire quota from any State could be raised from the white population," Dunham wrote angrily in his initial report. "It seems to me that, until the whites are willing to assume this burden, they should act in a decent manner toward the colored troops."[39] Echoing this sentiment, camp YMCA officials urged the military authorities to endorse their endeavor to provide equal service for all soldiers.

The position of Camp Merritt's YMCA mirrored the order Major General J. Franklin Bell had given in Camp Upton, New York, when clashes between white and black troops began in April 1918. When a few white men from a newly arrived Texas regiment walked into a camp YMCA, they were stunned to see two black soldiers inside writing letters. "Being unaccustomed to such scenes, the group threw them out the window," Charles Williams reported.[40] Bell assembled his officers the next morning and told them that all recreational facilities, including YMCA buildings and theaters, remained open to white and black troops. Bell warned them that hereafter "the officers in charge of both parties would be held strictly responsible for the acts of their men."[41] Men who disobeyed these orders would never, he promised, get overseas.

The principles outlined in this verbal order appealed to those who felt that army officials had the power to improve societal race relations. General Staff officials let Bell's order stand, but they had no intention of seeing it as a precedent. Captain G. B. Perkins, chief of the Military Morale Division, agreed with Emmett Scott that Bell's speech "met the situation squarely" but based his conclusion on the erroneous assumption that Bell was censuring only northern troops. A similar order, he argued, was "likely to be interpreted somewhat differently when both the white and the colored soldiers are from the Southern section of the Country or when the white soldiers in the camp come from the Southern states and the colored soldiers come mainly from the Northern states."[42] Certainly, the northern location of Camp Upton explained the indifference of neighboring civilians to Bell's order, and in the South, civilian protest had already forced many changes in camp racial policies. Without explicitly noting their obvious unwillingness to see such a general policy in place, General Staff officials argued that the army did not have the power to enforce a mandate for integrated recreational facilities. Perkins concluded that if the YMCA secretaries had been more conciliatory toward white soldiers in Camp Merritt, the riot never would have occurred. In the future, Perkins recommended, when racial friction emerged "some wise person, preferably colored . . . should talk to the [black] soldiers, advising them regarding their conduct and urging them to use every reasonable means to avoid disturbances."[43]

As might have been expected, given this interpretation of events, the Camp Merritt authorities made little effort to convict the guards of killing Private Frye. The one black NCO called to testify at the trial two months later could not identify which guard had shot and killed Frye, so the guards were acquitted. "It appears that there has been an unfortunate miscarriage of justice in connection with this affair," Loving noted dismally.[44] Black troops passing through Camp Merritt after the riot continually questioned

YMCA secretaries about the fate of the white assailants.[45] The response they received demonstrated to them that once again army authorities had refused to punish white troops for an unjust attack on black soldiers.

The General Staff's conclusion championed the principles that Major General Charles C. Ballou, commander of 92nd Division, had outlined for the black troops training in Camp Funston, Kansas. Ballou's infamous Bulletin # 35 ordered black soldiers to stop pressing for equal treatment when they visited the town next to camp. Ballou issued the bulletin to defuse a heated dispute between black soldiers and white civilians after a theater owner refused to admit a member of the 92nd Division. Ballou instructed his troops in their responsibility to avoid antagonizing nearby civilians. Although the theater owner had broken the law by discriminating against the black sergeant, Ballou stated, "the sergeant is guilty of the GREATER wrong in doing ANYTHING, NO MATTER HOW LEGALLY CORRECT, that will provoke race animosity." Ballou told his troops to stay out of places where whites did not want them, or they would suffer severe consequences. "White men made the Division," he said, "and they can break it just as easily if it becomes a troublemaker."[46] General Staff members concurred fully with this sentiment after the Camp Merritt riot. The "cases of unsatisfactory relations add weight to the opinion that the separation of the two races within the army organization is the policy of wisdom," intelligence officers concluded after the war.[47]

Army officials' receptivity to strident segregationist demands revealed their concern about disciplinary control as much as it unveiled their own racist beliefs. The choices that army officials made during the war reflected how vulnerable they felt, or made themselves, to the weight of white soldiers' racial preferences, but the army paid a price for exacerbating the sense of isolation from the war's purpose that their status as noncombatants already had thrust upon black soldiers. The army's blatant discrimination in favor of whites precipitated enormous anger and hostility among the black rank and file, and disciplining this increasingly alienated segment of the army population further distracted army officials from the military goal of winning the war.

The Repercussions for Black Soldiers

The army's tendency to appease white opinion both within and without the military had serious long-term repercussions for black U.S. soldiers. In early policy discussions about how to assign black recruits, General Staff officials never doubted the army's ability to train these men for combat, especially since black units had compiled illustrious records in the Civil War and the Spanish-American War. Instead, they spoke of balancing political and manpower demands. By the spring of 1918, however, the General Staff began for the first time during the war to justify its decision to limit the number of black combat units in terms of defects inherent in the black race. "The poorer class of backwoods negro has not the mental stamina and moral sturdiness to put him in the line against opposing German troops," Colonel E. O. Anderson concluded in a memorandum on the black draft in May 1918. "The enemy is constantly looking for a weak place in the line and if he can find a part of the line held by troops composed of culls of the colored race, all he has to do is to concentrate on that."[48] These same officials now argued that black soldiers found the adjustment to army life harder than whites. "The negro is frequently not accustomed to orderliness, moral or physical discipline, not even to ordinary cleanliness and sanitation. One colored private had complained bitterly because he had to comb his hair and take a bath every day," a typical intelligence bulletin read.[49] Army authorities also claimed that they could not trust a racial group who seemed more committed to winning their own political battles than to victory on the battlefield. Officials speculated that German propagandists had infiltrated black communities and planted stories that black servicemen served as shields for white soldiers at the front. Such rumors circulated so widely by June 1918 that the War Department cabled Pershing to send them a publishable statement refuting these charges.

The army responded to this supposed subversive threat by launching a comprehensive investigation into black soldiers' activities.[50] Intelligence officers compiled mountains of reports detailing the intentions of "troublemakers" to raise questions of equality and opportunity. Black troops concerned with these issues soon became dissatisfied with their army life, intelligence officers concluded, and were likely to instigate racial disturbances. Numerous operatives cited German propaganda as the cause of black soldiers' dissatisfaction, not the mistreatment black soldiers complained of to investigators. The stinging critique German propaganda pamphlets offered of racial segregation in American society had haunting accuracy. "Can you go to a restaurant where white people dine, can you get a seat in a theatre where white people sit, can you get a pullman seat or berth in a railroad car? . . . there is nothing in the whole game for you but broken bones, horrible wounds, broken health or death," leaflets that

German aviators dropped among the few American black troops near the front lines proclaimed.[51]

After the war, this image of the black soldier as "the enemy within" stuck. Postwar studies noted that while African-Americans' subordinate position in civilian society taught them to depend on white men for leadership, the injustice blacks often encountered bred strong feelings of resentment against whites. "It would be futile for us to try to believe that the negro has no particular state of mind against us, he undoubtedly has," cautioned one postwar report.[52] Rather than using this collection of evidence to create policies designed to remove the reasons for resentment and the appeal of enemy propaganda, the war induced a new, damaging period of institutional racism, in which officials viewed African-American soldiers as incompetent, untrustworthy, and dangerous.

Whenever racial friction emerged in any camp during the war, black troops were usually the ones who lost their pass privileges, received additional quarantines, or were court-martialed. When black troops directly questioned discriminatory quarantine rules, army officials simply responded that all soldiers had to endure quarantines to check the spread of infectious diseases through army training camps.[53] Privately, however, army officials acknowledged these lengthy quarantines kept black troops under supervision in one section of the camp. In a few camps, troops took matters into their own hands and organized efforts to rush the gates and get into town for the night. Most of the men Ely Green led in a charge of the gates one night at Camp Stuart, Virginia, an auxiliary camp near Newport News, had not left camp since entering the army. Scheduled to depart for France the next day, "I began thinking to how I would love to hold a little brown baby in my arms once more. I hadnt [sic] been close to a woman in a month. The men were talking of breaking camp. They were restless, I knew. I was too," Green recalled.[54] The men eluded the guards by throwing blankets over the perimeter fences and obstructing the guards' view of the escapees. Green cautioned the men to stick close together throughout the evening. "Dont [sic] any one get lost," he counseled them. "If you do you will be court-martialed. We must stick together." This strategy worked well, because only Green, the group's ringleader, got caught when the men returned to camp, and even he was released to sail with his unit the next day.

Many black soldiers who broke rules formulated to limit their interaction with white soldiers had less luck and got a quick and severe reminder of their second-class status. "The military police," at Camp Sevier, Charles Williams reported dismally "is composed of all southern soldiers, who are careful to see that the Negro soldiers stay in their place."[55] MPs regularly threw black soldiers into the guardhouse, where their jailers indiscriminately beat them, put them to work, or let them go. Private Adams Glatfeller, training in Camp Gordon, Georgia, approvingly noted to his brother the trepidation he observed in the black prisoners who occasionally marched through camp. "You know they are afraid of a white person," Glatfeller wrote.[56] Officials hoped the severity of the punishments given to black soldiers would deter other rebellious black soldiers from challenging army authority. When three black soldiers were convicted of raping a white woman outside Camp Dodge, Iowa, camp officials decided to hang them publicly so that everyone in the camp, white and black alike, would see the swift retribution aberrant black soldiers received.[57]

Such tactics successfully subdued many black soldiers, but they also left them dispirited, sentiments clearly reflected in a heart-wrenching letter Private Stanley Moore wrote to his sister from Camp Travis, Texas:

My dear Sister,

Your letter received and always glad to hear from you. I can't say that I like the Army life, it is a hard life to live and they are so mean to the colored boys here. They curse and beat them just like they were dogs and a fellow can't even get sick. Oh! it is an awfully mean place. I will be so glad when they send me away from here.[58]

Moore soon got his wish, and reported to his sister that things had improved for him in his new army home in Camp Funston, Kansas. His good luck did not last long, however, because medical examiners soon classified him as unfit to serve overseas and sent him back to Camp Travis.

Army officials made supervising black soldiers a high priority, but not supplying them. The equipment and housing requirements of white troops took precedence over the needs of black troops when the army allocated scarce resources. Inadequately housed and clothed black noncombatants consequently endured hardships more appropriate to the front line than in a stateside training camp. Some of the worst conditions existed in Camp Hill, which housed the black stevedores working at the Newport News embarkation port. "During the coldest weather Virginia has experienced in twenty-five years, the stevedores lived in tents without floors or stoves," forcing some to stand out around fires all night to avoid frostbite, Williams reported. Promised clothing within a month of their arrival in camp, these men worked in the sleet and snow loading and unloading ships "without overcoats, rain coats, or even good shoes." These men had nowhere to bathe, nor did they receive a change of clothing until January 1919. "Cases are known," Williams continued, "where men had only one suit of underwear for two or three months. As a result, many of them were covered with vermin."[59]

Conditions like these seriously impaired the morale of black noncombatant soldiers. Added to reduced military training opportunities, these miserable living conditions further weakened their resolve. Most did not receive adequate housing or recreational facilities until after the war, when demobilizing white soldiers vacated their quarters. First Lieutenant Howard Jenkins, a morale officer in Camp Travis, reported encouragingly that moving black soldiers into barracks, improving rations, securing three afternoons off for the men, and opening a YMCA recreational room "have been important factors in decreasing A.W.O.L.s and other offenses to a very small percentage."[60] This improved morale came too late to do the army much good.

Black troops gained significant social freedom while serving overseas, however. "A new race riot was staged in Winchester[,] England[,] between the southerners in the Camp Wheeler outfits and American negroes who were camped there," the debarkation intelligence officer reported to Washington. "It was reported, as has been reported many times before, that people in England always give American Negroes a big reception and show them big times. . . . The negroes of the outfit, it was said, began boasting about it to the southerners at Winchester and a free for all fight followed."[61] Nothing angered southern white troops more than friendships or sexual relationships between Frenchwomen and black soldiers. Sergeant Green, the same soldier who engineered the escape from Camp Stuart discussed above, was walking back to camp from St. Nazaire one afternoon with a group of white soldiers when they came upon a line of black troops waiting in line outside a whorehouse. "There was about fifteen Negro soldiers standing in line as if they were going mess. These white souldiers [sic] began yelling at these Negro souldiers telling them that not to get too use to white womans. You wont have them when you get to America," he recalled. "The Negroes yelled back: 'Go to Hell.'"[62] First Lieutenant William Powell reported from St. Sulpice that "almost daily there are reports coming into this office of the growing friction between the white and colored soldiers in this camp." The point of contention once again was competition for Frenchwomen. One Sunday, Powell saw a crowd of black soldiers gathering, and asked one of them what the problem was. "He replied, 'that a white guard had pulled a gun on a black boy who was talking to a white woman' and there 'would be trouble' if this continued."[63]

French people, unfortunately, "do not look upon the Negro exactly in the same way that the white people of America do," Brigadier General W. S. Scott, the commanding general at St. Sulpice, concluded, although white American soldiers did their best to enlighten them.[64] Black soldiers soon discovered that white U.S. troops were busy spreading rumors among the civilian population that blacks were rapists, thieves, and had tails.[65] Anxious to develop a strong working relationship with their new allies, French military officials tried to eliminate these offensive interracial relationships. Colonel Linard, a member of the French Mission attached to the U.S. Army, advised French Army headquarters to alert French officers that praising black soldiers and allowing unlimited interracial contact between friendly French civilians and black soldiers hurt white American troop morale.[66] Sexual encounters between black soldiers and Frenchwomen even troubled those lobbying for equal treatment. Major Loving, a stalwart defender of black soldiers throughout the war, nonetheless advised the War Department to ship black soldiers back home quickly once the Armistice had been signed. Black soldiers, like all other soldiers, he warned, would seek sexual diversions after the war, and because no white man "wants to see colored men mingling with white women . . . I cannot see anything but an American race war in France."[67]

Throughout the war, the army nearly always sided with white soldiers when they complained about unjust racial practices. These accommodations, coupled with the disciplinary revolution under way in nonracial matters, illustrate the powerful institutional position that white troops occupied. As the war wore on, winning the allegiance of these troops became more and more important to army officials. They increasingly viewed citizen soldiers as comrades whom they could count on for future political support, rather than antagonists. It soon became apparent, however, that the army had little ability to direct citizen-soldiers' budding political consciousness. Encouraged to contemplate the nation's democratic war goals, both white and black citizen-soldiers developed ideas of their own about where American priorities should lie in the international crusade being pursued by the United States. The problem of discipline and loyalty came to encompass more than whether soldiers would obey unquestioningly or maintain peaceful race relations. American officials soon realized that the more faith U.S. soldiers invested in the democratic purpose of the war, the more determined they became to forge relations with the French and Germans that reflected their own definition of national war goals.

CITIZEN-SOLDIERS ENTERING A TRAINING CAMP

On their way to their training camp, these civilians carry flags from their community send-off and are wearing their best clothes to begin their new life as soldiers. *Source:* National Archives, College Park, Md.

ILLUSTRATION OF THE SIMILARITY BETWEEN BOXING AND
BAYONET FIGHTING

A cult of aggressiveness formed around boxing in the training camps. This posed picture illustrates the similarity between boxing and bayonet fighting, a comparison that explains why army officials liked the activity so much. *Source:* National Archives, College Park, Md.

A TRAINING CAMP BOXING CLASS IN PROGRESS

In sharp comparison to the preceding posed picture, this photo captures the chaos and high spirits that reigned when men were let loose during these classes to practice the manly art. *Source:* National Archives, College Park, Md.

FRIENDSHIP BETWEEN AN AMERICAN AND A FRENCH SOLDIER

Here the general respect each had for the other's fighting abilities during the war is shown. *Source:* National Archives, College Park, Md.

A HELMET SAVES A SOLDIER'S LIFE ON THE WESTERN FRONT

Soldiers developed strong beliefs in chance and fate on the Western Front. According to one legend, each man would be killed by a shell with his number on it. *Source:* National Archives, College Park, Md.

A RUINED FRENCH CHURCH

This photograph of a field hospital in a ruined church offers a striking portrait of the toll of combat on the American forces and the destruction they witnessed. *Source:* National Archives, College Park, Md.

COLLECTING SOUVENIRS ON THE WESTERN FRONT

Some soldiers went to extreme lengths to satisfy their mania for collecting souvenirs that showed that they had been at the front and had had contact with the enemy. *Source:* National Archives, College Park, Md.

BLACK SOLDIERS HAUL AN ARTILLERY PIECE

Most black soldiers performed manual labor while overseas. The implication that the soldiers have simply replaced animals in hauling this artillery piece underscores even further the dehumanized view of black soldiers that solidified during the war among the army brass. *Source:* National Archives, College Park, Md.

ENGINEERS AT WORK

In a beautifully composed photo, engineers complete a variety of noncombatant tasks, seemingly far from the front. *Source:* National Archives, College Park, Md.

BLACK AMERICAN SOLDIERS HELP A FRENCH CIVILIAN
REBUILD HIS HOME

The work of these black soldiers in helping this French civilian rebuild his
house can be seen as an example of the positive relationships that developed
between the French and African-Americans during the war. *Source:* National
Archives, College Park, Md.

AN AMERICAN OFFICER AND A GERMAN OFFICER

The two shake hands after the Armistice, foreshadowing the quick reconciliation between the two armies and peoples. *Source:* National Archives, College Park, Md.

AMERICAN SOLDIERS SIGHTSEEING IN PARIS

After the war, the U.S. Army adopted a liberal leave policy to appease disgruntled citizen-soldiers in hope of improving veterans' future attitudes toward the army and France. *Source:* National Archives, College Park, Md.

VETERANS LOBBY CONGRESS DURING THE 1932 BONUS MARCH

Americans debated whether this was a coup d'état in the making or a gathering of poor men petitioning the government. *Source:* Underwood & Underwood. From the Herbert Hoover Presidential Library, West Branch, Iowa.

CAMP MARKS IN THE SUMMER OF 1932

Camp Marks was the main Bonus Army encampment in Washington, D.C. *Source:* Herbert Hoover Presidential Library, West Branch, Iowa.

5

FORGING THEIR OWN ALLIANCES

AMERICAN SOLDIERS' RELATIONS WITH THE FRENCH AND THE GERMANS

The German resumption of unconditional submarine warfare in 1917 had provided the immediate justification for the American declaration of war. But President Woodrow Wilson soon offered the American people larger, more grandiose goals than protecting the right of neutral ships to use international waters. Although the president had called upon the European powers in January 1917 to conclude a "peace without victory," Wilson now saw the war as an opportunity to achieve the greatest victory of mankind. In his war message on April 2, 1917, Wilson entreated the American people to make the world "safe for democracy." During the following months, Wilson articulated his revolutionary vision more fully. In his Fourteen Points, Wilson transformed the clash between European imperial powers into a war to establish self-determination, free trade, and an international governing association. If accepted, Wilson's ideas would result in the dismantlement of the colonial empires that had made the European nations world powers, and at the same time propel the United States into a commanding position in the international community. For the United States, the war became a way to reorder the world in its own image by spreading its distinctive democratic culture.

Reflecting the tone set by their commander in chief, army officials imbued their troops with a clear idea of what distinguished the U.S. Army from all others by cataloging the superior qualities of the American soldier for their wartime recruits. Firsthand contact with their allies and enemies gave American soldiers many chances to promote American methods of fighting and the American way of life. American soldiers' relations with French and German nationals also had a political dimension.[1] High-ranking officials in each army realized that good relations between American soldiers and the French were essential in order for the alliance to work effectively. How much power did American soldiers have to shape Franco-American wartime and postwar relations? How much ability did American and French officials have to mold American soldiers' views on international affairs? These questions consumed the American and French officials assigned to monitor and shape American soldiers' political views.

Wartime Alliances

From the beginning, how Americans viewed the French reflected their own beliefs about themselves. U.S. Army officials cultivated the distinctive American qualities that, they believed, would render their nation's army victorious where others had failed. "Berlin can not be taken by the French or the British Armies or by both of them," General H. B. Fiske, who devised the AEF training program, confided to his colleagues. "It can only be taken by a thoroughly trained, entirely homogeneous American Army."[2] AEF officials knew that they depended on Allied generosity to help train and arm their mass army. They sought, however, to accept the insights that Allied instructors offered without letting their failed strategies contaminate the fresh approach that Pershing hoped to interject into Western Front strategy.[3] Like American officers, French observers realized that American soldiers took admonitions to fight aggressively to heart. "Even if much weaker than his adversary, the American never retreats," one French instructor noted after observing boxing matches in stateside camps.[4] Yet too much emphasis on character and not enough on acquiring the skills needed to fight from the trenches might spell disaster for the U.S. Army, warned some French instructors.

American officials predicted that exposure to American methods would inject new spirit into demoralized Allied troops.[5] Their army racked by mutinies in the spring of 1917 after a series of failed offensives at Chemin des Dames, French officials expected the same results.[6] With satisfaction, French postal censors noted a new buoyancy in French soldiers' letters now that the Americans had entered the war. "More and more the Kaiser must curse Christopher Columbus's discovery," exclaimed one French soldier.[7] Once the Americans began arriving in force in 1918, their enthusiasm and energy reminded many French soldiers of themselves in 1914.[8] "Our soldiers note the aggressive spirit that animates our allies: 'They think that they are in a bad sector because it is too quiet: their dream is to fight hand to hand,'" a French censor quoted from one French soldier's letter in June 1918.[9] Such naïveté was understandable in novices, but few French soldiers expected it to last. "They want to attack," a French soldier reported, but "when the moment comes perhaps they will change their minds. It is when one does not know something that one finds it easy to do."[10]

The most generous French soldiers emphasized the ways in which strong, brave Americans would complement the wisdom the French had accumulated, creating a formidable alliance. Others, however, hoped for much less. Optimists expected every American soldier who entered the line to give a French soldier a chance to rest in the rear.[11] Pessimists feared that while Americans took over quiet sectors to perfect their training, French soldiers would find themselves primarily assigned to areas of active fighting. Soldiers with this view worried that "these people are only strong in talk," not action, and correctly believed that the French would still do the bulk of the future fighting.[12] What "marvelous lessons" could the Americans teach them? To one French soldier, the improvements the Americans had already made to French ports answered this question. "The Americans are very capable of making the most of all the resources of France," this soldier noted. "We count on them to bring us their mentality and methods."[13] Americans, however, had other ideas about the contributions they could make, and their list did not include giving French soldiers a rest, freeing them from custodial duties along the front, or injecting American engineering expertise into the French economy.

The send-off American civilians gave their troops reinforced the popular American conviction that they were off to save France from certain defeat. As Henry Dillard's unit made its way from Virginia to its embarkation camp in New York, cheering crowds met it at every train stop. "The entire trip was quite a triumphal procession," Dillard wrote to his mother.[14] A march past a Confederate soldiers' home in Richmond elicited a "rebel yell" from the aging veterans, who lined up to salute the doughboys. Young girls crowded train platforms to shake their hands, and Red Cross workers handed them sandwiches and coffee. The first American soldiers to arrive in France found little to contradict their self-image as designated saviors. The public euphoria that greeted their arrival augmented the mandate these American troops had received at home to save Western civilization. The widespread domestic publicity given to this glowing reception succeeded in bolstering French morale.[15] "The Yankees are quite wonderful," French civilians told each other, "Their love for France is truly extraordinary and it is necessary to hear them talk of Lafayette to understand how grateful and devoted they are to us."[16] The French population understood the reference to France's help in the American War of Independence and the symbolism of Pershing laying a wreath on the marquis de Lafayette's tomb on his first day in Paris.[17] It took the French populace longer to realize that the Americans would expect a similar outpouring of gratitude once they had saved France. In time, disappointed Frenchmen would come to appreciate that the American soldiers' love of France only went so far. French intelligence officers already noted in their confidential reports that American troops had some selfish reasons for fighting, such as protecting their country against German aggression, creating a world-class army, and gaining respect from the French Army.[18]

In the early months of American participation, however, French soldiers felt satisfied to have, as one noted after the Second Battle of the Marne, "at least some allies that we can count on."[19] French soldiers had ample opportunity to become acquainted with American soldiers. Twenty-five U.S. divisions served for varying periods with the French Army, while only nine divisions served with British units.[20] The passive posture American troops observed in quiet French sectors along the Western Front convinced green American troops that the French had indeed lost their will to fight. Soldiers wounded in the Lorraine sector elaborated upon this familiar theme when they told an undercover investigator that the French fired on the Germans as little as possible. When these troops described the "live-and-let-live" system in their sector, the investigator noted, they "said that the Boche and poilu did their washing together and hung the clothes upon the wire."[21] Although American troops would eventually establish their own trench routines, early on they condemned this inertia as freely as their leaders.

Other expectations American soldiers brought to France went unfulfilled. Little remained of the resplendent French countryside in the war-torn areas American troops occupied. A consistently rainy climate, coupled with the destruction wrought by alternating bands of occupying soldiers, had turned this part of France into a muddy and barren milieu. The destitute conditions inhabitants endured in the devastated regions appalled American soldiers. Hardened by war, these peasants had tired long ago of billeting soldiers and of competing with them for scarce resources. Consequently, these French nationals reacted indifferently to the Americans' arrival. Having magnanimously come to rescue France, American soldiers viewed this lack of interest as ingratitude. "Life in France for the American soldier meant marching in the dirt and mud, living in cellars in filth, being wet and cold and fighting," the chief of staff of the 4th Division noted at the close of the war. "He had come to help France in the hour of distress and he was glad he came but these French people did not seem to appreciate him at all."[22] The French also found it difficult to understand the American mentality. "You could not imagine a more extraordinary group than this American Army," exclaimed one French soldier in a letter home after training an American regiment.

> There is a bit of everything, some Greeks, some Italians, some Turks, some Chinese, some Indians, some Spanish, and even a reasonable number of Huns. . . . This does not seem to bother them. But doesn't this seem to you a strange outlook? As for me, I could hardly see myself fighting against my country even if I had left it a long time ago. They don't seem to remember it. . . . Did I tell you the story of the soldier from my regiment who was debarking in France and saw his German brother as a prisoner working at the port? . . . There are among the Americans the sons of French emigrants and the sons of Hun emigrants. I asked the French son if the Germans could be trusted to fight against their brothers or cousins, and he said without hesitation, "yes!"[23]

Their multi-ethnic army gave the Americans a few surprising moments as well. The discovery that some German prisoners of war were former immigrants to the United States captivated the imagination of American soldiers, who wondered why these men were "fighting in the wrong uniform." First Lieutenant Oswald Moore met German prisoners who had lived in Jersey City, and spoke with one who thought his son might be serving in the American army. "Sometimes it's a small world after all," an astounded Moore noted in a letter home.[24]

Confusion about each other's cultures rarely affected the ability of the two sides to fight together effectively. Mutual endorsements of their respective fighting abilities flowed freely. Changes Pershing ordered to quell the paranoia apparent within his staff facilitated the American soldier's growing regard for the French. General Fiske was convinced that the French were conspiring to undermine the American training program.[25] He based his suspicions, in large part, on a memorandum General Philippe Pétain, the French commander in chief, had distributed among French officers, which instructed them to teach American troops the value of heavy artillery and trench warfare. Fiske chose to ignore the fact that in the same memorandum Pétain cautioned his officers that defensive training should enhance, not diminish, American rifle expertise. Pershing shared Fiske's desire to rid his army of Allied advisors and also worried that the French were using joint training to further their cause of amalgamation. Although Pershing allowed American troops to train in quiet trench sectors with Allied divisions, he never wavered in his commitment to create an independent American army. Pershing rejected all Allied schemes that he simply train infantrymen and then turn them over for amalgamation into the French or British Army.[26] But Pershing also knew by June that unchecked outbursts by his divisional commanders and staff denigrating the French threatened to undermine the cooperative war effort. After learning that the French had received reports from their liaison officers that detailed American contempt for the French Army, he ordered his commanders to halt their rhetorical attacks on French military expertise.[27] Tacit disparagement of the French continued, but Pershing's order curbed open belittlement of the French in official circles. Two months later, the U.S. Army finally took over its own sector and rear-area training, and apprehension that the French were covertly trying to amalgamate the two armies diminished.

American troops serving with French units saw the scope of Allied aid to their force. Before long, initially disdainful American soldiers were moderating their opinions about their French comrades. "The average infantryman who spent but a few weeks in training in France and spent the remainder of his time fighting, frequently with the support of French artillery has, as a rule, considerable respect for the French," noted one Military Intelligence Division officer.[28] Many American divisional commanders also developed a more positive view of the French Army after fighting alongside the French, perhaps because Pershing encouraged them to regard the French more favorably. After the Armistice, GHQ officials asked their commanders to compare the relative effectiveness of the American and French armies. Few American commanders claimed, as GHQ officials often did, that American troops dominated every collaborative effort. Although 38 percent declared that the Americans contributed more to joint operations than the French, the rest either saw no difference (27%), said that it was impossible to estimate (13%), refused to answer (13%), or proclaimed the French role more significant (9%). Many described veteran French troops as exceptional fighters and gave high marks to French artillery, medical, signal, and air units. When rating the relative efficiency of American units as compared with French units, 34 percent claimed that the Americans were more efficient, 33 percent felt them equal, 11 percent rated the French more efficient, 9 percent could not judge, and 13 percent offered no comment.[29]

Although American soldiers still viewed themselves as more daring than the French and occasionally charged that the French were letting them "do the dirty work," good relations existed between troops of the two armies.[30] French soldiers noted with pride that American soldiers "had profited enormously from the lessons and advice, to the point of being as good as their French instructors and comrades."[31] More than one French soldier expressed annoyance over how the Americans wasted matériel and lives, but "one cannot count the number of them [French soldiers] who write that the Americans fight like lions," reported a censor after reading soldiers' mail in August 1918.[32] French soldiers noted one grating development by the fall of 1918: the steady American refrain that they were ready for the war to end. "They are waiting for the peace with a lot more impatience than us, which is very strange," noted one French soldier in October 1918. "They haven't even been fighting for that long. What would it be like if they had four years to their credit!"[33] American troops, however, never needed to develop much endurance, because rumors of peace flowed freely by October.

The Germans provided a different sort of model. The Americans had many ways to distinguish themselves from the Germans, especially because well-publicized reports of German atrocities gave Americans a moral imperative to conquer the forces of evil. A long tradition of reverence for Germany also existed in the United States, however. During their wartime encounters with the Germans, particularly with German prisoners and the retreating German Army, American soldiers had the luxury of deciding how to treat a defeated enemy. These overtures in the final days of the war laid the foundations for critical developments in the postwar period that would affect American soldiers' relationships both with the French and with their own officers.

The Germans

If American commanders and soldiers at times questioned the worthiness of the French as allies, they never doubted that they had found a formidable and somewhat admirable foe in Germany.[34] On the one hand, wartime propaganda depicted the Germans as beastly savages who raped and pillaged the people they conquered. On the other hand, army officials had enormous respect for Germany and its emergence as a military, industrial, and cultural leader at the turn of the century. American officers had emulated the preeminent German military system ever since Germany's overwhelming victory in the 1870–71 Franco-Prussian War. Regular army officials fashioned many of their modern reforms on the German model, including the concept of a General Staff, the comprehensive officer school system, and universal military training proposals.[35] Other Americans shared this prewar admiration for German achievements. Since 1850 a steady stream of German immigrants had infused American culture with an appreciation for the productivity and ingenuity of the German people. Until 1915, German-Americans retained strong ties to their homeland without alienating themselves from mainstream American society. Even hard-core nativists considered these prosperous businessmen, farmers, and skilled workers reputable immigrants. When war broke out in Europe, however, British propaganda, a series of highly publicized German attempts to sabotage munitions shipments from the then-neutral United States to the Allies, and U-boat attacks on merchant vessels turned public opinion against the close-knit German-American community. By the time the United States entered the war against Germany, a burgeoning anti-German hysteria was sweeping the country.[36]

Army officials, however, still held the German Army in high regard. In October 1917, General Robert Lee Bullard noted in his diary that he secretly believed that the United States had entered the war too late to defeat the powerful German Army. Pershing detected a similar note of pessimism among other AEF generals, and on December 13, 1917, he sent each one a confidential memorandum that chastised them for doubting the U.S. Army's ability to win. "A conservative firmness and faith in our cause is not inconsistent with a serious estimate of an enemy's forces," Pershing reminded his generals.[37] American confidence rebounded during the spring, but respect for the German enemy remained intact even after the Allied victory.[38]

The close quarters in which American and German troops waged war along the Western Front created numerous opportunities for American troops to test their own convictions about their enemy. Many soldiers preferred to view the Germans as an evil force, which they had come to destroy. "I [now] think they were just ordinary people, [but] then, of course, we were trained to hate them," Corporal Charles Hill recalled.[39] American soldiers understandably detested those pulling the triggers of opposing guns, Private Fred Ross noted. "Chaplains tried to dissuade us not to hate them, but I fear their efforts were futile in most cases," he declared. This impersonal perspective no doubt helped many soldiers survive at the front, where soldiers lived by the motto "Kill or be killed." German intelligence officers concluded that many American soldiers obviously believed their government's claim that the Germans took no prisoners, noting that U.S. troops appeared terrified of surrendering, even when trapped.[40]

Some American soldiers succumbed to the temptation, however, to tear down the barrier between them and the young men opposing them on the battlefield. Private Emmett Riggin openly boasted that his artillery squad named their gun the "Hun Hunter." Nonetheless, he was unnerved when he stumbled upon a dead German soldier standing upright with a spade in his hand, as if preparing to dig a hole in which to hide. In death, the German soldier's frozen posture betrayed the last desperate moments of his life. His back had been blown off during the most recent American artillery barrage, which Riggin had helped launch. "I called for Dill [my comrade] to come and see this pitiful sight, and Dill expressed his surprise and sympathy also," Riggin noted in his diary.[41]

Yet for most American soldiers, budding empathy for the Germans did not come from a growing perception of the universal horrors of combat. These men felt they could afford to be chivalrous to defeated German soldiers who did not dispute the Americans' claim to victory. The quest for souvenirs aroused considerable interest in German prisoners of war, but American troops also seemed intent on making friends with them. "Our soldiers fed them, gave them cigarettes and fraternized with them to such an extent that orders had to be issued to put a stop to such intercourse as Corps Headquarters found prisoners so treated were difficult to question," Lieutenant Colonel J. A. Baer reported in the fall of 1918.[42] The illicit relationships that German and American combatants risked toward the end of the war also suggested that victorious American troops wanted to be reconciled immediately with their defeated opponents. Americans soldiers made a profound judgment when they halted their belligerent stance before officially ordered to cease fire. There are few cases of fraternization as well documented as a late October incident involving the 26th Division, a somewhat unique episode in the annals of the American war experience. Nonetheless, this battlefield encounter has an instructive value that transcends the titillating aspects of an engrossing battlefield negotiation between opposing armies, one that foreshadowed the more pervasive reconciliation that U.S. soldiers would initiate with the Germans, in defiance of their orders, after the Armistice.

Although many Western Front soldiers established "live-and-let-live" rituals during the course of the war, opposing troops rarely consorted directly with one another, because few were willing to seem to be conspiring openly against their nation or to risk detection by their own officers. Many, no doubt, also questioned the sincerity of enemy invitations to meet. In October 1918, however, active fraternization between the 102nd Infantry Regiment and German soldiers began when small groups of German soldiers initiated shouting conversations across no-man's-land. These hesitant overtures soon evolved into covert meetings in the early morning fog. By the time Sergeant Major Julius Wax, who spoke German, conversed with these Germans on October 19, 1918, they were welcoming American soldiers into their trenches at night. The Germans explained to Wax, as they had told previous visitors, that they believed the war was almost over. "They also say that they could shoot our men frequently but when ordered to do so by their officers they fire over their heads, going on the assumption that the war is too near an end to kill unnecessarily and that they are not barbarians," Wax noted.[43] As an additional gesture of goodwill, the soldiers assured Wax that American troops could come out safely and bury their dead.

The crux of these mid-October conversations for American soldiers centered on their counterparts' admission of defeat, a concession, however, that created a dilemma. Private Ernst Volz claimed that the American soldiers who visited his trench to barter for alcohol told him that, with peace so near, they had no desire to fight the Germans anymore either, asking, "Why should we take each other's lives?"[44] The Germans refused to surrender out of fear that both they and their families would suffer repercussions if they were taken prisoner without their officers. The Americans perceived no honor in pursuing a beaten army whose soldiers asserted that their own government was holding them hostage in the front lines. So, secure in the knowledge that they had already won the war, members of the 102nd, 103rd, and 104th Infantry chose to protect themselves and their defeated enemy with ritualized mock shelling as they each waited for the war to end officially. But soldiers on both sides refused to divulge what units they belonged to, how many men lay in reserve, or when they expected a relief. The taboo placed on discussing vital military information perhaps explains why these soldiers never considered themselves traitors.

Frontline troops of the 102nd Infantry Regiment did not realize, however, that Wax submitted his observations to divisional headquarters. Headquarters officials responded by ordering an immediate barrage on the German trenches, which effectively ended fraternization in this area.[45] At least headquarters officials gave this version of events during the official investigation that ensued. But Wax, the commanding regimental officer, and the commanding brigade officer contradicted these assertions. Wax claimed that headquarters had ordered him to visit the German lines one last time on October 21 to persuade the Germans to give themselves up before the artillery barrage began. Wax maintained that he was sent to warn the Germans that "something was going to happen" unless they surrendered. American officers, bound by their own sense of honor, felt "this warning was considered just . . . [because] the Germans in that Trench had made clear efforts to spare our men," the commander of the 102nd Infantry, testified. The plan to take the Germans prisoner, and possibly avoid resuming hostilities, backfired when the German soldiers refused to surrender. Headquarters officials denied that either they or General Clarence Edwards, the division's commander, had ever authorized Wax's visit or message. Edwards made the mistake of discussing this fraternization episode with General Hunter Liggett, who had recently taken over command of the First Army from Pershing. Edwards intended to relay information about poor morale in the German Army, but instead he lost his job when an infuriated Liggett apprised an equally unforgiving Pershing of this episode. Pershing, who had wanted to remove this "National Guard" commander for a long time, within two days reassigned Edwards to a post in the United States.[46]

Yet despite the new divisional order prohibiting fraternization, cordial relations continued unabated in the adjoining sector between soldiers of the 104th Infantry Regiment and their German neighbors. When the 103rd Infantry Regiment took over the sector on October 25, soldiers from the 104th passed along their shelling protocol. Soldiers from the 103rd soon accepted an invitation to visit the German trenches themselves. While exchanging tobacco and brandy, American and German soldiers rehearsed the salient points of their pact, which included shooting high and signaling if ordered to raid or to snipe at the enemy line. The German frontline troops intentionally directed artillery fire away from their American friends during the required barrages by sending up red flares that signaled their own artillery to lengthen their range. Like the Americans, German soldiers passed these rituals on to the soldiers who relieved them to avoid any interruption in cordial relations.[47]

The relative safety Americans and Germans secured through these agreements improved life along this part of the front line tremendously.

While visiting a 103rd Infantry outpost, no more than thirty yards from the German line, a surprised Captain Joseph H. W. Hinkson saw American and German troops sitting out in plain view of each other around fires. "While I stood there I saw one of the Germans stand up and take off his hat and wave it at us," Hinkson noted, and witnessed the corporal in charge reply with a wave of his hand.[48] Such blatant gestures of friendship could not go undetected for long, and Hinkson's report to divisional headquarters prompted Lieutenant Colonel C. M. Dowell, the 103rd Infantry's new commanding officer, to take matters into his own hands. Disguised as a private, Dowell walked unrecognized through the trenches for a few hours. There he observed the telltale signs of American soldiers walking freely about outside their trenches in full view of enemy snipers and saw fires burning brightly throughout the enemy lines. The fires, Hinkson had already learned, signaled that the pact still held.[49] Continuing his covert interrogation, Dowell asked this soldier:

Q: Why do you suppose he [the German] shoots high? Why does he not snipe at you?
A: Well, I suppose it's because we don't shoot at him.
Q: You don't shoot at him either?
A: No, we don't.
Q: Why not?
A: Well, he would shoot back and besides we have orders not to shoot except where it is absolutely necessary.
Q: Who gave you those orders?
A: The fellows from whom we took over. . . .
Q: Has the Boche been in the habit of showing himself?
A: Oh yes, sometimes they come over and talk to us. Mostly they want tobacco. Sometimes they brought rotten rum which they wanted us to drink with them but I was always leery of it.

When asked why they saw no Germans out that particular afternoon, the soldier replied that they were hiding because the Americans had orders to snipe at their lines. How could the Germans know this was planned for later that day, Dowell asked. "I suppose somebody told them," came the reply. "Not long ago when they made a raid on us they told us it was going to happen. They said they would whistle when they were going to shoot or throw grenades," and they had kept their promise when the time came, the soldier added.[50] After this enlightening walk, an astounded Dowell urged headquarters to remove his regiment from the line immediately. His recommendation came too late, however, for by the time his report reached headquarters, the Armistice was in effect.

When the clock struck 11:00 on the morning of November 11, 1918, elation was strongest along the front lines.[51] "Everyone knew if he made it to eleven A.M. he would be o.k. and I never saw a more scared bunch of soldiers," Private Robinson Shepard recalled. "Somehow we had not paid much attention before, but now we were most anxious to live until eleven o'clock."[52] Shepard's sector experienced sparse shelling, but First Lieutenant Moore waited through a heavy barrage that morning. Seven minutes after the cease-fire went into effect, his sector finally quieted down. The profound silence that engulfed the Western Front lasted only a few moments before French, British, German, and American troops walked out onto no-man's-land and together rejoiced that they had survived the most destructive war in history. At fifteen minutes past the hour, Moore looked over the top and saw American and German soldiers, who minutes before had been huddled in the ground avoiding each other's artillery fire, shaking hands. "Not fifty yards away were about thirty Germans exchanging salutations with a bunch of our doughboys, swapping things and having a general good time, all accompanied by much cheering and singing from other points," Moore wrote home that day. Moore soon joined in the festivities, walking into the middle of no-man's-land to accept a cigarette from a German soldier. That night the Germans launched their remaining signal flares, a magnificent firework display, which filled the sky throughout the evening.[53]

What did this victory mean to American soldiers? Their conclusions often put them at odds with their French colleagues. To the French, the Allied victory would not be complete until the future of their boundaries was secure and their thirst for revenge against the Germans abated. The French intended, according to one French general, to "be as hard on the Boche as they would have been hard on us."[54] For American soldiers, victory meant quickly establishing democracy in Germany, returning home, and never coming back again to sort out a European conflict. When the French dismissed the Americans' claim that they were the war's true victors or condemned American soldiers' reconciliation with the Germans, they inadvertently attacked a group that many in power believed would become a potent postwar force. Both American and French officials worried about how American soldiers, who were increasingly expressing opinions and engaging in behavior that contradicted the official position of the U.S. government, might affect the peace process.

The Postwar World

With the German Army on the run, Pershing advised holding out for unconditional surrender, advice not heeded.[55] Pershing may have doubted the wisdom of an armistice, but the announcement pleased everyone else in the U.S. Army, who congratulated themselves on winning the war.[56] In January, the AEF General Staff sent the American Commission to Negotiate Peace a comprehensive analysis of the U.S. Army's pivotal contributions. Army officials expected this information to help the commission secure a prominent role in the peace negotiations. GHQ claimed exaggeratedly that the U.S. war effort had dwarfed those of France, Britain, and Germany in size, scope, and quality. This report downplayed the U.S. Army's dependence on Allied supplies and instead detailed the transportation infrastructure the Americans would eventually leave for the French. The authors of this report gave the American troops who had fought under French command during the German 1918 spring offensives full credit for stopping the German march to Paris at Château-Thierry in June and for the success of the Allied counterattack that summer.

AEF staff officials, however, saved their most illustrious praise for the operations they had conceived and commanded themselves. They based the U.S. Army's claim to have singlehandedly saved France on its troops' success in overcoming the Germans in hilly, densely forested terrain during the St. Mihiel and Meuse-Argonne offensives. "It is notorious that while we were fighting to the limit in the Argonne, the French Army was doing little more than observing the enemy with a view to taking over positions abandoned by the enemy. The British were doing little more. . . . But the American divisions in their ranks were given the most difficult enterprises, suffered the heaviest casualties, and by their energy and dash were in a very large measure instrumental in pushing forward the Allied lines," surmised the author of this report.[57]

American soldiers heartily agreed that they were indeed the only true victors of the war. Even those American soldiers willing to concede some glory to the French Army remained stubbornly hostile to French civilians. "The French soldier is all right," an intelligence officer heard one group of American soldiers fume, "but damn these French civilians."[58] French villagers, soldiers surmised, ungratefully focused on the property American soldiers damaged or the food they pillaged, rather than on how they

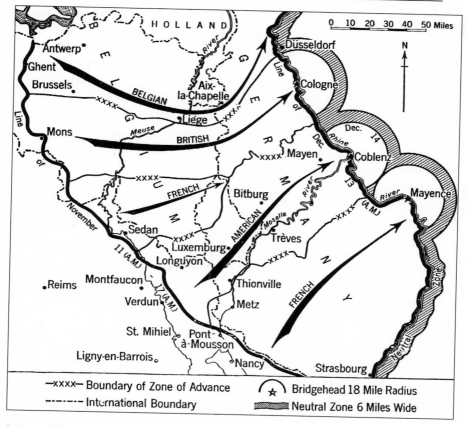

Map 2. The Occupation of the Rhineland after the Armistice. American and Allied Advance to the Rhine, November 17–December 14, 1918. *Source:* American Battle Monuments Commission, *American Armies and Battlefields in Europe: A History, Guide, and Reference Book* (Washington, D.C.: GPO, 1938; reprint, Washington, D.C.: Center of Military History, 1995), p. 487. *Note:* Mayence is French for Mainz.

had rescued France in her hour of need. Instead of thanking them, French proprietors overcharged American soldiers and refused to heed southern soldiers' requests that they ban black soldiers from their establishments.[59]

The Americans were on the lookout for slights, and the first blow came when the French decided to reduce the size of the bridgehead they would occupy. Besides requiring that German troops immediately evacuate Belgium, France, Luxembourg, and Alsace-Lorraine, the Armistice authorized Allied occupation of all of western Germany to the left bank of the Rhine and three eighteen-mile semi-circle bridgeheads around Cologne, Coblenz, and Mainz on the right bank (see map 2). It also created a demilitarized zone along the rest of the Rhine's right bank. Marshal Ferdinand Foch, the supreme commander of the Allied armies, had insisted on these terms, knowing that Allied control of the Rhine and all the major industrial cities and transportation hubs in western Germany would give the Allies an overwhelming battlefield advantage if the peace talks broke down and the war resumed. Rather than focusing on the overall strategic importance of this limited Allied occupation of Germany, American soldiers fumed over Foch's last-minute decision to give the U.S. Army only the northern part of the Coblenz bridgehead to occupy. Throughout the AEF, when asked why they disliked the French so much, American officers and soldiers incessantly recounted how this decision reduced the number of troops needed for the occupation force and abruptly ended the 5th Division's preparation for a "triumphant march into the enemy country." Watching French troops march through the American sector of the Rhineland on their way to occupy the area south of Coblenz originally assigned to the U.S. Army further incensed American troops. They "felt that this was not only an insult to the Division but to the entire American Army, and every American soldier deeply resents this treatment," an official explained to an investigator.[60]

The gracious reception American soldiers received in Germany prompted even more unfavorable judgments about the French. Most American soldiers soon agreed with the sentiment expressed by one that the Germans had "more respect for us than the British or the French. Oh, we get on first rate with them and they surely do a lot for us."[61] Warning that "familiarity breeds contempt," officials banned unofficial contacts between Americans and Germans, but to no avail.[62] In the Rhineland, American soldiers discovered a popular summer resort area filled with picturesque castles and tourist spas, all untouched by the ravages of war. After months in the wasted regions of France, these appealing surroundings, coupled with the residents' hospitality, provided a much desired respite from the war's devastation. The Germans, many soldiers attested, ungrudgingly offered them good meals and comfortable beds, charged reasonable prices for wine, and treated them like colleagues rather than unwelcome visitors. "Germany is not such a bad place to be," Corporal Ernie Hilton wrote earnestly to a friend at home. "There is a dutchman living at our place who fought against us in the St. Mihiel drive, and now we eat at the same table, share our tobacco and laugh at each other's experiences. This may sound rather queer to you but this is the way we are treated and the way we treat the Germans."[63] American troops also appreciated that demobilized German soldiers acknowledged that they had lost their will to fight after encountering fresh, energetic American soldiers.[64] Few French soldiers agreed with the American claim that "we won the war."[65] Some American soldiers spoke German, but ignorance of the language created few barriers for the rest when their hosts conveyed their goodwill through actions rather than words. "Shortly after they reach a town it is common enough to find that some old woman is baking cakes for them and giving them rooms in her house instead of the stable in which they are billeted," one officer complained. "This is a form of propaganda which it is practically impossible to combat."[66]

When some American troops began to say in conversation and in letters home that "we fought the war on the wrong side," U.S. Army officials realized that they had a serious problem on their hands.[67] The relatively comfortable life American soldiers found in Germany increased their disdain for the impoverished and miserly French. The soldier's daily experience with French parsimony lent credibility to untrue stories that the French government was demanding reparations from the U.S. government for property American soldiers had damaged, charged rent for the fields soldiers slept in, exacted tax on all the meat and ammunition purchased from the French during the war, and forced the U.S. government to buy French property at exorbitant prices for its wartime bases, which the Americans would have to sell at a loss. "Gossip, over heard largely thru Officers' messes and elsewhere, is tending to increase his [the American soldier's] . . . dislike for French business methods, whether individual or national, tending to make him feel that he is being stung, and that his nation is being stung," an intelligence officer noted.[68]

American soldiers' reconciliation with the German people irritated and worried the French and British.[69] Contradictory rumors circulated to explain this turn of events. Many French soldiers blamed the Germans for indulging the American ego in hopes of securing their support for a lenient peace. Others believed the Americans intended to recruit German officers to train their peacetime army, a rumor French intelligence officials investigated and discounted.[70] All clearly saw American naïveté on display. "Your attitude of victors is too noble," a French GHQ official noted in dismay to an American liaison officer. "[Y]our gentle attitude towards him [the German] tends to encourage his plans for revenge and another war."[71]

More than naïveté and ego, however, prompted American soldiers' reconciliation with the German people. Their quick reform of Germany into an apparently democracy-loving polity also served to justify the speedy repatriation of American troops. "They believe too easily that the maintenance of an army in Europe is due to the unjustified demands by the French," noted one French intelligence officer.[72] According to American soldiers, the French had created any problems they were having with the Germans. Rumors that French soldiers beat German civilians who did not salute when they passed, spitefully threw German residents out of their homes when seeking billets, maliciously destroyed furniture, defaced town buildings and churches, and looted shops flowed freely in the AEF.[73] American soldiers criticized the French for failing to realize, as they did, that this defeated populace appeared ready to establish a democratic government. Coupled with generally pleasant living conditions, the fact that the Germans "look upon the President of the United States as the 'greatest man of the day,'" one officer observed, "seems to have a softening effect on the soldiers."[74]

French intelligence officials found sympathy for their concerns among their American counterparts, who set out to investigate whether or not a carefully orchestrated German plot existed to entice American soldiers into protecting Germany from a harsh peace settlement. Despite their best efforts, searches for German agents in the U.S. Army proved futile, and officials eventually abandoned this explanation for American troops' antipathy toward the French.[75] American investigators also tested out another French theory that American soldiers "only suffered relatively minor losses and could not be in the same emotional state as those whose country was ravaged and whose close relatives were ruined, molested, and destroyed."[76] American soldiers should try to understand the French point of view, an American intelligence investigator told Colonel Paul Conger, chief of intelligence for the Third Army. Conger replied that nothing would justify unchecked aggression against a civilian population to American troops. This "was the very thing that America went to war for the purpose of exterminating," Conger told the investigator. "American troops would not do the very thing which they came over to fight against. He also stated that he knew of many instances where both officers and soldiers had stated that they were wondering after all if they had fought against the right people," the investigator reported.[77]

The war having been won, American soldiers seemed more interested in spreading the democratic ideals that would ensure their quick return home than in seeking revenge for war crimes. Kaiser Wilhelm II abdicated in November 1918, and a moderate socialist government was established in Germany. In January, the German government decided to hold national and regional elections. Realizing that the National Assembly selected during this election would draft Germany's new parliamentary constitution, Foch agreed to let elections take place in all the Germany territory under Allied control except Alsace-Lorraine (which he expected the pending peace treaty to return to France). Germany wanted a constitution just like the American one, German civilians told U.S. troops.[78] French soldiers, whose country had hitherto been the only republic in Europe, had their doubts about German intentions. To avoid reparation payments for the crimes Germany had committed, "they feign a republic," noted one French soldier dismissively.[79] The series of revolutionary and counterrevolutionary coup attempts that rocked Germany from the time of the Armistice to well over a year after the new constitution established the Weimar Republic revealed that many Germans remained uncommitted to parliamentary democracy. In the American sector, however, German officials maintained that the public's democratic impulses were genuine and gave the Americans credit for fostering interest in the upcoming elections. There were more votes cast in the American sector than in those areas held by the French and British, German officials told U.S. intelligence officers. "They account for this," a Second Division intelligence officer reported, "by saying that the German people are more or less ignorant of the method of voting and the necessity for it." This officer eagerly accepted German claims that before casting their votes "many went to the American soldiers who give them information and in general stimulated interest in the elections." The Germans making such statements correctly guessed that few Americans knew that imperial Germany had had a popularly elected Reichstag since 1871, which had voted enthusiastically for war in 1914. Instead, the Americans accepted that the war had been waged "against an autocratic government" and that these democratic elections "constituted a symbol of our victory."[80] By lauding the Americans for teaching them the art of voting, German officials no doubt hoped to foster American goodwill and distance themselves from the previous regime. American soldiers also, however, had some self-serving reasons for accepting this flattery without reservation. The quick rehabilitation of the Germans into a law-abiding, egalitarian people conveniently eliminated, in U.S. troops' minds, any reason for their prolonged deployment in Europe.

Paradoxically, while French soldiers doubted the ability of the Americans to bring about genuine reform in Germany, at least one of them believed that their continued presence in France would have a desirable political effect. "There are two million Americans here," he declared, "who would not be Bolsheviks for anything and who will have, I believe, a favorable influence in the workers' areas."[81] Americans did not want this responsibility. Realizing that resolving Europe's political problems involved more than educating Germans about democracy, the Americans had little incentive to prolong their stay. "They say that they are 'homesick,'" noted Captain Georges Bertrand, a French liaison officer; "they prefer to put an ocean between themselves and 'these excited peoples of Europe,' whose debates tire them."[82] Only regular army officers, for whom life in Germany was "as comfortable as along the Mexican border," expressed interest in staying.

Representatives serving on the American Commission to Negotiate Peace never intended to commit a permanent peacekeeping force to Europe. Indeed, American peace negotiators resented attempts to entangle the United States permanently in European affairs as much as American soldiers did. Nonetheless, the commissioners viewed the growing breach in the Allied alliance with alarm. "It is conceivable [that] Americans and Germans can be friendly without bad results," an AEF official reported to the commission, but he warned that this association was undoubtedly undermining the peace process. "The subject of the morale of the allied armies is perhaps not one for consideration of the Commission to Negotiate Peace, but the establishment of a real friendship between the armies seems of vital importance" to secure a future working friendship with the French.[83]

General Pershing shared the commission's concern over the exaggerated animus American troops had developed against the French. The extent of his concern prompted Pershing to discuss the rift between American and French soldiers with the president when he arrived at the peace conference. Unless dissuaded, Pershing noted in his diary after this meeting, "a good proportion of our men, if not the majority of them, who have been in the Army of Occupation will go home with a feeling of more respect for the Germans than for the French."[84] One concurring observer predicted that as soon as newspaper "articles began to appear showing the real feelings of our men towards the French, there would be a feeling of revulsion in the entire United States against France, so that our country would not only have the hatred of Germany, but of France as well."[85] During one briefing before the American Commission to Negotiate peace, former Chief of Staff Tasker Bliss, now the military representative on the commission, felt compelled to ask "whether, if it came to a show-down" over Germany accepting the Versailles peace treaty, American soldiers would fight. AEF officials reassured him that American soldiers would obey orders to resume the war, but the fact that Bliss even felt compelled to ask the question indicated the seriousness of the crisis that U.S. soldiers had triggered in the Franco-American relationship within three months of signing the Armistice.[86]

These developments worried French officials immensely, even though the disintegration of the German Army made renewed hostilities unlikely. Realistically, one French officer worried that U.S. soldiers would emphasize "the difference between the stay in Germany and the stay in France" when they returned home, with some potentially "severe consequences from the point of view of our national interest."[87] In an effort to reverse the tide, American officials reiterated their ban on fraternization, publicly denounced German cordiality as an insidious propaganda ploy, and gave soldiers passes to visit French resort areas.[88] These actions refuted the December prediction of a high-ranking French liaison officer that "the approach of the presidential election of 1920 did not permit American leaders" to insist on putting the Germans in their place.[89] With satisfaction, French officials witnessed the Americans' crackdown on their troops, which included arresting soldiers seen talking with German civilians and reserving cafes and public areas in occupied Rhineland towns for either civilians or soldiers. Visiting American dignitaries also urged American soldiers to moderate their views.[90] The French government reacted as well, providing constant reminders of France's gratitude to America by organizing a huge Fourth of July festival on the Champs Élysées, distributing a generous number of Croix de Guerre to American soldiers, and assigning French military officers still in the United States to speak at all American war-related ceremonies.[91] Still, the rioting that took place in Brest on June 28, 1919, the day Germany accepted the Versailles treaty, vividly illustrated the unraveling of the Franco-American relationship. This war-ending violence contrasted starkly with the cheers that had greeted the Americans' arrival and the Armistice. Second Lieutenant Charles Brady Ryan noted in his diary that cries of "la guerre [est] finie, Americans get out tout de suite" filled the streets. French sailors pulled down American flags in one section of town, and the ensuing mêlée caused casualties on both sides. American soldiers attacked the French sailors, prompting residents to drop bottles and rocks on the Americans from their second-story windows.[92]

It was telling that French and American officials focused on the potential influence returning soldiers might wield over American public opinion. These officials expected citizen-soldiers to take a stand and attempt to sway their government on critical postwar decisions. From France's point of view, the important issues included the peace treaty, potential financial aid to France, and a defense treaty with France to guarantee her borders against German aggression. The French government hoped that when American troops realized it was not opposing their repatriation, their former fond feelings for their wartime ally would return.[93] In an interview with French officials in July 1919, Theodore Roosevelt, Jr., one of the founders of the American Legion, a World War I veterans' organization, dispelled these hopes. In his estimation, American veterans' skepticism about continuing financial or military assistance to France was rooted in the negative images they retained of their personal postwar relations with the French.[94]

One group of American soldiers, however, was coming home with an extremely favorable view of the French. Among returning troops, only black soldiers expressed a preference for Europe over the United States in official surveys of soldiers' opinions.[95] Blacks stressed the differences between France and the United States, rather than between France and Germany.[96] "You know now that the mean contemptible spirit of race prejudice that curses this land is not the spirit of other lands," the Reverend F. J. Grimké told a group of returning black soldiers.[97] Soldiers from the four regiments that served directly with the French Army attested to the willingness of the French to let black men fight and to honor them for their achievements. Social interactions with French civilians—and white southern soldiers' reactions to them—also highlighted crucial differences between the two societies. Unlike white soldiers, African-Americans did not complain about high prices in French stores. Instead, they focused on the fact that "we were welcomed" by every shopkeeper they encountered. "One merchant in St. Die told a field officer in our Division . . . that the white soldiers 'come into my store and throw their money at me, but the black soldiers act as if it were a pleasure to trade with me and it is they that I welcome,'" an African-American officer told W. E. B. Du Bois.[98] French intelligence operatives confirmed that this was the general reaction of French merchants who dealt with both white and black American soldiers.[99] "The propaganda the southern crackers is [*sic*] spreading in France is going to do him more harm than good," noted one African-American sailor with satisfaction.[100] This sailor carried the photograph of a lynching around with him, and when he encountered Frenchmen who had been warned about "black rapist beasts," he responded by showing them this proof of white beastliness. The struggle to prevent the French from accepting southern demands for segregation, however, required constant effort by black soldiers. Unlike white U.S. soldiers, whose commitment to France wavered when the guns fell silent, American black soldiers continued their struggle to keep France free of American racial practices until the day they left for home.

France had its own history of segregation, rooted in its colonial heritage, a part of French culture that few American soldiers understood. The French government discriminated against the colonial wartime workers it brought to France by isolating them in separate housing and working environments to prevent contact with the civilian population, paying them less, and denying them the right to change jobs without approval. Racial tensions surfaced in French society when sporadic racial rioting broke out in 1917–18 during a moment of great frustration with the continuing war. In their attacks, white French targeted colonial workers, whom they blamed for working as strikebreakers, lowering the prestige of European women by establishing interracial relationships, and freeing more Frenchmen for the front.[101]

As positive symbols of military aid from abroad, the French generally treated colonial soldiers well, but they expected them to return to their native lands once the war ended.[102] The French welcomed African-American soldiers as temporary visitors who assumed their fair share of military responsibilities and, like all Americans, injected much welcome cash into the French economy.[103] These attributes do not alone, however, explain why France rejected the Jim Crow model demanded by white American soldiers, who were arguably providing even greater military and financial benefits to France. The forms of racial segregation developed for colonial workers and soldiers could have made it easy for the French to accept white American demands on this subject, but they did not. Every black soldier who chose to recount his wartime experiences included at least one story of encountering French civilians on the brink of accepting the advice of white Americans that they lock their doors against the black rapists, thieves, or savages coming to their town. The next segment of the story usually contained a passage in which an angry white soldier barged into a meal (or conversation, stroll, drink) that a black soldier was sharing with a French family to demand drunkenly that the black soldier leave. American black soldiers believed that they had successfully preserved French democracy from contaminating American influences when the head of the family refused the request. What caused this change of heart among the French people? To these soldiers, the answer was articulated perfectly in the testament of a French grandmother that "almost all the French love the blacks better than the whites because the blacks are so polite and nice." This lady, George Wilson assured Du Bois, "echoes the sentiment of a great many French people."[104] Elmer Carter concurred, claiming that "wherever the Negro soldier was stationed he soon won the admiration and respect of the inhabitants."[105] An informal survey by Du Bois of twenty-one French towns further confirmed these conclusions. Du Bois received an outpouring of praise for African-American soldiers who, as the mayor of Domfront wrote, "won the esteem and sympathy of all the population."[106] African-Americans thus ended the war with a clear image of France as a color-blind society.

These stories show, however, that African-Americans were not just passively enjoying the pleasures of French egalitarianism during their stay in France, but also attempting to ensure its survival through their own behavior. Friendship with a French family was a powerful experience, as was the realization that one's actions could make a difference in the universal struggle against racism. The moment of victory for many (whose chances on the battlefield were few) came in the simple phrase: the people "learned to love us."[107] French military intelligence officials confirmed that "many of the inhabitants of villages in which they [black troops] are stationed declare they like them better than whites."[108]

Black soldiers also received some inadvertent help from American army officials in their quest to ensure equal access to French people and institutions. American army officials intended to teach the French that black troops had criminal tendencies, but instead the unfolding of relations between American black soldiers and French civilians revealed the paradoxical results of internal U.S. Army policing. Regardless of the number of complaints lodged concerning the behavior of white troops, French liaison officers noted, "it seems that the officers completely disregard what their men do in the various occupied cantonments."[109] The contrast with the treatment reserved for black troops in the 92nd Division was stark. "Thanks to the severity of measures taken by the American commander, the misunderstandings and reported incidents have diminished quite noticeably," reported the liaison officer.[110] In keeping with the American racial mentality, officials punished infractions committed by black troops severely but failed to recognize any similarity between the behavior patterns of black and white soldiers. A steady stream of regulations sought to limit contact between African-American soldiers and French civilians. In some units, commanding officers forbade African-American soldiers to visit cafes; others took a risk if they had a conversation with a white woman or accepted an invitation into a French home.[111] Harassment from the American and French police meant that respectable women hesitated to go out with African-American soldiers, because they ran the risk of being branded prostitutes, Chaplain Joseph F. Simpson claimed.[112] African-American soldiers believed that these relationships thrived in spite of racist army policies, but it may also have been because of them.

Having warned the French inhabitants of the criminal tendencies of the black race, American army officials believed that the misbehavior of black troops confirmed the justness of their racial beliefs to the French. They were mistaken. Instead, the new regulations gave African-American soldiers a clear incentive to avoid giving French merchants, families, or cafe owners any reason to call the U.S. military police. To those who only saw the behavior of black troops improve as time went by, African-American troops soon appeared as ideal visitors. "The key note to French character," an officer attested was " 'whatever you do be polite about it' for they can forgive anything save meanness, boorishness, and impoliteness."[113] Villages now expressed a preference for black over white American troops. "Take back these soldiers and send us some real Americans, black Americans," wrote one village mayor after a group of rowdy white Americans disrupted the town.[114] The strict discipline required by U.S. Army officers and black soldiers' determination to prevent the spread of Jim Crow practices created a unique tie between the French and African-Americans, which continues even today.[115]

Black leaders in the United States eagerly awaited these troops' return. "[B]y the God of Heaven, we are cowards and jackasses if now that the war is over, we do not marshal every ounce of our brain and brawn to fight a sterner, longer, more unbending battle against the forces of hell in our own land," cried Du Bois in the pages of *The Crisis*.[116] The chief of the AEF Intelligence Bureau feared the same development, and alerted his officers in January 1919 to report any signs that black soldiers were organizing a secret organization to maintain "the social equality between the races as established in France."[117] William York confirmed that officers and enlisted men in the 92nd Division enthusiastically discussed this idea. "It is hoped that we may exert political influence and fight all kinds of discrimination," he told Du Bois in January.[118] The exact way to translate this euphoric experience overseas into concrete political changes in the United States, however, still remained unclear to many.

The French had undoubtedly found champions in black American soldiers. This support created a dilemma for French officials and, in some respects, a positive review from black troops troubled them as much as white soldiers' complaints. While they relished the moral high ground that African-American troops accorded them, these soldiers did not have the political power to turn such support into concrete financial aid for France. Instead, the interracial mingling accepted in French society contributed to some white Americans' image of France as a disagreeable place. The military attaché to the French embassy in Washington, D.C., worried privately to his superiors that resentful southern whites might hurt France's efforts to secure a favorable assistance package from the United States.[119] In 1920, charges from Germany that French colonial troops were terrorizing women in the Rhineland brought back the disturbing memories many white veterans still harbored of social equality in France. With diplomatic relations already souring over the issues of war debts and German reparations, publicity over the "shame upon the Rhine" recalled the offensive racial mixing between African-Americans and French women during the war. This scandal doomed any chance of rallying American public opinion behind financial or military aid to France.[120]

Encounters with foreign troops thus helped American soldiers reaffirm key components of their national sense of identity, which included a view of themselves as invincible, aggressive warriors, who were nonetheless chivalrous toward their defeated foes. Eventually, white Americans came to believe that they were pursuing loftier goals than the French, while black Americans received confirmation of their equality. The question of American soldiers' allegiance interested army officials intensely during the war, and even the French and Germans vied for their affections. Army officials did their best to stem the tide of U.S. soldiers' dissatisfaction with the French, which created serious problems in the postwar Franco-American relationship.

The U.S. Army's efforts to manage the political opinions of American citizen-soldiers, originally intended to ensure that they would fight effectively on the battlefield, were now directed at minimizing any disruption of the nation's foreign policy. With the war over, the army began to think more seriously about its own future too. Army officials made no attempt, however, to link their proposals for a strong permanent military establishment with a new constabulary role for the United States overseas. They intended to enact their reforms strictly within the confines of the nation's traditional preoccupation with self-defense and cultural cohesiveness. Increasingly, they began to count on returning soldiers' support to achieve these political goals.

By this point, citizen-soldiers also believed that their views mattered tremendously to the American public. Mass military service politicized this generation of soldiers, but not around the issues that interested the army the most. Citizen-soldiers increasingly doubted that the federal army deserved their postwar political support. These troops had helped introduce democracy to the Germans, but how well were democratic traditions faring in their own institutions? African-American soldiers led the charge by highlighting racial discrimination, but army officials had anticipated these complaints. Other attacks, however, against officer privileges, the court-martial system, and the organization's coercive disciplinary code, caught them off guard. As the government and public strained to decipher the message citizen-soldiers were bringing back about the ultimate meaning of the Great War for American society, army officials found themselves scrambling to salvage this potentially viable political constituency.

6

THE LEGACY OF THE WAR FOR THE ARMY

The Armistice came much more quickly than army officials had expected. Instead of planning for eventual demobilization, they had focused throughout the fall on building an ever larger and stronger army. As a result of President Woodrow Wilson's obsession with peace conference preparations and the immediate dismantling of the federal regulatory agencies that had controlled the wartime workforce, formulating an equitable and rational demobilization policy fell to the War Department. Realizing that a bungled demobilization could create havoc for the economy, society, and government, the War Department considered various plans, such as releasing soldiers when jobs became available for them at home, letting soldiers who had served the longest leave first, and having local draft boards decide when the men should return to their communities. All these proposals, however, involved more bureaucratic sophistication than the army possessed. The plan adopted, therefore, simply discharged men when the military rationale for their mobilization had ceased to exist.

In practice, this meant first releasing the 1.5 million men training in stateside camps, then bringing 2 million men home from overseas, in the following order: casuals, surplus and special service troops, troops in England, U.S. Air Service personnel, troops in Italy, combat divisions, and, finally, Service of Supply troops. Vast problems soon materialized when the army put this plan into motion. Horrendous winter weather and the ongoing influenza epidemic ravaged the troops crowded into French embarkation camps, where woefully unprepared army administrators tried to complete final physical and payroll records. Psychological tensions rivaled these physical problems. Angry over the indifference and inefficiency that they detected in the demobilization process, citizen-soldiers reacted especially violently to the army's insistence that they train and work for months after the cease-fire and continue to accept the social superiority of their officers.

During the demobilization period, the two distinct wartime trends toward granting citizen-soldiers a policy-making role in the military and treating them as political actors whose views mattered reached fruition. Thanks to the wartime innovation of monitoring soldiers' views, the army became acutely aware of citizen-soldiers' complaints about both the demobilization process and army life in general. Even traditionalists found it difficult to ignore this criticism, because they hoped to have veterans' support in upcoming budget and policy battles. With this future relationship in mind, and General Pershing's blessing, the army began an intensive campaign to appease citizen-soldiers during their last months in uniform.

For the most part, citizen-soldiers never knew that the army was monitoring and responding so intensely to their views, and they unhesitatingly took advantage of relaxed censorship regulations to contact their families and federal legislators to enlist their help to bring them home quickly and to vent their anger at army authoritarianism. The overwhelming public response to these complaints confirmed citizen-soldiers' suspicions that serving in the wartime army had magnified their own political authority. Attacks on the army's perceived mismanagement of its citizen-soldier population aired daily in Congress.

Censuring the Army

Dismantling America's vast wartime military machine was a task every bit as daunting as constructing it had been. Noncombatants especially understood the scope of work confronting the demobilizing army, and their feelings of neglect intensified once they faced the thankless tasks of cleaning up battle areas or dismantling stateside training camps. Private Julius Christensen, a member of the 3rd Pioneer Infantry, had spent the war salvaging the equipment that combatant units discarded on their long marches to the front, and, like all Americans, he celebrated when he heard that the fighting had stopped. Much to his dismay, however, Christensen soon realized that for him the true end to the war was still a long way off. The retreating German Army had left a trail of debris stretching all the way back to the Rhine, and Christensen's unit was soon marching along that path, blowing up discarded German ammunition. Initial euphoria gave way to a precariously fragile spirit in his company. "As long as I keep my health I don't care much but there are lots of guys disgusted with life. They think as long as the war's over they ought to be going home," Christensen wrote to his sister.[1] At home, noncombatants had the same sinking feeling. In Columbus, Ohio, seven hundred black soldiers working at the Army Reserve Depot unloading supplies and working in construction refused to work until the depot commander promised them more food. "They complained of food but their real grievance is that they want out of the army," Major J. W. Foyle told an Ohio newspaper reporter.[2] Work slowdowns provided other signs of the alienation of noncombatant army personnel during the demobilization period.

Combatants had their own reasons for despairing that they were no closer to returning home than they had been before the Armistice. AEF headquarters immediately curtailed their spontaneous peace celebrations and ordered them to begin heavy training. Until a peace treaty was signed, the army wanted to maintain an obedient, combat-ready force. These outraged troops evaded as many required drill sessions as possible. The AWOL rate skyrocketed in units within a day's travel of Paris. Combatants alternated between viewing their training either as meaningless busywork or as preparation for another, unstated, mission. When pressed a few months later, AEF officials claimed that the training had been necessary until the German Army completely disbanded. For good reason, this rationale failed to take hold among the troops. Brigadier General H. B. Fiske, head of AEF training, later acknowledged that he had seen this as a golden opportunity to create a trained cadre whom the regular army could call upon in future emergencies, giving the United States "for a long period a military asset not to be measured in dollars."[3] When the celebrated journalist Walter Lippmann, who was a captain in the Military Intelligence Division during the war, toured the AEF with members of the American Commission to Negotiate Peace, soldiers questioned him about the War Department's intentions. "They complain that they are not being told what the policy of the government is and they are full of rumors and fears about expeditions to Russia, projects for re-building France, permanent occupation, to collect indemnities, etc., etc.," Lippmann reported.[4]

Mounting evidence demonstrated to citizen-soldiers that army commanders were not only untrustworthy but incompetent supervisors of the demobilization process. To those who traveled home through the larger embarkation centers at Le Mans and Brest, the phrase "going through the mill" summed up their horrendous ordeal. The flu epidemic exacerbated the problems caused by overcrowding, as did the brutal winter weather. Three men in Private Myron Edwards's battalion died from influenza while they waited to return home at the Brest embarkation camp, including a close friend of his. "He went in our group all through the war without injury, then to die in a place like this," Edwards dismally observed.[5] If the public had any idea of the true extent of the flu-related deaths, one soldier, "who has been through the mill," wrote to the *Stars and Stripes*, many commanding officers would be facing both a court-martial and "a line of fathers on the other side when they landed that would make the old-time custom of running the gauntlet look like child's play."[6] Some, however, refused to wait patiently as the flu took its toll and administrators crowded more and more men into the embarkation camps. Soldiers in Corporal Lawrence B. Wright's company took to the streets one night, carrying red flags and shouting for their immediate release from the disease-infested Camp Pontanezen.[7] The protesters entreated Wright and the company's other noncommissioned officers to join them, but they refused. Instead, the NCOs spent the next few hours assuring the men that they would try to secure a definite sailing date if they abandoned their planned march on camp headquarters.

A wide range of exclusive privileges eased the burden that officers bore during the demobilization period. "It was hard for a soldier fighting for democracy to understand why it was improper for him to conduct himself as a social equal and on a social level with any fellow soldier," Private T. P. Wilson wrote angrily in his memoirs when he got home. With wartime censorship regulations lifted, soldiers forthrightly outlined their complaints in letters to the *Stars and Stripes*. Why, Private H. B. Dale asked the editors, did an officer's money buy more than his at army canteens, where large signs proclaimed: "No Candy, etc. For Enlisted Men." "Have we won Democracy?" Private George E. Simons asked, when only officers were entitled to basic material comforts in the U.S. Army. At home, drunken discharged men hurled abuse at officers on the street.[8] Soldiers' outrage threatened to explode into outright riot when enlisted men claimed all the seats in a new YMCA auditorium more than two hours before the evening's show. Fifteen minutes before show-time, an officer appeared and ordered the men sitting in the front rows to vacate their seats to make room for the officers who were just then arriving. "Someone in the back shouted, 'If these men have to give up their seats, let's all go,' " an observer reported. "Whereupon the whole house moved for the doors." The same officer then climbed back on stage and warned that if the men left, he would close the theater for two weeks. "After some discussion the men returned to their seats, except the 200 doughboys in front, whose places in the meantime were taken by officers," the same witness noted.[9]

This antagonism opened up the possibility that officers and soldiers would return to civilian life with very different opinions about the nation's military. Citizen-officers obviously enjoyed the full range of privileges available to them in the army, yet they also had some complaints about the treatment accorded them during the war. They believed, for example, that AEF officials only rewarded their own inner circle of professional soldiers with medals. Secretary of War Newton E. Baker had halted all promotions within the wartime army once the Armistice was declared, and this decision did not sit well with temporary officers, who, as one panel told Pershing, "have made good, yet have nothing to take back to civil life . . . [that] will prove it."[10] In January, Baker relaxed his earlier order and gave Pershing the power to fill vacancies by promoting a limited number of men up to the rank of colonel, but he forbade awarding promotions simply to thank temporary officers for their wartime service.

Citizen-officers also shared the enlisted man's desire to return home quickly. "Except that they know we [the officers] are in the same box and sympathize, we'd have trouble," noted Second Lieutenant Lawrence Richardson.[11] Captain E. Carlson found another example of shared convictions when he listened to a group of artillerymen on the USS *Aeolus* recall the time a runner from an advancing infantry unit had come back to tell them where to direct covering fire to protect progressing troops. The memory of how "the officer in charge of the artillery emplacement, being helpless to render assistance on account of being out of ammunition, broke down and cried like a child" remained utmost in their minds. Both officers and soldiers remained "very much embittered toward the Army on account of such instances," Carlson noticed.[12] This tendency to fault the army rather than their officers slowly seeped into the controversy surrounding officers' privileges. Gradually, a community of spirit emerged that cast rigid army regulations as the culprit. This perspective conveniently ignored the eagerness with which citizen-officers had embraced the rights conferred upon them, but T. P. Wilson explained the rationale behind this popular view. The existing hierarchy "was not the fault of officers nor of the men," he claimed. "It was the fault of a military system, inherited I presume, from the British."[13]

When officers reenacted the ceremonial "death of Sam Browne" on the transport ships bearing them home, they corroborated this conviction at the army's expense. Overseas officers wore a "Sam Browne" belt as part of their uniform, ostensibly to make them more easily identifiable on the field. The belt became a symbol of segregation between officers and soldiers, because it gave officers all the identification they needed to procure their social privileges. As might be expected, citizen-soldiers made many disparaging comments about "Sam Browne." Required to shed their belts once they returned to the United States, some citizen-officers initiated transport funerals for "Sam Browne," in which they made a great show of showing the enlisted men on board that they were gladly giving up this mark of privilege. An eyewitness account came from none other than Secretary Baker, who watched the ceremony in amazement when he returned from France upon the SS *George Washington*. According to Baker,

> the ship's band one night paraded around the deck, led by some junior officers, bearing signs of a jesting and jocular character pertaining to the death of Sam Browne. As the band went by the officers joined the procession, taking off their belts and carrying them in their hands. The several thousand soldiers on the ship saw the procession and cheered far into the night. And when General Haan himself joined the procession and took off his belt, the cheering was quite wild.[14]

General William Haan had no trouble joining in this shipboard celebration because shedding his belt conformed with army regulations, but his participation did not signal that the army was ready to discard officers' privileges.

Confidential investigations begun by intelligence and morale officials gave policymakers some insight into these and other concerns of the citizen-soldier population. Some internal disagreement arose, however, over how the army should respond to soldiers' grievances. Traditionalists saw nothing remarkable in the grumbling of a demobilizing army, but the reforming vanguard urged commanders to react to soldiers' discontent. All, however, wanted to control how and where citizen-soldiers expressed their opinions. AEF officials reprimanded citizen-soldiers who criticized the army or government in letters to their families or in their contributions to the *Stars and Stripes*, and banned the YMCA from sponsoring army-wide debates on whether President Wilson was serving the nation's interests at the peace conference.[15] AEF headquarters warned YMCA officials "that questions concerning the actions or policies of the President or the government, or in fact any international questions are not the proper subjects for debate or discussion" by soldiers.[16] Similarly, the Morale Branch kept most of its investigations secret, fearing that if they became common knowledge, citizen-soldiers might inundate it with criticism. The Morale Branch rarely surveyed soldiers openly, but instead distributed confidential lists of questions, which its operatives asked soldiers informally while circulating through the ranks.[17] Few citizen-soldiers ever knew that the army was monitoring their thoughts.

These secret investigations drew attention to aspects of military life that policymakers had rarely considered. Their subsequent uncertainty about the true importance of soldiers' opinions revealed their inexperience in analyzing this kind of information.[18] Some AEF policymakers expressed skepticism about the significance of investigators' findings, especially if their own policies came under fire. Major General J. W. McAndrew, the AEF's chief of staff, dismissed citizen-officers' request for a speedier review of citation lists, and Brigadier General Fiske vociferously denied accusations that his postwar training program was ill-conceived. Major General James Harbord, the head of the SOS, and J. A. Baer, a key AEF inspector general, however, lobbied for an immediate response to disturbing field reports.[19] Raymond Fosdick, chairman of the Commission on Training Camp Activities, joined them in demanding a change in army policy. If the army persisted with its strenuous training program, citizen-soldiers would return home and "prejudice a new generation against military preparation of any kind," including universal military training, Fosdick predicted after touring the occupying army. Lieutenant Colonel R. W. Case, who monitored troops aboard returning transports, concurred that the army would benefit if it retracted policies that offended citizen-soldiers, so that "the men leave the service with a proper attitude towards it, an attitude which will make them supporters of the Army and not antagonists." After interviewing black soldiers, however, Major William H. Loving doubted that any effort to improve segregated facilities could ease black soldiers' resentment. Discriminatory practices had created a "veritable hornet's nest of radicals" who blamed the army for their troubles, Loving noted.[20]

The most important convert from the traditionalist camp was Pershing himself. His postwar receptivity to the demands of citizen-soldiers was astounding for a general who unapologetically demanded complete obedience to his orders, signed letters "Believe Me Always," and had secretly given his officers permission to shoot soldiers who shirked battle. When Pershing received Fosdick's suggestions for postwar reforms, he asked

Fiske to review the document, because much of the report focused on the unpopular training program. Fiske dismissed Fosdick's report as nothing more than uninformed speculation that exaggerated the extent of troop discontent, an opinion Pershing might very well have shared during the war. Now, however, he chose to side with the reforming vanguard. Following a suggestion made by Lieutenant Colonel Theodore Roosevelt, Jr., Pershing had just called twenty temporary and National Guard officers to Paris to confer on why morale had plummeted in the victorious army. Like Fosdick, this panel advised Pershing to reduce the training load, award more decorations, publish the embarkation schedule, and expand recreational facilities.[21]

Unable to ignore the cumulative force of this advice, Pershing, who at this point was rumored to have presidential ambitions, ordered the AEF's adjutant general to send excerpts from Fosdick's report to all his commanding generals. Fosdick's report "gives, as few papers do, the point of view of the American civilian who has not been in the Army for more than a year, and who makes up the major part of the officer and enlisted personnel in our Army today," Pershing told his divisional commanders. After March 1, these commanders would set their own training schedules, and Pershing urged them to respect Fosdick's advice and minimize the number of hours troops drilled each day. He now conceded that it would take more than victory for citizen-soldiers to return "to the United States enthusiastic over their military experience," and agreed to pay the small price of these postwar concessions to ensure the long-term support for the army of veterans voting as a partisan bloc.[22]

From this point on, Pershing's accommodative attitude revolutionized policies in the demobilizing organization. AEF headquarters now let soldiers bring their souvenirs home and gave hospitalized men the option of returning with their units. When pressed to appoint morale officers to AEF units during the war, Pershing had refused, arguing that creating esprit de corps was one of a commander's primary duties, but he now reversed his earlier judgment and appointed morale officers to ensure adequate entertainment. Finally, headquarters' officials published a priority list giving the order in which units would return home, although not the exact timing.[23]

This response expanded patterns established during the war itself. Army officials had been unable to shape racial or disciplinary policies without taking some citizen-soldier preferences into consideration, and the same general principle prevailed when they tried to formulate viable demobilization policies. Officials never, however, engaged in any open dialogue with citizen-soldiers, and their hesitancy kept the latter from appreciating how hard AEF officials were working to appease them. Without censorship to curtail them, numerous citizen-soldiers appealed to their families and federal legislators to come to their aid. Suddenly, army officials faced the possibility that citizen-soldiers might assume the lead in rallying public opinion against, rather than in support of, the professional army.

Enlisting Outside Aid

Through the uncensored letters flowing across the Atlantic, families learned of the deplorable, unsanitary conditions in overseas embarkation camps, the long delays in pay, and the perceived unfairness of the demobilization schedule.[24] Armed for the first time with precise information about the circumstances in which their men now found themselves, and often urged by soldiers to take concrete action, many families took up their soldiers' cause with the War Department, the newspapers, and their congressmen.[25] Throughout the war, the War Department had received routine requests from families for information about missing allotment checks, wounded soldiers, or the belongings of dead soldiers, but nothing on the scale reached during the postwar period.[26]

Citizen-soldiers did not simply entrust their cause to civilians, however. In increasing numbers, they began to think about contacting their national representatives themselves. Toward the end of April, soldiers of the 8th Engineers held a mass meeting by the railroad tracks near their camp in El Paso, Texas, to discuss this option. After a soldier in the crowd pointed out that "you cannot try a whole battalion," the group decided to send an ultimatum to the adjutant general giving him ten days to release them before they went on strike. A hat was passed, and soon the ringleaders had collected enough money to send the telegram.[27] After the leaders had tried unsuccessfully to collect signatures on a petition, the next discussion of how they could "do something for themselves" centered on contacting their congressmen. The following day, the ringleaders declared that they would take the first step and send signed letters to their representatives. In France, men in the 336th Machine Gun Battalion watched a dozen proposed sailing dates from Nantes pass them by before they began "thinking of taking up a collection and sending a cable to some senator or congressman asking him to see if we couldn't get some word from home," Sergeant Walter O'Malley told his parents.[28] Soldiers who embarked at

Brest, however, did more than simply kick around the notion of contacting federal legislators. Upon their return to the United States, so many of them protested to Congress about disease-infested embarkation camps that Secretary Baker decided to visit them himself in hopes of heading off a congressional investigation.[29]

Congress quickly sensed the growing public empathy for citizen-soldiers' predicament. Troops often complained about the slowness of the mail service that brought them letters and newspapers from the United States, but it seemed to take no time at all for soldiers to hear when congressmen such as Representative John Tilson (R-Conn.) delivered sympathetic speeches on their behalf in Congress. Tilson, who based his original address on complaints he had received from soldiers' families, found himself inundated with letters from soldiers themselves. "The men are red hot," Tilson read aloud on the House floor from one machine gunner's letter. "Something should be done to punish these militarists. They are breeding bolshevism, anarchy, and socialism in the souls of men who were sterling patriots."[30] Expecting a sympathetic ear, other soldiers wrote to warn of the consequences if they were not released soon. "We have become more and more restless," one soldier explained to Senator William Borah (R-Idaho).[31] In France, "the 'old men' are literally speaking, becoming wild, anarchistic," Alfred Schak told Senator Thomas Walsh (D-Mont.).[32] Private Edward F. Mason wrote to ask Senator Borah why his noncombatant unit could not be replaced with civilian laborers. "Is it conceivable that the government would deliberately choose to save money by taking it out of the pockets of 200 young men, who are not rich and who already have given from eight months to a year to the service?" he wondered.[33] "The men are not as a whole sponsoring Bolshevism or anarchy," Private Harry Brandeberry wrote more reassuringly to Borah, "but they are chafing under their present environment and they are numerous enough to control politics should they desire to," he predicted.[34]

These letters raised the worrisome possibility that military service had radicalized citizen-soldiers. Congress, however, had other concerns. "These men are going to have their own say in our politics," Senator George Chamberlain (D-Oreg.) stated bluntly.[35] "Who is responsible for all this?" he asked, rhetorically echoing the question on millions of soldiers' lips. No doubt he was hoping that these same soldiers were listening when he replied: "[I]t isn't Congress, who did all that it could to improve the situation." Most congressmen did not disappoint those who wrote.[36] Representative James Gallivan (D-Mass.) warned his colleagues to investigate these charges immediately, because "the party which attempts to shield the guilty ones will go down to ignominious defeat."[37] Other congressmen took the approach of helping as many stateside constituents as possible. "I have already filed application for discharge but it seems useless unless you can receive aid from some reliable source on the outside," Private Guy McCool told Senator Borah after Senator Boies Penrose (R-Pa.) secured discharges for several of his friends from Camp Merritt, New Jersey.[38] Congressmen, like army officials, wanted to cultivate the loyalty of veterans, whom they expected to become a strong, partisan bloc of voters.

Black soldiers also felt their problems deserved national attention. "Hurray! Women can now vote for President," Charles Duncan wrote home to his mother. "Tell grandma when she rolls up to the polls in that auto you wrote me of for her not to forget to vote for a quick return for the boys in France, especially colored."[39] This request for family members to influence demobilization policy through voting was quite unusual. Their limited enfranchisement gave black soldiers little confidence that federal legislators would consider any appeal they made. These "Soldiers of America" (as one group of black soldiers from Columbus, Ohio, identified themselves on a petition they wrote) counted on civil rights organizations and black leaders to advance their cause. NAACP officials suspected that the army was delaying the demobilization of black troops so that they could perform the unsavory work of dismantling wartime training camps and reinterring the war dead, while white soldiers snatched up the best civilian jobs. The NAACP forwarded soldiers' letters to Emmett Scott, the official representative of black soldiers in the War Department, but his limited capacity to act became painfully obvious. Scott diplomatically suggested an official inquiry, but, not content simply to wait, W. E. B. Du Bois published the damning findings of his independent investigations in the pages of *The Crisis*.[40]

Any discussion of citizen-soldiers' post-Armistice agitation must also consider the protests of the 5,000 American soldiers stranded in the vicinity of the ice-locked port city of Archangel, Russia. For them "the signing of the armistice doesn't mean a damn thing," despaired a member of the mission.[41] This tenuous foray into North Russia was part of Wilson's effort to rechannel the Russian Revolution in a more democratic direction. To assist anti-Bolsheviks, the Wilson administration sent covert financial aid through Allied governments, smuggled in military supplies, conducted sabotage missions, organized an extensive intelligence-gathering operation, sent humanitarian assistance in 1919, and refused to establish diplomatic relations with the new Soviet Union.[42] Wilson preferred this "secret war" to direct intervention. The president hesitated to send troops to North Russia and Siberia because he worried that armed intervention might backfire and help the weak Bolshevik government unify the country against the foreign presence on their soil. The British took a different stand. Apprehensive that the Russians' separate peace with Germany in March 1918 would encourage the Germans to seize stockpiled Allied supplies in Russia and transfer large numbers of troops to the Western Front, the British pushed immediately for a military response. Having repeatedly rejected suggestions that American troops be amalgamated with Allied armies in France, Wilson finally agreed in July 1918 to participate in these expeditions as a gesture of goodwill toward the Allies.[43] Wilson also found a way to reconcile the mission with his principle of self-determination by arguing that the American presence would give the Russian people the protection they needed to express their desire for democracy.[44] As American troops disembarked in Russia, Wilson held out the possibility of a more extensive intervention if the Russians took advantage of this opportunity to organize an effective counterrevolutionary force.

Intervention in Russia

Two different rationales served as the basis for American intervention in North Russia and Siberia. In the case of Siberia, Wilson worried that Japan's intervention there on behalf of the Allies would cause anti-Bolshevik Russians still rankled by their country's defeat in the Russo-Japanese War of 1905 to join with the Bolsheviks to expel the Japanese.[45] The changing fortunes of the Czech Legion also complicated the situation. Stranded along the Eastern Front when Russia abruptly ended its war with Germany, the Czechs had first called on the Allies to expedite their transfer to the Western Front. The plight of these popular fighters battling their way out of the interior of Russia captured the imagination of Americans, and Wilson billed the American deployment as a mission to rescue the Czechs after word came that they were encountering Germans in their battles. Wilson, however, did not authorize the mission until the 40,000 Czech troops had established control over most of the Trans-Siberian Railway and appeared to be rallying a significant number of anti-Bolshevik Russians to their side.[46] The newly independent Czech government accepted their role as the fighting nucleus of Allied forces in Russia, in part to gain a bargaining chip at the peace conference. The 7,000 American troops sent as part of an Allied expedition that also included Japanese,

British, French, Chinese, Canadian, and Italian troops provided logistical support for the Czechs. After the Armistice, American troops guarded the Trans-Siberian Railway to keep supply lines open for the Czechs and to free White Russian troops for combat against the Red Army. With counterrevolutionary groups vying for control of Siberia, Major General William S. Graves, the expedition's commander, struggled to stay neutral, but it proved impossible for the Americans to avoid deadly clashes with rival White factions. In June 1919, Wilson finally chose to back Admiral Aleksandr V. Kolchak rather than the more popular moderate socialists, and American troops delivered 50,000 rifles to his forces. Wilson directed American financial aid to Kolchak until his government fell in November.[47] With dwindling support in Siberia and increased opposition at home, the Americans began withdrawing in January 1920, leaving the Czechs to fight and bargain their own way out of Siberia by turning Kolchak over to the Bolsheviks.

The American troops sent to Siberia were regular army troops from the 8th Infantry Division, who came directly from the Philippines and expected their overseas tour to continue regardless of the Armistice. Five thousand miles away, the drafted citizen-soldiers sent to North Russia had more reservations about what kinds of military missions the government could legitimately assign them to perform. In North Russia, the 339th Infantry Regiment, one battalion from the 310th Engineers, and the 337th Field Hospital and 337th Ambulance Company of the 85th Division joined 11,130 British, French, and locally recruited Russian soldiers to complete the Allied detachment. Sent to protect Allied supplies and the port in Archangel, to help rally anti-Bolshevik forces, and to keep a northern escape route open for the Czechs, American soldiers instead found themselves under British command and pursuing Bolshevik forces along an ambiguously declared "defensive" front that extended over 300 miles (see map 3). Wilson believed that he had authorized the advance of American troops into the interior only if the Russian people demonstrated an enthusiastic willingness to take up arms against the Bolsheviks.[48] The Russians, however, gave the Americans a lukewarm welcome, and Wilson accused the British of misrepresenting the extent of Russian support in order to further their goal of reopening the Eastern Front. He consistently rejected all British suggestions that the North Russian and Siberian expeditions be linked up to form a new front, because he believed that the war would be won or lost on the Western Front. U.S. troops also blamed the British for their predicament. "We are fighting for British interests and spilling good American blood and wasting good American lives for a cause that our government surely does not understand," Sergeant T. F. Moran angrily wrote to his mother. "I was always of the opinion that in 1776 we freed ourselves from their domain, apparently not, or else someone is speedily putting us back under their yoke," he speculated.[49] To quell these pervasive anti-British sentiments Colonel George E. Stewart, commander of the American Expeditionary Forces, North Russia (AEFNR), forbade soldiers to criticize either the British or their own government's decision to join the expedition in their private correspondence.[50]

Wilson quickly lost faith in this "experiment" and refused requests for further deployments once it appeared that his worst fears were coming true. Too small to inspire anti-Bolsheviks or indifferent peasants to run the risk of supporting the counterrevolution, the North Russian expedition helped the Bolsheviks save their faltering regime by galvanizing Russians to oppose the foreign invasion. Bolshevik propaganda successfully cast domestic opponents as collaborators with the invading powers, and easy victories against the outnumbered Allies made the Bolsheviks appear stronger than they were in 1919 and further discouraged dissidents from organizing armed resistance to them.[51]

Wilson did not, however, authorize the withdrawal of the American contingent before ice blocked the port of Archangel in November, thus guaranteeing that American soldiers would be fighting in North Russia until the spring. The breakdown in supply routes put Allied troops in a tenuous strategic position when American officials realized that enemy forces were growing. In mid-January, a rout by the revitalized Sixth Soviet Army at Shenkursk forced American troops to retreat fifty miles to the rear before they could stabilize the front.[52]

Outnumbered, unsure of their mission, and forced to slog through miles of frozen terrain to confront an enemy they could barely identify, the U.S. troops in Russia rapidly grew discontented. Scribbled notations in private diaries, intercepted messages from those trying to send the "truth" home, self-inflicted wounds, and timid responses to Bolshevik overtures of friendship reveal the extent of rebellion in the ranks.[53] Before leaving the United States, they had been told "of a cause to fight for, of honors to be won, wrongs to be righted . . . for the sake of democracy with a capital D," Sergeant Rodger Sherman Clark confided to his journal, but instead "the seemingly forgotten ANREF [sic] serves without honor; without a cause; without inspiration; without competent officers; without truth; without relief; without a flag."[54] Private indignation became public in the hand-

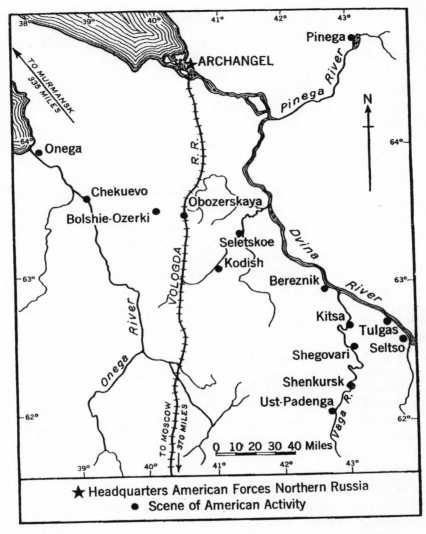

Map 3. American Forces in Northern Russia, September 4, 1918–August 5, 1919. *Source:* American Battle Monuments Commission, *American Armies and Battlefields in Europe: A History, Guide, and Reference Book* (Washington, D.C.: GPO, 1938; reprint, Washington, D.C.: Center of Military History, 1995), p. 432.

written petitions soldiers circulated. "The interest and honor of the USA are not at stake," B company declared in a March petition to their officers, noting, "we have accomplished the defeat of the German's whitch [*sic*] was our mission."[55]

Although pressed to explain the goals of the mission, army and administration officials remained uncharacteristically silent. Bliss received numerous requests from Dewitt Poole, the U.S. chargé d'affaires in North Russia, for a statement of purpose to appease the troops. A "frank statement from high authority would greatly lessen their discontent and end definitely the possibility of serious developments," Poole counseled throughout the winter. A flurry of apprehensive telegrams between AEFNR and AEF headquarters chronicled growing dissension within the American contingent. "Our troops are very much dissatisfied; winter clothing has been late in arriving and the friction existing between them and the British is not encouraging," Pershing told Bliss. "The situation seems to indicate withdrawal of our troops as the best solution."[56] In December, Senator Charles Elroy Townsend (R-Mich.) and Senator Hiram W. Johnston (R-Calif.) pressed the administration publicly to explain why American troops were in Russia.[57] Despite mounting domestic opposition, advice to withdraw from his military commanders, and his own conclusion that the expedition had failed, Wilson refused to make a public statement until he had spoken with Allied leaders at the peace conference.[58] Wilson hoped to extricate American troops without jeopardizing Allied support for his larger peace initiatives. In these discussions, the Wilson administration supported British Prime Minister David Lloyd George's suggestion that the Allies sponsor a meeting between all the various Russian factions struggling for control and rejected Winston Churchill's plan to mount an all-out attack on the Red Army. When Wilson's attempt to negotiate a diplomatic closure to the Allied intervention in the Russian Revolution failed, Bliss and Pershing persuaded the president to send an engineering unit to repair the railroads and facilitate the planned spring withdrawal.[59] A June evacuation was announced in February, but this information only haphazardly reached troops in the field, and others discounted it as rumor. Even those who believed it knew that until the thaw, little would change in their day-to-day situation. "To the Bolshevik soldiers," Private Kenneth A. Skellenger mused in his diary on March 9, "officially, we Americans know we have been ordered out of Russia by our President. . . . Homes and dear wives wait for us and no doubt for you. We wont [sic] make an attack on you. If you wait 2½ months we will be out of Russia."[60] Every American soldier had the same fantasy of arranging a truce that winter.

The impending withdrawal did not lessen soldiers' demands for a full explanation for the reasons behind the intervention. Poole did the best he could to interpret the government's policy, but an impromptu lecture he delivered to line officers only succeeded in impressing Second Lieutenant Charles Brady Ryan that "we're here because we're here."[61] What clearer demand for a legitimate policy to justify their deployment could there have been than First Lieutenant Carl H. Christine's demand, "WHERE IS OUR MONROE DOCTRINE?" in a subversive pamphlet he wrote entitled *Facts and Questions Concerning the N.R.E.F.*[62] "Widely circulated among the American troops at the front and the men consider that it fully covers their ideas regarding the reasons why American troops are kept here," the chief of the Military Mission scribbled on a typewritten copy he had confiscated.[63] The majority of soldiers believed that behind claims of guarding supplies or helping the Czechs evacuate through northern Russia lay a secret government plan to establish democracy in Russia. This conclusion raised a number of complicated questions, including the issue of self-determination, which American soldiers had trouble answering. "We had no right to come here to fight Russians. Bolsheviks are now fighting for their liberty and the Russian people should be allowed to straighten out themselves their difficulties," one sergeant proclaimed to his father.[64] If the Russians truly wanted democracy, they had yet to demonstrate that desire to many American troops. The Russians, Sergeant Edward Lenniv concluded, "like the Americans because we treat them good and have a president for a ruler instead of a Tsar or king." Yet although the average Russian peasant admired the American system "he doesn't want to fight for one like it," Lenniv noted.[65] And how was the outcome of the Russian Revolution important to American national security? "If these people want to fight among themselves, what is it to us?" asked Sergeant Carleton Foster, "if we want to stop a revolution let us go to Mexico. That is at home. If we have to but [sic] in, that is the place we should do it."[66] Christine aptly summarized the most important issue to American soldiers: "[I]s this [meddling] consistent with the principles of American democracy?"

In March 1919 word arrived in the United States that Company I troops had refused to load their sleds and return to the front.[67] As early as November 27, 1918, American officers expressed doubt that their troops would obey any further orders to attack. "Things are rather discouraging and hard to understand," noted one soldier in a December letter that U.S. censors intercepted. "The government has announced no policy for up here, yet here we are killing Bolsheviks and getting killed."[68] Confirmed by several soldier diaries, the March mutiny became a cause célèbre at home, where public opposition was already mounting against the mission.[69] Had there been a real mutiny? After their commanding officer agreed to listen to their questions, the men did in fact return to the front. Although given painstaking public analysis to deflate the importance of the event, the standoff was not an isolated incident.[70] In December, an American detachment in Kodema had left the field right before an attack. In January, Company K refused to return to Kodish after evacuating and burning it, causing "quite a commotion for a few hours," according to Corporal James Sibley.[71] In March, American and British sergeants in Obozerskaya agreed that if ordered to attack Bolshoe Ozerki, they would refuse, and members of the 310th Engineers threatened to strike if left behind when infantry troops departed in June.[72]

As the crisis in morale worsened, these citizen-soldiers reacted like their counterparts in France, putting great faith in those at home to end their plight. "We wonder," Christine wrote in his pamphlet, "what propaganda is at work in the States, which enables the War Department to keep troops here." Soldiers refused to believe that an informed public would support their continued deployment. Neither "President Wilson, or anyone else in America [has] the least conception of the situation," Moran protested in a letter home. "If they did they would pull us out of here without any hesitancy." Soldiers must inform civilians about Russia, a country Sergeant Silver Parrish described as a "land of ignorance, poverty, churches, and strife and loneliness."[73] Despite strict censorship, some soldiers stationed in northern Russia (most of whom hailed from Michigan and Wisconsin) managed to alert their families and friends to their difficulties. Clandestine letters were either smuggled out, passed through undetected in the cursory checks line officers often made of soldiers' mail, or forwarded by sympathetic officers, who sometimes also sent their own complaints home.[74] "Your letter just came and we were all mighty glad to hear from you," D. A. Commons replied to Second Lieutenant Ryan. Don't worry, Commons assured his friend, "there will be no let up on the demand till something is done. Detroit had a big meeting a few days ago and thousands of signatures have been secured to petition to Congress."[75] Besides petitions, a steady series of "indignation" meetings among parents, newspaper editorials supporting the "mutineers," and exhibits in downtown department stores displaying the overwhelming number of bizarrely fashioned clothes needed to survive an Arctic winter kept public attention focused on the fate of these troops.[76] Frazier Hunt, a correspondent for the *Chicago Tribune* who had been in Archangel, launched his own campaign to spread the truth about soldiers' troubles.[77] Private Kenneth Skellenger's hopes rose when he first heard "about Detroit yelling about [the] 339th in Russia," but he would have been ecstatic had he known that the governor of Michigan had been enlisted to consult directly with President Wilson.[78] By February, the only investigator who could report success in calming American soldiers did so by reassuring them that the 339th was the only regiment known by number throughout the United States. These soldiers, the investigator noted, "were especially pleased with the knowledge that the folks at home were talking about them."[79] That same month, Wilson's Senate enemies joined forces with anti-interventionists and nearly passed a resolution to bring American soldiers home from Russia (it was only defeated after Vice President Thomas Marshall broke a tie vote).[80]

In April, Brigadier General Wilds P. Richardson arrived to coordinate the evacuation, and American forces left when the ports reopened in June. As they debarked in France for delousing before continuing on to the United States, a few soldiers came down the gangplank shouting sarcastically, "Is the war over?"[81] Veterans of this expedition waged a lonely bureaucratic battle to bring home the bodies of their comrades who had died in the Arctic Circle. Armed with hand-drawn maps provided by former comrades, veterans representing the "Polar Bear" Association and Veterans of Foreign Wars made the rigorous journey back to northern Russia in 1929 to locate scattered American graves. The continuing nonrecognition of the Soviet Union made securing a visa difficult until Boris Skvivsky, the unofficial Soviet envoy to the United States, intervened. A clemency order from General Graves in Siberia had saved Skvivsky's life in 1919, and he now repaid the favor.

The expedition succeeded in bringing back eighty-six bodies for reburial in the United States.[82] "Natives often remarked 'What a wonderful place America must be to send men away over here for dead people,'" former First Sergeant Walter Dundon recalled in 1969.[83] In 1919, however, the American soldiers returning from Russia and France were focusing on the things wrong, not right, with America, especially the U.S. Army.

Reforming the Army

However gripping, soldiers' complaints about the army were usually ineffective agents for systematic policy reform. Congress readily held hearings to publicize the abuses, but in the end rarely decided to set policy for the army. One key exception, however, came when legislators agreed to work with former Judge Advocate General Samuel Ansell to reform the court-martial system. A barrage of soldiers' complaints backed up Ansell's criticisms of military justice. In the military justice system, courts-martial existed to help commanders discipline their troops, not as courts of law. Commanders had the power to prefer charges, to select the court-martial panels, and to review sentences. Some guidelines existed in the Articles of War for sentencing, but no safeguards protected accused soldiers from potential bias. As soon as the war ended, Ansell persuaded Baker to establish a clemency board in the Judge Advocate's Office to review all wartime sentences for excessive harshness. The astounding rate at which this board reduced sentences lent further credence to Ansell's critique.[84] In 73 percent of the 6,500 cases reviewed by September 1919, the sentences were either reduced or revoked. General Staff officials argued that delinquents deserved harsher penalties in time of war, but Ansell countered that justice was an absolute, not relative, concept. Senator George Chamberlain (D-Oreg.), who sponsored a reform bill, called Ansell to testify before the Senate Military Affairs Committee in February 1919.[85] When the 65th Congress adjourned in March, Chamberlain's bill died, but the senator prevailed upon Ansell to author a bill that he could introduce in the next session. Chamberlain originally proposed simply giving the judge advocate general the power to review all court-martial cases. Ansell, however, wanted the army to guarantee legal counsel for the accused, conduct investigations to decide whether a trial was justified, establish an independent board to review all appealed sentences, and assign enlisted jurors to court-martial panels when an enlisted man was on trial. Essentially, Ansell hoped to create a place for defense counsel, grand juries, a court of appeals, and the right to a jury of one's peers in the court-martial system. By narrowing the gap between the civilian and military justice systems, Ansell was proposing a fundamental change in the purpose that courts-martial served in the army.[86]

In early summer, Congress's attention momentarily turned to a somewhat different set of charges against the military justice system. Since April, former Sergeant Major James Beckman had been pressing Congress to consider a copy, which had somehow fallen into his possession, of a secret investigation into tortures and beatings at the AEF's Paris military prison.[87] That month, Senator Borah urged Beckman, who identified himself as a progressive Republican, to come forth with what Beckman promised to be "the greatest exposure in American history."[88] Beckman could not find any New York newspaper willing to print his charges until they were supported by a congressman. Reminding W. S. Patten of their wartime pact to "carry the fight to the limit," Beckman prevailed on Patten to show the incriminating documents to his new boss, Congressman Frederick Dallinger (R-Mass.).[89] A week later, Dallinger read Beckman's discoveries into the *Congressional Record* and Baker received a copy of the report for the first time.[90]

This report detailed how officers of the 27th Division had become suspicious when soldiers returning after long absences claimed that Paris MPs had incarcerated and beaten them because of minor irregularities in their leave orders. "That such brutality and inhuman treatment can exist in any institution under the control of Americans is unbelievable," divisional investigators reported after collecting affidavits from these former prisoners, "but the evidence is overwhelming."[91] After receiving their report, the inspector general of the Second Army Corps also visited the prison and interviewed prisoners.

In July, a few weeks before the Senate subcommittee hearings on Ansell's bill, Beckman recounted to House members how brutal prison guards had attacked junior officers, frontline soldiers, black noncombatant troops, and recovered convalescents who had been incarcerated but never charged with any specific crime. Representative Royal Johnson (R-S.D.), who had left Congress to enlist in the army and was wounded in the Meuse-Argonne campaign, supervised the House investigation into these charges.[92] Many ex-prisoners came to testify in person, but the official affidavits upon which Beckman based his initial charges delivered the most devastating blow to the army. In his sworn statement, Sergeant Thomas P. Hamill recalled that he had been in a courtyard with other prisoners while guards took three men into an adjoining shack to beat them. "Immediately cries and groans were heard from the barn . . . [and] for fully fifteen minutes these cries went on. The men were then kicked out, covered with blood and led to the hose to wash themselves and then led back [again] to the barn," he maintained.[93] Another soldier, Frederick Weiss, had said nothing when the Second Army Corps inspector general visited and asked any man who had been mistreated to step forward. Weiss had been beaten, but like his fellow prisoners, he chose to stay quiet because he feared the punishment he would face after the investigating team drove away.

The most dramatic moment of these hearings came when news leaked out that the brutal prison supervisor Lieutenant Frank "Hard-Boiled" Smith, a regular army officer, had been nearly beaten to death when he arrived at Fort Jay, Governor's Island, New York, to begin serving an eighteen-month sentence for mistreating prisoners.[94] The subcommittee subsequently traveled to Governor's Island to hear Smith's claim that he was being made the scapegoat for a corrupt system.[95] Smith's insistence that he had just been carrying out orders sat well with former National Guard officers. In their report, officers of the 27th Division implied that regular army prison guards only beat men from National Guard units, but in truth all soldiers knew to avoid the prison they called "the Bastille." Investigators in the 27th Division blamed "a spirit of intense hatred and hostility against the National Guard" for the beatings, especially since prison guards "who claimed to be Regulars" had shouted "National Guard son-of-a-bitch," and "God damn National Guard" when they assaulted prisoners.[96] National Guard advocates hoped that the public's growing disenchantment with professional soldiers during these investigations into prison abuse might bolster their fortunes in the upcoming debate with the regular army over how to divide defense responsibilities. The regular army, however, portrayed the whole episode as little more than an isolated case of abuse of power, not an officially condoned way to treat citizen-soldiers.

Soldiers' complaints about prison abuse received the focus they needed to exact permanent reforms in the military justice system from Ansell, who served as counsel for the House committee investigating prison conditions. Citizen-soldiers, in turn, invigorated Ansell's adjoining crusade in the Senate by illustrating the extreme importance of rights for the accused. The Senate committee heard testimony on Ansell's bill for four months. Ultimately, the threat that Congress might establish the dangerous precedent of setting organizational policy for the military gave army officials all the incentive they needed to offer revised Articles of War as a compromise. The new statutes required sworn charges, independent investigation into the merit of the charges, legal counsel for both the defendant and commanding officer, the creation of a trial judge position on the court-martial panel, and a permanent review board.[97]

The army did not, however, directly address the question of prison abuse or launch a wider investigation to learn whether the more traditional punitive disciplinary tactics or newer persuasive approaches to commanding men prevailed in military prisons. Ansell and his citizen-soldier allies also failed to change the philosophical basis of the court-martial system. According to the 1920 Articles, a commander was not obligated to follow the recommendations of the pretrial investigators or his own legal counsel. As important, enlisted men were still excluded from court-martial panels. The court-martial remained an executive, rather than judicial, body. Nonetheless, Ansell and his supporters forced the army to overhaul the Articles of War for the first time since the Revolutionary War, and pushed it one step closer toward the interpretation of military justice that it would eventually accept after its next encounter with citizen-soldiers in World War II.

This episode revealed that both the support of citizen-soldiers and good leadership were needed to transform vague congressional interest in military matters into desired institutional reform. Army officials knew they would need these same things to translate veterans' support for an expanded military into concrete legislative victories. They firmly believed that eventually most citizen-soldiers would champion a strong national military establishment like the one that had won the war for the Allies. Army officials felt that they had taken the first step toward securing the desired bloc of veterans' votes by modifying unpopular wartime army policies, but some members of Pershing's staff wanted to do more by helping citizen-soldiers organize into one powerful veterans' organization.

Veterans and the Army

With the Grand Army of the Republic's (GAR) legacy of a strong partisan veterans' organization before them, it appeared obvious that at some point World War I veterans would form an organization for themselves. The GAR's loyalties remained firmly with the National Guard, a fitting orientation, because most Civil War soldiers had served in local units. AEF officials yearned for a similarly powerful society that would be able to rally veterans' votes for the regular army whenever national defense legislation went before Congress.[98] It would be foolish to leave the organization of this veterans' association to chance, Brigadier General W. A. Bethel, the AEF's judge advocate general, argued, because "this society is expected to be the most important military society of its kind ever organized in the United States Army."[99] Envisioning an organization that created a permanent bond between veterans and army, Bethel wanted each division to send one delegate representing the regular army and one representing citizen-soldiers to Paris to organize a veterans' society before they went home. Pershing refused to approve this plan. Blatantly creating their own veterans' lobbying group would generate tremendous suspicion about exactly how extensive a presence the army wanted to establish in postwar society, Pershing warned his staff. He ordered them to let the situation "work itself out," rather than sow the seeds of distrust in the public's mind.[100] The most Pershing would do was endorse the "Comrades in Service" movement sponsored by the Chaplain's Office and wartime welfare organizations.

Before long, however, a more spontaneous opportunity for AEF officials to affect the course of veterans' affairs presented itself. In late January, four citizen-officers who had been actively involved in the prewar universal military training movement met and in the course of their evening's conversation began to ruminate about forming a veterans' association themselves. Lieutenant Colonel Theodore Roosevelt, Jr., 1st Division, Lieutenant Colonel Eric Wood, 83rd Division, Lieutenant Colonel George A. White, 41st Division, and Major Bill Donovan, 42nd Division, all had extensive military and civilian connections. An example of the influence enjoyed by the former president's son came a few weeks later, when Pershing asked Roosevelt to advise him on the morale problems then plaguing the army. Roosevelt suggested that Pershing convene a panel of twenty citizen-officers, and during this meeting of carefully selected officers, Roosevelt had no trouble persuading his peers that they should seize the moment to organize a veterans' society. The group adjourned with a plan to hold a much larger caucus in one month, and the conception of the future American Legion was complete.[101]

AEF officials did not create the American Legion but, as GHQ officials had noted in January, soldiers in uniform needed some help from army authorities to organize a society. After the war, the American Legion's founders tried to downplay this support as much as possible to counter the charge that their organization was just a pawn for the army. Legionnaires preferred to think that they had founded their society in spite of the army. Pershing, they pointed out, had not even wanted them to meet for a second time and had only grudgingly agreed after organizers protested that all their plans were already in place.[102] Legionnaires speculated that Pershing felt that their movement threatened the success of the "Comrades in Service" association that he had endorsed. In a similar vein, they noted, GHQ had refused to print an informational pamphlet for the Legion organizers to distribute among the troops. One would not expect such obstacles from a benefactor, legionnaires argued.

Pershing had always expressed reservations about facilitating the creation of a veterans' organization, however, and his hesitancy to authorize the March meeting reflected this reluctance. Others in his inner circle had far fewer qualms. Brigadier General Robert C. Davis, the AEF's adjutant general, gave organizers free use of the military mail and wire system to disseminate word of the proposed organization throughout the army. The officers who served on the temporary steering committee were stationed throughout France, but they had little trouble securing the leave they needed to plan the Paris caucus. Even Bishop Charles Brent, organizer of "Comrades in Service," agreed to merge with the Legion.[103] Consequently, whether or not legionnaires wanted to admit it, many important AEF figures backed the Legion from the beginning.

The actions of Brigadier General D. E. Nolan, another avid Legion supporter, betrayed the interest that the AEF's Intelligence Division had in assuming an even larger role in veterans' affairs. Nolan encouraged the *Stars and Stripes* to publicize the Legion's second caucus and exchanged ideas with the paper's editors on the best way to popularize the new society among the troops. Second Lieutenant Mark Watson, who sat on the paper's review board, confided to Nolan that "a glance at the colonels and majors forming the inner group scares me a lot."[104] The March caucus should include considerably more enlisted men, Watson cautioned, because "if universal service is to be pushed through it must have the heartiest support of the men, not the officers, who have been in universal service." Watson understood his audience. In addition to denouncing it as a GHQ creation, critics commonly charged during the first few months that the Legion catered primarily to officers. Legion founders countered that they had issued an open invitation to the March meeting, but conceded that few enlisted men had been able to secure the passes or funds needed to attend. In the end, enlisted men only accounted for fifty of the five hundred delegates. Stories in the *Stars and Stripes* disguised this fact, however, by highlighting the ways in which enlisted men had participated in the conference. The paper proclaimed the Legion a "true democracy."[105] The Legion's later advice for post organizers specifically tried to maintain this image: "After speech, have motion made to organize into Post. Have chairman select ten enlisted men and five officers to ask for charter."[106]

At the Legion's first domestic meeting, in St. Louis, controversy swirled around two different democratic issues: the question of membership for professional soldiers and black veterans. "Some delegates from Southern States were prepared to fight against allowing negroes to become members or to walk out, while others from northern States, notably Major Hamilton Fish [who had served with the 369th Infantry], were prepared to make a fight for full equality for negroes," reported the Intelligence informant attending the St. Louis caucus.[107] Competing white and black delegations from Louisiana forced the race question out into the open.[108] A separate state delegation of black veterans had come to press for full membership rights before the national caucus. The decision to seat the white delegation and send the black delegation home respected a compromise negotiated in Paris that left chartering decisions up to individual states.[109] Needless to say, southern legionnaires' determination to exclude black veterans from their organization, even in segregated posts, thinned the ranks of potential legionnaires considerably in the affected states.[110] In 1925, the Legion recognized 100 black posts, with an overall membership of 1,862, out of approximately 380,000 potential members. By 1930, the Legion could boast 3,557 black members, but the number of posts had dropped to 43.[111]

At the same St. Louis meeting, "after a long discussion, [the executive] committee finally recommended admission of Regular Army men by vote of 23 to 14," the Military Intelligence Division's director, Brigadier General Marlborough Churchill, reported to the chief of staff.[112] When the Legion met for its first formal convention in November, delegates railed against the arrogance of General Staff officials who claimed a lion's share of the credit for the Allied victory.[113] Legion supporters of universal military training (UMT) vowed to oppose any proposal that gave control of the program exclusively to the War Department, and others pushed plans to allot citizen-officers half of the positions on the General Staff in any future wars.[114] Yet in spite of the Legion's initial disdain of the regular army, army officials remained determined to forge a bond with it. After attending the first Legion convention, General Haan optimistically predicted that veterans' anger at the regular army would weaken. How much their attitude improved, he emphasized, "will depend largely upon the Regular Army."[115]

In the first big postwar battle the regular army faced over UMT, it failed to garner much veterans' support for its proposals, despite surveys showing that 94 percent of the officers and 88 percent of enlisted men agreed that UMT offered a host of personal and societal benefits.[116] With its own ranks divided over what plan to put forward, army officials never effectively focused veterans' attention on any one plan. The war persuaded some, including Pershing, to support a short universal training program that preserved the citizen-soldier principle. Others, however, including Peyton March, the chief of staff, remained steadfastly loyal to the Uptonian principle of a large, professional peacetime army. After finding an ally in Secretary Baker, March emerged temporarily as a stronger force in determining which plan the army would lobby for first.

This fracture in its opponents' camp gave the National Guard ample opportunity to steal the spotlight. The Guard discovered that it could channel affinity for the character-building benefits of military service into renewed support for locally controlled reserve training programs.[117] With the March-Baker proposal dead by the following legislative year, Lieutenant Colonel John McAuley Palmer and Pershing chose to promote their own version of nationalized universal training in alliance with civilian UMT organizations. By this time, however, the partisan debate over the merits of the League of Nations made the coalition-building necessary to pass any comprehensive military service program impossible. When the National Defense Act of 1920 was finally passed, it basically perpetuated the compromise legislated in the 1916 Defense Act. The National Guard retained its status as the primary manpower reserve, subject to General Staff supervision and congressional funding.

By 1920, it appeared clear that army officials had overestimated the interest veterans would have in shaping the postwar defense establishment. The Legion maintained a Military Policy Committee and always conferred with the General Staff before submitting its annual recommendations on defense-related legislation to Congress and the president, and it subsequently exerted some effort to popularize UMT and to secure more funding for the peacetime army in the interwar years. But these efforts interested few veterans. Military service had indeed politicized this wartime generation, but their agenda diverged widely from that of the professional army.

Rather than using their votes to shape the professional military establishment, citizen-soldiers' postwar influence came in the form of lessons that army officials drew from their wartime collaboration. The World War I experience gave advocates of management theories concrete examples upon which to base their argument that persuasive tactics should be included as part of a professional officer's formal education.[118] General Douglas MacArthur, who became superintendent of West Point in the fall of 1919, succumbed immediately to this pressure by introducing courses on human management into the military academy's curriculum.[119] In response to the dramatic increase in desertions in the first postwar year, the Morale Branch reformulated a wartime study to analyze the reasons for desertion among regular army troops.[120] Similarly, the Intelligence Department suddenly deemed the political loyalties of regular army troops worth studying when it appeared likely that the army would have to deploy troops to defuse the wave of labor and racial unrest sweeping the country in the fall of 1919.[121] Even Secretary Baker expected the postwar era to witness the birth of a different kind of peacetime army. "We have given our pledge that the New Army shall be a really democratic institution, not a thing apart from the people, but essentially a part of the people, by and for whom it exists," Baker wrote to the chief of staff in February 1920. To achieve this goal, Baker continued, regular army officers and NCOs needed to express "human interest and sympathy for the thoughts and feelings of the young civilian who dons our uniform" in peacetime.[122]

The supposition that the army should make formal, premeditated adaptations to satisfy its lowest-ranking members generated debate between traditionalists and reform-oriented officials, as it had during the war. When the Morale Branch was dissolved in 1921, the momentum for reform waned and, unlike wartime troops, regular army troops could not exert enough pressure to force traditionalists to concede.[123] Without strong civilian political connections or sheer numbers on their side, regular army soldiers never attained the same authority within the peacetime establishment that citizen-soldiers had enjoyed.

The army began studying the attitudes and behavior of citizen-soldiers exclusively to perfect its preparations for building the next mass army. The Army War College (the most prestigious educational institution for professional officers) diligently drew pertinent lessons for the future from the regular army's first sustained interaction with a conscripted citizen force. Class after class examined the successes and failures of the wartime army's deliberate attempts to improve morale, as well as the problems army officials inadvertently caused for themselves by neglecting some prominent citizen-soldier demands. The army, claimed Major Donald H. Connolly, needed to unravel how it had dampened citizen-soldiers' initial enthusiasm for military service, leading to "an opposition to officers in general and the regular army in particular, that lasted for years after the war."[124] After comparing the morale of the American, Allied, and German armies, the 1935 student committee concluded that in the next war, the army should require soldiers to undergo explicit political training, put all welfare and recreational activities under army control, avoid using untrained troops in battle, distribute more medals, award more promotions to temporary officers, and anticipate the need for an equitable and efficient demobilization plan.[125]

The issue of racial discord also permeated the discussion over what lessons the war had to offer. The 92nd Division's black and white officers feuded over whether incompetent whites or racially inferior blacks had caused it to fight so poorly. Ultimately, the army used the 92nd's dismal battlefield record to condemn the leadership abilities of black officers. Postwar army officials charged that the commitment of the 92nd Division's black officers to racial equality undermined their ability to serve the army. Black officers applied a racial perspective to every situation, asserted Lieutenant Colonel Allen Greer, chief of staff, 92nd Division, in response to an official postwar survey on the performance of black officers. "Their principal idea was not that they were in the service to fight for their country, but that they were there for the advancement of their racial interests."[126] White officers in the 92nd Division asserted both during and after the war that black officers showed racial favoritism, encouraged their men to challenge white authority figures, and were cowards. These stereotypes reinforced the army's dedication to the racial status quo.

Harder to measure than the veterans' vote, these institutional legacies reflected the ongoing influence of World War I citizen-soldiers on the development of the American military establishment. Future generations would serve in mass conscripted armies whose character and customs World War I citizen-soldiers had played a substantial role in creating. Veterans, however, neither knew nor cared that the army continued to study their wartime relationship. Rather than concerning themselves with the disciplinary structure of the army, Great War veterans were trying to understand how the war experience had shaped their own lives.

7

WAR MEMORIES

REEXAMINING THE SOCIAL CONTRACT

The homecoming year proved fitful. The restlessness apparent in the wave of soldiers' protests showed no signs of abating, even though their primary demand to return home had quickly been met. Unable to hold a job, William Henkelmen wandered along the "scenic route in box cars all over America," behavior indicative, according to former Sergeant Major W. H. Biggar, of "the soldier trying to find himself."[1] Biggar and Henkelmen did not know each other, but no doubt, had they met, Biggar would have understood Henkelmen's nervousness. "I arrived home last June, and have held at least a dozen positions since that time without finding one suited to my ideas at that time," Biggar divulged. These men returned to an equally unsettled society. The immediate cancellation of lucrative wartime contracts plunged the country into a severe recession. Fears that this unsettled economic environment would become the breeding ground of political radicalism preoccupied officials. In these opening months of the Red Scare, politicians, industrialists, and policemen linked practically every dissenting voice to a Bolshevik plot to overthrow the government.

It seemed to many that the country was coming apart in 1919. During this unstable period of strikes and escalating racial violence, the Post Office discovered thirty-four bombs addressed to prominent Americans, and terrorists exploded dynamite outside the home of Attorney General A. Mitchell Palmer, the man heading the Justice Department's hunt for Bolshevik terrorists. These attacks gave credibility to Palmer's claim before a House committee that "on a certain day which we have been advised of" radicals were planning "to rise up and destroy the Government at one fell swoop."[2] In response to this perceived revolutionary threat, Palmer raided the homes and offices of suspected radicals and deported a few hundred aliens with ties to radical organizations. The Red Scare convinced many Americans that unchecked immigration imported dangerous political ideas from overseas and threatened their economic, cultural, and political institutions. In the next few years, the United States would pass the most restrictive immigration legislation in its history.

Fears that exposure to the postwar political upheavals sweeping through Germany and Russia might have radicalized returning servicemen led to government surveillance of them as well. In addition, Americans worried, as they have after all wars, whether men conditioned to kill could resume normal lives as productive and peaceful citizens.[3] Veterans provided ample proof of the difficulties they faced. A "number of ex-servicemen in prison . . . got into trouble during the restless period of settling down," a Legion spokesman acknowledged in 1922.[4]

Besides the personal challenges of readjusting to civilian life, this generation also faced the test of finding out whether it had a collective political voice. During the first five years of postwar civilian life, veterans became a true war generation. Sharing the war experience did not itself guarantee the creation of such a community. It only emerged after American veterans had nurtured a collective memory of the war experience.[5] At first, with veterans lending their support to differing causes, it seemed that no common political agenda would emerge. The Wilson administration wanted to sever its relations with veterans immediately to dissuade them from thinking, as Union veterans had after the Civil War, that they deserved any further monetary or medical benefits. World War I veterans accepted the general consensus that Civil War veterans had taken advantage of government largesse, but they soon came to argue that the social compact created by national conscription rendered all comparisons with the Civil War pension experience irrelevant.[6]

By 1920, veterans increasingly agreed, as one told Theodore Roosevelt, Jr., that during the war "they were in the country's employ at the request of the country."[7] To those who asked, Roosevelt did his best to explain their reasoning. "To begin with in considering this problem you must take as a premise the draft," he noted.[8] During the war, the federal government had decided who worked in civilian society and who entered the military. Civilian workers had received the highest wages in American history, while citizen-soldiers labored for thirty dollars a month. Even worse, the federal government had bought the cooperation of industrialists by letting them keep their exorbitant wartime profits. In veterans' eyes, the government now had the postwar responsibility of compensating soldiers fairly. "All we seek is justice," explained one veteran, "and justice likewise demands that some of these [war] profits be now conscripted to pay this debt to the returned soldier."[9]

During the war, an array of feminist and black organizations attempted to construct a social contract with the state: in return for loyal wartime service, they would receive recognition of social, political, and professional equality.[10] By 1918, African-American leaders realized with bitterness that their campaign had failed, while women contented themselves with a constitutional amendment that recognized their right to vote but did not address questions of social and professional equality. Veterans now stepped up to define the terms of their social contract with the state. Unlike women and blacks, veterans did not focus on their contract as a way to advance their position in American society. Demanding rewards for their service would have put them in the same category as the much-maligned Civil War veterans. Instead, Great War veterans based their claim on the proposition that they should not be unfairly punished for having done their civic duty with diminished social and economic prospects upon their return home.

From 1922 on, with veterans secure in their knowledge that the federal government had the power to redistribute war-accumulated wealth, the campaign for adjusted compensation intensified. Veteran C. M. Carter's battle cry, "let us demand our rights," signaled the end of veterans' passive and fractured stance as to their expectations of the state.[11] Despite an unpromising start, therefore, veterans eventually found a collective political purpose.

A Fractured Beginning

The shift in attention toward how the civilian world had conducted itself during the war came gradually, a product of much pondering by citizen-soldiers over exactly what the state had denied them during their stint in uniform and what society withheld from them now that they had returned. High unemployment among veterans obviously fueled their discontent. The War Department's Employment Service promised that "no service man will be considered demobilized until a job has been found for him."[12] American Legion boasts of having placed 700,000 veterans in jobs during a 1922 jobs drive, however, attested to the gravity of the protracted veterans' unemployment crisis.

Concerned that unemployed veterans posed a threat to domestic peace, administration officials attributed disruptive potential even to the innocuous desire to improve one's postwar life. Black veterans found themselves castigated for moving North in the last leg of the migratory wave that had begun in 1917 with black workers seeking higher factory wages and freedom from Jim Crow practices.[13] Military officials had reason for concern, because the arrival of hundreds of thousands of blacks destabilized the racial status quo of many northern cities.[14] When wartime prosperity evaporated and black strikebreakers willingly crossed the picket lines of whites-only unions, racial tensions escalated to dangerously violent levels in many cities, especially Chicago. Returning to their southern communities did not ensure a tranquil return for black soldiers, however. There, whites nervously anticipated that black veterans had returned as revolutionaries, and this fear sparked at least thirty race riots in 1919. "The month of July has been marked by the explosion of racial riots, which . . . are far from being finished," reported the military attaché to the French embassy in Washington, D.C., as southern and northern whites endeavored to put blacks "back in their place."[15] Of the seventy-seven black citizens killed by mobs in 1919, ten were former soldiers.[16]

Government investigators also spoke with concern about white veterans who tried to improve their economic position.[17] "Some of the unemployment is due to the fact that men that have no trades dislike to go back to laborers' wages and, therefore, endeavor to obtain positions as clerks, salesmen and other occupations for which they are not at all fitted," a U.S. Employment Service official grumbled.[18] In forcefully conservative terms, the government urged all veterans to return to their communities and families as quickly as possible. Informational pamphlets distributed to troops on the ship home entreated them to stay away from cities and social agitators, to register with the government's employment service, to stick with the job they secured, and to keep their expectations reasonable. "You have probably been broadened by your Army experience," the soldier was advised. "This does not mean that you will better yourself by taking up a new kind of work . . . advancement will come more rapidly if you go back to the job where you are known."[19] If a soldier had resolved to change his occupation, the Agriculture Department sought to persuade him to consider moving to the country. Above all, the Employment Service urged all returning soldiers to remember that "what you do in the first few months after your discharge is liable to make or break you for the rest of your life."[20] Others offered veterans more than advice. Some cities gave them positions in their police departments, and the Ford Motor Company created jobs solely for veterans.[21]

In 1919, citizen-soldiers expressed their general discontent with the army, the government, their homecoming, and their precarious economic situation in various ways. In the paranoid climate of the Red Scare, officials took special note of any discontent that seemed to indicate a turn to the left. "Some of the men, disappointed with their treatment or progress in the army, have become very active Bolshevists," a Military Intelligence Division officer reported.[22] Their protests with red flags, suspicions that they had been a source of cheap labor for the government in France, and anti-imperialist comments in Russia reveal a radical edge to the outlook of some citizen-soldiers. "After being up here fighting these people I will be ashamed to look a union man in the face," Silver Parrish confided to his diary two months after securing the signatures of his entire platoon on a petition denouncing their continued involvement in the Russian Revolution.[23] As a self-described "working man," Parrish railed against the capitalist forces that created such dismal living conditions for the Russians. "The majority of the people here are in sympathy with the Bolo [Bolsheviks] and I don't blame them, in fact I am 3/10ths Bolo myself," he wrote in his diary.

On the other hand, fighting in northern Russia did not guarantee that a soldier returned home with Bolshevik sympathies. "The 339th soldiers can surely carry back a good message. They have seen what it means, and it ought to be unhealthy for any agitators to start their propaganda in the shops around Detroit," Charles Brady Ryan wrote to his family two months before heading home.[24] This comment raised the chilling possibility that men trained in the art of killing would use violence to express their political views. Indeed, veterans seemed ready to explode over almost any issue. "Ex-servicemen who think they didn't get a square deal while in the service" disturbed the army's 1920 recruiting efforts.[25] Veterans also attended mass meetings in Los Angeles protesting rent profiteering and made guerrilla attacks on the red flags of radical demonstrators.[26] Underlying this disgruntlement lay a general feeling that the government had broken some implicit promise to them, one that they were beginning to define more clearly.

Veterans bore a heavy grudge against all levels of government. In postwar interviews, returning soldiers complained about their involuntary isolation from domestic politics during the war. One group contended that they should have "had the right to vote in state elections" whether or not they could pay their poll taxes.[27] Another, incensed over the newly ratified Prohibition Amendment, had no qualms about openly assailing "the so-called 'scurvy trick,' played on them by the 'pussy-foots,' and the 'narrow-monded [sic], bigoted hypocrites who stayed at home and talked.' "[28] More suggestive of events to come, however, was the returning soldier's certainty, noted by one demobilization camp officer, "that he has rights and privileges peculiarly his own."[29]

Some military intelligence officials saw little reason for concern, believing that the general wave of discontent would pass when veterans found jobs. "The American veteran is not attracted by anything which is more than mildly radical," Major W. C. Smiley contended, a claim backed up by French observations about the political tendencies of American troops and the strict anticommunist platform of the American Legion.[30] This reassuring conclusion, however, mattered less and less as the first Red Scare created a climate in which any tinge of radicalism doomed an organization or individual to heavy surveillance and repression. Military analysts believed that radical organizations were seeking to profit from the unstable environment. These groups, they reasoned, hoped that if they had veterans as members, the government would be more tolerant of their organizing activities.[31] Intelligence officers became disturbed by the size of soldier audiences lured to radical meetings by pamphlets distributed at camp gates, which sometimes offered attendees a new set of civilian clothes. To the Military Intelligence Division, all this amounted to a carefully crafted plot to tempt recently trained fighting men, who undoubtedly knew little about the ultimate revolutionary purpose of these groups, into the dissidents' ranks.[32] Agents even filed hard-to-believe reports of planned infiltrations by radicals into the strictly anti-Bolshevik American Legion.[33] Some army officials, however, went beyond simply reporting these developments. They decided to act.

The Red Scare gave army officials another reason besides increased military budgets to forge a strong relationship with the Legion. The anti-army atmosphere of the first Legion convention did not deter Colonel Gordon Johnson from trying to obtain "practical support from the Legion" in quelling domestic disturbances.[34] This request came directly on the heels of General Leonard Wood's decision to deputize two hundred white legionnaires in Omaha, Nebraska, to help federal troops track down suspects responsible for a September race riot.[35] Despite their shared disdain for communism, Legion organizers rejected the idea of working so closely with the army. "It did not seem to occur to Colonel Johnson or anybody else that this is clearly in violation of law," scolded War Plans Director Major General W. G. Haan after hearing Johnson make his proposal to the assembled legionnaires. "I was more than pleased to see that these young men, boys most of them, readily brought out the fact that this would be the maintenance of a private army or a private armed force," he noted, assured that the matter had been laid to rest by the Legion's rejection of Johnson's proposition.[36]

Seven months later, however, the commander of the Western Department renewed the call to organize secret reserves of platoons, companies, and regiments within the Legion's ranks. Ignoring the misgivings of Legion leaders, the director of the Military Intelligence Division, Brigadier General Marlborough Churchill, encouraged these schemes, and some local Legion posts responded well to them. Well-equipped units at a local level, the Western Department commander argued, would be critical if the emergency declaration of martial law anticipated in the army's War Plan White (a secret defense plan that anticipated using the army to quell domestic disturbances) ever came to pass.[37] Independent reports from Western states, especially from Los Angeles, where the "Legion is allied with the police and have promised active support," indicated that in these localities semi-official alliances had already developed.[38] Despite Churchill's willingness, "in the most discreet manner," to pursue an analogous liaison on a national level, Haan refused to consider these proposals.[39] The Legion's national headquarters also stood firm. A neutral posture became increasingly important as the membership rolls of posts controlled by reactionary forces stagnated, and the Legion worried about its public image as a front for the army. Consequently, Legion National Adjutant Lemuel Bolles balked at cooperating with any "preparations to lay upon them [legionnaires] a greater burden than is laid upon other citizens" when approached by Churchill allies in the early 1920s.[40] Local posts likewise received recommendations from national headquarters to disentangle themselves from their compacts with local authorities.

The Labor Alternative

In its quest to speak unilaterally for veterans, the American Legion faced some competition in the early 1920s. "We will have to do some missionary work for the Legion among the working men," admitted the Michigan member of the 1920 Americanization committee.[41] Indeed, why join the Legion at all, when, in 1919, a host of other veterans' organizations offered an array of choices more clearly aligned with class interests?

"The purpose of the Workers, Soldiers, and Sailors Council is to assist and facilitate the unification of the working class," resolved a soviet in Tacoma, Washington, during its initial organizing meeting three months after the Armistice.[42] Uncoincidentally, these councils made their first, and strongest, showing in the Pacific Northwest.[43] In this prewar stronghold of the radical Industrial Workers of the World (IWW, or Wobblies) labor union, 30,000 soldiers assigned to the Spruce Production Division had worked side by side with civilian lumbermen among approximately 234 lumber mills during the war.[44] Poor working conditions, bidding wars among competitors, and IWW-led strikes had brought production of spruce intended for aircraft manufacture to a standstill. Determined to halt a labor turnover rate that soared to 600 percent a year, the War Department threatened to replace all striking workers with soldiers. Colonel Brice P. Disque, commander of the Spruce Production Division, came up with the idea of introducing a measure of industrial peace into the forests by forcing employees and employers into a company union, the Loyal Legion of Loggers and Lumbermen (LLLL). Instead of providing the anticipated "antidote for the poison of 'wobblyism,'" Disque's mandated eight-hour day and stricter sanitation standards, longtime goals of IWW organizers, seemed to breathe new life into the movement.[45] The IWW went underground and maintained a sizable presence within the LLLL.[46]

Disque's faith in his own troops' conservatism notwithstanding, citizen-soldiers grew close to their civilian fellow workers. Although singularly subject to military discipline, little else separated soldier spruce lumbermen from their civilian counterparts. Paid civilian-scale wages, soldier lumbermen had to purchase their board, clothing, and equipment from company stores. This alone gave soldiers a firsthand appreciation of the oppressive working conditions in lumber camps in the Northwest. In remarkable contrast to the self-congratulatory tone that permeated official Spruce Division accounts, Captain C. A. Turner charged that "three of my men were killed in one logging camp, one crippled for life and eight or ten injured . . . and we did not produce one foot of aéroplane spruce in twelve months' work." His company of 130 men, he testified before the Senate committee delegated to investigate the wartime aviation industry, had been "sold into slavery" solely to benefit private business.[47]

Events on November 11, 1919, offered a poignant illustration of the vehemence with which radical and reactionary forces took up arms against each other in this section of the country after the war. Legionnaires selected a parade route for the first anniversary of the Armistice in Centralia, Washington, that went past the IWW hall. The Wobblies correctly took this as a sign that the legionnaires intended to raid the hall. When the expected assault began, the prepared IWW members quickly killed three legionnaires leading the charge and wounded several others. A flee-ing Wobbly and ex-serviceman, Wesley Everest, shot and killed one of his pursuers before the crowd dragged him to the county jail. Later in the night, the mob reappeared and took Everest to the river, where they hanged him and mutilated his corpse.[48] Events in this region revealed little agreement or shared purpose among veterans, who instead aligned them-selves with an array of different political causes.

Immediately after the war, rather than defining a distinct political agenda for veterans, all veterans' organizations shared the aspiration to re-integrate returning soldiers quickly into the central political disputes of the day. The Legion, for instance, aligned itself with anti-Bolshevik and immigration causes, and some more radical groups reached out to the labor movement. These radical groups hoped to build returning soldiers' vague complaints about being sent out on scab jobs by the Employment Service into firm support for unionism.[49] Marvin G. Sperry, organizer of the Pri-vate Soldiers and Sailors' Legion, believed that "the failure and neglect of the government" regarding workers and veterans provided ample basis for a mutually beneficial relationship.[50] Hoping to excite interest in the plight of the unemployed veteran, groups like Sperry's sent soldier speakers to union meetings.[51] The World War Veterans (which absorbed the Soldiers, Sailors, and Marine Protective Association in 1919) and the Private Sol-diers and Sailors' Legion prohibited members from scabbing. In return, an impressive array of unions endorsed the World War Veterans, includ-ing the Amalgamated Metal Workers of America, the American Labor Alliance, and the American Federation of Labor (AFL).[52] This stamp of approval helped the organization post a 100,000 membership figure in the early 1920s, with strongholds in Chicago, St. Paul, and Des Moines. One investigator estimated that over 90 percent of those who belonged to the Private Soldiers and Sailors' Legion also belonged to a labor union. For a short while, this alliance forced the government to recognize the organi-zation. Given the Private Soldiers and Sailors' Legion's strength in indus-trial working-class communities across the nation, "it is believed that a refusal to tender this organization an invitation [to a White House recep-tion for veterans] would cause a considerable reaction from labor union ranks," advised a special investigator in 1921.[53]

Even the anti-union American Legion had to reckon with the popularity of the World War Veterans. The Legion made a limited attempt to reach out to labor by courting the AFL, the most conservative trade labor union supporting the World War Veterans. Noting their similarly strong stands against radicals and immigrants, one recruiter bragged of having "signed up many members of our unions" after showing "them where the American Legion and the A.F. of L. legislative committees agree on practically 90 per cent of the bills proposed before the two houses at Washington."[54]

Faced with concerted efforts to break them, however, labor-oriented veterans' organizations such as the World War Veterans lost momentum in 1922. The social climate in general had become distinctly inhospitable toward labor. Faced with an 11.7 percent unemployment rate, increased ethnic and racial discord within its own ranks, and steady government intervention on the side of business in labor disputes, the seven-year mobilization of labor ground to a halt. With some justification, the failure of the alliance between veterans and unions could be laid on the government's doorstep. Burdened with smear campaigns against their leaders, news blackouts, and meeting disruptions—all orchestrated by government agents—it was a wonder that these organizations did as well as they did.[55] The Legion's success and labor unions' postwar difficulties bespoke a truism of modern American life. For large-scale organizing activities to succeed in the early 1920s, at least tacit government support was necessary.

Besides this help from the government in destroying a main competitor, the Legion's decision to focus on adjusted compensation also enticed veterans to join. It is noteworthy that this policy shift came as a result of demands from the rank and file. "Members of Congress seem at a loss to know which of the 78 bills which have been introduced in the House the soldiers prefer to have passed," Representative James G. Strong (R-Kans.) admitted in the summer of 1919.[56] By 1922, it became clear that the majority of veterans wanted adjusted compensation, a crusade that the Legion was now prepared to lead.

Creating a Veterans' Agenda

Firmly entrenched on the margins, if not in the heart, of the political system of their time, the leadership of the American Legion had nothing to fear when its lobbyist John Thomas Taylor warned that the adjusted compensation fight was "wholly and solely a question of politics and strategy here in Washington." Taylor himself admitted that "we have the situation very well in hand."[57] As a legislative battle, the fight for adjusted compensation ultimately boiled down to securing enough votes in the House and Senate to override a certain presidential veto.[58] The Legion knew that President Warren Harding had "never admitted the Legion's Adjusted Compensation argument," and that President Calvin Coolidge had vetoed the 1924 act, despite a certain override, simply to "be able to say that he did the best he could."[59] When it came to adjusted compensation, Harding and Coolidge agreed with their Democratic foe Woodrow Wilson that men should not receive a bonus for fulfilling their duty as citizens. This conservative view encapsulated the government's hope that it could forge a temporary bond with conscripted citizens, then sever the relationship quickly and cleanly. Harding and Coolidge parroted Wilson's belief that the Great War had indeed ushered in a dramatically new kind of war experience. According to them, the country had finally fought a war in which debts to its fighting troops had been paid in full upon their demobilization. The government only offered demobilizing soldiers the option to convert their War Risk insurance into permanent life insurance, although they would have to continue making premium payments as they had during the war.

Government officials interpreted early reports about returning soldiers' indifference to a bonus and rejection of a pension as a sign that citizen-soldiers had accepted the government's terms. This was not as complete a misreading of citizen-soldiers' mood as it would later seem. At their first convention, largely dominated by the founders, the Legion straightforwardly rejected a bonus claim, proclaiming that they would be satisfied with any spontaneous recognition offered by the nation. "No serpent had ever entered our rainy Eden in Burgundy to whisper 'adjusted compensation,'" a veteran opponent of the measure accurately declared in 1922.[60] His self-righteous anger revealed World War I soldiers' remarkable vulnerability to charges that they were no better than their treasury-robbing Civil War predecessors. Determined to distinguish themselves by refusing to demand a monetary reward for their service, citizen-soldiers responded to army polls much as Wilson had hoped they would.

The first call for adjusted compensation came from the more radical veterans' organizations. The Private Soldiers and Sailors' Legion's Marvin G. Sperry offered a rationale for his position that, ironically enough, would soon take root and flourish within the American Legion. "It was by the laws and action of the United States government that upon the private soldier, sailor and marine were placed the burdens, hazards and losses of the world war," Sperry told a reporter from the *Little Rock Arkansas Gazette*.

"Only by the laws and action of the United States government can these burdens be removed and those hazards and losses to some extent be compensated."[61] A year after Sperry's interview, *The Home Sector* published a straw poll in which veterans, ten to one, supported the awarding of a cash bonus or a farm.[62] Alone, this poll revealed nothing more than veterans' well-known willingness to accept whatever the nation kindly offered. Increasingly, however, veterans' pronouncements sounded a less patient, more demanding, note, which changed the interpretation given to such polls. "The debated bonus for soldiers is necessary and only just," resolved a Pennsylvania Legion post, echoing the hope of one veteran's wife that if "they could start even with the world," their readjustment problems would disappear.[63] Bolder, more forceful declarations came in the following years. "As I recollect," legionnaire Frederick Alger declared, a few million men "were yanked out of their ordinary walks of life, deprived of their earning capacity and in many tens of thousands of cases were obliged to leave dependents with no adequate means of support."[64] The constant refrain of noncombatant troops that they were "not here from choice, but were assigned" to the rear, a soldier's denunciation that "we are powerless to help ourselves to return home," and another's lament that "for nine long months we have waited Uncle Sam's pleasure" were examples of soldiers' wartime recognitions that the state had seized complete control of their lives.[65] The memory of impotence in face of the omnipotent wartime state soon became a key factor in the mentality of World War I veterans.

"By what theory of Americanism can the members of the [American] Legion justly claim that they alone made sacrifices," demanded Elbert Hamlin in a letter to the Legion's national commander, echoing Armand Bang's conviction that "without the industrial soldier behind him, the soldier in the field would not have been worth a nickel."[66] Combatants and noncombatants answered that they had served in a wartime army, "willingly perhaps," veteran Henry Lindsley explained, "but nevertheless through force of the government."[67] Forgetting the community members who had served on local draft boards and made case-by-case decisions, veterans now held the federal government solely responsible for their induction into the military.

This memory of complete submissiveness to the will of the state took on new meaning during the postwar recession. Seven hundred thousand "jobless men hold honorable discharges from the army and navy . . . the visible evidence of valor," a Legion spokesman noted, "but they won't pass for a meal ticket, and the landlord declines to receive them in payment for the rent."[68] Suddenly, the verbal commendations of 1919 did not compensate for the disproportionate financial burden that soldiers had borne since 1917. Supported by vivid memories of civilian opportunities lost on account of their wartime service and contemporary evidence of widespread war-profiteering, veterans focused on the financial, rather than physical, hardships of military service.

Preserving the Wartime Class Divide

Many arguments surfaced against a veterans' bonus in the early 1920s. Within the veterans' community, former officers who viewed support for adjusted compensation as a final duty to their troops broke with those who believed that they had to protect these men from debasing themselves. Civilian efforts to divide and conquer by questioning the real hardships imposed on those who had never left the country resonated poorly among veterans. After all, they argued, all had been at the mercy of the federal government, powerless to determine in what capacity they served. By 1922, this counted for more than time at the front. Other critics resented what they perceived as an effort to put a price on patriotism. The politicians lined up against adjusted compensation offered more imaginative reasons for rejecting veterans' claims. Congressman Thomas Connally (D-Tex.), a veteran, warned that paying the bonus would disturb the racial status quo in the South, because the black veteran "will not chop cotton nor pull corn, nor pick cotton nor plow, so long as his cash bonus lasts."[69] President Warren Harding, on the other hand, rejected the proposed 1922 plan as offering too "niggardly" a gift.[70]

The most effective counter, however, came from the Chamber of Commerce, which raised the stakes considerably by linking rejection of the bonus to the successful implementation of Secretary of the Treasury Andrew Mellon's proposal for economic recovery, which was based on the proposition that the country could not afford both adjusted compensation for World War I soldiers and a tax cut. Faced with open challenges by this well-financed and politically effective businessmen's organization, veterans quickly discarded their complaints about the high wages that war workers had received and focused their anger on the large profits that industrialists had accumulated during the war. They were resolved, as one of the veterans, E. G. Adams, put it, "to go to the limit, just to show the Chamber of Commerce 'who won the war.'"[71] Drawing the battle lines, the American Legion released statistics charting the astronomical profits made by war contractors and offered evidence that Chamber members were threatening employees who refused to write to Congress opposing the bonus proposal. "Sometimes I think I am almost bolshevist in my feelings against the vested interests that are opposing this Adjusted Compensation bill," came a startling admission from a Legion department commander.[72] Tensions mounted further when members alerted the Legion's national headquarters that only those wealthy enough to have a telephone had received ballots in a 1922 *Literary Digest* survey that claimed to have found a generally negative public attitude to adjusted compensation.

An ex-serviceman's confession that he did "not feel so law abiding and patriotic as I might toward a Government that compelled me to go fight for the Noble Cause of making sixteen thousand new millionaires" suggested the broadening feeling among veterans that the government had exploited them during the war. Like many of his former comrades, this veteran exhibited a disillusionment immediately recognizable to any reader of interwar literature. He identified with those who "couldn't help fighting any more than we could," rather than with civilians on the home front, and forthrightly admitted his rage at wartime profiteers, "every one of which I would feel a greater pleasure in hanging than some of the poor [G]erman boys that we killed over there."[73] Yet veterans had more support than they might sometimes have realized. Polls of workers and women gave clear majorities to the adjusted compensation proposal.[74] Even internal surveys within the Chamber of Commerce revealed that the majority of chambers favored some kind of settlement in the shape of farms, homes, or vocational education to settle the wartime debt.[75] Petitions from the governors of thirty-three states and wide majorities each time the House of Representatives voted on adjusted compensation proposals provided further evidence that the nation wanted to remunerate its veterans further.[76] Mellon's fiscal miscalculations provided the final jolt. The fiscal year 1922 ended with a $313 million surplus instead of the predicted $24 million budget deficit, the figure Mellon had used to argue that the country could not afford a bonus. When he miscalculated again the next year with an infamous "billion dollar error," public support for a bonus for veterans stiffened.[77]

When it became apparent that too many choices over how to receive adjusted compensation might lead to a fourth consecutive legislative defeat, American Legion leaders chose in 1924 to settle for payment in the form of bond certificates that would reach maturity in 1945. The Legion's decision to accept government bonds, the preferred option among Legion leaders, rather than the cash settlement widely demanded by members in 1920, caused little dissension in the recovering economy of 1924.

The American Legion notion of "de-profitizing war" fueled other policy initiatives as well. In 1922, the Legion's Military Affairs Committee began pondering the problem that had "created such bitter hostility" and began to lobby for a universal draft.[78] In the next war, the Legion demanded an equitable "use by the Government of its power" to employ soldiers, workers, and property in national service, thus acknowledging that the United States would never fight another major twentieth-century war without conscripts. By adopting the measure, the government would recognize its lapses during the Great War and correct its treatment of future generations. The active role they could play in refining the contours of their sons' anticipated military experiences made the proposal attractive to veterans. The Legion did not succeed in the fight for a universal draft, but it would follow the same strategy of drawing lessons from veterans' wartime experience during the campaign for the GI Bill in 1944.

When the War Department reviewed the Legion's plan for a universal draft, officials conceded that "the state owes it to the soldier who goes to war."[79] This acknowledgment revealed how widely accepted veterans' views on conscription had become by 1922. Comparing this renegotiation of the wartime social contract with the struggles of other generations or populations to define what the state owed them highlights the importance of this episode in the history of entitlements and the welfare state.

In many respects, the nation was founded on the idea of special benefits for veterans. The pensions awarded to disabled soldiers by the First Congress and the service pensions granted in 1818 were the first national selective monetary entitlements in American history.[80] Both Revolutionary War and Civil War veterans waged long and ultimately successful campaigns to broaden an initially limited definition of which veterans deserved pensions (officers, the disabled, the impoverished) to a more expansive, inclusive one. In both cases, the eventual willingness to grant nearly every veteran a service pension had more to do with the political exigencies of the moment—a sudden romanticism about the Revolution during the turmoil of the Jacksonian period, and the need to recruit veterans into the Republican Party to win closely contested elections in the later nineteenth century—than it did with changing notions of entitlement.[81] The dilemma of defining who deserves federal aid permeates the history of the welfare state, including debates over mothers' pensions in the 1920s, social security in the 1930s, and welfare in the 1990s.[82] Within a clearly identified population segment—Revolutionary and Civil War veterans, mothers, senior citizens, the unemployed—whose poverty does the state have a responsibility to help alleviate? World War I veterans shared with these groups the tendency to define legitimate state aid as money that replaced wages lost through no fault of their own. The aspect of their crusade that would set veterans apart from other groups for the rest of the century came when they limited efforts to separate deserving from undeserving veterans. Proposals floated to grant adjusted compensation only to combatants, to overseas veterans, or to those demonstrating need went nowhere.

Some distinctions existed. Veterans received a quarter more per day for each day they had served overseas, and only those who had served for sixty days received adjusted compensation.[83] On the whole, however, adjusted compensation established the principle that all veterans who served in time of total war were deserving, in contrast to mothers, the aged, or previous generations of veterans, whom the government divided into contested categories of deserving and undeserving. The authoritarian power that the modern state had assumed over their lives justified all veterans' claims to redistributive federal entitlements, and this argument would form the foundation of the more generous GI Bill in 1944. The logic of entitlement emerging from the nation's experience with conscription during World War I thus helps explain why rights of the GI Bill type applied only to veterans and never became the prelude to expanding social welfare benefits to the entire population.

Having accepted the link between conscription and adjusted compensation, the War Department feared in 1922 that extending the authoritarian grip of the state to include wartime workers would make them eligible for later claims against the state. The vision of an army of civilian workers demanding pensions for their period of forced national service dampened military officials' interest in a universal draft. Unable to garner support from the War Department, and realizing the impossibility of a Chamber of Congress endorsement after assaulting its members as evil war profiteers, Legion leaders courted a hesitant AFL by moderating their inflammatory rhetoric and focusing on the need for strict wage and price supports. Labor leaders, however, opposed any measure that prematurely tied their hands in bargaining with the federal government.[84] The greatest support for the universal draft idea came from the White House. Proposals to invest the president with the wartime authority to control the nation's manpower and material resources with minimal congressional interference drew avid support from Harding, Coolidge, and Herbert Hoover. In 1924, a presidential election year, both the Democratic and Republican parties included the measure in their party platforms.[85] Eventually, Hoover convened the War Policies Commission in 1931 to study the proposal formally.

The White House's steady interest in universal draft propositions, the strong ties veterans maintained with Congress during the adjusted compensation debate, and professional soldiers' membership in the Legion demonstrated the extensive relations that veterans maintained with the state in the postwar period. These dynamic links with the postwar state thwarted the Wilson administration's effort to make a clean break with its wartime troops in 1919. In addition, one-quarter of all federal employees hired during the interwar period were veterans who had chosen to reinject themselves into the state apparatus as civil servants.[86] Their unique right to government-funded health care, awarded in 1924, further underscored the strong ties developed between veterans and the state in this period.[87]

The adjusted compensation cause had emerged from a groundswell of interest on the part of individual members. Nonetheless, Legion leaders never had the power to mobilize the rank and file to lay down a "barrage" on Congress upon "command" for the measure. "The Legion is not old enough, and does not understand the meaning of orders or directions from the National Headquarters," explained its legislative affairs advocate John Thomas Taylor.[88] Taking stock of these internal difficulties within the Legion helps arrest the tendency to conflate Great War veterans with legionnaires. At times, the Legion provided an invaluable forum for debate among veterans. Yet, from the beginning, the Legion came under constant assault from more radicalized segments of the veterans' community, left black veterans behind in its effort to construct a national coalition, and accepted the resignation of more well-to-do veterans who disavowed the adjusted compensation crusade. The Legion never restricted itself solely to preserving veterans' distinct societal status. The Legion's Americanism, encompassing concerns about Bolshevism, immigration, and sponsorship of multiple community service projects, affiliated the organization with a host of similarly oriented civilian organizations. The Legion can rightly, therefore, be considered both a vital link in the veterans' network and one of the myriad patriotic voluntary associations that dotted the American landscape after the war.[89] Correspondingly, Great War veterans did not confine their political activities to the approved resolutions of Legion conventions or even to veterans' organizations. A former Legion commander, Hanford MacNider, actively organized a veterans' service league within the Republican Party in 1924 to prepare veterans for leadership of the party in 1928, for example, and working-class veterans used street demonstrations to communicate with the American people and government during the 1932 Bonus March. In the coming years, veterans would strike out beyond the confines of the Legion to continue renegotiating their social contract with the state.

8

"THE YANKS ARE STARVING EVERYWHERE"

THE BONUS MARCH

American veterans of the Great War won a major legislative battle in 1924 when their claim for adjusted compensation became law. As the urgency accompanying the 1919 recession passed, having to accept a bond in lieu of a cash payment aroused little complaint among veterans. For the rest of the decade, the issue seemed settled. Then the economy collapsed. It took Americans a while after the stock market crash of 1929 to realize that the economic crisis would not pass quickly. One by one, veterans revived calls for an immediate cash payment. At first glance, this second phase of the reckoning with the country over the terms of the social contract implicit in World War I conscription seems remarkably similar to the first. The nation once again found itself ensnared in debates over what had or had not occurred during the war.[1]

A paralyzing malaise settled over Americans, stunned by the quickness with which their economic fortunes had reversed. President Hoover urged private charities to expand their work, companies to retain workers on their payrolls, and banks to keep lending. Finally, in 1932, Hoover took an important step by agreeing to lend banks and large corporations funds through a new agency called the Reconstruction Finance Corporation (RFC). World War I veterans also struck out on a new course by presenting immediate payment as a way to spur the consumer spending needed for recovery, a modest version of the Keynesian deficit spending that eventually would restore jobs during World War II. At first, veterans confined their lobbying to the traditional channels of letter-writing and Legion conventions. In 1932, however, a group of working-class veterans took veteran political activism in a bold new direction with the Bonus March.

Over time, this debate centered less on the past and more on the present. When thousands of veterans descended on Washington in a mass demonstration that lasted nearly two months, the government challenged their popularity by branding them a dangerous and unstable special interest group. The World War I generation believed their financial problems deserved special attention, because they had been uniquely handicapped in the competition for scarce jobs and the government had agreed that it owed them money. The public, however, sympathized with the Bonus March out of the conviction that Hoover was not expanding government services fast enough to mitigate widespread suffering among the working people of the nation. Attempting to resurrect public interest in the long-term consequences of conscription, veterans instead helped the nation frame the debate over the government's responsibility to its Depression-hobbled citizens. Their success in helping the public conceptualize a new domestic role for the federal government in relieving the suffering of the unemployed came about in a most unexpected way.

A Veterans' Depression

Veterans suffered severely during the economic crisis. When the government allowed loans of up to 50 percent against the face value of the adjusted compensation certificate in February 1931 (an effort by Congress to stem the demand for full payment), within five months, over half of the surviving 4.3 million veterans took it. This loan involved considerable long-term loss for veterans, because the 4.5 percent interest rate (lowered in 1932 to 3.5 percent) would consume the remaining principal by the time the bonds matured in 1945. Veterans Administration (VA) findings that 65 percent used their loans to buy food, pay rent, or meet payments on furniture or a car reflected the immediacy of their needs.[2] Another 20 percent invested their money, but this figure included farmers buying seed for crops or homeowners making mortgage payments to avoid foreclosure. American Legion post commanders in the hard-hit cotton areas of the South used the most convincing argument they could imagine to refute all suggestions that veterans would squander this loan. "There was great apprehension in this state as to the manner in which the negro veteran would use his money," reported the Louisiana commander. He cited the example of a black veteran who "had gotten in debt and in order to pay his bills had borrowed several hundred dollars in a loan company charging

3½% per month or 42% per annum, this being a legalized rate of interest for such companies making loans of $300.00 and less in this state."[3] The interest penalty inflicted by the federal government paled in comparison, allowing this veteran to improve his financial situation significantly.

The political demonstrations a year later revealed that the small boost provided by the loans did not mitigate the widespread distress captured by detailed census studies in 1930 and 1931, which showed tremendous hardship among veterans. They were clearly suffering, but were they disproportionately afflicted? Veterans believed so, and the numbers backed up that claim.[4] According to a special unemployment census released in 1931, 11.7 percent of men in the 30–54 age group were unemployed. Taking that figure as a starting point, Veterans Administration officials expected to find 502,202 unemployed veterans. Instead, they found 800,000. Approximately 21 percent of the 20.7 million men in the 30–54 age group were veterans of the Great War, yet veterans made up 32.9 percent of the unemployment within that cohort. Veterans Administration officials struggled to reduce these numbers, arguing that at least 50,000 were unemployed as a result of service-related disabilities and already received a government subsidy. Overall, 10.2 percent of World War I veterans collected disability benefits from the government in 1931.[5] With this reduction, the Veterans Administration believed that only 30.8 percent of all unemployed men between the ages of 30 and 54 were able-bodied veterans, and that 17.4 percent of all veterans were unemployed. This still meant that veterans suffered a nearly 50 percent higher unemployment rate than their age cohort as a whole. Conceivably, mixing veterans into samples representing the overall population of men between 30 and 54 skewed overall unemployment figures upward, raising the possibility of an even greater discrepancy between veterans and nonveterans in terms of unemployment. One rare VA study comparing veterans and nonveterans in this age group supported this possibility, concluding that veterans exhibited more economic need and remained out of work longer.[6]

These statistical studies supported veterans' claims that the war years had set them back in the race with their civilian counterparts for a share of the nation's wealth. "We understand that your chief objection is that Veterans are [not] a special class," wrote James Turner to President Franklin Delano Roosevelt from Bennettsville, South Carolina. "May I submit this thought: When we were suddenly taken from our ordinary pursuits of life and thrust into a uniform, some serving here, others abroad, as I did, were we not then a special class?"[7] The Depression did, however, put a new twist on this old refrain. Suddenly, this generation faced the prospect of starting over, not just once, but twice in their lives. Acknowledging that many Americans had lost everything in the worsening economic crisis did not mean that veterans now viewed the playing field as level. Stories about the imminent loss of a home, the catastrophe of four successive crop failings, the inability to clothe children, and the shame of finally going on relief were sadly enough quite common. But veterans told two stories of starting over. Their stories of hardship started with coming back in 1919 to find "foreigners" in their factory jobs, women in clerical positions, the chance to learn a skill gone, a postwar recession in the farming community that endured throughout the so-called "Roaring Twenties," an incapacitating sensitivity to noise, "jumpy nerves," or struggles of hard work and thrift to acquire a small house and garden. They then told of losing a job, home, farm, or family after 1929. The future suggested the possibility of yet more upheaval. "It looks as if there might be another war quite soon," D. V. Simpson noted in a 1935 letter to Roosevelt. "Most of us who were in the last would be expected to fight in the next. But *we feel that we have not been paid for the last!*"[8]

Veterans faced having to reinvent their lives again a mere twelve years after their previous attempt to do so. "Mr. President, the average age of the veteran today is 42 to 47 years. Should business warrant increase[d] employment, how many business houses would employ men between these ages?" wondered Herbert Nicholas.[9] "Even if there was work to be had what chance has the overseas veteran to compete with the younger man?" echoed a veteran from Providence, Rhode Island.[10] Knowing that they were no longer young, single men, these men refused to wait for their money, because "we will all be dead by 1945 at the rate we are now trying to exist," as one veteran told Roosevelt.[11]

As with other men struggling to survive, staying off the dole became a quest to preserve self-respect. The adjusted compensation certificate tucked away in four million homes across the nation, however, gave veterans unique hope of finding an immediate way out of their downward spiral. To receive their bonus payment now instead of later "will make us feel like men again," explained Ed Fischer.[12] In the official view of General Frank Hines, director of the Veterans Administration, veterans would ultimately take better care of their families by leaving them the adjusted compensation certificate in the event of their untimely death before 1945. In these cases, the widow could collect immediately.[13] The notion of adjusted compensation as a de facto life insurance policy struck a favorable note among some wives of unhappy unions. Agnes Brewington, suffering in a violent, alcoholic marriage, did not hesitate to convey her feeling that "the bonus should not be given [to] the veterans to squander but should be left to be used for his burial and the family . . . after they have sacrificed so much for the veteran since the war."[14] Living with a veteran disposed to violent outbursts, which she blamed on his combat experience, convinced Brewington that she was as much a victim of the war as her husband. Those wives who descended on Washington with their spouses during the Bonus March may not all have agreed with her conclusion that their husbands would only waste the money on drink, but they certainly accepted that their husbands' quest had become their own as well. To at least one government observer, "the women are more outspoken and bitter in their denunciation of the Government than are the men."[15] Many letters to the White House and Congress about the veterans' bonus were now from interested wives. Husbands and wives might not have shared the army experience, but the political struggle for immediate payment became a joint endeavor in many households across the nation.

Amid the rancorous political debate over immediate payment, a troubling new question arose. Was their present predicament affecting the way the country remembered their past achievements?[16] "On my way to the Post Office recently," Carl Sanderson wrote to Congresswoman Virginia Jenckes (D-Ind.),

> I passed several small boys playing along the street, one of these small lads had on (probably his dad's) an overseas hat, a lad a little larger than the one wearing the hat made a remark about the hat, whereupon the little fellow wearing the hat was heard to remark, my dad was a soldier he was over fighting the [G]ermans, and he has bullet wounds to prove it, the larger lad says that is nothing, he is a big bum anyway, the little fellow wants to know why his dad is a bum, and the larger lad replys [sic], why my father says he is, because he lays around and want[s] work.[17]

Those carrying placards with the inscription "Wilson's Heroes, Hoover's Bums" during the Bonus March blamed the president and his failed economic policies for this predicament. Still, as the above story illustrates only too well, seeing themselves through the eyes of children as nothing more than middle-aged failures provided continued evidence to disheartened veterans that the country had let them down.

The Bonus March made clear the concrete political dimensions to the personal dilemmas of starting over and aging among veterans. Who would speak for the pro-bonus veteran became an open question once the American Legion sided with the administration.[18] Many veterans in 1924 had believed passionately in their cause, yet never considered taking their movement to the streets. To its supporters, the Bonus Expeditionary Force (BEF) represented democracy in its purest form. To its detractors, it epitomized the violent threat trained ex-servicemen would always pose. Most important, after an eight-year absence, veterans once again thrust themselves to the forefront of the American political stage.

Challenging Legion Leadership

Although initially lukewarm to the idea of increased loans against the adjusted compensation certificate, in 1931, the Legion fought for the measure with a carefully constructed member survey that detailed the positive good the loan money brought to devastated communities across the nation.[19] Legion posts dutifully reported that cash from the loans rippled outward to benefit extended family, merchants, and banks. VA Director Frank Hines disagreed, concluding from his surveys that the payments had a negligible impact on the economy.[20] The Legion's defense of loans against the adjusted compensation certificates, however, camouflaged a growing erosion in its standing as the legitimate voice of the veterans. "Our Legion Boys are wondering if the American Legion has sold out to political intrigue and boloney [sic]," a post commander wrote from Holyroad, Kansas, to the national headquarters in 1932.[21] "Why this silence?" on the bonus question, he asked. By then, Legion officials had already sacrificed much credibility among veterans to appease the administration. The descent began in 1930, when President Hoover made an appearance before the Legion's national convention and the delegates obediently tabled a resolution calling for immediate payment. Overwhelmed by the outcry from their membership, the Legion's Executive Committee met four months later to calm the internal strife without breaking with Hoover. The Legion leadership, the committee claimed, believed in "the principle of immediate cash retirement" but had to respect the convention's resolutions and therefore could not sponsor any enabling legislation.[22]

These tensions died down later in the month, when Congress approved the loan provisions and Legion headquarters stepped up to defend veterans' legitimate need. As the next national convention neared, however, another showdown loomed. Influential Republican legionnaires hoped to bolster Hoover's faltering public image with a strong anti-bonus speech.[23]

Hoover kept his supporters waiting until the last minute before accepting the invitation to address the Legion, however, deciding a dramatic buildup would help his speech deliver the desired punch. Theodore Joslin, secretary to the president, gloated privately in his diary about keeping such a big story from the press, but noted that the decision took its toll on White House staff. "Ye gods what a job in a few days," Joslin exclaimed in his journal, "when writing a speech to him [Hoover] is as great an ordeal as childbirth to a woman!"[24] When the big moment arrived, Hoover delivered a rather predictable speech, calling upon the Legion to exhibit self-denial and courage until the economic situation improved.[25] Once again, the convention deferred to the president's wishes, this time defeating an immediate payment resolution by a vote of 902–507.[26]

The occasion may have provided Hoover with a chance to improve his stature as a leader, but it did exactly the opposite for Legion officials. On the heels of this convention, post after post responded with resolutions of support for a cash settlement. This time Legion leaders stood firm. When the president repeated his stand against the bonus in his 1932 State of the Union address, some congressmen proved as defiant as the rebel Legion posts. In its first session, the Seventy-Second Congress debated no fewer than thirty-four versions of payment legislation.[27]

Theodore Roosevelt, Jr., and Hanford MacNider, two of the Legion's founders, repeatedly pressured the current national commander to reject the call for immediate payment. Their interest in influencing the political activities of veterans reflected more than their current status as members of the Republican administration. In 1924, feeling ignored at the National Republican Convention, Theodore Roosevelt, Jr., concocted the idea of organizing veterans into a Republican Service League (RSL) so that they could have a voice in party affairs. Organizing "within our party, our particular generation" delivered at least six states in the Midwest and West to the Republicans in 1924, MacNider gleefully claimed.[28] "Our day [for control of the Republican Party] is coming fast enough," he predicted. Like MacNider, Theodore Roosevelt, Jr., spurned any suggestion that the RSL merge with the national organization. By doing so, "we would automatically loose [sic] our identity," and with it the chance for veterans to take over the reins of power within the party, he argued.[29] To that end, MacNider did not hesitate to help contain the Legion in 1931, even though he had pushed hard as its commander in 1922 to secure the adjusted compensation settlement. "Most of your friends . . . don't think you are right . . . when you have the Legion, as an organization, go on record as being opposed to a measure that at least ninety per cent of its membership favors," a lifelong friend of MacNider's wrote him after the Legion's latest anti-bonus resolution.[30] MacNider, however, was acting on his belief that veterans' political future lay within the Republican Party, not in using the Legion to secure additional benefits.[31]

Ironically, MacNider's prophecy of inspired political leadership by veterans was about to be fulfilled in a wholly unforeseen way. In the spring of 1932, a few hundred veterans in Portland, Oregon, decided to make a statement radically different from the resolutions, petitions, and letters normally used to press veterans' claim with the administration. They resolved to march across the country and make a personal appeal to Congress and the president. Capturing the interest of the press after a standoff with railroad officials in East St. Louis, this ragtag group inspired veterans from other communities to launch their own drives toward Washington, D.C.[32] As the movement picked up steam, it became evident by late May that thousands of veterans were coming to Washington with the intention of camping on the front lawn of the Capitol until Congress voted favorably on the bonus question. The Bonus March had begun without either the Republican Service League or the American Legion in sight.

The Bonus March

After the stock market crash, small groups of veterans made little-noticed pilgrimages to Washington, D.C., to present petitions to the federal government. None gained the momentum of the Oregon group, which traversed the country in twenty days. On May 29, this contingent rode into the nation's capital atop eighteen trucks provided by the Maryland National Guard to discover that their trek had become a full-fledged mass movement. Veterans were arriving en masse from all parts of the country, propelled toward Washington by their own initiative and by local governments intent on seeing that they did not lose heart and settle along the way. The Oregon contingent's experience set the pattern for those who followed. For the most part, the Portland men found towns gracious enough to feed them. The railroads were not as accommodating. When the B and O Railroad refused to move the cars that veterans had seized in East St. Louis, local authorities stepped in with an offer of transportation to the state line.[33] The state governments of Indiana, Maryland, Ohio, Pennsylvania, and West Virginia did the same.[34]

Their quest captured the imagination of a public eager to see how Hoover would respond to their evident poverty. The capital had already received two other groups of marchers, first, a group of 4,000 communists in December, who demonstrated for two days, and then a three-day rally of 15,000 unemployed in February, led by a Pittsburgh priest, James R. Cox. Watching thousands picketing during the latter event, Senator Clarence Dill (D-Wash.) said to a fellow senator: "Suppose ten other cities sent ten thousand unemployed here and they came in and took charge of the House and the Senate. What would we do about it? Do you think you'd get an army to come here and kill them?"[35] At the end of July, when Hoover decided the time had come to evict the Bonus Marchers, the U.S. Army would finally have a chance to answer that query.

Given the true grassroots character of the movement, the Bonus March posted impressive numbers, averaging 15,000 in strength, with a peak of 20,000 in mid-July. Newcomers steadily replaced men who either got discouraged or were called home, and thousands of others completed at least part of the journey before turning back, bringing the total close to 40,000 veterans who marched at some point.[36] Thousands of other veterans who stayed at home supported the marchers with cash donations, supplies, and letters to Congress and Hoover.

The collective organizational experiences of the marchers paid off immediately. Like any self-respecting veterans' group, they immediately elected a leader, set up community rules to govern their Washington encampments, sent recruiting parties to solicit members and contributions, learned to welcome distinguished visitors and members of the press, and policed themselves to keep the taint of scandal from undermining their public appeal. Camp commanders registered new arrivals, made assignments to fatigue duties, organized three mess calls a day, and soon had a working post office and camp newsletter in place. The veterans also enjoyed nightly boxing matches and baseball games, which evoked memories of their training camp days.

Replicating their army camp days also included maintaining a haphazard pattern of segregation. Roy Wilkins claimed that black and white veterans pitched their tents near each other, ate together, and stood interspersed on the Capitol steps.[37] He castigated the army once again for claiming that black and white soldiers had to be separated during the war to maintain discipline. Few official reports corroborated this view of general racial harmony, however. Communists participating on the fringes of the march criticized the "extensive policy of segregation" in the main veteran encampment, and military intelligence observers noted that black and white veterans separated themselves during parades.[38] While making the journey to Washington, D.C., black and white veterans from Texas and Oklahoma traveled in one group, but black veterans marched, rode, and ate separately.[39] Other black veterans Wilkins interviewed claimed, however, that on their journey with southern white veterans, they had eaten and slept in the same whites-only establishments many times. This suggestion of racial unity marking the beginning of the march unraveled by the end. In the final days, with the frustration of their failed movement building, many veterans left for home because they expected violence, and, a military investigator reported, "many of these seem to think that it will be race trouble."[40] Black veterans participated in the Bonus March, but no realignment in race relations among veterans occurred during the demonstration.

The marchers originally intended to camp on the Capitol grounds, but the District of Columbia's police chief, Pelham D. Glassford, successfully marshaled them across the Anacostia River to the Anacostia Flats, two miles southeast of the Capitol. Until Congress voted on an immediate payment bill in the third week of June, the lobbying routine consisted of visiting individual congressmen, picketing outside on the Capitol steps, and trying to see the president. From Camp Marks, as they called their main encampment, the veterans could easily walk across a bridge each day to demonstrate. The ability to lift the drawbridge gave the police chief a way to contain the movement if ever it turned violent.[41] A retired brigadier general who had commanded a field artillery unit in France, Glassford sympathized with his fellow veterans, and with Hoover's approval, he secured army rations, tents, medicine, and field hospitals for them.[42] When the movement grew too big for the Anacostia Flats, Glassford negotiated the use of abandoned federal buildings downtown. His detractors believed that he encouraged the movement, but Glassford maintained that he had been doing "everything possible to avoid trouble—has been yielding to the marchers on minor points, ordinances, letting them use unoccupied buildings, and so on so as not to do anything to shape public sentiments in favor of the marchers as against the authorities," a military intelligence observer reported in July.[43] Yet, this officer, continued, Glassford "fears that sooner or later there will be some important thing on which the police cannot yield and that then there will be some trouble."

If sympathizers like Glassford considered violence possible, critics certainly believed that a communist coup was in the making from this self-styled "army." The Communist Party indeed played a minor role in the Bonus March. Upon hearing of the Oregon contingent's cross-country trek, the Party saw an opportunity to attract new members and gain national publicity.[44] A small cell of communist activists arrived and set up a camp downtown under the auspices of the Workers' Ex-Servicemen's League. Their nightly meetings attracted about a hundred veterans or so on average, including a large cadre of undercover agents, who dutifully reported every word spoken, much of it complaints about the communists' exclusion from Camp Marks by BEF leaders.[45] Reports from the twenty other smaller camps should also have given the president some peace of mind. "The rank and file blame the banks, big business, and politicians for everything," reported one agent, hastening to add that the conversation in the noncommunist camps "reminds one much of that heard around a country store near election time."[46] The deputy chief of staff, Major General George Van Horn Moseley, acknowledged six years later that most marchers "took action wherever possible to eliminate communistic leadership."[47]

Concerns about possible violence, communist-inspired or otherwise, immediately affected Hoover.[48] He refused all invitations that required him to appear in public, because, as Joslin recalled, "there are too many assassins here now."[49] White House visitors and staff noted that getting rid of the Bonus Marchers dominated conversation between Hoover and his advisors day and night.[50] Meanwhile, veterans grew angry with a president who steadfastly refused to meet with their representatives or accept their petitions.[51] The veterans, who had come to present their grievances personally to the president, never succeeded in getting an audience with him.

Some Washingtonians shared Hoover's disdain of the marchers. Good riddance, said John Le Gorce when the marchers fled the city. After a while, according to Le Gorce, the veterans "began to intimidate citizens in their demands for food and supplies, particularly in the Southwest section of Washington where they would picket grocery stores and markets and when women came out with their baskets of food for the home would accost them and in an insistent voice ask if they really needed all that food at home when there were hundreds of people starving."[52]

Le Gorce's account did not do justice to the more respectable ways Bonus Marchers found to keep their movement financially afloat. True, the veterans depended on the cash and food donations that arrived daily at the camp. Eight German and Austrian war veterans (now naturalized American citizens) argued, however, that, "the American veterans who treated us like human beings" during the postwar occupation had already earned the food the group brought to Camp Marks.[53] But farmers personally delivering milk or vegetables, bakers bringing loaves of bread to the camp, and builders donating piles of lumber to shore up the shanties dotting the Anacostia landscape had to prepare themselves beforehand for the men who would crowd around them asking for a day's work.[54] Selling the camp newspaper, the *B.E.F. News,* and manning drink stands on street corners around town also put change in veterans' pockets. Joe Angelo won the prize for most inventive when he had himself buried alive and charged onlookers to chat with him through the stovepipe that served as his tombstone. Even without the threat of violence and vagrancy, however, other reasons existed to disband the camp. District health officers and military intelligence officials worried that unsanitary camp conditions were preparing the way for a major epidemic in the muggy, humid summer weather, and the 350 veterans receiving treatment each day in a military aid station downtown seemingly confirmed this fear.[55]

On June 17, when the Senate took up a House-approved bill that incorporated the inflationary tactic of simply printing the money needed to pay the veterans' bonus, Washington waited to see if the movement would fulfill critics' predictions of violence. The merging of the bonus issue with inflationary fiscal policies spelled certain defeat in the Senate, especially when the Senate Finance Committee issued a negative report on the bill. As the Senate went through the motions of debate, sweaty veterans listened in the gallery, while thousands of others massed on the Capitol steps, hoping that fortune might favor them. At the White House, Hoover and his advisors worried that wavering senators might be intimidated by the numbers of Bonus Marchers milling around outside and leave it to the president to veto the bill. Three hundred armed guards waited in reserve with instructions to close and guard the gates of the White House in case the bill did pass. Despite the mounting tension, Hoover remained defiant in front of his aides. "Don't worry about the veterans coming down here," the president reportedly snapped. "I'll have that bill back before Congress with my veto in ten minutes."[56]

To pass the time, the crowd outside the Senate whipped through a litany of their old war songs, and the impromptu sing-along also included a parody of the AEF's signature song, "Over There."[57] The rousing words they had sung as soldiers—"Over there / Over there / Send the word / Send the word / Over there / That the Yanks are coming / The Yanks are coming / The drums rum-tumming everywhere"—fourteen years later had changed to:

> All you here—here and there
> Pay the bonus, pay the bonus everywhere
> For the Yanks are starving,
> The Yanks are starving,
> The Yanks are starving everywhere.

Just before the evening vote, the police raised the drawbridge over the Anacostia River, and sent police details to watch the two other bridge crossings.[58] At 8:20 P.M., the Senate defeated the measure by a vote of 62–18. "Prepare yourselves for a disappointment, men," the BEF commander, Walter Waters, announced to a silent crowd.[59] As the senators waited within for the riot to commence, Waters shouted above the murmuring crowd, "We are not telling you to go home. . . . Go back to your camps!"[60] After singing a hearty rendition of "America," groups of men began trickling toward Camp Marks. The evening had passed without incident.

Now that Congress had voted, officials expected the marchers to pack up and leave. As a token gesture, Congress lowered the rate of interest on loans against the adjusted compensation certificate to 3½ percent. Hoover also signed legislation allowing veterans to borrow train fare home against their adjusted compensation certificates, interest-free, to facilitate their exodus. A few thousand took the money, but rather than evaporating, most of the Bonus Army remained.[61] The flamboyant Royal Robertson, who had arrived with a contingent from California early in July, helped rally the protesters once more by staging a sit-in on the Capitol grounds.[62] When the Capitol police put a stop to veterans sleeping there, Robertson responded with a well-publicized "Death March," during which constant rotations kept the veterans parading around grounds made soggy by a sprinkler system purposely left on all night.[63] Their presence so disturbed Vice President Charles Curtis that he sent Chief of Staff Douglas MacArthur an order for troops to clear them away, which Glassford intercepted and canceled, a decision Hoover supported. The sight of sixty Marines arriving and departing from the Capitol grounds within the span of fifteen minutes created rumors among the veterans that the soldiers had refused to act against men who had also worn the uniform.[64] This rumor proved long-lasting, and after the forceful eviction of the Bonus March two weeks later, MacArthur had to deny arresting four hundred Marines for refusing to march "against their brother veterans."[65]

When Congress adjourned on July 16, the time had surely arrived for the veterans to admit defeat and start for home. But still thousands lingered, and the administration decided to press the issue. First, on July 21, the Treasury Department revoked its permission to use a row of downtown federal buildings scheduled for demolition. The District of Columbia commissioners ordered veterans to evacuate these buildings immediately, and gave the inhabitants of other camps, including Camp Marks, until August 4 to vacate the city. Glassford stalled for time, and Waters tried unsuccessfully to secure a permanent camp from Secretary of War Patrick Hurley.

"The psychological effect of the many false starts that have been made towards evicting the Bonus Marchers is sure to give the Bonus Marchers the idea that they have the authorities 'bluffed,'" Assistant Chief of Staff Colonel Alfred T. Smith warned MacArthur on July 27, 1932. Smith predicted that these false starts had "undoubtedly lessened to a great degree the chance of evicting the Bonus Marchers without the use of force." On July 29, Glassford had a chance to test this prediction when he began clearing the Pennsylvania Avenue Treasury buildings between 3rd and 4½th Street. The police had to carry out a few of the veterans living in the condemned row, providing newsworthy photographs for the press.[66] Satisfied with this progress, Glassford left to urge the District commissioners to accept a piecemeal eviction.[67] Rather than reassuring the District commissioners, Glassford's visit prompted them to visit the site and make their own determination of the situation.

With veterans and police facing one another across the police line established in front of the newly vacated building, tempers were running high. A few minor scuffles between the two sides broke out, only to die back down. In another occupied building, down the row on the corner of Pennsylvania Avenue and 4½th Street, two veterans began tussling around 2:15 P.M. Police officers immediately entered the building to break up the fight, only to discover an angry pack of veterans waiting for them. Before anyone truly knew what had transpired, punches, bricks, and gunshots filled the air, and one veteran lay dead on a stairway. Another would die of his wounds within a week. Three police officers left the scene bleeding.

The District commissioners had just returned to their offices when news of the mêlée arrived. They immediately called President Hoover, who "asked if the Chief of Police had himself said he could not manage the situation, and if they were sure he could not," the president's wife reported a few days later in a personal letter to her son.[68] Hoover demanded their request for troops in writing. The commissioners immediately sent a note asking that the police "be given the assistance of Federal troops, in maintaining law and order in the District of Columbia."[69]

When the order came, Washington-based troops had been on alert for two months.[70] In preparation, the army had secretly transferred tanks to Fort Myer, given troops anti-riot training, readied a small force to protect the White House and Treasury at a moment's notice, and developed an operational plan.[71] In accordance with this plan, one squadron of cavalry troops, two battalions of infantry, a headquarters company, a mounted machine gun squad, and six whippet tanks assembled on the Ellipse, the public lawn behind the White House. "The Chief of Staff, General MacArthur, said that he would go out and take command," Dwight Eisenhower, then a chief aide to MacArthur, recalled some years later.

Well, I thought it had the aspect of a riot rather than a great big military movement, and so I told him that I thought this was inadvisable; that the Chief of Staff should not dignify the incident by going out himself. But he said that this was a very serious test of the strength of the Federal Government; that he was going, and that I was going as his aide. In those days we all went in civilian clothes normally, so I had to go home and get into my uniform (chuckle) and come back and meet him, and we went out on this expedition.[72]

Quite a sight soon proceeded down Pennsylvania Avenue: MacArthur in full uniform sitting in a staff car, the cavalry on horseback, five tanks, and the remaining troops on foot, with one company under the command of Major George Patton. It took less than two hours to evacuate the area. "The blue haze of gas that hung like an ominous pall over the section of shanties and condemned Federal buildings [was] . . . reminiscent of scenes in war-torn France," the Associated Press reported to newspaper readers across the country.[73] Soon, the downtown camps blazed, fires having inadvertently been started by flawed gas candles and tear gas containers used to clear the area.[74]

Although the troops had ammunition in their guns, they only used their bayonets to herd the veterans out of the buildings and into the gathering crowd of spectators. "There apparently existed a feeling that soldiers would not forcibly act against the self-styled 'former-buddies,'" Lieutenant Colonel L. A. Kunzig later reported.[75] When the veterans realized their mistake, the cheers that had initially greeted the troops quickly turned to boos and profanity. The crowd was soon picking up tear gas containers before they exploded and hurling them back at troops.[76]

At 9 P.M., after a dinner break, the troops received orders to "proceed to the Anacostia Flats and evacuate Bonus Marchers from that property."[77] The troops arrived at the bridge by 10 P.M., and gave the veterans another hour to evacuate the camp. The angry crowds of civilians blocking the bridge hurled more than insults at the troops.[78] When the latter entered the encampment at the appointed hour, it was already burning, and the army later asserted that the veterans had set it afire before they left.[79]

In deciding to cross the Anacostia River and attack Camp Marks, MacArthur ignored explicit orders from Hoover to limit troop activity to the downtown camps.[80] When Hoover realized later in the evening that MacArthur was disobeying his original order, he told Hurley to forbid MacArthur to cross the Anacostia Bridge. Van Horn Moseley claimed in his memoirs that he personally delivered the message to MacArthur and later sent Colonel Clement H. Wright, secretary of the General Staff, to repeat it.[81] According to Van Horn Moseley, MacArthur "was very much annoyed in having his plans interfered with in any way until they were executed completely." Eisenhower confirmed that the orders were sent down, but recollected: "I went up to the General and said, 'There's a man here who has some orders about this.' He said, 'I don't want to hear them and I don't want to see them. Get him away.'"[82] The detailed narrative First Lady Lou Hoover wrote to her son soon after the eviction reported that the president had received a late evening telephone call from the field (from either MacArthur or a messenger, she was not sure) informing him that MacArthur wanted to turn all the veterans out and burn the camps. "Daddy did not agree with him . . . he didn't like the idea of driving them out in the night. So he refused his consent to the plan."[83]

In the political turmoil that followed, Hoover chose to stand by MacArthur, however. The closest he ever came to acknowledging the latter's insubordination publicly came in his 1952 memoirs, when he briefly acknowledged: "I did not wish them driven from their camps . . . our military officers, however, having them on the move, pushed them outside the District of Columbia."[84] Hoover had even earlier hesitations about backing MacArthur's self-serving version of events. "[I]f MacArthur is putting out this kind of stuff, I shall tell what really did happen, and it will do MacArthur no good," he wrote to his former secretary Lawrence Richey after coming across a critical newspaper column in 1934.[85]

In the press conference that MacArthur gave in the middle of the night, he claimed that he had liberated the besieged people of Washington from the grip of a force whose terrorizing presence rivaled that of any he had seen during the war.[86] Veterans across the country, however, saw a differ-ent parallel between their war experience, the tear gas attack, the burning of the camp, and official justifications for the assault. Comparisons to "the destruction of the homes of the Belgians by the Kaiser's army" became a familiar refrain in letters of protest sent to Washington over the next few weeks.[87] A Pittsburgh veteran denounced the president's day-after public statement as "a lot of propaganda, just like the propaganda about the Ger-mans during the war."[88] Percy Hocking noted that, unlike MacArthur, he remembered that "these people were *my* war time comrades" during the war.[89]

Two highly controversial international conferences on war debts and disarmament were occurring at the same time as the Bonus March, and some protestors linked these war-related events in their letters. As the march ran its course, diplomats meeting in Lucerne, Switzerland, were trying to find a way to restore financial health to Europe. The Americans refused to agree to any plan that linked the reduction of Germany's stiff reparation payments to a corresponding lessening of Allied war debts to the United States.[90] If Hoover ever doubted this stance, the Bonus March showed the extent to which the American public firmly opposed forgiv-ing the Allied war debt. After all, wrote one woman from Oklahoma City, "charity begins at home."[91] Critics also mentioned the ongoing World Disarmament Conference in Geneva. "Our country has talked and talked to foreign countries against using tanks and gas in war, but you in turn ordered them turned out against our own men, women and children," H. L. Caldwell wrote angrily from Evansville, Indiana.[92]

When he awoke the following morning, Hoover seems to have given little thought to the larger repercussions of the Bonus Army eviction. When told of the telegrams lambasting the operation, he told Joslin: "That's all to the good. . . . Tell the press when they come in that I have received scores of telegrams from communist organizations all over the country threatening me and the government."[93] Pressing his advantage, Hoover swiftly ordered Justice Department and grand jury investigations. The administration delivered the shocking news that a collection of com-munists and criminals had camped out in the Capital and had buried guns and dynamite in Camp Marks.[94] The administration also went to great lengths to point out that the two eviction-related deaths had been at the hands of the D.C. police, not the U.S. Army.

Meanwhile, the Bonus Marchers attempted to reorganize their move-ment in Johnstown, Pennsylvania. Talk of forming a more permanent political organization, the Khaki Shirts, encouraged the demonstrators to stay. They hung on despite the evident inability of Johnstown to provide the supplies and sanitation needed to sustain their encampment.[95] The scope of Glassford's contribution to the infrastructure of the movement became more evident every day. After a frustrating week, the veterans formally disbanded with the help of donated railroad and truck rides home. The Bonus Marchers disappeared back into the anonymous ranks of the poor and unemployed.

Criticism of the Bonus March eviction soon affected Hoover's reelection campaign. Each American Legion or Veterans of Foreign Wars (VFW) post resolution condemning the president's manhandling of the Bonus Marchers guaranteed at least one article in the local paper. The president's secretaries responded to every resolution identically, occasionally with the desired results. "I have read the official reports on the matter, which you sent me, and it is my sincere belief that a great many of the members of the Post had been misinformed on this subject," VFW Commander Victor B. Galloway wrote from Dearborn, Michigan. Official refutations could not, however, head off a VFW resolution censuring Hoover for using troops to evict the Bonus Army. Losing the support of the pro-bonus, 100,000-member VFW paled in significance, however, in comparison to the possibility that the politically more powerful American Legion might follow suit. Hoover's friends in the Legion acknowledged that they could not prevent a pro-bonus stand that year. Instead, MacNider and others claimed victory when they stopped the Legion from censuring the president publicly for the Bonus March debacle.

Where did the veterans and Hoover stand vis-à-vis the sentiments of the rest of the country throughout this exchange? Seemingly, the harder Hoover worked to put the issue to rest, the more he succeeded in fanning the flames anew. "For heaven's sake lay off the veterans' bonus army," a Republican newspaper editor from Buffalo, New York, advised Hoover's staff.[96] Like the rest of the country, Buffalo was tiring of claims that a movement the majority of veterans supported was not, in fact, peopled by veterans. "This outrage of calling out one set of soldiers to fight the World War heroes of 1918 has lost you more votes than any other event in the past four years," warned John Mullen, a veteran.[97] Those around Hoover feared that Mullen might be right.

"I am not discouraged," General George E. Leach had written Hoover from the Legion convention. "[A]ll the votes in this country are not veterans."[98] Perhaps not, but the Bonus March eviction symbolized to many nonveteran voters exactly what was wrong with the government in Washington. As Franklin D. Roosevelt would demonstrate, the majority of Americans had no trouble agreeing that veterans should wait to receive their adjusted compensation payment. The pertinent issue now became how history would remember this phase of the Great War experience. Most nonveteran voters viewed the Bonus March as a test of the president's humanitarian impulses, and they intended to punish him for failing.[99]

The Poor Man's Lobby

Nonveteran critics writing Hoover did not care whether or not the Bonus Marchers had posed a real military threat or deserved payment. Instead, they used the incident to define Washington's responsibility to the nation. In calling out the troops, Hoover had followed the time-honored practice used by earlier presidents to end the great strikes of the nineteenth century. Part of the country, notably the business class, celebrated this show of militant leadership. The rest saw the need for change in the march's unfortunate end. The first wave of analysis focused on the constitutional right of all American citizens to petition their government. "The unemployed have only one way of making their plight public knowledge: through demonstrations," Peter Guldbrandsen explained to the president from Berkeley, California.[100] By contrast, the poor could never hope to match the resources available to the "war profiteers, maintaining themselves in marble palaces," the professional "parasite" lobbyists who could afford "to buy the approval of Congress for their requests," other correspondents argued.[101] These writers jumped easily from celebrating the Bonus Marchers as a poor man's lobby to questions about why Hoover continued to oppose direct aid to individual citizens. "The poor American, according to you, has too much pride to accept a meal or shelter from his government, but the 'big banker' and 'big organized business' [receiving help from the RFC] . . . does not have to worry about his pride," fumed Louis Kirchheiner, who had watched returning Bonus Marchers trudge past his house in Baltimore.[102] The working class now had a tangible symbol to help them express their evolving preference for a more active state. "The unemployed of this country owe a debt of gratitude to the men who made the bonus march to Washington, D.C.," Frank Murray wrote, protesting the eviction. To those who had watched events unfold, he said, "it seems illogical for the federal government to shirk its duty" to the unemployed and needy any longer.[103]

These vocal citizens were far ahead of presidential candidate Franklin D. Roosevelt in envisioning a new role for the government in American society. The Bonus March served as the catalyst for an avalanche of demands for direct unemployment relief, but Roosevelt initially focused on cutting, not expanding, government expenditures. Those who supported Hoover's forceful eviction of the Bonus Marchers understood the intent of these declarations even sooner. In them, they saw the unraveling of American society. "It is astounding how the old-fashioned ideas of self-reliance and independence seemed to have been pushed into the background by the feeling that the Government should take care of everybody," Frederick Gambrill wrote to Hoover in the middle of the controversy.[104] The Washington Board of Trade sent out a request asking communities to contain future marches before they reached the capital. By providing transportation to the initial Bonus Marchers, state governments had symbolically made the problem of relief a federal one. The White House had considered granting transport to the Bonus Marchers "nothing short of a breakdown of State Government."[105] But along with numerous individual citizens, many state governments now agreed that the country needed a federal solution to the Depression crisis.

Although the issue of adjusted compensation faded into the background, it did matter that the men who symbolized the plight of the poor were veterans. Who better to represent how far one could fall, from hero to bum, in the present economic climate? Who better to differentiate the honorable, hard-working American poor from undeserving vagrants? Moreover, if it mattered that the protesters were veterans, then the war that had given them their purpose for coming to Washington continued to be important as well. Veterans would never have attempted the march if not for the distinct, ongoing relationship the Great War had created between them and the federal government. At the very moment of their most transcending leadership, the distinct impact of the war upon their generation could still not be forgotten.

A New Administration, New Problems, and New Solutions

Like the rest of the country, veterans did not know what to expect from Franklin D. Roosevelt. In many respects, Roosevelt began where Hoover had left off, calling for a federal bank holiday and using the Reconstruction Finance Corporation to fund an array of New Deal programs.[106] In an irony that Hoover would never forget, Roosevelt promised to bring fiscal discipline back to federal finances. World War I veterans, however, intimately understood the president's desire for balanced budgets. One of Roosevelt's first pieces of legislation, the Economy Act of 1933, repealed all public laws concerning veterans' benefits. Eleven days after Congress agreed to wipe the veterans' slate clean, Roosevelt issued a set of twelve executive orders listing the benefits he intended to reinstate. In saving the country $4.6 million, Roosevelt reduced the compensation to veterans with service-related disabilities by half, struck nearly 100,000 from the disabled rolls, and eliminated veterans' general hospitalization benefits. In making these reforms, Roosevelt was again following Hoover's lead. To save administrative costs and to undercut veterans' political strength, Hoover had melded the Bureau of Pensions, National Homes for Disabled Volunteer Soldiers, and the Veterans Bureau into the new Veterans Administration.[107] By 1930, disability allowances to Civil War and Spanish-American War veterans were openly acknowledged as nothing more than old-age pensions.[108] The thought that within fifteen years, the country might have to assume the same burden for four million World War I veterans sent shivers through the Hoover administration. "They have already put the Government in the hospital business on a very large scale," warned one internal White House memo.[109] As Civil War and Spanish-American War veterans passed away, the Bureau of Pensions and National Homes for Disabled Volunteer Soldiers would stake their survival on incorporating World War I veterans into the pension system. Fighting against pensions on one front rather than three would give the White House greater odds of prevailing, argued the White House Committee on the Coordination of Veterans Matters.[110]

The reduction of benefits for disabled veterans brought an immediate outcry from veterans' organizations. The Bonus March had rendered the Legion irrelevant in veterans' politics for most of the year, but the Economy Act cuts revived it. Roosevelt's budget director, Lewis Douglas, tried to calm the waters by raising allowances slightly, but anecdotal tales of bureaucratic injustice poured into the White House mailroom. In Kansas City, for example, newly reclassified veterans released from soldiers' homes owned no civilian clothes, so they wandered away in old uniforms.[111]

The polio-stricken president gave no indication of personal concern for the heart-breaking hardships disabled ex-servicemen faced, but he eventually reacted to growing public concern that the government had deserted too many of the war wounded. Congress moved even sooner, limiting the reductions the president could make to service-related disability pensions and restoring "presumptively service-connected cases" at a reduced rate to the government rolls. For his part, Roosevelt established a Board of Veterans' Appeals in July and again raised disabled pension rates. "To speak frankly," read an internal White House memo, "we will either go this far or have something worse thrust down our throats by the next Congress."[112]

In the fall, Roosevelt found an opportunity to foster public support for his austere approach to veterans' benefits when he accepted an invitation to address the American Legion's National Convention. Roosevelt's supporters understood the long-term political advantages of making a "courageous appearance" before the Legion, especially if "the contrast with a former chief executive's attendance" stuck in the public's mind.[113] During his talk, Hoover had told veterans that "no man can doubt the character and idealism of men who have gone into the trenches in defense of their country," and asked them to show the same spirit in the present crisis.[114] Roosevelt chose a more combative tone. The president's words echoed the letters coming into the White House mailroom from supporters labeling themselves the other "90 percent of the people," "the army of the rest of us who stayed at home and bought liberty bonds," or simply the "common people."[115] The war had taught the importance of national unity, Roosevelt lectured. "The fact of wearing a uniform does not mean that he [the veteran] can demand and receive from his Government a benefit which no other citizen receives," Roosevelt asserted.[116] The president had struck the right chord, and the public congratulated him for making a stand against self-interest. "It goes back to the fundamental principle that the individual must be sacrificed for the good of the state," noted H. D. Derrick from Tennessee.[117]

For the next year, the Legion focused on restoring previous pension rates for service-connected disabilities, returning 30,000 presumptive cases to the rolls, reinstating general hospital privileges for all veterans and securing aid for the widows and orphans of enlisted men. The Legion prevailed in each case but the latter. The president's requests for the famous large-scale relief programs that characterized the New Deal shattered the budget-balancing mood in Congress, and the legislative body overrode a presidential veto to restore most of the old veterans' benefits system in 1934.[118] After a year of haggling, World War I veterans landed on their feet with only slight damages to the benefits program they had so carefully constructed since 1919. But Roosevelt also won. By vetoing the liberalizing legislation, the president got credit for taking a principled stand and had avoided discussion of adjusted compensation for more than two years.

Determined to learn from the past, Roosevelt's advisors wanted to keep the "common man" appeal of down-and-out veterans to a minimum. A 1933 bonus march drew about 3,000 veterans to Washington in May. With a stronger communist presence among them, Roosevelt had a more legitimate red card to play than Hoover had ever possessed. The president's advisors, however, chose control over combat. The government welcomed the marchers as conventioneers, and footed the bill (out of profits from the wartime newspaper *Stars and Stripes*) for accommodations on a military base ten miles from the city, food, and transportation to and from the camp. To placate the marchers, the president agreed to review the severity of Economy Act cuts and met with their leaders.[119] His wife even visited the veterans' camp at Fort Hunt. When the time came for the marchers to leave, the administration offered them some of the 25,000 places reserved for veterans in the new Civilian Conservation Corps (CCC).[120] Bonus March participants immediately took twenty-five hundred spots, and the government gave the rest train tickets home.[121] This pattern was repeated in 1934, when the last bonus army assembled in Washington.[122] Despite the urging of organizers to turn down CCC jobs and to stay put until the bonus was paid, approximately 600 of the 1,500 participants requested placement in a CCC camp as the march wound down.[123]

Veterans were now making their way to Washington year-round in a slow trickle to demand (and receive) immediate enrollment in CCC camps.[124] The director of emergency conservation work protested that veterans were breaking the rules by not applying through state unemployment offices, but the White House told him that because "of the very difficult situation caused by the veterans in Washington, it is absolutely necessary to enroll them and send them to CCC camps."[125] During 1935, the VA guaranteed placement in either a Federal Emergency Relief Administration transient camp, a Works Progress Administration (WPA) work project, or a VA hospital to the thirty veterans who came to its offices each day seeking relief.[126] These multiple options, WPA official Lawrence Westbrook noted, "will fully take care of all worthy veterans who really want to work, and any veteran who refuses to take advantage of the opportunity afforded thereunder will thereby demonstrate beyond question that they are not entitled to any assistance or consideration."[127]

For the 213,000 middle-aged veterans who spent time in the Civilian Conservation Corps during the Depression, CCC work was like stepping into a time capsule.[128] If they had downed spruce in Army-run lumbering camps, built bridges in France, or cleared forests for encampments, then much of the work they performed in the CCC was familiar to them. As during the war, a government agency decided whether one was physically fit and determined where and when one worked.[129] Enrollees once again received a serial number, vaccinations, penalties for going AWOL or deserting, and certificates of valor for acts of heroism. The requirement that three-quarters of their compensation go directly to their dependents bore more than a passing resemblance to the wartime regulation on which it was modeled.[130] The provision to pay enrollees with no designated dependents only one-fourth of their pay, with the rest going into a savings account, recalled the way wartime officials had tried to control unruly troops.

CCC officials made no claims that these jobs would give veterans a fresh start, recognizing that CCC work was unlikely to mitigate the lifelong impact of the Great War on this aging veteran cohort. Opportunities missed in youth could not now be retrieved. In sharp contrast, CCC officials claimed that the camp experience helped young men "get a start in life" by giving them a "fixed daily schedule," job training, camp schools, a chaplain, and regular physical exams. "If these men look alert, if they are courteous, willing to grasp each opportunity, if they plod ahead and do not get discouraged easily, if they have the habit of work and the attitude of cooperation, if they are good citizens, then the Civilian Conservation Corps can feel that its youth rehabilitation program has been justified," the CCC director wrote in his 1939 annual report.[131] In the 1930s, the leg up provided by work experience, the positive attitudes of employers toward CCC experience, and the chance to save money gave some young men involved in CCC work the chance to distinguish themselves from their peers. World War I veterans, however, provided living examples that the historical moment would ultimately determine whether military-style training helped a young man advance. No one thought to point out that the middle-aged veterans entering the CCC ranks had already tested the claim that military training improved career prospects.[132] Rather than raising this sticky question, the CCC ignored it. The administration wanted to use the CCC to quell veteran activism, not to confirm that serving in the wartime military had put veterans at a comparative disadvantage.[133]

Putting veterans back in military-style units may have addressed the problem of Bonus Marchers, but it did not stop the issue of immediate payment of a veterans' bonus from becoming a hot legislative topic again in 1935. The Legion now firmly favored immediate payment, and veterans writing directly to Roosevelt poked holes in his argument against adjusted compensation. "When you passed special Legislation for a particular class of farmers to destroy cotton, a particular class of wheat farmers to destroy

wheat, a particular class of hog owners last year to kill hogs, is this consistent with your policy of not wishing to aid a particular class?" queried
James Turner of South Carolina.[134] Even previous supporters of the president's position had to agree. "[G]overnmental largess in so many directions has changed my opinion," wrote M. V. Birney from his Wall Street
office.[135]

The president remained unswayed. When he vetoed the 1935 bonus bill,
he did his best to ensure that his message reached the largest possible audience by personally delivering the veto to the House of Representatives.
For the first time, millions of Americans heard a presidential veto on the
radio.[136] The high profile given to the veto announcement generated over
fifty boxes of mail to the White House rehashing the ongoing dispute over
whether or not the Great War had created a unique relationship between
the government and conscripted soldiers.

This time, however, a speech could not stop the forces gathering in
favor of immediate payment. A noticeable shift in public opinion had occurred. In a November 1935 poll, 55 percent signaled their willingness for
the government to pay the bonus.[137] By an even greater margin of four to
one, Americans receiving relief from the government supported immediate payment. Besides benefiting from the general feeling that a few million
more dollars in government expenditures did not matter any more, the
worrisome situation in Europe also swung some public sympathy back the
veterans' way. The ensuing restrictions on the American armaments trade
in the first Neutrality Act enhanced the feeling, expressed to the president
by one veteran, Herman H. Glasser, that World War I had been "a war
we were dragged into in order to protect the investments of our Napo-
leons of finance and industry who had over extended themselves in giving
credit to some of the warring nations."[138] Congressional investigations the
same year into war profiteering also created a sympathetic environment
for veterans' claims that they were still paying for the government's past
mistakes.

By 1936, a presidential election year, Congress finally had the votes to
override a presidential veto.[139] Within four months, over 98 percent of veterans had received full payment on their certificates, with interest against
loans taken after 1931 being forgiven.[140] This money only provided a temporary boost for veterans. In 1937, the number of unemployed veterans
actively seeking work dropped 30 percent, while over half of the veteran
enlistees indicated that they intended to leave their CCC jobs immediately once the bonus was paid.[141] Near capacity enrollment in the CCC

and a 12 percent veteran unemployment rate returned within two years.[142] Veterans found it easier to find jobs, however, as the economy geared up for wartime production.

Throughout the 1930s, World War I veterans served as symbols of both the plight of the common man and the danger of special interest politics. At a time when the federal government was dramatically expanding the role it played in the personal lives of individual citizens, veterans eventually became just another group seeking to clarify the government's responsibility to ensure their well-being. In 1943, World War I veterans received one last opportunity to convince American society that conscription created a unique social contract between citizen-soldiers and the federal government. This time the results were truly revolutionary.

THE GREAT WAR'S FINAL LEGACY
TO THE COUNTRY: THE GI BILL

The Servicemen's Readjustment Act (1944), commonly known as the GI Bill, is rightly celebrated for the renewal that unemployment, education, and housing loan benefits gave millions of World War II veterans. The law marked a poignant ending as well. The signing of the GI Bill two weeks after American troops landed on the Normandy beaches of France did not signal the end of their war. Instead, 1944 marked the symbolic exit of World War I veterans from the national political arena after more than twenty-five years in the public spotlight. The GI Bill is rarely remembered as the final legacy of World War I to the nation. Yet ignoring Great War veterans' authorship of the GI Bill results in an imperfect understanding of why the law took the form it did when it did. Line by line, the most comprehensive piece of social welfare legislation the United States has ever known, it illustrated in vivid detail the struggles World War I veterans had endured to give meaning to their social contract with the state. For the first and perhaps only time, wartime military service became a stepping-stone to a better life. The final legacy of World War I created one of the most prosperous, advantaged generations in American history.

Once the United States had entered World War II, ensuring that history did not repeat itself became the primary objective both of the U.S. Army and of Great War veterans. To learn from its past experiences with conscripted civilians, the General Staff ordered a series of studies of the army's previous experience with black soldiers, courts-martial, relations between American and Allied soldiers, collecting soldiers' votes, desertions, and demobilization.[1] Hoping to avoid the psychiatric breakdowns observed among shell-shocked soldiers during the Great War, the army at first tried to weed out (through induction center rejections or discharges) those who seemed predisposed to mental breakdowns. Eventually realizing that this practice created a way, so feared at the beginning of World War I, for malingerers to avoid military service, the army then reverted to the battlefield treatments used effectively twenty-five years earlier.[2] Picking up where the Morale Division had left off in 1919, the soldiers' opinion studies undertaken by Samuel Stouffer and his colleagues in the Research Branch of the Information and Education Division of the War Department provide some clues about how much influence civilian soldiers wielded within the new wartime army.[3] The Stouffer studies were vastly more sophisticated than the rudimentary efforts of previous morale investigators, but their intent was the same. Hoping to perfect the collaboration between citizen-soldiers and the army, the Stouffer group provided commanders with detailed reports of soldiers' predilections, including discussions of how some army policies had inadvertently hurt morale. The Research Branch, for example, compiled an impressive amount of evidence that infantrymen felt their branch, which bore the brunt of actual fighting, had the lowest status of any combatant service branch. As a result, the chief of staff initiated a systematic campaign to improve the prestige of the infantry by raising their pay, awarding them distinctive medals, and publicizing the feats of infantrymen throughout the service.

The racial attitudes of white soldiers continued to be important to army officials in World War II. The Research Branch's monumental finding that shared combat experiences could change racial attitudes did not affect institutional policy until after the war. In December 1944, shortages of infantry riflemen replacements in Europe compelled army officials to ask black noncombatants who had received some rifle training to volunteer as replacement riflemen in white units. These men were organized into fifty rifle platoons and distributed among white rifle companies. White officers and enlisted men spoke highly of the volunteers' performance, with over 80 percent noting that black soldiers performed "very well" in combat.[4] Although many doubted that they could live amicably on post with black troops, 93 percent of the officers questioned and 60 percent of enlisted men claimed that blacks and whites had gotten along "very well" while fighting side by side, with all others responding "fairly well." This was "in spite of the fact that two thirds of each group had begun, according to their own retrospective reports, with relatively unfavorable attitudes toward serving in a mixed company. In a similar fashion, the bulk of both groups (77 percent) reported that their feelings had become more favorable since serving in the same unit with Negro soldiers," the Stouffer group recounted.[5] White soldiers' willingness to fight with black soldiers during combat emergencies in World War II helped convince the ever-present reform faction within the army that integration was possible. After a postwar investigative committee, the Gillem Board, recommended revising army racial policy, President Harry Truman issued an executive order in 1948 guaranteeing equality of treatment and opportunity in the armed forces.[6]

Once again, the army hoped to secure veterans' postwar support for expanded defense funding, and this time, it used troop surveys to devise demobilization policies avoid to the mistakes made during World War I.[7] The Research Branch surveyed 20,000 soldiers on the most equitable way to discharge wartime troops and discovered that they wanted the army to award points to each soldier that reflected his days in combat, time overseas, number of children, and length of service. This wartime research made it possible for President Roosevelt to claim that the point system was "based on the wishes of the soldiers themselves."[8] The end of the Pacific war came sooner than expected, however, disrupting these carefully laid plans. The army was in the midst of preparing for a massive invasion of the Japanese islands when the dropping of two atomic bombs caused Japan to surrender. Scrambling to demobilize its wartime force quickly, the army soon abandoned the point system and instead released men when it no longer needed them. As in 1919, overseas soldiers were furious when their return home was delayed, and widespread protests broke out in the Pacific and Europe in 1946.[9]

The smoldering resentment of officers' privileges and court-martial practices presented one final similarity between the two world wars. In 1946, the army and public conceded that the time for permanent reform had arrived. Many of the reforms instituted by the 1946 Doolittle Board echoed proposals made after World War I by Raymond Fosdick, chairman of the Commission on Training Camp Activities.[10]

In these ways, the lessons and precedents of World War I remained relevant in the military establishment. World War I veterans, however, had little interest in monitoring the influence conscripted soldiers had within the army, even though they had set the precedents that gave these soldiers their institutional power during World War II. Instead, World War I veterans focused on ensuring that the nation learned the appropriate lessons from the adjusted compensation debacle.

Public attention turned to the problem of welcoming veterans home as early as 1943, when Roosevelt used the end of a July fireside chat on the progress of the war to warn the country against "waiting to do a hasty, insufficient and ill-considered job at the last moment."[11] Mail to the White House suggested a warm response to Roosevelt's general proposals for mustering-out pay, unemployment insurance, educational benefits, and adequate medical care. Seventy percent of those responding to a 1944 Gallup Poll even offered to pay extra taxes for these veterans' benefits.[12] However, the head of the VA, General Frank Hines, warned the president against expecting the country to let him solve the problem alone. "We again hear the same talk of high wages at home while the men are fighting abroad," Hines cautioned. These statements raised Hines's suspicions that another bonus crusade was in the making.[13] The president still opposed adjustment compensation, but he had not helped his case by acknowledging in his fireside chat that servicemen "have been compelled to make greater economic sacrifice . . . than the rest of us."

The president, it turned out, had little to fear in choosing to remain neutral during the subsequent legislative debates over the GI Bill. Rather than seizing on his words to legitimate the principles they had long espoused, American Legion officials intended to repackage these concepts to make them politically viable. This wartime generation, Harry Colmery, the original author of the GI bill and a former Legion commander, stated, "should be aided in reaching that place, position, or status which they had normally expected to achieve, and probably would have achieved, had their war service not interrupted their careers." But a new vocabulary emerged to explain the GI Bill. "How well we all know that the words adjusted compensation and pension are dynamite to many people," noted one Legion official.[14]

The American Legion's omnibus bill competed with 640 bills introduced in Congress to provide a solution to the veterans' problem.[15] The freshness of the scars inflicted over the previous twenty years surfaced when veterans came to testify before congressional subcommittees. "You can remember that you and I came back as returning heroes. Nothing was too good for us. The streets were draped with flags and the people were cheering," Congressman Errett Scrivner (R-Kans.) recalled to Omar Ketchum, commander of the VFW. "That was the first day," Ketchum interjected. "Well, within the first month," Scrivner replied. "But it was not long after that that we were called every name under the sun."[16] On the Senate side, American Legion Commander Warren Atherton spoke with confidence to the committee chair. "You, Senator [Bennett] Clark [D-Miss.]," he said, "having been the first national commander of the American Legion and knowing the conditions which prevailed for returning World War I veterans in 1917–18, realize the value of making this preparation."[17]

No one present at these hearings disputed the need to plan properly this time around for the ex-servicemen's return to society. What they were guarding against, however, depended on how one interpreted the preceding twenty-four years. For some advocates, the revolutionary potential evident in the soldiers' demonstrations of 1919 and the Bonus March necessitated keeping as many veterans as possible off the streets.[18] The type of law Congress passed, Colmery told the Senate subcommittee holding hearings, would determine if this veteran generation would be a "force for good or evil in the years to come."[19] Others, however, worried about a backlash if the benefits were too generous. The Disabled American Veterans (DAV) preferred to call the Legion's omnibus bill "the ominous bill." Chairman Millard Rice warned that "if the wrong approach is made toward the solution of the economic needs of millions of able-bodied veterans . . . then I fear that the ultimate result, some years from now, would be another Economy Act."[20] "Ominous" also summed up the feelings of those who feared the return of the Depression's dark days. Educational benefits, they argued, might slow the reentry of veterans into the job market.

The Legion had some dramatic moments after ignoring advice that it chop up its GI Bill into more manageable chunks, rather than continue to press for a complete benefits package. In March, at the request of five smaller veterans' organizations, several congressmen introduced an adjusted compensation bill in lieu of the GI Bill of Rights.[21] With this division in veterans' ranks threatening to confuse the nation over which path to pursue, the Legion rallied its members to make their wishes known. Behind-the-scenes negotiations brought the VFW into line behind the Legion bill.[22] The Legion worked diligently to organize a grass-roots campaign and prepared promotional materials for its 12,000 posts to use in rallying local support. Posts received suggested radio interviews, press releases, and letters and telegrams for congressmen, as well as short trailer films for legionnaires to take to the local movie theater.[23] The earlier decision of the Hearst newspaper chain to support the bill as a way to highlight the shortcomings of the Roosevelt administration's social welfare programs also helped influence public opinion in favor of the proposal.[24] Inside the Legion command center in Washington, members mounted a huge wall chart to portray the results of their daily canvas of Congress and the work of the 149 House members who belonged to the Legion. On May 10, in a well-publicized ceremony on the steps of the Capitol, Legion officials delivered petitions bearing a million signatures to the House leadership.[25]

Congressman John Rankin (D-Miss.), a legionnaire, who chaired the House World War Veterans' Legislation Committee, provided the most gripping, nail-biting moments. The Senate passed an omnibus bill on March 24, but the House version remained mired in Rankin's committee until May 3. In April, the Mississippi congressman focused his objections on the bill's unemployment provisions. In public hearings, he recalled the "goldbrickers" he had known during World War I who would have relished a chance to loaf at government expense.[26] Privately, Legion officials noted that, in executive sessions, Rankin was "using the line that it will result in too high remuneration without work for Negro veterans in the South."[27] Rankin also wondered aloud whether adjusted compensation better served former farmers from the South and West who had no intention of attending college. Throughout this period, the Legion worked hard writing compromise drafts to appease Rankin. The draft of the bill finally reported out of Rankin's committee on May 3 limited educational and employment benefits and raised the maximum loan amount.[28] The version that passed the House 387–0 on May 18 sharpened these modifications.

In the joint Senate-House Conference Committee created to hammer out differences between the two omnibus bills, compromise came quickly on education and loan benefits. Deadlock soon developed, however, over a relatively minor issue: whether or not the VA should have supervisory or administrative responsibility over the Veterans' Employment Service.[29] With the final conference committee vote set for the morning of June 10, 1944, Rankin refused to cast the proxy vote of an absent member in favor of supervisory responsibility. Legion officials raced to track down Congressman John S. Gibson, a Democrat who had returned to Georgia. Those enlisted in the search included a telephone operator, who rang his house every fifteen minutes, a local radio station, which put out a news alert for Gibson to call home, and the state police, who went on the lookout for his car.[30] Returning home late in the evening after spending the day hunting, Gibson agreed to take an army flight back to Washington from nearby Waycross air base. This plan fell through when the only available plane succumbed to mechanical problems, but the officer in charge provided a car to a commercial air field in Jacksonville, Florida. After boarding a 2:20 A.M. flight to Washington, Gibson arrived in time to cast the key vote.[31] In the final version of the bill, a board chaired by the administrator of Veterans' Affairs was established to monitor veterans' job placement by the U.S. Employment Service.

The housing loan and unemployment compensation provisions of the GI Bill clearly owed a debt to New Deal innovations such as the long-term, low-interest mortgages first offered in 1933 by the Home Owners Loan Corporation, the unemployment compensation provisions of the 1935 Social Security Act, and the creation of the 1933 Veterans' Employment Service within the U.S. Employment Service. The largesse of the New Deal years also made the proposal seem less like special class legislation (the main objection FDR had to paying the bonus early), and more like a subset of the general social welfare assistance now available to Americans classified as deserving poor. The public and government intended simply to enfold veterans in the system of entitlements available to a broad cross-section of Americans. Dixon Wecter, in his pathbreaking study of veterans in 1944, spoke for the majority of Americans when he refused to see GI Bill–granted access to national health care as special class legislation. Wecter argued that the "broader ideas of social responsibility which have sprung with the New Deal" made national health insurance inevitable, "which means that [soon] the ex-soldier as civilian will share a universal protection."[32] Although influential commentators like Wecter denied veterans the right to special entitlements, the notion of them as a specially disabled group had stuck. "The fact that selective service has become the basis for recruiting our armed forces—that a man's losses in time, opportunity, or health while in the service are no longer voluntary but risks exacted by the State—has fostered a greater sense of Federal responsibility in his retraining and reemployment," Wecter wrote.[33] Foreshadowing the debate that would swirl around affirmative action programs in the late twentieth century, the question centered on whether veterans' benefits restored equality by rectifying past injustices or whether they bestowed advantages and created a specially entitled class. The public had sanctioned adjustment compensation as the former in the 1920s and rejected the bonus as the latter after the Bonus March. Commentators like Wecter soothed Americans with the idea that the majority of the benefits provided by the GI Bill simply leveled the playing field that the selective service system had made uneven, and that the remainder would soon be extended to non-veterans. In reality, the legislation created the most privileged generation in American history.

The GI Bill went further than any previous New Deal program by providing equal benefits without regard to class, race, gender, or (by 1945) age. The access to free medical care and bonus payments that had set World War I veterans apart paled in comparison to the way the GI Bill established the veteran as a unique social class in American society. State laws governing mortgages became irrelevant to 3.7 million working-class veterans, who needed no down payment to acquire a house in the new suburban subdivisions, and to thousands of others seeking a farm or a business. Federal Housing Administration restrictions that only approved loans for homes in areas with electricity and sewers did not apply to veterans.[34] Female veterans had independent access to benefits for themselves and their children, unlike their civilian counterparts, whose social security benefits depended on whether or not their husbands lived at home. The law provided the same unemployment benefits for all veterans, regardless of what line of work they intended to pursue after the war. This provision overrode state and federal laws that denied unemployment compensation to agricultural and domestic workers, rules that effectively excluded many blacks and Hispanics from receiving jobless benefits. The GI Bill also set up a system of federally administered unemployment benefits at a standard rate of twenty dollars a week for veterans, in contrast to state rates for civilians that varied from two to twenty-two dollars weekly.[35] Overall, 9 million veterans received unemployment benefits after the war, although the average of seventeen weeks' assistance fell far below the fifty-two weeks allowed.[36] Only one exception existed to these efforts to ensure that all veterans had full use of these benefits to recover their financial losses: Congress refused to grant unemployment compensation to veterans who participated in strikes. Veterans did, however, gain the right to turn down a scab job without jeopardizing their unemployment rights. There would be no repeat of state employment bureaus sending ex-servicemen to break strikes as they had in 1919.[37]

It is hard to exaggerate the importance of the GI Bill in twentieth-century American history. For the first time, serving in the wartime military became a way to enter the middle class. The economic stability provided by the GI Bill in education, home ownership, and medical care came at the right historical moment in the life of both individuals and the nation.[38] Until amended in 1945, the initial law required veterans who

entered the service after age twenty-five to prove that the war had interrupted their education in order to receive more than a year of educational
benefits.[39] The original bill's creators correctly concluded that younger veterans had the best chance of using education to repair their civilian lives.[40]
Colmery warned that "many of the older group taken under selective service, leaving wife and children and sacrificing position and business[,] may
have a more serious problem of readjustment than the younger ones."[41]
The GI Bill's expansion of the VA's hospital system, coupled with easier
access to government health care in the next few years, proved to be a more
substantial way to help older veterans.[42] Paradoxically, the men who had
entered military service later in life had more health problems throughout
their lives, even though they were less likely than younger recruits to have
experienced combat in World War II.[43]

University education helped younger veterans advance because this opportunity came along at the right personal and historical moment. Giving
free college tuition to men who as a group averaged only a sixth grade
education would have made little sense after World War I. The discovery
of this educational deficit, coupled with stricter child labor laws, had encouraged a new domestic emphasis on education in the interwar years.
By World War II, the average serviceman had completed the second year
of high school. This veteran could readily see how military service had
prevented him from finishing high school or attending a college or technical school.[44] Approximately 80 percent of the 2.2 million veterans who
received a GI Bill–sponsored college education were returning students,
while 5.4 million took vocational job training courses.[45] An education as
an engineer, accountant, or even a plumber meant little, however, without
a job after graduation. Defying all predictions forecasting a new Depression, educated World War II veterans benefited from and contributed to a
postwar economic boom that kept the unemployment rate below 5 percent.
The singularity of this historical moment is underscored by life-course research on the Vietnam War. Military service did not have the same positive
effect on the socioeconomic status of Vietnam veterans. Substantial aid
to college-bound students in the 1960s and 1970s and scaled-back veterans' benefits meant that military service once again became time lost for
veterans rather than the path to increased occupational and educational
opportunities.[46]

As expected, the issue of adjusted compensation came up again after
World War II, but the bonus concept had been discredited by its ineffec-
tiveness as a relief measure and its earlier role in rallying veterans against

the government, and little came of such proposals.[47] The concept of compensating veterans for the hardships of living overseas and for the length of time they spent away from high-paying civilian wartime jobs remained relevant, however. The amount of mustering-out pay, for instance, differed for those serving at home and overseas, while education and unemployment benefits depended upon the length of one's service.[48]

The only adjustment to wartime service pay came after returned soldiers learned that the army had paid officers for furlough days not taken when they left the service. Congress retroactively adjusted enlisted men's wartime wages to include unused furlough days by giving them a bond that matured in five years.[49] Recognizing that a bond in lieu of cash left a sour taste in the mouths of those who remembered the Bonus March, Congress agreed in 1947 to let veterans redeem their bonds immediately. As a result of their fathers' hard work planning their homecoming, World War II veterans expressed overwhelming satisfaction with the help given to them by the federal government.[50]

World War I veterans had made a long and difficult journey from 1917 to 1944 to establish the principle that total war gave soldiers and the state a mutual obligation to ensure each other a safe and prosperous future. Starting with adjusted compensation and ending with the GI Bill, World War I veterans forced the government to accept responsibility for redistributing profits and opportunities from advantaged civilians to disadvantaged veterans in the aftermath of total war. The executive branch found itself transformed forever by its experience in conscripting a mass national army to fight the Great War. World War I soldiers shaped critical policies and practices of the army and modern state, and created the piece of social welfare legislation that played a key role in generating the unprecedented prosperity Americans enjoyed in the second half of the twentieth century.

NOTES

Introduction

1. In April 1918, all distinctions between regular army, National Guard, and national army (conscripted) divisions were formally eliminated and all became units of the United States Army.

2. The total force raised during the war numbered 4,412,533, including 3,893,340 soldiers, 462,229 sailors, 54,690 marines, and 2,294 Coast Guard troops. Of the 3,893,340 soldiers, 2,810,296 (72%) were conscripted. Office of the Provost Marshal General, *Second Report of the Provost Marshal General to the Secretary of War on the Operations of the Selective Service System to December 20, 1918* (Washington, D.C.: GPO, 1919), p. 227.

3. John W. Chambers, *To Raise an Army: The Draft Comes to Modern America* (New York: Free Press, 1987), pp. 41–71.

4. Ibid.; Eliot A. Cohen, *Citizens and Soldiers: The Dilemmas of Military Service* (Ithaca, N.Y.: Cornell University Press, 1985); David R. Segal, *Recruiting For Uncle Sam: Citizenship and Military Manpower Policy* (Lawrence: University Press of Kansas, 1989).

5. Chambers, *To Raise an Army*, pp. 136–38, 167–70.

6. Harold Wool, *The Military Specialist: Skilled Manpower for the Armed Forces* (Baltimore: Johns Hopkins Press, 1968).

1. Establishing a National Army

1. The Selective Service system contained five classifications. Class I was composed of men eligible to serve immediately. Class II and III included temporarily deferred married men and skilled workers in industry and agriculture; Class IV contained married men with economic dependents and key business leaders, while those unable to meet physical and mental requirements were placed in Class V. After December 15,

1917, Class I registrants with the appropriate skills could still volunteer for the Surgeon General's, Engineers, Signal, and Quartermaster's branches. Draft-eligible men could enlist in the navy or marines until July 27, 1918. All voluntary enlistment ceased in August 1918. At the end of the same month, Congress extended the draft-eligible ages from 21–30 to 18–45. John W. Chambers, *To Raise an Army: The Draft Comes to Modern America* (New York: Free Press, 1987), p. 191. Office of the Provost Marshal General, *Second Report of the Provost Marshal General to the Secretary of War on the Operations of the Selective Service System to December 20, 1918* (Washington, D.C.: GPO, 1919), pp. 22, 227.

2. John Dickinson, *The Building of an Army: A Detailed Account of Legislation, Administration and Opinion in the United States, 1915–1920* (New York: Century, 1922), pp. 90–92. Men enlisted in large numbers from northern urban areas, where support for the war and conscription was strongest, while few volunteered from dissenting sections of the Midwest and South.

3. Sgt. Henry Charles Ward, 343rd Field Artillery, 90th Division, memoir, p. 4. World War I Survey, U.S. Army Military History Institute Archives, Carlisle Barracks, Carlisle, Pa. (hereafter WWI, Carlisle—unless otherwise noted, the citation is a veteran's response to a retrospective questionnaire).

4. The General Staff training committee was formulated first as part of the War College Division, then became an independent bureau, the War Plans Division, in 1918.

5. Memorandum for the chief of staff, Nov. 3, 1917, p. 2, file # 8568-20; General Correspondence, 1903-19 (entry 296); War College Division and War Plans Division, 1900-1942; Textual Records of the War Department General and Special Staffs, Record Group 165 (hereafter 296/165, NA); National Archives, College Park, Md.

6. "General Court-Martial in the American Expeditionary Forces (AEF)," from Brig. Gen. W. A. Bethal, judge adv. gen., to Gen. John J. Pershing, Aug. 7, 1919, "Reports, Misc." folder, box 172. John J. Pershing Papers, Library of Congress (hereafter Pershing Papers, LOC).

7. Memorandum for the chief of staff, Feb. 4, 1918, p. 3, file # 8568-37; 296/165, NA.

8. By the end of the war, even regular army observers concluded that most men who deserted from the army in the first few months of the war did not understand the seriousness of this offense. 1st Lt. R. C. Shaw, "Analysis of the Causes of 200 Desertion Cases," Feb. 7, 1919, file # 1150, box 145; General Correspondence, 1917–21 (entry 8); Office of the Chief of Staff; Textual Records of the War Department General and Special Staffs, Record Group 165 (hereafter 8/165, NA); National Archives, College Park, Md.

9. Gen. Johnson Hagood, diary, vol. 1, Sept. 24–Oct. 23, 1917, p. 15. Manuscript Collection, U.S. Army Military History Institute Archives, Carlisle Barracks, Carlisle, Pa. (hereafter Manuscripts, Carlisle).

10. Cpl. Paul Murphy, 309th Infantry, 78th Division, "An Account of My Personal Experience in World War I," Apr. 1, 1963, p. 9. WWI, Carlisle.

11. Memorandum for Captain Perkins from Capt. E. R. Padgett, Aug. 30, 1918, Camp Meade file, box A10; Correspondence Relating to Morale at Army Installa-

tions (entry 377); War College Division and War Plans Division, 1900–1942; Textual Records of the War Department General and Special Staffs, Record Group 165 (hereafter 377/165, NA); National Archives, College Park, Md. Col. Henry Shaw to the surgeon general, Dec. 12, 1917, p. 6, file # 702, box 1090, Decimal Correspondence File, 1917–25 (entry 37); General Records of the Adjutant General's Office, Record Group 407 (hereafter 37/407, NA); National Archives, College Park, Md.

12. Pvt. Oscar Carl Heig, 332nd Machine Gun Battalion, 86th Division. WWI, Carlisle.

13. Pvt. Henry L. Henderson, 358th Infantry, 90th Division, diary. WWI, Carlisle.

14. Col. E. G. Payton, quoted in "Control of Men as Part of an Officer's Training," May 5, 1929, file # 357-18, Army War College Curriculum Files. U.S. Army Military History Institute Archives, Carlisle Barracks, Carlisle, Pa. (hereafter Curriculum, Carlisle). "A Study in Morale," Jan. 30, 1919, Camp Grant File; 377/165, NA.

15. Memorandum for Captain Perkins, Aug. 30, 1918, Camp Meade file; 377/165, NA.

16. 1st Lt. Milton E. Bernet, 314th Supply Train, 89th Division, "The World War—As I Saw It," p. 34. WWI, Carlisle.

17. Greager Clover to father, July 31, 1917, "The Great War from the Point of View of the Virginia Soldier," p. 242. Miscellaneous letters and diaries, box 6, Virginia War History Commission; Virginia State Archives, Richmond, Va. (hereafter Virginia State Archives).

18. Having underestimated its own need for skilled men and overestimated the number of relevantly skilled men available from the draft, the army allowed men to volunteer for specialist training courses in colleges throughout the country offered during the entire war. Chief WO Hartley S. Newman, "A Study on Student Army Training Corps WWI," Sept. 1942, file # 7200-DD, p. 60, Thomas File; Records of the Historical Section . . . (entry 310); War College Division and War Plans Division, 1900–42; Textual Records of the War Department General and Special Staffs, Record Group 165 (hereafter 310/165, NA); National Archives, College Park, Md.

19. Pvt. Robinson Shepard, 301st Signal Battalion, 76th Division, "Memories of World War I." WWI, Carlisle.

20. Pvt. George A. Prentice, 104th Infantry, 26th Division, diary. WWI, Carlisle.

21. In addition to the officers trained directly by the army, technical and specialist agencies commissioned 70,000 civilians who were experts in their respective fields, while the army promoted 16,000 soldiers from the ranks. Edward Coffman, *The War to End All Wars: The American Military Experience in World War I* (New York: Oxford University Press, 1968), pp. 55–58.

22. Samuel Gompers, president, American Federation of Labor, to Baker, June 12, 1917, pp. 3–4, "G, 1917" folder. Newton E. Baker Papers, Library of Congress (hereafter Baker Papers, LOC).

23. Memorandum for the chief of staff, June 16, 1917, "G, 1917" folder. Baker Papers, LOC.

24. Russell Weigley, *History of the United States Army* (New York: Macmillan, 1967) and *Towards an American Army: Military Thought from Washington to Marshall* (New

York: Columbia University Press, 1962); Walter Millis, *Arms and Men: A Study in American Military History* (New York: G. P. Putnam, 1956).

25. Lt. Col. R. G. Peck to commanding general, 1st Army, Oct. 12, 1918, file # 1602; Reports, Studies, Monographs . . . of the First Army in France During World War I, Historical File, 1917–19 (entry 24); Office of the Commander-in-Chief, 1917–20; Textual Records of the AEF, 1917–23, Record Group 120 (hereafter 24/120, NA); National Archives, College Park, Md. Memorandum for the chief of staff, Dec. 8, 1917, file # 10049-15; 296/165, NA.

26. Provost Marshal General, *Second Report*, pp. 110–14. See also Chambers, *To Raise An Army*, pp. 196–98.

27. Provost Marshal General, *Second Report*, p. 115.

28. Memorandum for the chief of staff, Mar. 30, 1918, p. 1, file # 10871-2; 296/165, NA. See also Maj. Charles H. Collins, "Farm Labor in Wartime, 1917–1918," Feb. 15, 1943, file # 7200-OO, Thomas File; 310/165, NA.

29. "Outside Camp News," Foreign Speaking Soldiers Bulletin, June 6, 1918, file # 10564-47; Security Classified Correspondence and Reports, 1917–41 (entry 65); Office of the Director of Intelligence (G-2), 1906–49; Textual Records of the War Department General and Special Staffs, Record Group 165 (hereafter 65/165, NA); National Archives, College Park, Md.

30. "Inside the Camp News," June 5, 1918, file # 10564-47 (10); 65/165, NA.

31. Intelligence officer, Camp Hancock, Ga., to chief, Military Morale Section, Aug. 19, 1918, file # 80-106; 65/165, NA.

32. Chief, Military Intelligence Section, to K. W. Strzelec, Feb. 6, 1918, file # 10565-37; 296/165, NA. Transcript of captured intelligence report from 7th German Army, June 17, 1918, file # 80-71; 65/165, NA.

33. The postwar army subsequently used the "foreign-speaking" soldier issue to solicit support from civilian voters. Recruit Educational Centers that Americanized alien recruits became a major, and well-publicized, part of the army's postwar expansion plan. The War Plans Division expected the idea to "meet with nationwide approval, since it makes for better citizenship and for a higher order of Americanism." Memorandum for the adj. gen., July 29, 1919, p. 2, file # 7519-154; 296/165, NA.

34. The war ended before organization of these units was complete. Memorandum for the chief of staff, May 17, 1918, file # 10050-168. Memorandum for the adj. gen., July 31, 1918, file # 10762-21. Memorandum for the chief of staff, Oct. 21, 1918, file # 10762-35. All in 296/165, NA.

35. Nancy Gentile Ford, " 'Mindful of the Traditions of His Race': Dual Identity and Foreign-Born Soldiers in the First World War American Army," *Journal of American Ethnic History* 16, no. 2 (1997): 35–57.

36. Russell Lawrence Barsh, "American Indians in the Great War," *Ethnohistory* 38, no. 3 (1991): 276–303; Thomas Anthony Britten, "American Indians in World War I: Military Service as Catalyst for Reform" (Ph.D. diss., Texas Tech University, 1994). These authors credit the stereotypes of Indians as natural warriors for the acceptance of Native Americans by white soldiers. Separate Indian units had been tried, and dis-

carded, in the 1890s. Most Indian groups resisted segregation as contrary to their goals of assimilation. They also worried that segregation would lead to a reclassification of Indians from white to colored. Bruce W. White, "The American Indian as a Soldier, 1890–1919," *Canadian Review of American Studies* 7 (1976): 15–25.

37. Army officials resisted commissioning any more than the one class of black officer candidates who attended the Fort Des Moines Camp because they believed that racially inferior black men were incapable of leading, that it was impossible to assign equally ranked white and black officers to the same command, and that the number of college-educated black men was too small to justify another camp. Memorandums for the chief of staff, June 12, 1918, file # 8142-150, and Aug. 31, 1917, file # 8142-18, both in 296/165, NA.

38. Memorandum for the chief of staff, July 31, 1917, file # 8142-13; 296/165, NA.

39. The army had encountered similar opposition from civilian communities when it closed frontier posts after 1890 and assigned black regular army regiments closer to established communities. Black soldiers entered these towns at a time when recently passed segregating and disenfranchising legislation had heightened racial animosities. Black troops further destabilized race relations when they refused to obey these new Jim Crow laws. In 1906, without a trial, the army discharged 167 black regular army soldiers accused of raiding and killing civilians in Brownsville, Texas. Marvin Fletcher, *The Black Soldier and Officer in the U.S. Army, 1891–1917* (Columbia: University of Missouri Press, 1974).

40. Memorandum for the secretary of war, Aug. 21, 1917, file # 8142-17; 296/165, NA.

41. W. E. B. Du Bois, *Darkwater*, p. 602, in *The Oxford W. E. B. Du Bois Reader*, ed. Eric J. Sundquist (New York: Oxford University Press, 1996).

42. Memorandum for the secretary of war, Aug. 24, 1917, file # 8142-17.

43. Robert V. Haynes, *A Night of Violence: The Houston Riot of 1917* (Baton Rouge: Louisiana State University Press, 1976).

44. Arthur Barbeau, Florette Henri, and Bernard Nalty have meticulously documented the harsh discrimination and abuse black soldiers faced, a direct outcome, they conclude, of the prejudiced and stereotypical image policymakers had of blacks. See Arthur Barbeau and Florette Henri, *The Unknown Soldiers: Black American Troops in World War I* (Philadelphia: Temple University Press, 1974), and Bernard C. Nalty, *Strength for the Fight: A History of Black Americans in the Military* (New York: Free Press, 1986).

45. Barbeau and Henri, *Unknown Soldiers;* Nalty, *Strength for the Fight.*

46. Congressman R. Y. Thomas, Jr. (D-Ky.) to President Woodrow Wilson, Feb. 20, 1918, file # 3735, ser. 4. Woodrow Wilson Papers, Library of Congress (hereafter Wilson Papers, LOC).

47. Col. Hugh Johnson, deputy provost marshal general, to Wilson, Feb. 23, 1918, file # 3735, ser. 4. Wilson Papers, LOC.

48. Pioneer infantry units were trained to work just behind the front at work that required more technical skill than the tasks labor units performed. These troops needed

some infantry training so that they could fight as last resort reserves or defend themselves if overrun during an enemy offensive. Memorandum for the chief of staff, July 21,
1918, file # 8142-176; 296/165, NA.

49. In *Making Men Moral: Social Engineering During the Great War* (New York:
New York University Press, 1996), Nancy Bristow offers a compelling look at the complex relationship that total war created between the federal government and local
communities through the CTCA. Especially noteworthy is Bristow's conclusion that
CTCA reformers were partly responsible for the general demise of Progressive reform
after the war. Progressives were long seen as the victims of a postwar backlash against
democratic idealism, but Bristow provides a case study of Progressives whose zeal-
ousness in backing their cultural vision with the power of the state caused alarm. See
also Jennifer Diane Keene, "The Fight for Fitness: Athletic Training Among Enlisted
Men in World War I" (MA thesis, George Washington University, 1987).

50. A copy of this form letter from 1st Lt. Marion C. Patton, 327th Field Artillery,
to Henry Moss, St. Paul, Minn., Feb. 14, 1919, is in Eugene A. Moss, 84th Division,
WWI, Carlisle.

51. Charles Davenport and Albert G. Love, *Defects Found in Drafted Men: Statistical Information Compiled from Draft Records* (printed for use of the Senate Committee
on Military Affairs, 66th Cong., 1st sess., Washington, D.C., 1919), p. 74.

52. Observations of Maj. George Draper in Memorandum for the chief of staff,
July 26, 1918, file # 7541-117; 296/165, NA.

53. "Replacement of Personnel in the A.E.F.," p. 10, file # 3347, Thomas File;
310/165, NA. Leonard Lerwill, *The Personnel Replacement System in the United States
Army*, Dept. of the Army Pamphlet no. 20-211 (Washington, D.C.: Dept. of the Army,
1954), pp. 174–76.

54. Memorandum for the director of operations, General Staff, Nov. 20, 1918, file
10773-116; 296/165, NA.

55. U.S. Surgeon General, *Physical Examination of the First Million Draft Recruits:
Methods and Results*, Bulletin No. 11 (Washington, D.C.: GPO, 1919), p. 140.

56. Memorandums for the chief of staff, Mar. 12, 1918, file # 9796-172, and Mar. 8,
1918, file # 7431-19, both in 296/165, NA.

57. Col. Henry A. Shaw, Medical Corps, to the surgeon general, Dec. 12, 1917, file
702, box 1090; 37/407, NA.

58. Memorandum for the chief of staff, June 18, 1918, pp. 5, 14, file # 10195-25;
296/165, NA.

59. John Carson, "Army Alpha, Army Brass, and the Search for Army Intelligence," *Isis* 84, no. 2 (1993): 278–309.

60. 1st Lt. Edwin Spies to adj., Training School for Sanitary Troops, First Depot
Division, Oct. 3, 1918, file # 353, box 821; 37/407, NA.

61. "Negro Personnel in the War," Statistical Section Report # 138, Army War College Library. Brig. Gen. Paul B. Malone, "Report on Education," folder # 268; "Reports of the Commander in Chief . . . World War I" (entry 22); Office of the Commander in Chief, 1917–20; Textual Records of the AEF, 1917–23, Record Group 120
(hereafter 22/120, NA); National Archives, College Park, Md.

62. Maj. William S. Foster, "Data Relating to Illiteracy in the Drafted Army," file # 758, Thomas File; 310/165, NA.

63. Brig. Gen. Hugh S. Johnson, "Draft Problems," file # 287A-22. Curriculum, Carlisle. Guy V. Henry, Jr., autobiography MS. Guy V. Henry Papers, Manuscripts, Carlisle.

64. For discussion of the ways in which propaganda purportedly influenced soldiers' views of the war, see Mark Meigs, *Optimism at Armageddon: Voices of American Participants in the First World War* (New York: New York University Press, 1997).

65. Course at the Army War College, 1935–36, Subject: Morale, file # 1-1936-6, p. 65. Curriculum, Carlisle. Pvt. Joseph M. Cunningham, 101st Field Artillery, 26th Division, memoir. WWI, Carlisle.

66. Baker to Wilson, July 11, 1919, "W, 1919" folder. Baker Papers, LOC.

67. Baker to Wilson, Oct. 1, 1917, "W, 1917" folder. Baker Papers, LOC.

68. It is difficult to ascertain how representative the class background of the drafted population was of the population at large. Limited surveys of combatant units after the war revealed the predominantly unskilled and rural backgrounds of drafted troops, which, Fred Baldwin argues, accurately reflected the overall working-class character of American society at this time. See Fred Baldwin, "The Enlisted Man During World War I" (Ph.D. diss., Princeton University, 1964), p. 58, and all of ch. 2.

69. Clarence J. Bertler, Camp Headquarters, Camp Grant, Ill., letter to U.S. Army Military History Institute, Mar. 1, 1989. WWI, Carlisle.

70. Memorandums for the chief of staff, May 28, 1918, file # 10195-20, and July 29, 1918, file # 7519-122, both in 296/165, NA. Lt. Col. H. E. Stephenson, "Procurement of Occupational Specialists by Selective Service in the World War," Oct. 7, 1932, lecture at the Army War College. Curriculum, Carlisle.

71. Bernet, "World War—As I Saw It" (cited n. 16 above), p. 128.

72. Terrance Gough, "The Battle of Washington: Soldiers and Businessmen in World War I" (Ph.D. diss., University of Virginia, 1997), pp. 449–67, 523–24.

73. Paul A. C. Koistinen, *Mobilizing for Modern War: The Political Economy of American Warfare, 1865–1919* (Lawrence: University Press of Kansas, 1997), pp. 244–53.

74. Gough, "Battle of Washington," p. 538.

75. Bernet, "World War—As I Saw It," p. 10.

76. Henry Warren Jones, Headquarters Co., 90th Division, letter, Oct. 7, 1917. Sgt. Joseph Correll, Headquarters Co., 80th Division. Both in WWI, Carlisle.

77. Sgt. Henry Charles Ward, 343rd Artillery, 90th Division, memoirs, p. 16. Sgt. Frank Grace, 346th Infantry, 87th Division, letter to mother, June 20, 1918. Both in WWI, Carlisle. "The Individual Mind in Relation to Military Service," Memorandum for the director, G-1, Oct. 9, 1927. Curriculum, Carlisle.

78. 1st Lt. Billie E. Paul, Camp Shelby, Miss., to chief, Military Morale Section, Dec. 14, 1918, file # 10218-244; 65/165, NA.

79. Intelligence officer, Camp Jackson, S.C., to chief, Military Morale Section, Dec. 2, 1918, file # 10218-244 (80). Intelligence officer, Camp Meade, to chief, Military Morale Section, Oct. 30, 1918, file # 10218-244 (10). For more positive assessments, see

memorandums to chief, Military Morale Section, Oct. 31, 1918, file # 10218-244 (23), and file # 10218-244 (5). All in 65/165, NA.

80. Capt. Wilson L. Townsend, intelligence officer, Camp Logan, Tex., to chief, Military Morale Section, Dec. 2, 1918, file # 10218-244 (58); 65/165, NA.

81. Maj. W. H. Loving to chief, Military Morale Section, Nov. 2, 1918, file # 10218-280; 65/165, NA.

82. Le Mans intelligence report to Capt. Charles D. Gentsch, G-2, 83rd Division, Oct. 31, 1918; Reports Relating to the Morale of American Troops, 1917–18 (entry 195); General Staff, 1917–19; Textual Records of the AEF, 1917–23, Record Group 120 (hereafter 195/120, NA); National Archives, College Park, Md.

83. Cpl. Kenneth W. Jones, 316th Sanitary Train, 91st Division, "Memories of World War I," p. 61. WWI, Carlisle.

84. Sgt. Antonio E. McAdam, 315th Sanitary Train, 90th Division. WWI, Carlisle.

85. Cpl. Edward August Schafer, 102nd Infantry, 26th Division, memoirs, p. 8. WWI, Carlisle.

2. Americans as Warriors

1. Memorandum for chief of staff, Oct. 30, 1917, file # 639-173; memorandum from adj. gen. to all department commanders, Nov. 23, 1917, file # 639-174; memorandum from adj. gen., "Enforcing Training Requirements," Jan. 4, 1918, file # 7541-66. All in 296/165, NA.

2. Col. H. O. Williams, insp. gen., to adj. gen., July 31, 1918, "WD—Camp Sherman—Report of Inspection" folder, box 207; 310/165, NA.

3. Abstract of Inspection Report, 3rd Division, April 6, 1918, file # 10896-2; 296/165, NA. Maj. H. B. Fiske, "Training in the A.E.F.," lecture at the Army War College, Apr. 21, 1920, pp. 10–11, file # 215-70. Curriculum, Carlisle.

4. Pvt. William Graf, 315th Sanitary Train, 90th Division, "My Experience in the Army During World War I." Capt. Roy E. Meyers, 114th Field Artillery, 30th Division, diary. Sgt. Charles R. Blatt, 305th Engineers, 80th Division, "Over There with the Eightieth." All in WWI, Carlisle.

5. Memorandum for the insp. gen., July 31, 1918, file # 7431-71; 296/165, NA.

6. Sgt. Richard McBride, Sr., 328th Infantry, 82nd Division, "Passing in Review: Memoirs of World War I." Cpl. Kenneth W. Jones, 316th Sanitary Train, 91st Division, "Memories of World War I." Both in WWI, Carlisle. Memorandum to the insp. gen., Apr. 6, 1918, file # 10896-2; 296/165, NA.

7. Course at the Army War College, 1935–36, Subject: Morale, file # 1-1936-6. Curriculum, Carlisle. Brig. Gen. H. B. Fiske, assistant chief of staff, G-5, AEF, "Report of G-5," June 30, 1919, pp. 31–33, folder # 215; 22/120, NA.

8. Secret bulletin to First Division, Aug. 11, 1918, "First Division: Memoranda and Instructions" folder, box 14, Charles P. Summerall Papers, Library of Congress (hereafter Summerall Papers, LOC). A three-month divisional training program in France to acclimate troops to conditions on the Western Front was supposed to follow a four-month stateside training program, but few soldiers received this much training.

9. "Catechismal Edition Infantry Drill Regulations: Corrected to November 1,

1917," and "Infantry Drill Regulations: Corrected to May 6, 1918," quoted in Kenneth E. Hamburger, *Learning Lessons in the American Expeditionary Forces* (Washington, D.C.: U.S. Army Center of Military History, 1997), pp. 23–24.

10. Pvt. Jack Walter Ninneman, 23rd Engineers. WWI, Carlisle.

11. Col. J. G. Hannah, "Inspection of Camp Greene," box 207; 310/165, NA.

12. Harold Wool, *The Military Specialist: Skilled Manpower for the Armed Forces* (Baltimore: Johns Hopkins Press, 1968), pp. 17, 195. By Wool's definition, all infantry, artillery, cavalry and armor units contain only line combat positions. Wool describes craftsmen as soldiers with skills in trades like construction or metalwork, while technicians included telegraph and telephone operators and medical attendants. The World War I U.S. Army contained, Wool estimates, 1,234,000 ground combat troops (39.6%); 853,000 service workers (27.4%); 421,000 craftsmen (13.5%); 232,000 mechanics and repairmen (7.4%); 211,000 technical troops (6.8%); and 164,000 administrative troops (5.3%). He does not include the 549,000 unclassified recruits still training at the end of the war in his calculations.

13. Col. P. S. Bond, 107th Engineers, 32nd Division, to chief of staff, Jan. 5, 1918, file # 7541-62; 296/165, NA. Chief WO Hartley S. Newman, "A Study on Student Army Training Corps," Sept. 1942, p. 58, file # 7200-DD, Thomas File; 310/165, NA.

14. "Whether it should be so or not, it is apparently a fact that such units are not regarded, either by the men in them, or by other soldiers, as on par with the regular fighting organizations," reported a morale officer. "Morale of Negro Soldiers," Aug. 23, 1918, Negro Soldiers file, box A9; 377/165, NA.

15. Maj. W. H. Loving, Camp Pike report, Sept. 27, 1918, file # 10218-280. See also Charles Williams's report on Camp Beauregard, Nov. 30, 1918, file # 10218 (unmarked). Both in 65/165, NA.

16. Memorandum for the chief of staff, May 16, 1918, file # 8142-150; 296/165, NA.

17. Charles Williams, "Special Report on Conditions at Camp Hill, Newport News, Virginia," file # 10218 (unmarked); 65/165, NA.

18. Memorandum for the secretary of war, July 28, 1918, "H, 1918" folder. Baker Papers, LOC.

19. C. L. Brosius, CTCA athletic director, to J. E. Raycroft, undated letter, "Southern Department" folder, Correspondence of the Athletic Division, 1917–19 (entry 398); Commission on Training Camp Activities; War College and War Plans Division, 1900–1942; Textual Records of the War Department General and Special Staffs, Record Group 165 (hereafter 398/165, NA); National Archives, College Park, Md. Brig. Gen. Jas. A. Ryan, Camp Travis, Tex., to J. E. Raycroft, Feb. 18, 1919, Camp Travis folder; 398/165, NA.

20. Charley White, boxing instructor, Camp Custer, Mich., quoted in *Battle Creek Enquirer*, clipping in "Camp Custer" folder; 398/165, NA.

21. Pvt. Mortimer L. Myers, 302nd Ambulance Train, 77th Division. WWI, Carlisle.

22. Kenneth Jones, "Memories of World War I." Irving Crump, *Conscript 2989: Experiences of a Drafted Man* (New York: Dodd, Mead, 1918), p. 57.

23. Timothy K. Nenninger, "American Military Effectiveness During the First

World War," in *Military Effectiveness*, vol. 1: *The First World War*, ed. Allan R. Millett and Williamson Murray (Boston: Allen & Unwin, 1988), pp. 143–45, 151–52.

24. Memorandum from the Inspector General's Office, Dec. 11, 1918, folder # 123; 22/120, NA. See report from 2d Lt. Leland Stevenson, Oct. 18, 1918, "M.P." folder; 195/120, NA.

25. Donald Smythe, *Pershing: General of the Armies* (Bloomington: Indiana University Press, 1986), p. 196.

26. Capt. Charles D. Gentsch, Le Mans Classification Camp Intelligence, Oct. 22, 1918; 195/120, NA.

27. Chaplain James R. Laughton, 80th Division, "The Cross in the Tempest: Personal War Experiences." WWI, Carlisle.

28. Pvt. T. P. Wilson, 317th Infantry, 80th Division, memoir, Rockbridge County folder, Virginia State Archives.

29. Memorandum from the Inspector General's Office, Dec. 11, 1918.

30. Col. George Marshall, quoted in Allan R. Millett, "Over Where? The AEF and the American Strategy for Victory, 1917–1918," in *Against All Enemies: Interpretations of American Military History from Colonial Times to the Present,* ed. Kenneth J. Hagen and William R. Roberts (Westport, Conn.: Greenwood Press, 1986), p. 249.

31. Nenninger, "American Military Effectiveness," pp. 138, 146.

32. "Our Military System As It Appeared to America's Citizen Soldiers," response to question # 5, (9-5-19 to 10-8-18) file, box 821, decimal # 353; 37/407, NA. Question 5 reads: "Considering that you would want to be *100% trained* before *risking . . . your own life* in a battle, what per-cent of that training and efficiency do you consider you have acquired?" (p. 6). The average response, with training time ranging between one month and 18 months, was a 72 percent efficiency rating.

33. Pvt. Frank J. Boldt, 341th Infantry, 86th Division. Pvt. Gus M. Kantrud, 305th Infantry, 77th Division. Joseph McLaughlin, "The Great Northern Story," Coast Artillery Corps. Pvt. Charles Vernon, 364th Infantry, 91st Division. Pvt. Guy B. Woodson, 357th Infantry, 90th Division, "While in the 357th Infantry of the US Army." All in WWI, Carlisle.

34. Sgt. Fred E. Ross, 317th Infantry, 80th Division. WWI, Carlisle.

35. T. P. Wilson memoir (cited n. 28 above).

36. Tony Ashworth, *Trench Warfare, 1914–1918: The Live and Let Live System* (New York: Holmes & Meier, 1980), describes how British troops who occupied quiet sectors during the war used inertia, ritualism, and peer pressure to reach unspoken truces with German soldiers. Ashworth argues that the live-and-let-live system empowered soldiers to determine, not just how the war was fought, but how they personally experienced war.

37. Cpl. Edward Schafer, 102nd Infantry, 26th Division, memoir. WWI, Carlisle.

38. Cpl. Elmer T. Roden, 306th Infantry, 77th Division. WWI, Carlisle.

39. Cpl. Ernie Hilton, 353th Infantry, 89th Division, letter to Grace, Aug. 11, 1918. Pvt. Wiley Chase Goudy, 314th Field Artillery, 80th Division. 1st Lt. Lee Harrison, 111th Infantry, 28th Division, memoir. All in WWI, Carlisle.

40. Pvt. Clarence H. Stuhldreher, 363rd Infantry, 91st Division. WWI, Carlisle.

41. D. Clayton-James, *The Years of MacArthur,* vol. 1 (London: Leo Cooper, 1970), p. 156, cited in Ashworth, *Trench Warfare,* p. 126.

42. Cpl. Paul Murphy, 309th Infantry, 78th Division, "An Account of My Personal Experience in World War I," p. 25. Wagoner Fred Wadsworth, 305th Ambulance Company, 77th Division. Both in WWI, Carlisle.

43. The General Staff focused during the first year of the war almost exclusively on raising combat divisions, without outlining a coherent system for training and assigning replacement troops. The War Plans Division drastically reduced stateside training time to meet Pershing's overwhelming demand for replacements in the fall of 1918. John J. Pershing, *Final Report of General John J. Pershing, Commander-in-Chief, American Expeditionary Forces* (Washington, D.C.: GPO, 1919), p. 616. Memorandum for dir. of operations, Nov. 20, 1918, file # 10773-116; 296/165, NA.

44. Milton B. Sweningsen, 138th Infantry, 35th Division, "My Four Days under Fire." WWI, Carlisle.

45. Quotation from memorandum for General Spinks, Office of the Inspector General, Oct. 11, 1918, file # 1008; General Correspondence, 1917–19 (entry 588); insp. gen.; Administrative Staff, 1917–19; Textual Records of the AEF, 1917–23, Record Group 120 (hereafter 588/120, NA); National Archives, College Park, Md. For similar comments and discussion of insufficient training of replacement troops, see memorandum to the commander in chief, Oct. 26, 1918, file # 13599-A-131; General Correspondence, 1917–19 (entry 6); Office of the Commander in Chief, 1917–20; Textual Records of the AEF, 1917–23, Record Group 120 (hereafter 6/120, NA); National Archives, College Park, Md. Insp. gen., Report on 77th Division, Oct. 6, 1918, folder # 120; 24/120, NA.

46. Memorandum for Inspector General's Office, Dec. 11, 1918 (cited n. 24 above), p. 30.

47. Pvt. Michael H. Byrne, 361st Motor Transport Corps and 165th Infantry, 42nd Division, diary. In Karl B. Bretzfelder Papers, Manuscripts, Carlisle.

48. Harrison, 28th Division, memoir (cited n. 39 above). Pvt. Paul Holsen, 308th Infantry, 77th Division. WWI, Carlisle.

49. Smythe, *Pershing,* p. 192. Nenninger, "American Military Effectiveness," p. 147. Kantrud, 77th Division (cited n. 33 above).

50. Pvt. Arthur J. Nelson, 181st Infantry, 91st Division. WWI, Carlisle.

51. Woodson, "While in the 357th Infantry" (cited n. 33 above).

52. For related examinations of the cultural response to trench warfare and its significance, see Paul Fussell, *The Great War and Modern Memory* (New York: Oxford University Press, 1975), and Eric J. Leed, *No Man's Land: Combat and Identity in World War I* (New York: Cambridge University Press, 1979). Fussell examines the imaginative, creative response of British soldiers to their war experience. In his view, their myths, poems, stories, and tales together reveal the new ironic perspective soldiers developed during the war. Leed examines soldier culture (primarily of German soldiers, although he asserts that his analysis holds for British, French, and American troops

as well) as a text that reveals how soldiers confronted the disjunction between the initial civilian expectations these men had of soldiering and their own actual military experiences during the war.

53. Bernard Eubanks, 316th Military Police Train, 91st Division, "My Small Part in WWI," p. 13. Myers, 77th Division. 1st Lt. Milton E. Bernet, 314th Supply Train, 89th Division, "The World War—As I Saw It." All in WWI, Carlisle.

54. Hilton to Grace (cited n. 39 above), Jan. 27, 1919.

55. Pvt. Raymond F. Corkery, 102nd Field Artillery, 26th Division, diary entry, June 16, 1918. Sgt. Stephen V. Morray, 305th Ambulance Train, 80th Division. Both in WWI, Carlisle. Pvt. Norman Roberts, 323rd Infantry, 81st Division, diary. Virginia State Archives.

56. Lt. Col. J. A. Baer to insp. gen., AEF, Sept. 22, 1918, file # 247/1; 588/120, NA.

57. Eric Dean, *Post-Traumatic Stress, Vietnam, and the Civil War* (Cambridge, Mass.: Harvard University Press, 1997), pp. 29–34, 207, contends that although all soldiers in battle suffer some form of psychiatric breakdown, the sustained artillery fire of World War I produced the worst kind.

58. Murphy, "Account," p. 44 (cited n. 42 above).

59. Laughton, "The Cross in the Tempest" (cited n. 27 above).

60. Edward A. Strecker, "Military Psychiatry: World War I, 1917–18," and Albert Deutsch, "Military Psychiatry: World War II, 1941–1943," in American Psychiatric Association, *One Hundred Years of American Psychiatry* (New York: Columbia University Press, 1944), pp. 385–416, 419–41.

61. Chief Surgeon M. W. Ireland to adj. gen., AEF, Oct. 1, 1918, file # 12622-A18; 6/120, NA.

62. Maj. Gen. James Harbord to Maj. Gen. Leonard Wood, 89th Division, Camp Funston, Oct. 11, 1917. James Harbord Papers, Library of Congress (hereafter Harbord Papers, LOC).

63. Allied commanders who hoped to push Pershing toward amalgamating U.S. troops with Allied units continually criticized his use of limited shipping space to transport noncombatant troops. During one meeting, an exasperated Pershing pointed out to Marshal Ferdinand Foch, the supreme allied commander, that the French Army would also suffer if the U.S. Army did not bring more laborers into France. Pershing, diary entry, June 1, 1917, box 4–5; Pershing Papers, LOC. Edward Coffman, *The War to End All Wars: The American Military Experience in World War I* (New York: Oxford University Press, 1968), p. 129.

64. Maj. Charles H. Collins, "Farm Labor in Wartime, 1917–1918," Feb. 15, 1943, file # 7200-OO, Thomas File; 310/165, NA.

65. Memorandum for the adj. gen., Sept. 25, 1918, file # 10871-31; 296/165, NA.

66. Maj. Oliver S. McCleary, "The Shortage of Essential War Materials in the Lumber Industry and the Handling of the Labor Problems," Aug. 1940, file # 7200-L, Thomas File; 310/165, NA.

67. Charles Williams, "A Brief Report on Conditions Among Colored Soldiers at Camp Eustis, Va.," Feb. 14, 1919, file # 10218; 65/165, NA. "Morale in Armies," course at the Army War College, 1928–29, Oct. 24, 1928, pp. 41–50. Curriculum, Carlisle.

68. *Army and Navy Register* 65, Feb. 15, 1919, p. 197, and Feb. 22, 1919, p. 233.

69. All departments with supply functions, formerly part of the Line of Communication, were grouped into the Service of Supply in February 1918. By August 1918, the commanding general of the SOS communicated directly with the War Department, rather than working through AEF general headquarters, to settle supply matters not involving questions of policy.

70. Wool, *Military Specialist*, p. 195.

71. Memorandum for insp. gen., Jan. 25, 1919, file # 1034-1; 588/120, NA.

72. Harbord to Pershing, Dec. 4, 1918. Harbord-Pershing Correspondence; Harbord Papers, LOC.

73. Gen. R. L. Bullard to adj. gen., Jan. 6, 1919, file # 21043; 6/120, NA.

74. Pvt. Henry W. Stewart, 56th Pioneer Infantry. WWI, Carlisle.

75. Sgt. John J. Devine, 59th Pioneer Infantry. Walter Hart, 5th Engineers. WWI, Carlisle.

76. Melvin S. Wroolie, 311th Supply Train, 86th Division, "My Experiences in WWI." WWI, Carlisle. Intelligence Report, Newport News, Va., Jan. 7, 1919, file # 80-163; 65/165, NA.

77. Pvt. Vincent Everett, 29th Engineers, diary entry, Sept. 25, 1918. WWI, Carlisle.

78. Pvt. Nelson M. White, 114th Engineers, memoir, Norfolk County folder; Pvt. James Baxter Douglas, 17th Engineers, diary, Nottoway County folder. Virginia State Archives.

79. Smythe, *Pershing*, p. 184.

80. Sgt. John Mansfield, 51st Pioneer Infantry, diary. WWI, Carlisle.

81. Influenza spread quickly in crowded camp barracks, especially among new recruits who had not yet built up any immunity to common camp diseases. As the fall offensives wore on and recently arrived replacements began to enter combatant divisions, increasing numbers of combat soldiers contracted Spanish Influenza. Alfred Crosby, Jr., *Epidemic and Peace, 1918* (Westport, Conn.: Greenwood Press, 1976), pp. 150–70.

82. Pvt. Joseph N. Kern and Pvt. Elmer Denzer, both in the 161st Depot Brigade, Camp Grant, Ill. WWI, Carlisle. Warned about the malingering habits of troops, army doctors often ignored initial complaints from ill men and sent them back to work. In the first year of the war, the Medical Department aggressively inspected water supplies and sewage systems to control the spread of contagious diseases in training camps. Most stateside camps experienced short epidemics of measles or spinal meningitis, which medical officers contained primarily through quarantines. When influenza swept across the country, however, understaffed army hospitals soon became so crowded that ill men had nowhere to go except their barracks. Col. T. G. Donaldson, "Investigation of Camp Funston," Feb. 4, 1918. Baker Papers, LOC. Brig. Gen. M. W. Ireland to Pershing, file # 12876-R; 6/120, NA.

83. Brig. Gen. Charles G. Dawes and Brig. Gen. George Van Horn Moseley, "Review of the Report of the Inspector Covering the Operation of the YMCA," May 10, 1923, folder # 6, box 352. Pershing Papers, LOC.

84. Sgt. Charles R. Blatt, 305th Engineers, 80th Division, "Over There with the Eightieth." WWI, Carlisle.

85. 1st Lt. Harry Logsdon, 315th Sanitary Train, 90th Division. WWI, Carlisle.

86. Wagoner Charles McKinney, 315th Field Artillery, 80th Division. WWI, Carlisle.

87. Pvt. Elmer Goodrick, 341st Field Artillery, 89th Division, letter to sister Helen, Sept. 5, 1918. WWI, Carlisle.

88. Lt. Col. Frederick Palmer, "Report on Conditions at Port of Embarkation," Jan. 22, 1919. Baker Papers, LOC.

89. "The Negro in the Army," memorandum for the director, Military Intelligence Division, app. D, pp. 7–8, file # 10218-279 (10); 65/165, NA.

90. Memorandum for the chief of staff, May 16, 1918 (cited n. 16 above).

91. Pershing, diary entries, July 30, 1918, and Aug. 3, 1918 (quoted), box 4–5, Pershing Papers, LOC. For a similar response to importance of engineer work, see Gen. Robert Lee Bullard, diary # 9, Oct. 17, 1918. Robert Lee Bullard Papers, Library of Congress (hereafter Bullard Papers, LOC).

92. Col. John Stephen Sewell to Harbord, chief of staff, AEF, Nov. 9, 1917, file # 5011-A; 6/120, NA.

93. Pvt. Paul E. Maxwell, 314th Field Artillery, 80th Division. WWI, Carlisle.

94. Cpl. Robert L. Harbison, 320th Infantry, 80th Division, letter to parents, Nov. 1, 1918. WWI, Carlisle.

95. Pvt. Everett Taylor, 101st Infantry, 26th Division, letters to family, Oct. 27, 1918, and Dec. 14, 1918. WWI, Carlisle.

96. There was ongoing discussion during the war over whether medals should be used as incentives to fight or as recognition for bravery. Memorandum for the chief of staff, Sept. 13, 1917, file # 12622-O; 6/120, NA. Harbord to Pershing, Sept. 7, 1918, and Sept. 10, 1918, Harbord-Pershing Correspondence. Harbord to Gen. J. W. McAndrew, Jan. 31, 1919, and reply, Feb. 3, 1919. "World War Military Activity" folder, Harbord Papers, LOC. For similar complaints about delays in decorating soldiers, see memorandum to the adj. gen., June 5, 1918, file # 913-1-A. Memorandum for commander in chief from A. W. Brewster, insp. gen., July 12, 1918, file # 367-1. Both in 588/120, NA. See "Historical and Psychological Aspects in Use of Awards," and "The Detection of Merit, Bravery, and Valor," supplements no. 1 and 2, Oct. 7, 1926, file # 333-1. "Morale as Affected by Definite Plans and Directives, by Rewards and Punishment and by Leadership and Training Methods," Mar. 14, 1922, # file 226-3/A. All in Curriculum, Carlisle.

97. Harbord to adj. gen., AEF, Apr. 18, 1919. Harbord Papers, LOC. The Medal of Honor, established by Congress in 1862, was the army's most prestigious award for distinguished acts of valor and bravery under enemy fire. Criteria for the Medal of Honor were therefore much higher than for Distinguished Service awards.

98. Memorandum for the chief of staff, Sept. 13, 1917, pp. 7–10. General Order No. 12, Jan. 6, 1918, file # 12622; 6/120, NA.

99. Maj. Gen. F. J. Kernan, headquarters SOS, to commander in chief, AEF, Mar. 16, 1918, file # 12622-B; 6/120, NA.

100. General Order No. 110, July 7, file # 12622-Z-20; 6/120, NA. Soldiers with less than six months' service overseas received a blue chevron. Time toward the chevron began as soon as a soldier left an American port and ended when he returned to one. Sgt. Maj. Henry Warren Jones, Headquarters Co., 90th Division, letter home, Mar. 14, 1919. WWI, Carlisle.

101. Wound chevrons were the other decoration adopted by the army during the war, and only certain types of wounds were considered legitimate war injuries. Men did not receive a chevron for wounds received during training, for slight injuries that did not require medical treatment, or for shell shock.

102. *Army and Navy Register* 64, Dec. 28, 1918, p. 737, and Dec. 21, 1918, p. 707; ibid. 65, Jan. 4, 1919, p. 6.

103. Pvt. Emmett Riggin, 60th C.A.C., diary. Virginia State Archives. Sgt. Vincent Garske, 348th Field Artillery, 91st Division. WWI, Carlisle. Lt. Col. J. G. McIllroy, "Investigation of Alleged Robbery of Dead," Mar. 18, 1919, file # 276-6; 588/120, NA. Lt. Col. Baer to insp. gen., Sept. 22, 1918 (cited n. 56 above).

3. The Meaning of Obedience

1. "General Training Principles Governing the Training of Units of the AEF," file # 7541-60; 296/165, NA.

2. Memorandums for the chief of staff, June 4, 1918, file # 8568-78 (quoted), and July 13, 1918, file # 8568-88, both in 296/165, NA. Governor of North Carolina to Secretary of War Newton Baker, July 10, 1918, file # 10481-38; 65/165, NA.

3. Memorandum for the chief of staff, Jan. 22, 1918, file # 8575-40; 296/165, NA. The War Plans Division rejected this proposition after the judge advocate general warned that the American people would never accept a decision to execute men who had deserted "from training and mobilization camps far removed from the theatre of hostilities." See also memorandum for the chief of staff, p. 3, June 4, 1918.

4. Edward Gemmer, 305th Infantry, 77th Division. In Alfred Graichen file, 77th Division, WWI, Carlisle.

5. General Order No. 56, Apr. 13, 1918, in "A Study on Court-Martial Cases of Men in Combat, AEF 1917–1918," July 1942, file # 7200-F, Thomas File; 310/165, NA. AEF judge advocate general to the chief of staff, May 1, 1918, file # 11730-L; 6/120, NA.

6. Cpl. Fred Anson Tyrell, 102nd Infantry, 26th Division. WWI, Carlisle. Chief of staff, 1st Division, to Lt. Col. Walter Grant, G-3, GHQ, May 10, 1918, file # 11730-L; 6/120, NA.

7. Baker to President Woodrow Wilson, May 1, 1918, and undated May 1918 letter. Both in "W, May 1918" folder. Baker Papers, LOC. Memorandum for the chief of staff, Apr. 1920, file # 8568-155; 296/165, NA.

8. Gen. John Pershing, personal and confidential letter, to Maj. Gen. Henry T. Allen, 90th Division, Oct. 24, 1918, "1918 (Jan.–Sept.)" folder, box 11. Henry T. Allen Papers, Library of Congress (hereafter Allen Papers, LOC).

9. Brig. Gen. W. A. Bethel, AEF judge advocate general, to commander in chief, Oct. 21, 1918. This letter was distributed to division commanders and is found in several

collections of private papers, including the Allen Papers, LOC, in the Commander of the 90th Division, "1918 (Jan.–Sept.)" folder, box 11, and 80th Division Collection, "Embarkation/Debarkation" folder, box 4. WWI, Carlisle.

10. General Order, No. 56. "A Study on Court-Martial Cases of Men in Combat, American Expeditionary Forces, 1917–1918." "General Court-Martial in the AEF," AEF Judge Advocate's Office, Aug. 7, 1919, "Reports. Misc" folder, box 172. Pershing Papers, LOC. Securing the time, officers, and witnesses to conduct a court-martial was a cumbersome task, and AEF officials discouraged officers from convening them. A general court-martial of five officers was only convened to try major offenses. GHQ recommended that penalties for minor offenses be assigned by a single officer in a summary court-martial, while intermediate offenses were to be handled by special courts-martial consisting of three officers, which could award a maximum sentence of six months.

11. Cpl. Paul Murphy, 309th Infantry, 78th Division, "An Account of My Personal Experience in World War I," p. 53. WWI, Carlisle.

12. Adj. Gen. to commanding general, GHQ, AEF, Aug. 8, 1918, file # 12118-G. Maj. Gen. Robert L. Bullard, 1st Division, to Gen. J. W. McAndrew, chief of staff, July 22, 1918, file # 12118-B. Both in 6/120, NA.

13. Robert Lee Bullard, *Personalities and Reminiscences of the War* (Garden City, N.Y.: Doubleday, 1925), pp. 266–67.

14. Capt. Emmett W. Smith, 18th Infantry, to commanding general, 1st Division, Sept. 24, 1917, file # 83; 588/120, NA. Gen. John A. Lejeune, commanding general, 2nd Division, to commander in chief, AEF, Oct. 16, 1918, file # 12223-A-279; 6/120, NA. Capt. George Thompson, salvage officer, to regulating officer, Noisy-le-Sec, Nov. 4, 1918, file # 17721-A107; 6/120, NA.

15. Hunter Liggett, *A.E.F.: Ten Years Ago in France* (New York: Dodd, Mead, 1928), pp. 206–7.

16. Maj. Gen. A.W. Brewster, insp. gen., AEF, to the chief of staff, Oct. 21, 1918, file # 12223-A-290; 6/120, NA.

17. Ibid. Secret Headquarters memorandum, 1st Division, Aug. 11, 1918, "First Division: Memoranda and Instructions" folder, box 14. Summerall Papers, LOC. "Notes by Inspector General—12 September 1918–11 November 1918," folder # 123; 22/120, NA. Inspector General Division reports on 82nd Division and 4th Division in file # 120; 24/120, NA.

18. 1st Lt. Harry A. Logsdon, 359th Ambulance Company, 90th Division, diary. WWI, Carlisle.

19. Pvt. Milton L. Smith, 308th Machine Gun Battalion, 78th Division, diary. WWI, Carlisle.

20. Brig. Gen. W. W. Atterbury, director of transportation to chief of staff, Feb. 15, 1918, file # 12876-D; 6/120, NA. Maj. Gen. A. W. Brewster to chief of staff, Aug. 28, 1918, file # 252; 588/120, NA.

21. Capt. F. J. Fitzpatrick, 508th Engineers, to C.O. 1st Battalion, 23rd Engineers, July 21, 1918, file # 252; 588/120, NA.

22. AEF judge advocate general to chief of staff, May 1, 1918. General Order No. 78, May 25, 1918, file # 11730-L; 6/120, NA.

23. Lt. Col. George P. Tyner to M. R. Hilgard, acting chief of staff, G-4, Aug. 8, 1918, file # 252; 588/120, NA. Brewster to chief of staff, Aug. 28, 1918.

24. Sgt. Henry Charles Ward, 343rd Field Artillery, 90th Division, memoirs, p. 11. WWI, Carlisle.

25. Lt. John J. Maginnis, 301st Infantry, 76th Division, memoirs. WWI, Carlisle.

26. Memorandum for the chief of staff, Feb. 15, 1918, file # 10766-21; 296/165, NA. Col. Robert C. Humber, "Absence Without Leave at Ports of Embarkation During World War I," Feb. 1943, file # 7200-LL, Thomas File; 310/165, NA.

27. Sgt. Richard McBride, 328th Infantry, 82nd Division, "Passing in Review: Memoirs of World War I, 1917–AEF–1919," pp. 27, 36. WWI, Carlisle.

28. Pvt. G. W. Reed, 117th Train Headquarters, 42nd Division, diary entry, Nov. 5, 1917. Pvt. Frank J. Boldt, 341st Infantry, 86th Division. Sgt. Joseph Correll, Headquarters Detachment, 80th Division. Roger Bonney, 161st Field Artillery, 86th Division. Melvin Wroolie, 86th Division, memoir. All in WWI, Carlisle. Pvt. T. P. Wilson, 317th Infantry, 80th Division, memoir, Rockbridge County folder, Virginia State Archives. Memorandum for the chief of staff, Apr. 2, 1918, file # 8082-101; 296/165, NA.

29. See, e.g., "Summary of Fort Leavenworth Report," Nov. 22, 1919, file # 1150, box 145; 8/165, NA, a review of the service crime records of approximately 2,000 prisoners in Fort Leavenworth in the fall of 1919 by Capt. Randolph Shaw, who noted in a subsequent analysis of crimes committed from March 15, 1919, to March 17, 1920, that "a marked reduction may be expected in military offenses as intoxicating liquors are made more difficult to obtain," as when national prohibition took effect. "Analysis of Apparent Causes of General Court-Martial Offenses . . . from March 15, 1919, to March 17, 1920," Apr. 26, 1920. See also, "Analysis of the Causes of 200 Desertion Cases," Feb. 7, 1919. Both in file # 1150, box 145; 8/165, NA. Memorandum for McIntyre, Feb. 14, 1919, file # 1010-17; 8/165, NA.

30. Dissenting Opinion of Lt. Col. W. A. Castle, Jan. 5, 1918, file # 10124-83; 296/165, NA.

31. Memorandum for the chief of staff, Feb. 27, 1918, file # 6292-31; 296/165, NA.

32. Acting chief of staff, G-2, 4th Division, to acting chief of staff, G-2, GHQ, AEF, May 17, 1919, file # 10314-414 (25); 65/165, NA. Lt. Col. C. H. Goddard, "A Study of Anglo-American and Franco-American Relations During World War I" (July 1942), file # 7200-E, pt. 2, Thomas File; 310/165, NA.

33. Memorandums for the chief of staff, Nov. 16, 1917, p. 2, file # 10040-8, and Jan. 5, 1918, file # 10124-83, both in 296/165, NA. For a discussion of Pershing's wish to limit the doughboy's monthly pay to $10, see also Felix Frankfurter to Baker, Aug. 15, 1917, "F, 1917" folder, Baker Papers, LOC. For effect of loan drives, see memorandum on soldiers' pay, Sept. 6, 1918, file # 80-53 (7); 65/165, NA. Straightforward bureaucratic bumbling also created numerous delays in paying soldiers overseas. Quartermaster officials often failed to rectify payrolls before troops sailed to France, or to pay soldiers regularly after they went into battle or the hospital. By the end of the war, the gov-

ernment owed some soldiers hundreds of dollars in back pay, which they had been eligible to receive overseas. "Inspector of Disbursements, Chief Quartermaster, Report for Year Ending December 31, 1918," Jan. 3, 1919. In Charles E. N. Howard Papers, Manuscripts, Carlisle. Memorandum for General Anderson, Jan. 21, 1919, "Inspection of Demobilization Activities" folder, box 224; 310/165, NA.

34. "Notes by Inspector General—12 Sept. 1918-11 November 1918," p. 31 (cited n. 17 above). "Methods and Results of Training, 81st Division," file # 7541-76; 296/165, NA. "Report of Inspection of the troops at Camp Sherman, Ohio," 84th Division, July 31, 1918, "WD—Camp Sherman—Report of Inspection" folder, box 207; 310/165, NA. "Report on Training of the 107th Engineers," Jan. 5, 1918, file # 7541-62; 296/165, NA.

35. Horace Hobbs, inspector of 26th Division and commanding officer, 101st Infantry, letter to wife, Aug. 26, 1918. Horace Hobbs Papers, Manuscripts, Carlisle. Maj. Gen. Leonard Wood to adj. gen., Apr. 30, 1919, file # 250.4; 37/407, NA.

36. Pershing, cable No. 178-S, Sept. 24, 1917, in "Report of G-5 Divisional Training," p. 10, folder 246; 22/120, NA. Memorandum for the adj. gen. of the army, Mar. 4, 1918, file # 10754-9. Memorandum for acting chief of staff (G-2), July 1, 1918, file # 1692-H. Both in 6/120, NA. "Present War Department Morale Plans," Course at the Army War College, 1933-34, file # 401-7. Curriculum, Carlisle. Capt. H. E. Pace, "The Why of Military Courtesy," *Infantry Journal* 15 (July 1918): 51-56. Maj. Gen. David C. Shanks, "Management of the American Soldier," ibid. (Oct. 1918): 298-99. 1st Lt. Warren J. Clear, "The Inevitable Reflection," ibid. (Mar. 1919): 719-20.

37. Untitled morale memorandum, file # 80-78; 65/165, NA. Raymond Fosdick, chairman, Commission on Training Camp Activities, to Baker, Apr. 17, 1919, "F, 1919" folder. Baker Papers, LOC. Maj. Gen. Eli A. Helmick, lecture, "Leadership," Army War College Course, 1923-24, file # 270-67. Curriculum, Carlisle.

38. David M. Kennedy, *Over Here: The First World War and American Society* (New York: Oxford University Press, 1980), pp. 88-92.

39. Nancy Bristow, *Making Men Moral: Social Engineering During the Great War* (New York: New York University Press, 1996).

40. The mutinies that swept through the French Army in 1917 provided American officials with a vivid example of the threat pacifist political ideas allegedly posed to the war effort. Rather than analyzing the mutinies as a response to three years of futile assaults against German machine guns, French Army officials latched onto the contact furloughed soldiers had had with civilian pacifist organizations as the main cause of the mutinies. The new commander in chief, Henri Philippe Pétain, ordered closer supervision of pacifist assemblies and tighter press censorship, gave troops furloughs home, and waited for the Americans before launching another major offensive. See "Morale and Discipline in the French Army in the Spring of 1917," file # 8121-X; 6/120, NA.

41. "Informal Conference on Morale," Apr. 12, 1918. "Report on Second Conference of Morale," May 15, 1918. Both in box 131; 310/165, NA. Thomas M. Camfield, " 'Will to Win,'—The U.S. Army Troop Morale Program of World War I," *Military Affairs* 41 (Oct. 1977): 125-28. For Col. E. L. Munson's plan see, memorandum for the

surgeon general, Mar. 2, 1918, file # 7519-107. For Maj. Gen. J. F. Morrison's plan, see memorandum for the chief of staff, Feb. 26, 1918, file # 7519-106. Both in 296/165, NA. For organization of Morale Division, see memorandum for the chief of staff, Aug. 29, 1918, file # 80-1 (25); 65/165, NA.

42. "Suggestions for Morale Officers," Morale Circular No. 1, "Morale Circular, 1918-1919" folder, box 77; 310/165, NA. The Commission on Education and Special Training, which supervised the army-sponsored technical training and reserve officer courses on college campuses, also offered a War Issues Course toward the end of the war. See Stephen D. Wesbrook, "Historical Notes," in *The Political Education of Soldiers*, ed. Morris Janowitz and Stephen Wesbrook (Beverly Hills, Calif.: Sage Publications, 1983), pp. 251-84.

43. Capt. Charles D. Gentsch, Le Mans Classification Camp Intelligence, 83rd Division, Sept. 5 and Sept. 12, 1918; 195/120, NA.

44. Capt. Charles D. Gentsch, 83rd Division, Oct. 27, Sept. 1 (quoted), and Sept. 3, 1918; 195/120, NA.

45. Pvt. Henry L. Van Landingham, apps. C and G, letter collection, Richmond City folder, box 4, Virginia State Archives.

46. 2d Lt. Donald Dinsome, undated letter to mother, 103rd Field Artillery, 26th Division. WWI, Carlisle. Henry B. Dillard, letter to mother, Aug. 12, 1918. Henry B. Dillard Papers, Library of Congress (hereafter Dillard Papers, LOC). See also "Informal Conference on Morale," Apr. 12, 1918.

47. Memorandum, Feb. 23, 1918, quoted in Alfred E. Cornebise, *The Stars and Stripes: Doughboy Journalism in World War I* (Westport, Conn.: Greenwood Press, 1984), p. 8.

48. Lt. Col. Aristides Moreno, acting secretary of G-2, to Capt. Mark Watson, Jan. 17, 1919, and Watson's reply, Jan. 23, 1919, quoted in Cornebise, *Stars and Stripes*, p. 10.

49. Untitled memorandum, June 17, 1918, file # 80-71; 65/165, NA.

50. "A Study in Morale," Jan. 30, 1919, Camp Grant file; 377/165, NA.

51. "Report on Second Conference of Morale," May 15, 1918, p. 6.

52. Memorandum for the chief of staff, Feb. 4, 1918, file # 10288-10; 296/165, NA.

53. In the Civil War and World War II, civilian politicians took the initiative to resolve problems in collecting soldiers' votes to bolster their respective chances in the 1864 and 1944 presidential elections. In the Civil War, at the request of the Republican party, many northern regiments furloughed soldiers to return home and vote for Abraham Lincoln. States also authorized officers to collect the votes of their regionally based units. In World War II, procedural problems in getting absentee ballots to and from soldiers in a timely manner resulted in only 28,000 servicemen out of 5.7 million casting ballots in 1942. Two years later, after much pushing from Franklin D. Roosevelt, Congress simplified the voting process but still only one-fourth (2.6 million) of the armed forces cast ballots. See *The Public Papers and Addresses of Franklin D. Roosevelt*, vol. 13: *Victory and the Threshold of Peace, 1944-45*, ed. Samuel I. Rosenman (New York: Harper & Brothers, 1950), pp. 114-16; Mary R. Dearing, *Veterans in Politics: The Story of the GAR* (Baton Rouge: Louisiana State University Press, 1952).

54. Acting secretary of war to Wilson, Oct. 9, 1918, reprinted in Capt. Charles H. Collins, "Soldier Voting," Aug. 1942, pp. 1–2, 7, 17, file # 7200-X, Thomas File; 310/165, NA.

55. "Balloting Overseas in 1917," in Collins, "Soldier Voting," pp. 110–18.

56. The War Department agreed in November 1917 to allow qualified state election officials to visit domestic training camps to collect votes for state and local elections and provided registration lists, facilities, and officers' aid. The army claimed that the military vote was quite small in 1917, perhaps indicating that soldiers had little interest in voting. In 1918, more states heeded the army's requests and adopted an absentee ballot procedure for stateside soldiers, but election officials reported that the domestic military vote again was small. General Order No. 144, Nov. 16, 1917, and General Order No. 63, June 28, 1918, as well as Rhode Island, Connecticut, and Massachusetts voting plans. All in Collins, "Soldier Voting," pp. 7, 14, 19–21, 80, 90–92.

57. Memorandum for the chief of staff, Apr. 10, 1918, file # 10288-13; 296/165, NA. This memorandum reflects Ketcham's rationale for collecting a vote, but was never actually sent to the Chief of Staff's Office.

58. Memorandum for the chief of staff, AEF Judge Advocate's Office, Nov. 26, 1917, file # 10288-10; 296/165, NA. Memorandum for the secretary of war, May 1918, "Voting by Soldiers with the AEF," in Collins, "Soldier Voting," pp. 66–76. Memorandum of the judge advocate general, Jan. 19, 1918, in ibid., p. 71.

59. In the spring, the War Department drew up a list of conditions states had to meet to collect overseas soldiers' votes. The army refused to let frontline soldiers vote except through the mail, to furnish comprehensive lists of state residents serving in the army, to suspend censorship to protect the secret ballot, to require officers to validate votes, or to ensure the safe delivery of mail ballots. General Order No. 63, June 28, 1918. Acting Secretary of War Crowell to Wilson, Oct. 9, 1918. Acting judge advocate general to Baker, May 31, 1918. Governor of Nebraska to Wilson, Mar. 22, 1918. New York voting plan. All in Collins, "Soldier Voting," pp. 14–18, 77–78, 86–89. See also memorandums for the chief of staff, Aug. 17, 1918, file # 10288-20, and Oct. 5, 1918, file # 10288-30, both in 296/165, NA.

60. The work of the Morale Division has been underrated by historians, who have only examined its wartime, not its postwar, activities. See Camfield, "Will To Win," and Wesbrook, "Historical Notes."

4. Racial Violence and Harmony in the Wartime Army

1. Brig. Gen. C. H. Barth, 81st Division to adj. gen. of the army, Aug. 31, 1917, file # 8142-21. See also memorandum for the chief of staff, July 31, 1917, file # 8142-13. Both in 296/165, NA.

2. Memorandum for the chief of staff, May 6, 1919, file # 8142-199; 296/165, NA.

3. "Replacement of Personnel in the A.E.F. in France," pp. 5–7, file # 3347, Thomas File; 310/165, NA. Leonard Lerwill, *The Personnel Replacement System in the United States Army*, Dept. of the Army Pamphlet no. 20-211 (Washington, D.C.: Dept. of the Army, 1954), pp. 174–76.

4. Governor Theo G. Bilbo, Jackson, Miss., to President Woodrow Wilson, Apr. 5, 1918, file # 3735, ser. 4. Wilson Papers, LOC.

5. *New Orleans States*, Apr. 24, 1918, newspaper clipping in "Military—General Newspaper Clippings, 1918, January–April" folder, box C-376. National Association for the Advancement of Colored People Papers, Library of Congress (hereafter NAACP Papers, LOC).

6. Emmett J. Scott, *Scott's Official History of the American Negro in the World War* (Chicago: Homewood Press, 1919), p. 104. Charles Williams, *Sidelights on Negro Soldiers* (Boston: B. J. Brimmer, 1923), pp. 31–32.

7. Secretary of War Newton Baker to Wilson, Apr. 27, 1918, file # 3735, ser. 4. Wilson Papers, LOC.

8. Baker to Wilson, July 1, 1919, file # 152, ser. 4. Wilson Papers, LOC.

9. The Intelligence Division also maintained relationships with moderate black advancement organizations throughout the war, hoping to obtain information from them about the morale of black troops and black laborers. The division expected these organizations to funnel government propaganda back into black communities and to encourage black citizens to support the war effort. These black advancement organizations included the NAACP, National Race Congress, Council of Federated Churches (black members), and League for Equal Rights. See "Morale of Negro Soldiers and Negro Civilian Population," Aug. 23, 1918, Negro Soldiers folder, box A9; 377/165, NA.

10. Scott, *Scott's Official History*, pp. 49, 62.

11. Memorandum for the chief of staff, Apr. 20, 1919, file # 10218-361 (1); 65/165, NA.

12. Charles Williams, "Inside the Camp," file # 80-97; 65/165, NA.

13. Charles Williams, "Special Report on Conditions at Camp Hill, Newport News, Virginia," file # 10218 (unmarked); 65/165, NA.

14. Of the approximately 1,250 educated black men who attended the Des Moines training camp between June 18 and October 15, 1917, 629 were commissioned. Having provided an ample number of company officers for the existing black combatant units, the school closed. Noncombatant units were officered by whites. See Hal S. Chase, "Struggle for Equality: Fort Des Moines Training Camp for Colored Officers, 1917," *Phylon* 39, no. 4 (1978): 297–310.

15. From Headquarters Camp Pike to adj. gen., July 15, 1918, file # 8142-178; 296/165, NA.

16. William Lloyd Imes, Young Men's Christian Association (YMCA) secretary, to Scott, Aug. 18, 1918, file # 10218-209 (15); 65/165, NA.

17. Charles Williams, "Report from Camp Hancock," Oct. 20, 1918, file # 10218 (unmarked); 65/165, NA.

18. Charles Williams, "Military Police," Oct. 31, 1918, file # 10218 (unmarked). For a similar incident, see intelligence report from Camp Pike, Arkansas, Dec. 9, 1918, file # 10218-224. Both in 65/165, NA.

19. When white MPs ejected black soldiers from a YMCA building in Camp

Travis, Tex., the soldiers showered them with rocks they picked up as they poured out of the building and into the street. "Then the officer of the day, a First Lieutenant, came on the scene and he too like the rest had to make his escape by taking refuge in the YMCA building," the YMCA secretary, Scott B. Joyce, reported to Scott, Sept. 4, 1918, file # 10218-216; 65/165, NA.

20. "Investigation into Treatment of Colored Soldiers at Camp Funston, Kansas," Aug. 12, 1918, file # 293-1; 588/120, NA. Also see Williams, "Inside the Camp," file # 80-97.

21. "Investigation Concerning Disorderly Conduct of 370th Infantry, Passing Through Belfort," Aug. 14, 1918, file # 203; 588/120, NA.

22. Cpl. Lloyd Blair, 317th Ammunition Train, 92nd Division. WWI, Carlisle.

23. Pvt. Roy Chesebro, 161st Depot Brigade, Camp Grant file. WWI, Carlisle.

24. Memorandum for the chief of staff, Mar. 28, 1918, file # 8142-107; 296/165, NA.

25. Maj. William H. Loving, "Report on Camp Zachary Taylor," Kentucky, Sept. 23, 1918, file # 10128-280. Charles Williams, "Report on Camp Dix, N.J.," July 31, 1918, file # 10218. Both in 65/165, NA.

26. Williams, "Inside the Camp," file # 80-97. Maj. William H. Loving to chief, Morale Section, Washington, D.C., Nov. 24, 1918, file # 10218-279 (8); 65/165, NA.

27. In civilian society, strong racial prejudices were always evident during race riots but were rarely their sole cause. Robert Haynes, for example, has argued that the most notorious clash of the entire war, the 1917 Houston riot between white civilians and black regular army soldiers, was precipitated by disappointment over failed Progressive city reforms, an influx of rural black migrants who were unwelcome in the black community, and a dispute between the police chief and veteran policemen. The status of black regular troops, recently arrived from Camp Logan, Texas, declined after black civilians saw them obeying, rather than challenging, local Jim Crow customs. The riot began when a soldier tried to stop white policemen from beating a black woman, but the soldiers received little support from fearful black civilians, who refused to hide or aid fleeing mutineers. Robert V. Haynes, *A Night of Violence: The Houston Riot of 1917* (Baton Rouge: Louisiana State University Press, 1976).

28. Testimony of Pvt. Fred Carrier, 17th Battalion, U.S. Guards, Dec. 16, 1918, in official report on Charleston riot, file # 10218-272; 65/165, NA.

29. Official report on Charleston riot, p. 5.

30. Ibid., p. 7.

31. Ibid., p. 8.

32. Maj. Gen. Henry G. Sharpe, commander of Southeastern Department to Tristam T. Hyde, mayor, City of Charleston, Dec. 20, 1918, file # 10218-272 (6); 65/165, NA.

33. Another example of how white and black soldiers cooperated in distinct military situations comes from the occasional reports of robberies describing crimes black and white soldiers committed together. Memorandum to G-1, general headquarters, AEF, Mar. 20, 1919, file # 11440-A-236; 6/120, NA.

34. Memorandum on Camp Meade, Md., to chief, Military Morale Section, Aug. 9, 1918, file # 10218-199. YMCA secretary, Camp Travis, Tex., to Scott, Sept. 4, 1919,

file # 10218-216. Imes to Scott, Aug. 18, 1919. Charles Williams, Report on Camp Upton, N.Y., Aug. 12, 1918, file # 10218 (unmarked). Report on Camp Devens, Mass., Aug. 21, 1918, file # 10218 (unmarked). Report on Camp Lee, Va., undated, file # 10218 (unmarked). All in 65/165, NA.

35. Intelligence Office memorandum, Camp Shelby, Miss., Dec. 14, 1918, file # 10218-244 (81); 65/165, NA.Williams, *Sidelights,* p. 31. At the end of the war, only twelve camps housed separate YMCA facilities for black soldiers, which meant that in many camps black soldiers had nowhere to meet their visitors.

36. Loving to chief, Morale Section, Nov. 24, 1918 (cited n. 26 above).

37. Imes to Scott, Aug. 18, 1918 (cited n. 16 above).

38. Ibid.

39. Maj. L. B. Dunham to chief, Military Morale Section, Aug. 30, 1918, file # 10218-209 (4); 65/165, NA.

40. Williams, *Sidelights,* p. 32.

41. Capt. G. B. Perkins, chief of the Military Morale Division to Scott, Sept. 27, 1918, file # 10218-209 (23). Memorandum to Military Intelligence Division, Apr. 20, 1918, file # 10218-125. Both in 65/165, NA.

42. Perkins to Scott, Sept. 27, 1918.

43. Ibid.

44. Maj. William H. Loving to chief, Military Morale Section, Nov. 29, 1918, file # 10218-209 (26); 65/165, NA.

45. 1st Lt. H. O. Reardon, report on Camp Merritt, Nov. 6, 1918, file # 10218-244 (38); 65/165, NA.

46. Black combatant troops and black civilians immediately denounced this bulletin. The civilian black press demanded that General Ballou resign, and Scott wrote to ask why he had given such an inflammatory command. Ballou defended his order, claiming that the newspapers neglected to mention that he also had persuaded community officials to prosecute the theater manager, who was eventually fined ten dollars. His primary intention, he claimed, was to prevent race friction from undermining discipline in the camp. Scott, *Scott's Official History,* pp. 98–100.

47. "The Negro in the Army," memorandum for the director, Military Intelligence Division, Dec. 23, 1918, p. 4, file # 10218-279 (10); 65/165, NA.

48. Memorandum for the chief of staff, May 16, 1918, file # 8142-150; 296/165, NA.

49. "Morale of Negro Soldiers," Aug. 23, 1918 (cited n. 9 above).

50. In *Ethnic Soldiers: State Security in Divided Societies* (Athens: University of Georgia Press, 1980), Cynthia Enloe argues that state elites deliberately form "ethnic state security maps" by limiting the institutional role of ethnic groups they perceive as eager to overturn the established power structure of society.

51. Williams, *Sidelights,* pp. 70–71. "Cable History on the Subject Colored Soldiers, Compiled by the Cable Section," Cable # 1523, June 14, 1918, and Cable # 1335, June 19, 1918, "War Department Physical Improvement" folder, box 50; 310/165, NA. Also see Quander G. Hall to Capt. Harry Taylor, Aug. 22 and 23, 1918, file # 10218-71; 65/165, NA.

52. "Secret Study—Employment of Negro Manpower in War," file # 127-25. Mal-

vern Hill Barnum to Colonel Greer, Apr. 19, 1920, file # 127-21. Both in Curriculum, Carlisle.

53. "The Negro in the Army," Dec. 23, 1918, pp. 9–10.

54. Ely Green, *Too Black, Too White*, ed. Elizabeth N. Chitty and Arthur Ben Chitty (Amherst: University of Massachusetts Press, 1970), pp. 395–98.

55. Charles Williams, "Camp Sevier," Oct. 15, 1918, file # 10218 (unmarked); 65/165, NA.

56. Pvt. Adams F. Glatfeller, 326th Infantry, 82nd Division, letter. WWI, Carlisle.

57. A. C. Wilcox, 352nd Infantry, 88th Division. WWI, Carlisle.

58. Stanley Moore, quoted in letter from Haydee Moore to John Shillady, Dec. 30, 1918, "Military, General, 1918" folder, box C-374. NAACP Papers, LOC.

59. Williams, "Special Report on Conditions at Camp Hill" (cited n. 13 above). For a general overview of black soldiers' complaints, see "Summary of Complaints Received at National Office, N.A.A.C.P.," "Military General, 1919, January and February" folder, box C-374. NAACP Papers, LOC.

60. 1st Lt. Howard S. Jenkins, 165th Depot Brigade, Camp Travis, Feb. 26, 1919, to chief, Morale Branch, Camp Travis file; 377/165, NA. Charles Williams, "Report on Camp Eustis[, Virginia]," Feb. 14, 1919, file # 10218 (unmarked); 65/165, NA.

61. Le Mans intelligence report to Capt. Charles D. Gentsch, G-2, 83rd Division, Oct. 27, 1918, Classification Camp folder; 195/120, NA.

62. Green, *Too Black, Too White*, pp. 401–2.

63. 1st Lt. William G. Powell, June 6, 1918, file # 17599-D; 6/120, NA.

64. Brig. Gen. W. S. Scott, commanding general, Base Section # 2, to commanding general, SOS, June 22, 1918, file # 17599; 6/120, NA. The notion that untamed black male rapists were preying on virtuous southern women had recently become an obsession in the South. See Joel Williamson, *A Rage For Order: Black/White Relations in the American South since Emancipation* (New York: Oxford University Press, 1986), pp. 186–91.

65. Continuous charges of rape haunted members of the 92nd Division. Division commanders prohibited these men from all contact with Frenchwomen, and predicted a carnal rampage if black soldiers were not supervised closely. Black advancement organizations claimed that white officers had exaggerated the number of sexual assaults as part of their effort to discredit the service record of black combatants. See Williams, *Sidelights*, pp. 74–76; Arthur Barbeau and Florette Henri, *The Unknown Soldiers: Black American Troops in World War I* (Philadelphia: Temple University Press, 1974), pp. 142–44.

66. Colonel Linard, "Au sujet des troupes noires américaines," Aug. 7, 1918, série 7N, Bureau spécial franco-américain, carton 2257, Service historique de l'Armée de terre, Château de Vincennes, Paris (hereafter 7N, Vincennes). For the first published English-language version, see *The Crisis* 18 (May 1919): 16–17.

67. Maj. William H. Loving, memorandum for Gen. Marlborough Churchill, Nov. 18, 1918, file # 10218-256; 65/165, NA.

5. American Soldiers' Relations with the French and the Germans

1. In the midst of responding to widespread disobedience within its own ranks, the French Army had the intelligence apparatus in place to analyze the reaction of French troops to the Americans' arrival. For a discussion of French intelligence monitoring of the American war effort, see Jennifer D. Keene, "Uneasy Alliances: French Military Intelligence and the American Army During the First World War," *Intelligence and National Security* 13, no. 1 (Spring 1998): 18–36.

2. Brig. Gen. H. B. Fiske, secret memorandum for the chief of staff, July 4, 1918, in "Report of G-5," p. 31, folder # 215; 22/120, NA.

3. "General Principles Governing the Training of Units of the AEF," file # 7541-60; 296/165, NA. Gen. John J. Pershing, cable to Washington, D.C., Sept. 24, 1917, in "Report of G-5," "Divisional Training," app. no. 31, p. 10, folder # 246. Pershing, cable to Washington, D.C., Apr. 18, 1918, in "Report of G-5," pp. 36–37, folder # 215. Both in 22/120, NA.

4. "Le candidat inspecteur auxiliaire Mignot à M. le commissaire spécial, chef du service de sûreté de la mission française près l'armée américaine," Mar. 18, 1918, série 17N, Mission militaire française près l'armée américaine, carton 47. Service historique de l'Armée de terre, Château de Vincennes, Paris (hereafter 17N, Vincennes).

5. Pershing, cable to Washington, D.C., June 19, 1918, in "Divisional Training," p. 28. Pershing, cable to Washington, D.C., Apr. 18, 1918. See also John J. Pershing, *My Experiences in the World War* (New York: Frederick A. Stokes, 1931), 1: 11–12, 151–54.

6. "Morale and Discipline in the French Army in the Spring of 1917," file # 8121-X; 6/120, NA. Pershing to Secretary of War Newton Baker, July 9, 1917, reprinted in Pershing, *My Experiences*, 1: 96–99.

7. For quotation, see "Commission de contrôle postal militaire," Sept. 1, 1918, 2ᵉ Armée, série 16N, 2ᵉ bureau, Section de renseignements aux armées (SRA); Grand quartier général, carton 1397, Service historique de l'Armée de terre, Château de Vincennes, Paris (hereafter 16N, Vincennes). For suggestions on improving morale with talks on the subject of the vast American military aid arriving, see "Sujets des causeries que les officiers doivent faire aux soldats," June 5, 1917, 16N 2404, Vincennes.

8. "Appréciations des troupes françaises sur les troupes américaines d'après le contrôle postal en Mai 1918," 17N 47, Vincennes.

9. "Les américains et l'opinion française d'après le contrôle de la correspondance du 15 juin au 15 juillet 1918," 17N 47, Vincennes.

10. "Commission de contrôle postal militaire, IIᵉ armée," Sept. 8, 1918, 16N 1397, Vincennes.

11. "Bulletin confidentiel # 3 résumant la situation morale aux armées dans la semaine du 15 au 21 juillet 1917," 16N 2405. "Les américains et la guerre," Oct. 28, 1917, 17N 47. Both in Vincennes. André Kaspi, *Le temps des Américains: Le concours américain à la France en 1917–1919* (Paris: Université de Paris I, 1976), p. 126.

12. "Appréciations" (cited n. 8 above).

13. "Les américains et l'opinion française d'après le contrôle de la correspondance du 15 août au 15 septembre 1918," 17N 47, Vincennes.

14. Henry Dillard to mother, May 19, 1918. Dillard Papers, LOC. Pvt. Joseph W. Hussar, 319th Infantry, 80th Division. WWI, Carlisle.

15. Lt. Col. C. H. Goddard, "A Study of Anglo-American and Franco-American Relations During World War I" (July 1942), p. 6, file # 7200-E, pt. 2, Thomas File; 310/165, NA.

16. "Les américains et l'opinion française" (cited n. 13 above).

17. Kaspi, *Le temps des Américains*, p. 127. Pershing, *My Experiences*, 1: 91–95.

18. "Rapport récapitulatif pour la période du 1 au 31 mars, mission française près l'armée américaine," 17N 47, Vincennes. Mignot to commissaire spécial, Mar. 18, 1918 (cited n. 4 above).

19. "Les américains et l'opinion française d'après le contrôle de la correspondance du 15 juillet au 15 août 1918," 17N 47, Vincennes.

20. For discussions leading to this joint training, see letters exchanged between Pershing and Pétain, Dec. 28, 1917, and Jan. 6, 1918, in série 6N, Fonds Clemenceau, carton 141, Service historique de l'Armée de terre, Château de Vincennes, Paris (hereafter 6N, Vincennes). And see Kaspi, *Le temps des Américains*, pp. 110–15. Three of the latter nine divisions came under French control in the spring of 1918. Lt. Col. Calvin Goddard, "Relations Between AEF and BEF, 1917–1920," pp. 1–4, and "Franco-American Relations," p. 1, file # 7200-E, pt. 1 and pt. 2, Thomas File; 310/165, NA.

21. Memorandum to Capt. Charles D. Gentsch, Oct. 17, 1918; 195/120, NA.

22. Acting chief of staff, G-2, 4th Division, to acting chief of staff, G-2, GHQ, May 17, 1919, file # 10314-414 (25); 65/165, NA. Goddard, "Franco-American Relations" (cited n. 15 above), pp. 6–7. Also see Naval Intelligence report, Feb. 26, 1919, file # 10314-414 (11); 65/165, NA. Memorandum for the chief of staff, Jan. 5, 1918, file # 10124-83; 296/165, NA. French observers concurred that Lorraine peasants accepted the American arrival as coldly as they reacted to all the war's events. "L'état d'esprit des populations du secteur," 17N 47, Vincennes.

23. "Les américains et la guerre," Oct. 28, 1917 (cited n. 11 above).

24. 1st Lt. Oswald Moore, 107th Machine Gun Battalion, letter, Oct. 12, 1918. Oswald Moore Papers, Manuscripts, Carlisle (hereafter Moore Papers). Pvt. Leonard L. Brazeau, 305th Field Signal Battalion, 80th Division. WWI, Carlisle. Lt. Col. J. A. Baer to insp. gen., Sept. 22, 1918, file # 247 (1); 588/120, NA.

25. Fiske, secret memorandum for the chief of staff, July 4, 1918, in "Report of the G-5." Pétain, "Instruction of American Infantry Units Attached to Large French Units," May 1, 1918, app. 41, folder # 265; 22/120, NA.

26. Pershing to secretary of war, Jan. 17, 1918, reprinted in Pershing, *My Experiences*, 1: 293–97, 274–76.

27. Chief of staff, AEF, to all corps and division commanders, June 17, 1918, Goddard, "Franco-American Relations" (cited n. 15 above), app. 2.

28. Brig. Gen. D. E. Nolan, assistant chief of staff, G-2, GHQ, AEF, to director of MID, May 27, 1919, file # 10314-414 (23); 65/165, NA. "Conditions Among Troops at Mayet (July 31–August 5)," Aug. 6, 1918; 195/120, NA.

29. For commander survey, see Goddard, "Franco-American Relations" (cited n. 15 above), pp. 1–5.

30. Ibid., p. 7.

31. "Les américains et l'opinion française" (cited n. 13 above).

32. "Les américains et l'opinion française d'après le contrôle de la correspondance du 15 juillet au 15 août 1918" (cited n. 19 above).

33. "Commission contrôle postal militaire," Oct. 27, 1918, 16N 1397, Vincennes.

34. Thomas C. Leonard, *Above the Battle: War-Making in America from Appomattox to Versailles* (New York: Oxford University Press, 1978), pp. 59–73, argues that the desire to defeat a formidable opponent reflected Americans' need to reaffirm their own self-worth through a chivalrous war effort, and that the Germans were the most satisfying opponent they had faced since fighting among themselves in the Civil War.

35. The preeminent military theorist Emory Upton was especially captivated by the Prussian military system. Russell Weigley, *History of the United States Army* (New York: Macmillan, 1967), pp. 276–81, 314–17, 335–41, argues that Upton proposed numerous reforms based on the German model that were untenable in the United States, such as eliminating citizen-soldier organizations, establishing a large peacetime army, and reducing civilian control over the military.

36. John Higham, *Strangers in the Land* (New York: Atheneum, 1978), pp. 25, 123, 195–98, 205–12, 304–5.

37. Robert Lee Bullard, diary entry, Oct. 28, 1917, Diary # 9. Bullard Papers, LOC. Commander in chief to commanding generals, Dec. 13, 1917, folder # 3, box 2. Summerall Papers, LOC.

38. In their published memoirs, Generals Robert Bullard, James Harbord, and Douglas MacArthur all admitted their professional admiration for the defeated enemy. See Leonard, *Above the Battle*, pp. 77, 221.

39. Cpl. Charles Hill, 364th Infantry, 91st Division. Fred E. Ross, 317th Infantry, 80th Division. Joseph Hussar, 319th Infantry, 80th Division. All in WWI, Carlisle.

40. For refusal of U.S. troops to surrender, see "Combat Value of American Troops," Apr. 23, 1918, intelligence officer of [the German] GHQ, in U.S. Army, Department of the Office of Military History, *United States Army in the World War, 1917–1919*, vol. 11: *American Occupation of Germany* (Washington, D.C.: GPO, 1948; reprinted Washington, D.C.: Center of Military History, 1988), p. 290.

41. Pvt. Emmett Riggin, 60th C.A.C., diary, Virginia State Archives. Pvt. James H. Turner, 159th Infantry, 80th Division. Cpl. Ralph T. Moran, 103rd Infantry, 26th Division. Sgt. Charles R. Blatt, 305th Engineers, 80th Division, memoir. All in WWI, Carlisle.

42. Lt. Col. J. A. Baer to insp. gen., Sept. 22, 1918 (cited n. 24 above). On American chivalry in World War I combat, see "Americans in a Major Operation," memorandum for [the German] chief of the general staff of the field army, Sept. 22, 1918, reprinted in *United States Army in the World War*, 11: 414.

43. Sgt. Maj. Julius Wax, 3rd Battalion, 102nd Infantry, 26th Division, Oct. 19, 1918, file # 299-13; 588/120, NA.

44. "Special Examination of Six Prisoners, All of the 12th company, 33rd Land-wehr Regiment, 1st Landwehr Division, captured November 6," Nov. 6, 1918, "26th Division" folder, box 16. Hugh Drum Papers, Manuscripts, Carlisle (hereafter Drum Papers).

45. Interrogation by Col. J. A. Baer of Lt. Col. E. E. Lewis, commander, 102nd Infantry, and of Sgt. Wax. Memorandum for insp. gen., AEF, Dec. 1, 1918. All in file # 299-13; 588/120, NA.

46. Edward Coffman, *The War To End All Wars: The American Military Experience in World War I* (New York: Oxford University Press, 1968), pp. 330–31. Donald Smythe, *Pershing: General of the Armies* (Bloomington: Indiana University Press, 1986), pp. 215–16.

47. Lt. Col. C. M. Dowell, commander, 103rd Infantry, to Brig. Gen. Charles H. Cole, commanding general, 52nd Infantry Brigade, Nov. 12, 1918, "26th Division" folder, box 16. Drum Papers, Manuscripts, Carlisle.

48. Statement of Capt. Joseph W. Hinkson, 311th Machine Gun Battalion, Nov. 5, 1918, "26th Division" folder, box 16. Drum Papers, Manuscripts, Carlisle.

49. Dowell to Cole, Nov. 12, 1918. Hinkson statement, Nov. 5, 1918.

50. Dowell to chief of staff, 26th Division, Nov. 7, 1918, file # 299-13; 588/120, NA. The division commander immediately relieved the commanders of the 3rd Battalion and 52nd Infantry Brigade for failing to visit the line. Statement of Brig. Gen. Charles H. Cole, 52nd Infantry Brigade, file # 299-13; 588/120, NA.

51. 1st Lt. Nathaniel Stimson, 53rd Pioneer Infantry, letter to mother, Nov. 23, 1918. Pvt. A. B. Danagher, 33rd Division, recollection. Both in Armistice box, WWI, Carlisle.

52. Pvt. Robinson Shepard, 301st Signal Battalion, 76th Division, "Memories of World War I." WWI, Carlisle.

53. Moore, 107th Machine Gun Battalion, letter, Nov. 11, 1918. Moore Papers, Manuscripts, Carlisle.

54. Lt. Col. Paul H. Clark, director of the American Military Mission, French GHQ, to Gen. John J. Pershing, Nov. 8, 1918. Letters sent to General Pershing by [Lt.] Col. Paul H. Clark, chief, American Military Mission, French General Headquarters, containing military intelligence, Mar.–July 1918 (entry 18); Private Papers of General of the Armies John J. Pershing, Record Group 200 (hereafter 18/200, NA); National Archives, College Park, Md. The letters in this file actually end in June 1919, not July 1918.

55. Pershing to Allied Supreme War Council, Oct. 30, 1918, reprinted in John J. Pershing, *My Experiences in the World War* (New York: Frederick A. Stokes, 1931), 2: 366–77.

56. See, e.g., "The American Military Factor in the War," Jan. 14, 1918, file # 811.20/1; General Records of the American Commission to Negotiate Peace, 1918–31 (entry 27); Records of the American Commission to Negotiate Peace, Record Group 256 (hereafter 27/256, NA); National Archives, College Park, Md.

57. "American Military Factor in the War," p. 16.

58. Nolan, assistant chief of staff, G-2, AEF, to director, Military Intelligence,

May 27, 1919 (cited n. 28 above). For other complaints against French civilians, see "Relations Between American and French Armies," Jan. 17, 1919, "Joseph C. Grew, December 1918–February 1919" folder, box 247, Tasker Bliss Papers, Library of Congress (hereafter Bliss Papers, LOC).

59. Acting chief of staff, G-2, 4th Division, to acting chief of staff, G-2, GHQ, May 17, 1919 (cited n. 22 above). Memorandum for Colonel Moreno, GHQ, AEF, Apr. 2, 1919, file # 20327-A-654; 6/120, NA. Memorandum for Gen. Marlborough Churchill, "Negro Troops in France," Nov. 18, 1918, file # 10218-256; 65/165, NA. "French Soldiers Like Negro Yanks," *Topeka Plaindealer*, Oct. 11, 1918, in "General News Clippings, September–Oct., 1918" folder, box C-377. NAACP Papers, LOC.

60. Naval Intelligence report (cited n. 22 above), Feb. 26, 1919, p. 5; "Misunderstanding Between Americans and French," Jan. 23, 1919, file # 10314-414 (10); 65/165, NA; Report to chief liaison officer on conditions in occupied territory, Feb. 3, 1919, and Memorandum to commander in chief, AEF, Jan. 19, 1918, in Goddard, "Franco-American Relations" (cited n. 15 above), apps. 5 and 6; Lt. Col. Paul H. Clark to Pershing, Jan. 5, 1919; 18/200, NA. For the terms of the Armistice, see Martin Gilbert, *The First World War: A Complete History* (New York: Holt, 1994), p. 500.

61. "Relations Between American and French Armies" (cited n. 58 above), pp. 3–4, Jan. 17, 1919. Leonard, *Above the Battle*, pp. 68–73, suggests that American soldiers always intended to reconcile immediately with the Germans, whom they saw as much closer to them in temperament and accomplishment than the French. He describes their psychology during the war as loving the sinner, hating the sin.

62. "Rapport N° 32, Capitaine Hendrick, officier de liaison," Dec. 4, 1918, 17N 47, Vincennes.

63. Cpl. Ernie Hilton, 353rd Infantry, 89th Division, letter to Grace, Dec. 26, 1918. WWI, Carlisle.

64. Enemy Order of Battle Subsection, Intelligence Department, GHQ, AEF, "Candid Comment on the American Soldier, 1917–1918, . . . by the Germans," pp. 57–58, file # 124-271 (1); 65/165, NA. Acting chief of staff, G-2, 4th Division, to acting chief of staff, G-2, GHQ, May 17, 1919 (cited n. 22 above).

65. "Contrôle postal militaire," X Armée, Dec. 8, 1918, 16N 1447, and Commission de contrôle postal, IV Armée, March 1919, 16N 1410. Both in Vincennes.

66. Memorandum for General Connor, Dec. 26, 1918, "American Forces in Germany" folder, box 373, Pershing Papers, LOC. Fraternization was easier to control in German cities because American soldiers lived in barracks. "Confidential Report on Alienation Between American and French," Mar. 26, 1919, file # 10314-414; 65/165, NA. Acting chief of staff, G-2, 4th Division, to acting chief of staff, G-2, GHQ, May 17, 1919 (cited n. 22 above).

67. Quotation from memorandum for General McIntyre, "Work of Morale Branch, Week Ending March 8, 1919," Mar. 13, 1919, file # 1010-17; 8/165, NA. See also, e.g., Naval Intelligence Report (cited n. 22 above), Feb. 26, 1919, p. 2; memorandum for General Connor, Dec. 26, 1918.

68. Nolan, assistant chief of staff, G-2, AEF, to director, Military Intelligence, May 27, 1919 (cited n. 28 above); acting chief of staff, G-2, 4th Division, to acting chief

of staff, G-2, GHQ, May 17, 1919 (cited n. 22 above); "Relations Between American and French Armies," Jan. 17, 1919 (cited n. 58 above); "Franco-American Relations" (cited n. 15 above), p. 19.

69. British Mission, GHQ, AEF, Dec. 10, 1918, weekly summary for week ending Dec. 7, 1918, WO106/499A. Directorate of Military Operations and Intelligence: Papers, WO 106, Public Records Office, London.

70. "Mission militaire française près de l'armée américaine, rendre comptes les territoires occupés par l'armée américaine," Mar. 13, 1919, 17N 48; Colonel Linard to président du conseil, Mar. 12, 1919, 7N 2249; Commissariat général des affaires de guerre franco-américaines, Jan. 24, 1919, 6N 137. All in Vincennes.

71. Captain LeBleu, secretary, 3rd Bureau, conversation quoted by Lt. Col. Paul H. Clark in a letter to Pershing, Dec. 22, 1918; 18/200, NA.

72. "Chef du 2ᵉ Bureau de la mission militaire française près de l'armée américaine, compte rendu des observations à Metz, Trèves, Coblence, Chaumont," Feb. 13, 1919, 17N 48, Vincennes.

73. Naval Intelligence report (cited n. 22 above), Feb. 26, 1919.

74. Lt. James Harten to intelligence officer, port of embarkation, Feb. 25, 1919, file # 10314-399; 65/165, NA. Memorandum for General Bliss, Dec. 17, 1918, "Naval Officers, November 1918–October 1919" folder, box 248. Bliss Papers, LOC. Memorandum for Major Brown, Feb. 5, 1919, file # 10314-399 (1); 65/165, NA. Naval Intelligence report (cited n. 22 above), Feb. 26, 1919, pp. 7–8.

75. Acting director, MID, to assistant chief of staff, G-2, AEF, Mar. 18, 1919, reprinted in Goddard, "Franco-American Relations" (cited n. 15 above), app. 4. Maj. L. B. Dunham to acting director, MID, Mar. 21, 1919, file # 10314-414 (18); 65/165, NA. Memorandum for Colonel Dunn, Mar. 17, 1919, file # 10314-414 (15); 65/165, NA.

76. "Mission militaire française près l'armée américaine, rendre compte des observations dans les territoires occupés par l'armée américaine," Dec. 13, 1918, 17N 48, Vincennes.

77. Naval Intelligence report (cited n. 22 above), Feb. 26, 1919, pp. 3–4.

78. "Commissariat général des affaires de guerre franco-américaines," Jan. 24, 1919 (cited n. 70 above).

79. "Correspondance étrangère," Nov. 18–24, 1918, 16N 1410, Vincennes.

80. "American Soldiers Teach the Art of Voting," Second Division Summary of Intelligence, Feb. 2, 1919, in "Candid Comment" (cited n. 64 above), p. 47. For quotation on the symbolic importance of elections, see "Supervision of Civil Legislative Organs," in *United States Army in the World War*, 11: 227–30; J. M. Winter, *The Experience of World War I* (New York: Oxford University Press, 1989), pp. 211–13.

81. "Commission de contrôle postal militaire, 3ᵉ Armée," Dec. 7–13, 1918, 16N 1404, Vincennes.

82. Capt. Georges Bertrand, "Mission militaire française près l'armée américaine," Mar. 27, 1919, 17N 48, Vincennes.

83. "Relations Between American and French armies" (cited n. 58 above), Jan. 17, 1919, pp. 6, 9. Memorandum to Capt. Edwin S. Ross, port of embarkation intelligence officer, June 21, 1919, file # 80-163 (103); 65/165, NA. Lt. Col. Paul H. Clark to Persh-

ing, Nov. 16, Dec. 4, and Dec. 23, 1918; Feb. 13, Feb. 24, and May 2, 1919. All in 18/200, NA.

84. Pershing, diary entry, Jan. 11 and 12, 1919, vol. 2: Sept. 2, 1918–July 30, 1919, box 4–5. Pershing Papers, LOC.

85. Naval Intelligence report (cited n. 22 above), Feb. 26, 1919, p. 3; memorandum for General Connor, Dec. 26, 1918 (cited n. 66 above).

86. Minutes of the Daily Meeting of the Commissionary Plenipotentiary, American Commission to Negotiate Peace, Feb. 15, 1919, p. v, file # 184.00101/15; 27/256, NA.

87. "Rapport du Lieutenant de Ham, officier de liaison adjoint," Feb. 8, 1919, 17N 48, Vincennes.

88. Lt. Col. Paul H. Clark, director of the American Military Mission at French GHQ, continually pointed out to French officials that Pershing had issued a general order prohibiting fraternization. During a personal tour of the occupied zone, Clark also elicited guarantees from unit commanders that they would improve enforcement of this order. Clark to Pershing, Jan. 5, 1919 (cited n. 60 above).

89. "Mission militaire française près l'armée américaine," Dec. 13, 1918 (cited n. 76 above).

90. "Compte rendu, Cap. Georges Bertrand, l'informateur spécial près l'armée américaine, Coblence," Apr. 1919, 17N 48, Vincennes.

91. For July 4 celebration, see correspondence, Apr.–June 1919 in 7N 2251, Vincennes. For distribution of Croix de guerre, see "Compte rendu, Cap. Georges Bertrand," Apr. 1919. For French officers attending stateside ceremonies, see General Collardet, military attaché, French embassy, Washington, D.C., to the French minister of war, "E.M.A. bureau spécial franco-américain," Apr. 30, 1919, 7N 2251, Vincennes.

92. 2d Lt. Charles Brady Ryan, June 29, 1919, diary entry. Papers of participants in the American Expeditionary Forces, North Russia, Michigan Historical Collections, Bentley Historical Library, University of Michigan, Ann Arbor, Michigan (hereafter UM).

93. "Mission militaire française près de l'armée américaine," Mar. 13, 1919 (cited n. 70 above).

94. Jean-Jules Jusserand, French ambassador, Washington, D.C., foreign affairs telegram no. 378, July 26, 1919, 6N 138, Vincennes.

95. Memorandum for Gen. Marlborough Churchill, Apr. 25, 1919, file # 10261-78; 65/165, NA.

96. For additional discussion of the African-American/French friendship, see Tyler Stovall, *Paris Noir* (New York: Houghton Mifflin, 1996), pp. 16–24.

97. F. J. Grimké, "Address of Welcome to the Men Who Have Returned from the Battlefront," in *A Documentary History of the Negro People in the United States*, vol. 3: *From the N.A.A.C.P. to the New Deal*, ed. Herbert Aptheker (New York: Carol Publishing Group, 1993), p. 242.

98. W. E. B. Du Bois, "The Black Man and the Wounded World," ch. 14, unnumbered pages of unpublished manuscript, box 57, W. E. B. Du Bois Papers, Fisk University, Tennessee (hereafter Du Bois Papers, Fisk).

99. "Rapport sur les relations franco-américaines, Mission militaire française près l'armée américaine, prévôté auprès de la 92ᵉ Division," Oct. 1, 1918, 17N 47, Vincennes.

100. Unsigned letter to Du Bois, June 10, 1918, ch. 10 notes, box 55, Du Bois Papers, Fisk.

101. Tyler Stovall, "The Color Line Behind the Lines: Racial Violence in France During the Great War," *American Historical Review* 103, no. 3 (June 1998): 737–69.

102. For West African soldiers' experiences in France, see Charles John Balsei, *From Adversaries to Comrades in Arms: West Africans and the French Military, 1885–1918* (Waltham, Mass.: Crossroads, 1979); Lucie Cousturier, *Des inconnus chez moi* (Paris: Editions de la Sirène, 1920); Marc Michel, *L'Appel à l'Afrique: Contributions et réactions à l'effort de guerre en A.O.F., 1914–1919* (Paris: Publications de la Sorbonne, 1982); Joe Harris Lunn, "Memoirs of the Maelstrom: A Senegalese Oral History of the First World War" (Ph.D. diss., University of Wisconsin, 1993).

103. Stovall, *Paris Noir*, p. 23.

104. George H. Wilson, Brest, France to Du Bois, July 19, 1919, box 62, Du Bois Papers, Fisk.

105. Elmer Carter to Du Bois, May 7, 1919, reel 8/500, W. E. B. Du Bois Papers, University of Massachusetts–Amherst (hereafter Du Bois, UM-A).

106. *The Crisis* 18 (May 1919): 12.

107. Louis H. Pomtock to Du Bois, Apr. 26, 1919, reel 8/43, Du Bois Papers, UM-A.

108. "Rapport sur les relations entre les militaires américains de la 92ᵉ Division et la population civile française," Aug. 31, 1918, 17N 47, Vincennes.

109. "Rapport de la prévôté auprès de la 26ᵉ Division sur les relations entre les soldats américains et la population," Aug. 1, 1918, 17N 47, Vincennes.

110. "Rapport sur les relations franco-américaines" (cited n. 99 above).

111. Arthur Barbeau and Florette Henri, *The Unknown Soldiers: Black American Troops in World War I* (Philadelphia: Temple University Press, 1974), pp. 108, 135, 142–43, 167. Chaplain Jos. F. Simpson to Du Bois, June 7, 1919, reel 8/927, Du Bois Papers, UM-A. Pomtock to Du Bois, Apr. 26, 1919 (cited n. 107 above).

112. Simpson to Du Bois, June 7, 1919.

113. Quoted in Du Bois, "The Black Man and the Wounded World" (cited n. 98 above), ch. 14.

114. Quoted in Michel Fabre, *La Rive Noire: De Harlem à la Seine* (Paris: Lieu Commun, 1985), p. 49.

115. Stovall, *Paris Noir*, tells the story of this unique relationship from World War I until the present.

116. "Returning Soldiers," *The Crisis* 18 (May 1919): 14.

117. Brig. Gen. D. E. Nolan, assistant chief of staff, G-2, to C.E. officers, secret, Jan. 31, 1919, 17N 46, Vincennes. Concern that Du Bois was responsible for radicalizing black troops brought *The Crisis* under heavy MID surveillance in the postwar period. See Theodore Kornweibel, Jr., *Seeing Red: The Federal Campaign Against Black Militancy, 1919–1925* (Bloomington: Indiana University Press, 1998), pp. 54–60.

118. William H. York, Co. K, 368th Infantry, to Du Bois, Jan. 25, 1919, reel 8/1055, Du Bois Papers, UM–A.

119. General Collardet, military attaché, French embassy, Washington, D.C., Aug. 6, 1919, 6N 136, Vincennes.

120. William R. Keylor, " 'How They Advertised France': The French Propaganda Campaign in the United States During the Breakup of the Franco-American En-tente, 1918–1923," *Diplomatic History* 17 (Summer 1993): 351–73; Keith L. Nelson, "The 'Black Horror on the Rhine': Race as a Factor in Post–World War I Diplomacy," *Journal of Modern History* 42 (1970): 606–27; Sally Marks, "Black Watch on the Rhine: A Study in Propaganda, Prejudice, and Prurience," *European Studies Review* 13 (July 1983): 297–334.

6. The Legacy of the War for the Army

1. Pvt. Julius Christensen, 3rd Pioneer Infantry, letter to sister, Dec. 15, 1918. Pvt. Everett Taylor, 101st Infantry, 26th Division, letter home, Dec. 14, 1918. Both in WWI, Carlisle. The AWOL problem was particularly great in noncombatant units; see Office of the Assistant Chief of Staff, G-2, Dec. 17, 1918, "MP" folder; 588/120, NA.

2. Maj. J. W. Foyle quoted in "Summary of Complaints Received at National Office N.A.A.C.P. from Colored Soldiers at Army Camps in United States, By Camps," in "Military, General 1918" folder, box C-374, NAACP Papers, LOC. For postwar non-combatant complaints about working alongside more highly paid civilian workers, see Charles Williams's reports for Camp Taylor, Dec. 30, 1918, file # 10218 (unmarked); Camp Meade, Feb. 8, 1919, file # 10218 (unmarked); and Camp Knox, Dec. 12, 1918, file # 10218-248. On the lax postwar work habits of white noncombatants, see "Morale of Troops, Newport News, Va.," Jan. 7, 1919, file # 80-163 (1). Investigators uniformly reported poor postwar morale; see December 1918 reports from Camp Sevier, Camp Sherman, Camp Jackson, Camp Beauregard, Picatinny Arsenal, and Camp Devens, file # 80-173. All in 65/165, NA.

3. Memorandum for the chief of staff, p. 4, Feb. 25, 1919, folder # 266; 22/120, NA.

4. Capt. Walter Lippmann to Brig. Gen. D. E. Nolan, assistant chief of staff, G-2, AEF, Jan. 15, 1919, "L, 1919" folder. Baker Papers, LOC. And see also Robert Davis, adj. gen., "Morale in the AEF," Feb. 14, 1919, "Fifth Army Corps: Other Intelligence Reports" folder, box 16. Summerall Papers. LOC.

5. Pvt. Myron J. Edwards, 30th Engineer Regiment, memoir. Capt. Roy E. Meyers, 114th Field Artillery, 30th Division, diary. Both in WWI, Carlisle.

6. "Letters Written to the *Stars and Stripes*," Jan. 13, 1919, file # 1038; 588/120, NA.

7. Cpl. Lawrence B. Wright, 25th Engineer Regiment, diary entry, Apr. 1919. WWI, Carlisle.

8. Pvt. T. P. Wilson, 317th Infantry, 80th Division, memoir, Rockbridge County folder, Virginia State Archives. Letters from Pvt. George Simons and Pvt. H. B. Dale in "Letters Written to the *Stars and Stripes*," Jan. 13, 1919. For problems between offi-cers and soldiers at home, see memorandum for General McIntyre, Dec. 10, 1918, file # 1010; 8/165, NA.

9. Raymond Fosdick, Commission on Training Camp Activities, to Secretary of War Newton Baker, Apr. 17, 1919, p. 3, "F, 1919" folder. Baker Papers, LOC.

10. Quotation from memorandum for the commander in chief, chief of staff, Feb. 15, 1919, file # 357-26; 588/120, NA. Memorandum on the morale of reserve officers, Oct. 11, 1919, file # 21660-T; 6/120, NA. "Morale," file # 1-1935-6, pp. 38–39. Curriculum, Carlisle. Memorandum for the director of operations, Apr. 8, 1919, file # 1010-32; 8/165, NA. For low officer morale, see memorandum for chief, Morale Branch, Feb. 24, 1919, file # 46542; 398/165, NA. Meyers, diary. Baker to Gen. John J. Pershing, Jan. 25, 1919, "B, 1919" folder. Baker Papers, LOC.

11. 2d Lt. Lawrence E. Richardson, 101st Field Artillery, 26th Division, letter home, Jan. 29, 1919. WWI, Carlisle. Memorandum for the commander in chief, chief of staff, Feb. 15, 1919. Memorandum on the morale of reserve officers, Oct. 11, 1919.

12. On board the USS *Aeolus*, citizen-soldiers refused to salute their officers, yet they recounted this sympathetic tale. "Attitude of Returning Personnel," Apr. 30, 1919, file # 80-163 (12); 65/165, NA. For soldiers' sense of distance from headquarters officials, see Maj. Gen. James Harbord, commander, Service of Supply, to Maj. Gen. J. W. McAndrew, AEF chief of staff, Jan. 31, 1919. Harbord Papers, LOC.

13. T. P. Wilson memoir (cited n. 8 above).

14. Baker to Pershing, Aug. 3, 1919, "Book file, Memoirs 1918–19," box 373. Pershing Papers, LOC.

15. Nolan believed that unchecked letter writing to the AEF newspaper would undermine discipline and ordered commanding officers to punish those who wrote unrestrained letters to the *Stars and Stripes*. "Letters Written to the *Stars and Stripes*," Jan. 13, 1919. AEF officials were also concerned about the number of uncensored letters reaching the United States now that the war was over. Memorandum for Colonel Moreno, Apr. 2, 1919, file # 20327-A-654; 6/120, NA.

16. Fosdick to Baker, Feb. 20, 1919, "F, 1919" folder. Baker Papers, LOC.

17. For instructions and list, see "Confidential Questionnaire," Camp Grant file; 377/165, NA. For concerns about confidentiality, see Col. E. L. Munson to morale officers, Feb. 6, 1919, "Cases for Investigation, February" folder, box A8; 377/165, NA.

18. Memorandums for General McIntyre, Feb. 14 and Mar. 13, 1919, file # 1010 (17); 8/165, NA. See also individual camp reports in Camp Grant, Camp Funston, and Camp Travis files; 377/165, NA, and in file # 80-163; 65/165, NA.

19. Harbord to McAndrew, Jan. 31, 1919, and McAndrew's reply to Harbord, Feb. 3, 1919. Harbord Papers, LOC. For Baer's suggestions, see memorandum on the morale of reserve officers, Oct. 11, 1919 (cited n. 10 above). For Fiske's defense of his program, see memorandum for the chief of staff, Feb. 25, 1919 (cited n. 3 above).

20. Fosdick, memorandum on morale in the AEF, Feb. 1, 1919, file # 80-34 (2); 65/165, NA. For Case quotation, see memorandum for the director of operations, Apr. 8, 1919 (cited n. 10 above); see also Lt. Col. Harry Hodges to Gen. Charles Dawes, Nov. 19, 1918, file # 8005-Q; 6/120, NA. Maj. William H. Loving to director, MID, Aug. 6, 1919, file # 10128; 65/165, NA.

21. For this officer meeting, see "First Meeting of the Caucus of the American

Legion," Mar. 15, 1919, file # 5777, Thomas File; 310/165, NA; memorandum for the commander in chief, chief of staff, Feb. 15, 1919 (cited n. 10 above). Fosdick, memorandum on morale in the AEF, Feb. 1, 1919.

22. Quotations from Davis, "Morale in the AEF," Feb. 14, 1919 (cited n. 4 above). For changes in training policy see memorandum for the chief of staff, Feb. 25, 1919 (cited n. 3 above).

23. For policy changes, see "First Meeting of the Caucus of the American Legion"; memorandum for Gen. McIntyre, Mar. 13, 1919 (cited n. 18 above); "Morale," file # 1-1935-6 (cited n. 10 above). For souvenirs, see memorandum for the director of operations, Apr. 8, 1919 (cited n. 10 above). For choice given to hospitalized men, see memorandum from the chief of staff, AEF, GHQ, Feb. 23, 1919, file # 15932-A-377; 6/120, NA.

24. Base Censor, AEF, "Report on 1st Army," Jan. 13, 1919, file # 1045. "Examination of Mail of 81st Division." Both in 588/120, NA. Memorandum for Colonel Moreno, Apr. 2, 1919 (cited n. 15 above). Also see letters in files cited above of 2d Lt. Lawrence Richardson and Pvt. Julius Christensen. And Pvt. M. J. Cunningham, Virginia State Archives.

25. Office of the Chief of Military History, "History of Military Demobilization in the U.S.," box 32. Peyton March Papers, Library of Congress (hereafter March Papers, LOC). *New York Times*, Feb. 16, 1919, sec. 4, p. 11.

26. Lt. Col. James O'Brien, "Loss of Effects of Deceased Officers and Soldiers in World War I," Aug. 1942, file # 7200-Z, Thomas File; 310/165, NA. *New York Times*, Jan. 3, 1919, p. 8. For congressional response to complaints from soldiers and their families, see also Theodore Conway, "The Great Demobilization: Personnel Demobilization of the A.E.F. and the Emergency Army, 1918–19: A Study of Civil-Military Relations" (Ph.D. diss., Duke University, 1986), pp. 90–100. John M. Lindley, "A Soldier's Also a Citizen: The Controversy over Military Justice in the U.S. Army, 1917–1920" (Ph.D. diss., Duke University, 1974), pp. 193–98.

27. Report, El Paso, Tex., Apr. 29, 1919, file # 10603-2; 65/165, NA.

28. Sgt. Walter O'Malley, 336th Machine Gun Battalion, 87th Division, letter to parents, Feb. 2, 1919. WWI, Carlisle.

29. Edwards, memoir (cited n. 5 above). *New York Times*, Jan. 3, 1919, p. 8; Feb. 8, 1919, p. 11.

30. *New York Times*, Feb. 16, 1919, sec. 4, p. 11.

31. Pvt. Harry Brandeberry to Senator William Borah, Aug. 19, 1919, "Discharges —Army, A-B," box 71. William E. Borah Papers, Library of Congress (hereafter Borah Papers, LOC).

32. Alfred Schak to Senator Thomas Walsh, May 26, 1919, "Soldiers Abroad" folder, box 205. Thomas James Walsh Papers, Library of Congress (hereafter Walsh Papers, LOC).

33. Pvt. Edward F. Mason to Borah, Apr. 30, 1919, "Demobilization, 1918–19" folder, box 71. Borah Papers, LOC.

34. Brandeberry to Borah, Aug. 19, 1919.

35. Chamberlain is quoted in a letter from General Collardet, military attaché,

French embassy, Washington, D.C., to the French minister of war, Jan. 2, 1919, 17N 9, Vincennes.

36. *New York Times*, Jan. 3, 1919, p. 8; Jan. 4, 1919, p. 6; Feb. 8, 1919, p. 11; Feb. 21, 1919, p. 7; Feb. 23, 1919, p. 12. Memorandum for chief, Morale Branch, June 12, 1919. Memorandum for the chief of staff, June 23, 1919. Both in Camp Grant file; 377/165, NA.

37. *New York Times*, Feb. 2, 1919, p. 17.

38. Pvt. Guy H. McCool to Borah, Camp Merritt, July 20, 1919, "Military Discharges" box 72. Borah Papers, LOC.

39. Charles Earle Duncan to Mrs. R. Duncan Scott, Apr. 27, 1919, reel 8/203, Du Bois Papers, UM-A.

40. Charles Williams, *Sidelights on Negro Soldiers* (Boston: B. J. Brimmer, 1923), p. 72. For the role of *The Crisis*, see Loving to director, MID, Aug. 6, 1919 (cited n. 20 above). For "Soldiers of America," see "Summary of Complaints," NAACP Papers, LOC (cited n. 2 above).

41. Clarence G. Scheu, Co. B, 339 Infantry, diary entry Jan. 10, 1919. Clarence G. Scheu Papers, UM.

42. David S. Foglesong, *America's Secret War Against Bolshevism* (Chapel Hill: University of North Carolina Press, 1995), p. 5.

43. The "good ally" thesis is advanced by Eugene P. Trani, "Woodrow Wilson and the Decision to Intervene in Russia: A Reconsideration," *Journal of Modern History* 48, no. 3 (Sept. 1976): 440–61, and John W. Long, "American Intervention in Russia: The North Russian Expedition, 1918–19," *Diplomatic History* 6, no. 1 (Winter 1982): 45–67. They rely on Baker's subsequent recollection of conversations in which, he said, Wilson claimed that he was against the Russian expeditions but explained, "my trouble is that we are fighting the war with allies." Baker to Peyton March, Sept. 7, 1927, "Ma-Mb, 1927" folder, box 150, Baker Papers, LOC. In *America's Secret War Against Bolshevism*, Foglesong, however, disagrees. In his estimation, the Wilson administration fought a long undeclared war against Bolshevism, of which military intervention formed just one part. Historians who have focused on the sending of regular army troops to Siberia have come to different conclusions over Wilson's motivation. Robert J. Maddox, *The Unknown War with Russia: Wilson's Siberian Intervention* (San Rafael, Calif.: Presidio Press, 1977), views it as a direct response to Bolshevism. Betty Miller Unterberger, *America's Siberian Adventure, 1918–1920: A Study of National Policy* (Durham, N.C.: Duke University Press, 1956), emphasizes Japanese ambitions to expand into Siberia.

44. Foglesong, *America's Secret War Against Bolshevism*, pp. 202–5.

45. Ibid., pp. 143–87.

46. Ibid., pp. 159–64.

47. Ibid., pp. 181–82.

48. The legitimate confusion over what Wilson had authorized in his aide-mémoire of July 17, 1918, is discussed in detail by Long, "American Intervention in Russia."

49. Sgt. T. F. Moran, 339th Infantry, to Anna Moran, Dec. 3, 1918, Field Censorship folder; General Correspondence, 1918–19 (entry 1537); AEF, North Russia, 1918–19; Textual Records of the AEF, 1917–23; Record Group 120 (hereafter 1537/120,

NA); National Archives, College Park, Md. For other reports that American soldiers believed the coalition force was sent to camouflage an imperialistic British scheme, see "Facts and Questions Concerning the N.R.E.F," Feb. 27, 1919, file # 24-327 (59); 65/165, NA; 1st Lt. E. O. Munn to Col. J. A. Ruggles, chief of American Military Mission, p. 3, Jan. 3, 1919, "Allied Offensive on Vologda Force Front" folder; Historical File, 1918–19 (entry 1540); AEF, North Russia, 1918–19; Textual Records of the AEF, 1917–23, Record Group 120 (hereafter 1540/120, NA); College Park, Md.; Ruggles to GHQ, AEF, France, Nov. 29, 1918, "AEF and American Forces in France, January–December 1918" folder, box 248. Bliss Papers, LOC; Adjutant, Base Section No. 3, SOS, to commanding officer, American Forces in Russia, Feb. 13, 1919, quoted in Lt. Col. Calvin H. Goddard, "Relations Between AEF and BEF Forces, 1917–1920," p. 17, June 1942, file # 7200-E, pt. 1, Thomas File; 310/165, NA.

50. For Colonel Stewart's orders, see commanding officer to 1st Lt. Henry Katz, Mar. 18, 1919; Memorandum: Violation of Censorship Regulations; Censorship Posters, Nov. 22, 1918. All in Field Censorship folder; 1537/120, NA.

51. Foglesong, *America's Secret War Against Bolshevism*, pp. 213–25.

52. Dewitt Poole, chargé d'affaires, U.S. Embassy, to American Peace Mission, Paris, Jan. 23, 1919, file # 861.00/154. Memorandum for the president, from Gen. Tasker Bliss, Feb. 12, 1919, file # 861.0146/6. Both in 27/256, NA. For firsthand accounts of averting disaster during this attack, see Edwin Arkins, 339th Infantry, diary entry Jan. 24–30, 1919, and Godfrey J. Anderson, "The 337th Field Hospital in North Russia, 1918–19," pp. 47–72, in Edwin Arkins Papers and Godfrey J. Anderson Papers, UM.

53. Diaries of Pvt. Charles Althen Simpson, Ambulance Co.; Cpl. James B. Sibley, Co. E, 339th Infantry Regiment; 2d Lt. Charles Brady Ryan, Co. K, 339th Regiment; George Albers, Co. E, 339th Infantry Regiment; Cpl. Cleo M. Colburn, Co. I, 339th Infantry Regiment. In, respectively, Charles Althen Simpson, James B. Sibley, Charles Brady Ryan, and Cleo M. Colburn Papers, UM.

54. Sgt. Rodger Sherman Clark, Co. C, 310th Engineers, "What Ails the AEF?" Apr. 23, 1919. Rodger Sherman Clark Papers, UM.

55. Petition in diary, Sgt. Silver Parrish, Co. B, 339th Infantry Regiment. Silver Parrish Papers, UM; Memorandum for Gen. Marlborough Churchill, Dec. 13, 1919, file # 24-327 (82); 65/165, NA; Mutinies in North Russia, July 1, 1919. All in Historical File; 1540/120, NA.

56. Dewitt Poole, chargé d'affaires, U.S. Embassy, to American Commission to Negotiate Peace, Feb. 13, 1919, file # 861.00/245; see also Feb. 20, 1919, file # 861.00/281; Mar. 31, 1919, file # 861.00/447. All in 27/256, NA. Pershing to Bliss, personal note, Dec. 1, 1918, "AEF and American Forces in France, Jan–Dec 1918" folder, box 248. Bliss Papers, LOC.

57. *The Papers of Woodrow Wilson*, vol. 53: *Nov. 19, 1918–Jan. 11, 1919* (Princeton: Princeton University Press, 1986), p. 583 nn. 5–6.

58. Baker to Wilson, Jan. 1, 1919, in *Papers of Woodrow Wilson*, 53: 580–84. Long, "American Intervention in Russia," pp. 62–63.

59. Bliss, diary, Feb. 8, 1919, box 244. Bliss Papers, LOC. Memorandum from Bliss to Wilson, Feb. 12, 1919 (cited n. 52 above).

60. Pvt. Kenneth A. Skellenger, Co. A, 339th Infantry, diary entry, Mar. 9, 1919. Kenneth A. Skellenger Papers, UM.

61. Charles Brady Ryan, diary entry, Dec. 14, 1918. Ryan Papers, UM.

62. Although for obvious reasons reluctant to admit authorship, 1st Lt. Carl Christine conceded that he had written *Facts and Questions Concerning the N.R.E.F.* as a personal letter home. He maintained that his comments accurately summarized the feelings of his men. How the document passed into the troops' hands remained a mystery. Some of Christine's fellow officers made copies for themselves on the night he wrote it, but during an official interrogation, each denied passing this tract on to enlisted men. See testimony, June 12–14, 1919, by 1st Lt. Carl H. Christine, Second Lt. Jesse W. Calhoon, 1st Lt. Albert M. Smith, 1st Lt. John Cudahy, Capt. Robert P. Boyd, Lt. W. H. Dresing. All of Company B, 339th Infantry, file # 24-327 (59); 65/165, NA.

63. Notation at the end of confiscated copy *Facts and Questions* . . . (cited n. 49 above).

64. Captain Prince, "Morale of American Troops on Diva Front," Feb. 2, 1919, in "Reports on American Morale" folder; 1540/120, NA.

65. Sgt. Edward Lenniv, Supply Company, 339th Infantry, letter to father, Oct. 22, 1918, Field Censorship folder; 1537/120, NA.

66. Sgt. Carleton G. Foster, Supply Company, 339th Infantry, letter to mother, Nov. 24, 1918, Field Censorship folder; 1537/120, NA. Christine quotation, *Facts and Questions* . . . (cited n. 49 above).

67. Poole to American Commission to Negotiate Peace, Mar. 31, 1919 (cited n. 56 above).

68. Unnamed soldier to brother, Dec. 5, 1918, Field Censorship folder; 1537/120, NA.

69. Colburn, diary entry, Mar. 30, 1919. Colburn Papers, UM. Simpson, diary entry, Apr. 3, 1919. Simpson Papers, UM.

70. Memorandum for Gen. Marlborough Churchill, Dec. 13, 1919; Mutinies in North Russia, pp. 9–12, July 1, 1919 (cited n. 55 above); Joel Moore, *The History of the American Expedition Fighting the Bolsheviks* (Detroit: Polar Bear Publishing, 1920), pp. 223–30; Sgt. Rodger Clark, "What Ails the ANREF?" (cited n. 54 above).

71. Sibley, diary entry, Jan. 4, 1919. Sibley Papers, UM. For Kodish, see also Charles Brady Ryan, diary entry, Jan. 8, 1919. Ryan Papers, UM. For Kodema, see Captain Prince, "Morale of American Troops" (cited n. 64 above).

72. Mutinies in North Russia, pp. 9–12, July 1, 1919 (cited n. 55 above). Simpson, diary entry, May 31, 1919. Simpson Papers, UM.

73. Parrish diary. Parrish Papers, UM.

74. Moore, *History of the American Expedition,* pp. 223–24. Colburn, diary entry, Feb. 11, 1919. Colburn Papers, UM. Clark to Iva, June 1, 1919. Clark Papers, UM; File 372.7, "Field Censorship File," 1537/120, NA. Baker to Wilson, Jan. 1, 1919 (cited n. 58 above).

75. D.A. Commons to Charles Brady Ryan, Feb. 15, 1919. Ryan Papers, UM. Example of petition in "Misc. Materials, 1918–19" folder. Michael Macalla Papers, UM.

76. Letter to Sgt. John Sherman Crissman, Co. A, 339th Infantry, from his mother,

Feb. 10, 1919, John Sherman Crissman Papers. Newspaper clippings in Walter McKenzie and Hugh D. McPhail Papers. All in UM.

77. Foglesong, *America's Secret War Against Bolshevism*, p. 228.

78. Skellenger, diary entry, Apr. 16, 1919. Skellenger Papers, UM. Long, "American Intervention in Russia," pp. 62–67.

79. Capt. J. A. Harzfeld to Col. J. A. Ruggles, Feb. 9, 1919, p. 4, "Reports on American Morale" folder; 1540/120, NA.

80. Long, "American Intervention in Russia," pp. 62–67.

81. *Chicago Tribune*, June 13, 1919, p. 1.

82. "Flashback: The War We Fought with Russia," *Sunday News*, Aug. 28, 1960, in Cpl. John Boron, Co. A, 339th Infantry, Boron Papers, UM. Macalla diary, 1929, and recollections in Macalla Papers, UM, and Sgt. Walter F. Dundon, Co. M, 339th Infantry, 1929 diary and recollections in Walter F. Dundon Papers, UM.

83. Dundon, "A Personal Experience Unique in the History of USA Wars," 1969 file. Dundon Papers, UM.

84. Memorandum for the chief of staff from E. H. Crowder, judge advocate general, Sept. 24, 1919, file # 1150; 8/165, NA. For support that the clemency board's actions generated for Samuel Ansell's reforms, see *Army and Navy Register* 65, Apr. 19, 1919, p. 493, and May 24, 1919, p. 669.

85. Senator George Chamberlain introduced a bill (S. 5320) on Jan. 13, 1919. Congressman Royal C. Johnson (R-S.D.) introduced an identical version (H.R. 15945) in the House of Representatives on Feb. 14, 1919. Lindley, "A Soldier's Also a Citizen," p. 195.

86. The Ansell-authored bill became S. 64, while Johnson introduced an identical bill in the House (H.R. 367). Ansell to Baker, Dec. 11, 1917, folder "A, 1917." Baker Papers, LOC. *New York Times*, Feb. 14, 1919, p. 1, and Feb. 16, 1919, p. 17. *Army and Navy Register* 65, Feb. 22, 1919, pp. 229–30. Lindley, "A Soldier's Also a Citizen," pp. 191–200, 226–35. William T. Generous, Jr., *Swords and Scales: The Development of the Uniform Code of Military Justice* (Port Washington, N.Y.: Kennikat Press, 1973), pp. 3–13.

87. For 27th Division report, see Lt. Col. E. H. Agnew, insp. gen., Jan. 3, 1919, file # 283-8, and "Treatment of AWOLs in Paris," Jan. 22, 1919, file # 283-21. Both in 588/120, NA. James W. Beckman, "The Bastile [*sic*], Farm No. 2 and the Stockade," pts. 1 and 2, "Court Martial Cases, 1918–19," box 70. Borah Papers, LOC.

88. Beckman to Borah, Apr. 19, 1919; Borah to Beckman, Apr. 22, 1919, "Court Martial Cases, 1918–19," box 70. Borah Papers, LOC.

89. Beckman to Borah, May 24 and June 9, 1919, "Court Martial Cases, 1918–19," box 70. Borah Papers, LOC.

90. *New York Times*, July 21, 1919, p. 10; *Army and Navy Register* 66, July 26, 1919, pp. 126–27.

91. Division inspector and division judge advocate general to commanding general, 27th Division, Dec. 26, 1918, file # 283/6; 588/120, NA; *Army and Navy Register* 66, Aug. 2, 1919, p. 152. Lt. Col. J. Leslie Kincaid to Congressman Frederick Dallinger (R-Mass.), letter reprinted in *New York Times*, July 28, 1919, p. 3.

92. *Army and Navy Register* 66, July 26, 1919, p. 98. Lindley, "A Soldier's Also a Citizen," p. 195.

93. Undated testimony of Sgt. Thomas P. Hamill and Cpl. Paul P. Boggs attached to 27th Division report, Lt. Col. E. H. Agnew, insp. gen., Jan. 3, 1919; Statement of Frederick Weiss, in report "Treatment of AWOLs in Paris," Jan. 22, 1919 (both cited n. 87 above). *New York Times*, July 16, p. 13; July 18, p. 5; July 23, p. 8; July 30, p. 3 (all 1919). *Army and Navy Register* 66, July 26, 1919, p. 98.

94. *New York Times*, July 18, 1919, p. 5.

95. Ibid., July 30, 1919, p. 3.

96. Division inspector and division judge advocate general to commanding general, 27th Division, Dec. 26, 1918.

97. Generous, *Swords and Scales*, p. 10.

98. Dixon Wecter, *When Johnny Comes Marching Home* (Boston: Houghton Mifflin, 1944), pp. 242–54. Stuart Charles McConnell, *Glorious Contentment: The Grand Army of the Republic, 1865–1900* (Chapel Hill: University of North Carolina Press, 1992). The GAR was founded about a year after northern troops had left the army and quickly aligned itself with the Radical Republicans in local and national elections. By the 1880s, the GAR had evolved into a middle-class fraternal organization that called upon the state and federal governments to care for the nation's veterans. In this age of patronage politics, the GAR secured ever increasing benefits for Union veterans from congressmen who desperately sought their votes.

99. Memorandum for the chief of staff, Feb. 5, 1919. Memorandum for the commander in chief, Feb. 1, 1919. Both in file # 5777, Thomas File; 310/165, NA. These officials went so far as to cable a request for copies of the constitutions and by-laws of existing military societies.

100. Pershing, pencil notation on memorandum for the commander in chief, Feb. 1, 1919.

101. William Pencak, *For God and Country: The American Legion, 1919–1941* (Boston: Northeastern University Press, 1989), pp. 49–55. Thomas A. Rumer, *The American Legion: An Official History, 1919–1989* (New York: M. Evans, 1990), pp. 8–18.

102. Pencak, *For God and Country*, pp. 53–54.

103. Bishop Charles Brent, address to Second Meeting of the Caucus of the American Legion, Mar. 17, 1919, file # 5777, Thomas File; 310/165, NA. For aid from GHQ source, see George A. White, "Cradle Days in the Legion," pp. 6, 11–12, photocopy provided by American Legion National Headquarters, Archives, Indianapolis, Indiana (hereafter ALNH). White acknowledged this aid but at the same time asserted that Legion activities vexed AEF officials. Also see Rumer, *American Legion*, pp. 15–17.

104. 2d Lt. Mark Watson, *Stars and Stripes*, to Nolan, Mar. 4, 1919, file # 5777, Thomas File; 310/165, NA.

105. Pencak, *For God and Country*, p. 54. White, "Cradle Days in the Legion," pp. 4–5.

106. Hints for speakers and organizers of posts, 1919 folder, ALNH.

107. Memorandum for the chief of staff, May 23, 1919, file # 10261–71 (18); 65/165, NA.

108. John Parker to Theodore Roosevelt, Jr., Apr. 15, 1919, "American Legion, 1919" folder, box 36. Theodore Roosevelt, Jr., Papers, Library of Congress (hereafter Roosevelt, Jr., Papers, LOC).

109. Pencak, *For God and Country*, pp. 68–69. In segregating black and white posts, the Legion was following the precedent set by the GAR. In the 1890s, the GAR had also faced dueling black and white delegations from Louisiana and had refused to seat the black delegates on technical, not racial, grounds. Although eschewing a formal policy of separate national encampments for black and white members, the GAR maintained a strict color line. McConnell, *Glorious Contentment*, pp. 213–18.

110. Only in four of the twelve states that made up the "Solid South" (North Carolina, Tennessee, Kentucky, and Virginia) would the Legion even consider applications for black posts.

111. For compilations of membership figures for black posts, see Administration and Organization, Class Post-Black File, ALNH.

112. Memorandum for the chief of staff, May 23, 1919. "It was only by using all my influence that I was able to prevent a membership clause excluding the regular army," Theodore Roosevelt, Jr., wrote to Col. W. H. Jordan, May 15, 1919, "American Legion, 1919" folder, box 36, Roosevelt, Jr., Papers, LOC.

113. Col. Gordon Johnson to Gen. Marlborough Churchill, director, MID, Nov. 21, 1919, file # 10261-128 (36); 65/165, NA.

114. See reports of Legion Military Policy Committee in "Committees—MPC" folder, ALNH.

115. Memorandum from Gen. William Haan to Gen. Marlborough Churchill, Nov. 28, 1919, file # 10261-128 (38). Colonel Johnson to Gen. Marlborough Churchill, Nov. 21, 1919. Memorandum for the chief of staff, May 23, 1919. Memorandum for Gen. Marlborough Churchill, June 3, 1919, file # 10261-78. All in 65/165, NA.

116. For officers, see memorandum for the chief of staff, file # 2225, Nov. 7, 1919; General Correspondence, July 1919–Oct. 1920 (entry 279); War College Division and War Plans Division, 1900–1942; Textual Records of the War Department General and Special Staffs, Record Group 165 (hereafter 279/165, NA); National Archives, College Park, Md. For enlisted men, see "Our Military System as It Appeared to America's Citizen Soldiers," file # 353 (9-5-19 to 10-8-19); 37/407, NA. An independent survey published in *The Home Sector*, a postwar veterans' magazine, reflected strong support for UMT among veterans who responded. *Home Sector*, Feb. 28 and Apr. 17, 1920, quoted in Wecter, *When Johnny Comes Marching Home*, pp. 371–74.

117. See John Chambers, *To Raise an Army: The Draft Comes to Modern America* (New York: Free Press, 1987), pp. 239–60. Richard S. Jones, *A History of the American Legion* (New York: Bobbs-Merrill, 1946), pp. 84–90. Raymond Moley, *The American Legion Story* (New York: Duell, Sloan & Pearce, 1966), pp. 150–55.

118. Morris Janowitz, *The Professional Soldier: A Social and Political Portrait* (Glencoe, Ill: Free Press, 1960), pp. 38–39. Lt. Col. Carl A. Bach, "When an Officer Really Leads His Men," folder 274; 22/120, NA; also reprinted in *Military Engineer* 67–72 (Apr.–Mar. 1921): 178. "Discipline vs. Threats," anonymous letter, *Infantry Journal* 25 (Mar. 1920): 789. Col. M. B. Stewart, "A Thirty-Minute Talk," *Infantry Journal* 16

(Dec. 1919): 491. Lt. Col. Weston Jenkins, "What Gave Birth to 'What Price Glory,' " *Infantry Journal* 30 (Jan. 1927): 8–11. Maj. Donald H. Connolly, "Control of Men as Part of an Officer's Training," May 5, 1929, p. 5, file # 357-18. Maj. Gen. Eli A. Helmick, "Leadership," file # 270-67, Command Course No. 67, 1923–24. "Morale as Affected by Definite Plans and Directives, by Reward and Punishment and by Leadership and Training Methods," Mar. 14, 1922, file # 226-3/A. All in Curriculum, Carlisle.

119. Gen. Douglas MacArthur to Baker, Nov. 7, 1919, and Baker's reply, Nov. 10, 1919, "M, 1919" folder. Baker Papers, LOC. For more on the introduction of human management courses, see Eli Helmick, "Demand for Better Human Leadership," *Military Engineer* 18 (July–Aug. 1926): 276–77. Maj. P. L. Ransom, "A Brief Study of Morale Factors in a Combat Division, First Division AEF," app. 2, in "Morale and Propaganda," G-1 Course, 1934–35, file # 1-1935-7. Curriculum, Carlisle.

120. Maj. E. N. Woodbury, "A Study of Desertion in the Army," Sept. 15, 1920, file # 10317-821; 296/165, NA. There were nearly 10,000 deserters out of the 69,000 new men who enlisted between 1919 and 1920, a rate vastly higher than the wartime desertion rate. For a discussion of regular army officers' reactions to the Woodbury study and these figures, see Robert Griffith, *Men Wanted for the U.S. Army: America's Experience with an All-Volunteer Army Between the World Wars* (Westport, Conn.: Greenwood Press, 1982), pp. 42–48. For other postwar studies in this genre, see "Analysis of Apparent Causes of General Court Martial Offenses . . . from March 15, 1919 to March 17, 1920," Apr. 26, 1920, file # 1150; 8/165, NA. Memorandum for the chief of staff, "Summary of Fort Leavenworth Report," Nov. 22, 1919, file # 1150; 8/165, NA. During the war, the Morale Branch had begun examining the reasons men deserted. See memorandum for chief, Morale Branch, Feb. 7, 1919, file # 1150; 8/165, NA.

121. Memorandum for chief of staff, "Attitude of Soldiers Towards Present Conditions of Unrest in Civil Life," Nov. 25, 1919, file # 80-200 (4); 296/165, NA, and file # 1010-47; 8/165, NA.

122. Memorandum for the chief of staff, Feb. 18, 1920, file # 250.01, box 528; 37/407, NA. On Baker's request, March circulated this letter to all army commanders. Baker was particularly fond of the educational programs begun during the demobilization period and the Americanization programs initiated to help absorb aliens during the war. See Annual Report of the War Plans Division, July 1919–June 1920, box 77; 310/165, NA. Memorandums for the adjutant general, July 29, 1919, file # 7519-154, and Sept. 1919, file # 8213-100. Memorandum for the chief of staff, Apr. 2, 1919, file # 9591-89. All in 296/165, NA.

123. Commentators on the problem of recruiting and retention suggested raising pay and reducing fatigue duties but were unwilling to go much further in modifying the authoritarian aspects of army life, which caused many enlisted men to leave the service. Griffith, *Men Wanted*, pp. 105–6.

124. Connolly, "Control of Men as Part of an Officer's Training," May 5, 1929, p. 5 (cited n. 118 above). Other studies or lectures at the Army War College drawing on Great War experience to examine problems of morale and leadership among wartime troops include lectures by Maj. Gen. Eli A. Helmick, "Relation of Psychology to

Leadership," file # 293A-61, Command Course No. 61, 1924–25; "The Individual Mind in Relation to Military Service," file # 341A-26, G-1 Course, 1927–28; and "Morale in Armies," G-1 Course, 1928–29. All in Curriculum, Carlisle.

125. "Morale," G1 Course # 1-1935-6, Report of Committee No. 6. Curriculum, Carlisle.

126. Lt. Col. Allen Greer, Apr. 13, 1920, file # 127-22. Also see responses from Col. Herschel Tupes, Brig. Gen. W. P. Jackson, and Maj. Gen. W. H. Hay in the Army War College 1919 Survey "Colored Troops in the U.S. Military Establishment," files # 127-15 through # 127-22. All in Curriculum, Carlisle.

7. War Memories

1. W. H. Biggar to Senator Thomas Walsh, Mar. 5, 1920, bonus file, box 264. Walsh Papers, LOC. William Henkelmen, Co. B., 339th Infantry Regiment, reminiscences. William Henkelman Papers, Archives of Labor History and Urban Affairs, Wayne State University, Detroit, Michigan (hereafter Henkelmen Papers, Wayne State).

2. S. Coben, "Postwar Upheaval: The Red Scare," in *The Impact of World War I*, ed. Arthur Link (New York: Harper & Row, 1969), p. 105.

3. For a classic debate on this subject, see Willard Waller, *The Veteran Comes Back* (New York: Dryden Press, 1944), and Dixon Wecter, *When Johnny Comes Marching Home* (Boston: Houghton Mifflin, 1944).

4. Report of the National Americanism Commission, 1920, p. 5, "Committees—Americanism, 1920–1927" folder, ALNH.

5. Classic works on the problem of collective memory include Maurice Halbwachs, *The Collective Memory*, translated from the French by Francis J. Ditter, Jr., and Vida Yazdi Ditter (New York: Harper & Row, 1980), and Roger Bastide, *Les religions africaines au Brésil* (Paris: Presses universitaires de France, 1960). Also see *Between Memory and History*, ed. Marie-Noëlle Bourguet, Lucette Valensi, and Nathan Wachtel (New York: Harwood Academic Publishers, 1990).

6. For an influential study on pension largesse that reflected the negative views held of pensions by 1918, see William Glasson, *Federal Military Pensions in the United States* (New York: Oxford University Press, 1918). On the first page of his study, Glasson specifically noted that "army pay and pensions are not matters of contract" and denied veterans the right to make any financial claim, even for wounds, against the state for simply having fulfilled their duty as citizens. The Supreme Court agreed, defining pensions (even if promised to entice enlistment) as solely within the power of Congress to grant, recall, increase, or diminish.

7. Theodore Roosevelt, Jr., to Senator Boies Penrose (R-Pa.), Oct. 15, 1919, box 11, and to R. J Caldwell (source of quotation), May 11, 1920, box 12. Roosevelt, Jr., Papers, LOC.

8. Theodore Roosevelt, Jr., to Edmond Tooney, Feb. 27, 1922, "General Correspondence, 1922, S–Z" folder, box 12. Roosevelt, Jr., Papers, LOC. Although he expressed support, Roosevelt was unwilling to play an active role in Legion affairs while pursuing a political career.

9. Heber G. Poland to Representative Wallace H. White (R-Maine), Aug. 26, 1919, "War Legislation" folder, box 31. Wallace H. White Papers, Library of Congress (hereafter White Papers, LOC).

10. Kimberly Jensen, "Women, Citizenship, and Civic Sacrifice: Engendering Patriotism in the First World War," in *Bonds of Affection: Americans Define Their Patriotism,* ed. John Bodnar (Princeton, N.J.: Princeton University Press, 1996), pp. 139–59.

11. C. M. Carter to Commander Hanford MacNider, Feb. 11, 1922, "Veteran Welfare—Adjusted Compensation—1922" folder, ALNH.

12. Col. W. E. Haseltine, March 1943, "Demobilization, Repatriation and Rehabilitation of Army Personnel, 1918–19," p. 21, file # 7200-W, pt. 2, Thomas File; 310/165, NA.

13. Col. John M. Dunn, acting director of Military Intelligence Division, Mar. 20, 1919, file # 10218-319 (4); 65/165, NA.

14. David M. Kennedy, *Over Here: The First World War and American Society* (New York: Oxford University Press, 1980), p. 280.

15. General Collardet, military attaché, French embassy, Washington, D.C., Aug. 6, 1919, 6N 136, Vincennes.

16. Bernard C. Nalty, *Strength for the Fight: A History of Black Americans in the Military* (New York: Free Press, 1986), pp. 125–27. Memorandum for the Director of Military Intelligence, July 23, 1919, file # 2198; 279/165, NA.

17. For concerns over crowding into cities, oil camps, and the desire for change, see Camp Travis Survey, June 5, 1919, Camp Travis file; 377/165, NA; and Lt. Col. D. S. Wilson, Camp Lee to chief, Morale Branch, June 10, 1919, file # 80-143 (4); 65/165, NA. For conservative estimations of soldiers' interest in changing professions, see memorandum for General McIntyre, Feb. 14, 1919, file # 1010 (17); 8/165, NA; and Camp Funston Surveys, Camp Funston file; 377/165, NA.

18. National Superintendent of Bureau for Returning Soldiers and Sailors to Capt. Eliot Frost, Morale Branch, Mar. 19, 1919, file # 10218-319 (3); 65/165, NA.

19. "Soldiers! Your Job and How to Get It," p. 2, in Pvt. Roy C. Brewer, 344th Field Artillery, 90th Division, WWI, Carlisle. Officials often insisted that soldiers buy their tickets with their travel allowances before they left the camp gates. These tickets were discounted if a soldier agreed to leave the area within twenty-four hours. "Demobilization, Repatriation and Rehabilitation of Army Personnel, 1918–19," pp. 7–9 (cited n. 12 above).

20. "Soldiers! Your Job and How to Get It," p. 2. For examples of encouragement to take up farm work, see reports from morale officer, Camp Lee, Apr. 12 and 19, 1919, Camp Lee file; 377/165, NA. For soldiers' resistance to this idea, see memorandum for General McIntyre, Mar. 13, 1919, file # 1010 (17); 8/165, NA.

21. March report from General Collardet, military attaché, French embassy, Washington, D.C., to French minister of war, Apr. 8, 1919, 6N 136, Vincennes.

22. File # 10110-913; 65/165, NA.

23. Silver Parrish, Co. B, 339th Infantry Regiment, Mar. 11, Mar. 18, and May 4, 1919 (source of quotation) diary entries. Parrish Papers, UM.

24. 2d Lt. Charles Brady Ryan, Co. K, 339th Regiment to Lou, Apr. 4, 1919. Ryan Papers, UM.

25. Recruiting officers' reports, quotation from Dec. 2, 1920, file # 10110-2187; also see Nov. 30, 1920, file # 10110-2187; Dec. 22, 1920, file # 10110-2237; and collection of reports in file # 10110-2179. All in 65/165, NA.

26. For protests on rent profiteering, see Military Intelligence report, Feb. 8–15, 1920, pp. 29–30, file # 10110-1683. For attacks on red flags, see memorandum for Gen. Marlborough Churchill, May 5, 1919, file # 10261-78. For veteran raids on socialist groups, see memorandum for Gen. Marlborough Churchill, Apr. 18, 1919, file # 10261-78; and report from R. E. Enright, police commissioner, New York City, May 9, 1919, file # 10110-920 (628). All in 65/165, NA.

27. Camp Travis Survey, June 5, 1919 (cited n. 17 above).

28. Memorandum to Capt. Edwin Ross, June 21, 1919, file # 80-163; 65/165, NA. Camp surveyors in Camp Funston recorded a similar consensus that the soldiers' vote should have been collected on this matter. Jewish Welfare Board response, Camp Funston Surveys (cited n. 17 above).

29. Memorandum for director of operations, Apr. 8, 1919, file # 1010-32; 8/165, NA.

30. Memorandum for Gen. Marlborough Churchill, Apr. 25, 1919, file # 10261-78; 65/165, NA.

31. Bulletin of Regular Army, Feb. 1–7, 1920, pp. 21–22, file # 10110-1683; 65/165, NA.

32. Supplement of the work and activities of the MID negative intelligence within the civilian population, 1919, file # 10110-1143; 65/165, NA.

33. Military Intelligence report, Mar. 20, 1920, pp. 40–41, file # 10110-1683; 65/165, NA.

34. Col. Gordon Johnson to Gen. Marlborough Churchill, Nov. 25, 1919; file # 10261-128 (36); 65/165, NA.

35. Clayton D. Laurie, "The U.S. Army and the Omaha Race Riot of 1919," *Nebraska History* 72, no. 3 (1991): 140–41.

36. Memorandum for Gen. Marlborough Churchill, Nov. 28, 1919, file # 10261-128 (38); 65/165, NA.

37. Assistant chief of staff, war plans and training, to director, War Plans Division, July 1, 1920; file # 6866; 279/165, NA.

38. Western Department intelligence officer to director of Military Intelligence, Dec. 16, 1919; file # 10261-128 (34); 65/165, NA.

39. Gen. Marlborough Churchill to Johnson, Feb. 12, 1920; file # 10261-144 (7); 65/165, NA.

40. Lemuel Bolles, national adjutant to D. John Markey, chairman, Legion Committee on Military Affairs, Apr. 28, 1922, file # 10261-71 (72); 65/165, NA.

41. Minutes of the Meeting of the National Americanism Committee, Jan. 19, 1920, p. 20, "Committees—Americanism—Minutes of Meeting" folder, ALNH.

42. Declarations of Principles of the Workers, Soldiers, and Sailors Council, file # 10261-61 (4); 65/165, NA.

43. Memorandum for Gen. Marlborough Churchill, May 5, 1919 (cited n. 26 above).

44. U. S. Army, *History of Spruce Production Division* (Portland, Oreg.: U.S. Spruce Production Corporation, 1919).

45. Maj. Oliver S. McCleary, "The Shortage of Essential War Materials in the Lumber Industry and the Handling of the Labor Problems," file # 7200-L, Exhibit A, p. 2, Thomas File; 310/165, NA.

46. Military Intelligence, Plant Protection, to chief signal officer of the army, Mar. 27, 1918, file # 10261-65(1); 65/165, NA.

47. Quoted in *One Big Union Monthly*, Oct. 1919, p. 25. Collection in Archives of Labor History and Urban Affairs, Wayne State University, Detroit.

48. Philip S. Foner, *History of the Labor Movement in the United States*, vol. 8: *Postwar Struggles, 1918–1920* (New York: International Publishers, 1988), pp. 214–25.

49. Interrogation of Soldiers and Sailors' Protective Association members, Jan. 23, 1919, file # 10261-59; 65/165, NA.

50. *Little Rock Arkansas Gazette,* Apr. 26, 1919, clipping, file # 10261-70 (36); 65/165, NA.

51. Inspector John G. Purdie, Apr. 22, 1919; file # 10261-60; 65/165, NA.

52. For endorsements, see M. J. Burns, director, Department of Justice, Bureau of Investigation, to director, MID, Feb. 3, 1922, p. 5, file # 10110-2283 (50). For prohibition on scabbing, see acting director of military intelligence to assistant chief of military intelligence, Southern Department, Aug. 31, 1920, file # 10261-70 (63). Both in 65/165, NA.

53. Notes to accompany lists of veterans' organizations, Dec. 9, 1921; file # 10261; 65/165, NA.

54. William Absolon, Chicago, Ill., to Paul McNutt, national commander, Dec. 5, 1928, "Universal Draft" folder, ALNH.

55. For examples of these MID and Justice Department activities, see files # 10261-60, # 10261-70, # 10261-66, and # 10261-115; 65/165, NA.

56. Representative James G. Strong (R-Kans.) to American Legion, Aug. 27, 1919, "Veteran Welfare—Adjusted Compensation, Mis. Correspondence, 1919" folder, ALNH.

57. John Thomas Taylor to Commander John Quinn, Dec. 15, 1923, "Veteran Welfare—Adjusted Compensation—1924" folder, ALNH. See correspondence in this folder and in the "Committees—Military Policy Committee" folder for Legion leaders' meetings with Presidents Warren Harding and Calvin Coolidge and with the congressional "soldier bloc."

58. Taylor to Quinn, Jan. 3, 1924, "Veteran Welfare—Adjusted Compensation—1924" folder, ALNH.

59. Gilbert Bettman, chairman, National Legislative Committee, to Legion commander, July 28, 1921, "Veteran Welfare—Adjusted Compensation—1921" folder, ALNH. Taylor to Quinn, Dec. 15, 1923.

60. Boyd Van Benthuysen to MacNider, Feb. 2, 1922, "Veteran Welfare—Adjusted Compensation—1922" folder, ALNH.

61. *Little Rock Arkansas Gazette,* Apr. 26, 1919 (cited n. 50 above).

62. *The Home Sector,* Apr. 17, 1920, pp. 7–8.

63. American Legion Post No. 177, Newport, Pa., Oct. 23, 1919. Mrs. William Johnson, Dec. 27, 1920. Both in "Veteran Welfare—Adjusted Compensation—1919–20" folder, ALNH.

64. Frederick Alger to MacNider, Feb. 16, 1922, "Veteran Welfare—Adjusted Compensation—1922" folder, ALNH.

65. Pvt. Dan Zelich to Senator William Borah, Aug. 12, 1919, "Discharges—Army, T–W" folder, box 72. Borah Papers, LOC. C. H. Perrine to Walsh, Jan. 25, 1919, "Soldiers Abroad" folder, box 205. Robert Brown to Walsh, Mar. 18, 1918, "Legislation, Army" folder, box 262. Both in Walsh Papers, LOC.

66. Elbert Hamlin to MacNider, Mar. 11, 1922, and Armand Bang to House Ways and Means Committee, Mar. 6, 1920. Both in "Veteran Welfare—Adjusted Compensation—Mis. Correspondence, 1922" folder, ALNH.

67. Henry D. Lindsley to Marquis James, Feb. 10, 1922, "Veteran Welfare—Adjusted Compensation—Mis. Correspondence, 1922" folder, ALNH.

68. James to H. F. Sherwood, May 5, 1922, "Veteran Welfare—Adjusted Compensation—Mis. Correspondence, 1922" folder, ALNH.

69. Representative Thomas Connally (D-Tex.), 1920 House Speech, Scrapbook, box 589. Thomas Connally Papers, Library of Congress (hereafter Connally Papers, LOC).

70. Visit to the president, May 25, 1922, "Veteran Welfare—Adjusted Compensation—1922" folder, ALNH.

71. E. G. Adams to MacNider, Feb. 2, 1922, "Veteran Welfare—Adjusted Compensation—1922" folder, ALNH.

72. Charles H. Cole, Department of Massachusetts, to MacNider, Mar. 8, 1922, "Veteran Welfare—Adjusted Compensation—Mis. Correspondence, 1922" folder, ALNH. For the Legion's ongoing and bitter dispute with the Chamber of Commerce, see Chamber of Commerce, Literary Digest Referendum, and Federal Clippings folders under the rubric "Veteran Welfare—Adjusted Compensation—1924," ALNH. These folders contain correspondence between the two organizations, reactions of members, and the Legion's own publicity campaign.

73. An ex-serviceman to Senator George William Norris (R-Nebr.), Feb. 11, 1922, veteran folder, box 23. George William Norris Papers, Library of Congress (hereafter Norris Papers, LOC).

74. John Thomas Taylor to Borah, Sept. 12, 1922, "Soldier Bonus, DC 1921–1922" folder, box 122. Borah Papers, LOC.

75. Chamber of Commerce, referendum no. 38, Mar. 9, 1922, "Veteran Welfare—Adjusted Compensation—1924 (Chamber of Commerce)" folder, ALNH.

76. "What Adjusted Compensation Is! The American Legion Explains," "Veteran Welfare—Adjusted Compensation—1924, February" folder, ALNH.

77. William Pencak, *For God and Country: The American Legion, 1919–1941* (Boston: Northeastern University Press, 1989), p. 199.

78. Military Affairs Committee minutes, June 26, 1922, "Universal Draft" folder, ALNH.

79. "Drafting of Labor in War," Office of the Assistant Secretary, War Department, May 24, 1922, "Universal Service" folder, ALNH.

80. Laura S. Jensen, "The Early American Origins of Entitlements," *Studies in American Political Development* 10 (Fall 1996): 360–404.

81. On Revolutionary War pensions, see ibid. On Civil War soldiers' pensions, see Stuart McConnell, *Glorious Contentment: The Grand Army of the Republic, 1865–1900* (Chapel Hill: University of North Carolina Press, 1992), and Theda Skocpol, *Protecting Soldiers and Mothers* (Cambridge, Mass.: Harvard University Press, 1992).

82. For debate over how politics and societal views on class and gender defined these deserving categories, see Linda Gordon, "Gender, State and Society: A Debate with Theda Skocpol," and Theda Skocpol, "Soldiers, Workers, and Mothers: Gendered Identities in Early U.S. Social Policy," *Contention* 2, no. 3 (Spring 1993): 139–83.

83. The World War Adjusted Compensation Act authorized payments of $1 for each day of domestic duty (up to $500) and $1.25 for each day of overseas duty (up to $625) served between April 5, 1917, and July 1, 1919, for all soldiers below the rank of major for service in excess of sixty days. Soldiers owed $50 or less received cash, others received a bond certificate that matured in 1945. Beginning in 1926, veterans could borrow as much as 22.5 percent of the certificate's face value.

84. See "Universal Draft" folder, ALNH, for details of Legion efforts to appease the AFL and the congressional lobbying campaign.

85. Ibid., "History of the American Legion's Universal Service Law, 1919–1935."

86. The addition of 10 points to disabled veterans' civil service ratings and 5 points for all other honorably discharged troops won veterans 159,332 federal positions between 1919 and 1930. Report of President's Advisory Committee on Veteran Preference, 1931. "Soldiers and Sailors Preference, 1931," folder, box 372, Subject File; Presidential Papers, Herbert Hoover Papers, Herbert Hoover Presidential Library, West Branch, Iowa (hereafter SF-HHPL).

87. Providing this care for non-service-related problems was not mandatory, but rather granted upon the discretion of the director of the Veterans' Bureau. The appointment of a sympathetic supporter, General Frank Hines, as director of the Veterans' Bureau in 1924 assured a generous application of this discretionary power. In 1937, for example, over a million veterans legally received care in federal medical facilities, with 141,500 hospitalized for treatment. Walter P. Dillingham, *Federal Aid to Veterans, 1917–1941* (Gainesville: University of Florida Press, 1952), p. 70.

88. Taylor to Quinn, Dec. 15, 1923 (cited n. 57 above).

89. The latter is admirably done by Pencak, *For God and Country*.

8. The Bonus March

1. William Pencak, *For God and Country: The American Legion, 1919–1941* (Boston: Northeastern University Press, 1989), pp. 175, 199, offers a somewhat different interpretation of the Legion's role in the adjusted compensation debate. According to Pencak, by focusing on war profiteers, the Legion successfully appealed to the public's

notion of America as a classless society and to general mistrust of the wealthy. In his account, class exploitation became the theme that secured public support for adjusted compensation legislation in both 1924 and 1936.

2. Frank T. Hines, Veterans Administration, to President Herbert Hoover, Aug. 28, 1931, "Veteran's Bureau, Economy Program 1932 and undated," box 358, SF-HHPL.

3. Commander, Department of Louisiana, to James Barton, national adjutant, American Legion, May 12, 1931, "Veteran Welfare—Adjusted Compensation—Federal Loans—1930–31," ALNH.

4. These figures are derived from information provided in Hines to Hoover, Aug. 28, 1931.

5. For the disproportionate number of veterans hospitalized for mental breakdowns, see "Hospitalization of Veteran Neuropsychiatric Patients, July 7, 1935, World War Veterans, 1934–35," box 1, Official File 95, President's Official Files, Franklin D. Roosevelt Papers, Franklin D. Roosevelt Presidential Library, Hyde Park, New York (hereafter OF, FDRL).

6. Relative Economic Need of Veterans Groups, "Speech Material—Veterans," file # 1820, President's Personal File, Franklin D. Roosevelt Presidential Library, Hyde Park, New York (hereafter PPF, FDRL).

7. James R. Turner, American Legion commander, Department of South Carolina, to FDR, May 16, 1935, "Soldier's Bonus—In Favor," box 4, OF 95, FDRL.

8. Dale V. Simpson, Marion, Ohio, to FDR, Apr. 15, 1935, "Soldier's Bonus—In Favor," box 4, OF 95, FDRL.

9. Herbert R. Nicholas to FDR, Apr. 27, 1935, "Soldier's Bonus—In Favor," box 4, OF 95, FDRL.

10. John Ryan, Providence, R.I., to FDR, Mar. 25, 1935, "Soldier's Bonus—In Favor," box 4, OF 95, FDRL.

11. Frank L. McAleer, Saranac Lake, N.Y., to FDR, Mar. 16, 1935, "Soldier's Bonus—In Favor," box 4, OF 95, FDRL.

12. Ed Fischer, Chicago, Ill., to FDR, 1935, "Soldier's Bonus—In Favor," box 4, OF 95, FDRL.

13. Statement of General Frank T. Hines, administrator of veterans affairs, before Senate Finance Committee, Feb. 3, 1931, "World War Veterans—Bonus Correspondence 1931," box 372, SF-HHPL.

14. Agnes Brewington to FDR, Mar. 20, 1935, "Soldier's Bonus," box 5, OF 95, FDRL.

15. Hines to President Hoover, July 22, 1932, "World War Veterans Bonus Reports—1931–32, July 25," box 376, SF-HHPL.

16. For a more general discussion of how America remembered the war see G. Kurt Piehler, *Remembering War the American Way* (Washington, D.C.: Smithsonian Institution Press, 1995), pp. 92–125. All remembrances (parades, monuments, cemeteries) emphasized the wartime unity of spirit and focused on hopes for lasting peace from the war to end all wars. The Legion took the lead in lobbying the federal government to make Armistice Day a national holiday and to place a sentry at the tomb of the Unknown Soldier.

17. Carl A. Sanderson to Congresswoman Virginia Jenckes, May 16, 1933, "Soldier's Bonus 1933," box 2, OF 95, FDRL.

18. These conflicting loyalties within the Legion parallel debates among Civil War veterans in the Grand Army of the Republic over service (as opposed to disability) pensions. In the 1880s, GAR rank-and-file supporters of the measure successfully faced off against elite posts and leaders. Supporters saw service pensions as part of the social contract: in return for saving the nation, they deserved public support. Detractors viewed it as payment for fulfilling a basic duty of citizenship. See Stuart McConnell, *Glorious Contentment: The Grand Army of the Republic, 1865–1900* (Chapel Hill: University of North Carolina Press, 1992), pp. 127–62.

19. Survey responses in "Veteran Welfare—Adjusted Compensation—Federal Loans—1930–31," ALNH.

20. Hines to Hoover, Mar. 31, 1931, and Aug. 12, 1931, "World War Veterans—Bonus Correspondence, 1931," box 372, SF-HHPL. Hines to Hoover, Aug. 28, 1931 (cited n. 2 above). Rogers Daniels, *The Bonus March: An Episode of the Great Depression* (Westport, Conn.: Greenwood Publishing, 1971), pp. 56–57.

21. Rev. M. L. Seybold, Holyroad, Kansas, to commander, American Legion, June 20, 1932, "Veteran Welfare—Adjusted Compensation—Federal—Immediate Cash Payment, 1931–32," ALNH.

22. James F. Barton, national adjutant to R. E. Jackson, Delaware Post No. 1, May 31, 1932, "Veteran Welfare—Adjusted Compensation—Federal—Immediate Cash Payment—1931–32," ALNH.

23. Congressman Royal C. Johnson (R-S.D.) to Hoover, Aug. 13, 1931, "Trips—Detroit, American Legion Convention," box 307, SF-HHPL. Senator Arthur H. Vandenberg (R-Mich.) to Hoover, Aug. 10, 1931, "Trips—Detroit American Legion Convention," SF-HHPL.

24. Theodore G. Joslin, secretary to the president, diary entry, Sept. 16 and 18, 1931, "Subject and Individual File," box 10, Theodore G. Joslin Papers, Herbert Hoover Presidential Library, West Branch, Iowa (hereafter Joslin Papers, HHPL).

25. Address of President Hoover to the Thirteenth Annual Convention of the American Legion, Sept. 21, 1931, "Veterans' Bureau, Speeches and Statements, 1930–32," box 359, SF-HHPL.

26. Barton to Jackson, May 31, 1932.

27. Daniels, *Bonus March*, pp. 53, 61.

28. First National Conference of Republican Service League, Mar. 27, 1925, "1924 General File—Circular Letters and Campaign Literature," box 87, Hanford MacNider Papers, Herbert Hoover Presidential Library, West Branch, Iowa (hereafter MacNider Papers, HHPL).

29. Theodore Roosevelt, Jr., to RSL members, Aug. 26, 1924, "1924 General File—Circular Letters and Campaign Literature," box 87, MacNider Papers, HHPL. The RSL mounted campaigns in 1928 and 1932, but it never again equaled the success it had in 1924.

30. Jay Williams to MacNider, May 25, 1932, "Canada, Minister to, 1932, January–June," box 46, MacNider Papers, HHPL.

31. MacNider to Theodore Roosevelt, Jr., Sept. 2, 1931, "Canada, Minister to, Correspondence, 1931, July–December," box 46. Theodore Roosevelt, Jr., to MacNider, Sept. 10, 1924, "1924 General File," box 87. Both in MacNider Papers, HHPL.

32. For an analysis of how forty newspapers and magazines covered the Bonus March, see Louis Liebovich, "Press Reaction to the Bonus March of 1932: A Re-Evaluation of the Impact of an American Tragedy," *Journalism Monographs* 122 (1990): 1–32.

33. Memorandum for the chief of staff, May 26, 1932, file # 10110-2452 (285a); 65/165, NA.

34. *St. Louis Post-Dispatch*, May 25, 1932, clipping in "World War Veterans—Bonus Press Comment, 1932, Jan.–June," box 373, SF-HHPL. Memorandum for the chief of staff, May 27, 1932, file # 10110-2452 (289a); 65/165, NA.

35. Senator Clarence Dill (D-Ohio), Oral History, p. 14, box 9, Herbert Hoover Presidential Library, West Branch, Iowa. Donald J. Lisio, *The President and Protest: Hoover, Conspiracy, and the Bonus Riot* (Columbia: University of Missouri Press, 1974), pp. 57–63.

36. Daniels, *Bonus March*, pp. 81–82. Memorandum for the chief of staff, June 20, 1932, file # 10110-2452 (347); 65/165, NA.

37. Roy Wilkins, "The Bonus Marchers Ban Jim Crow," *The Crisis* 39 (Oct. 1932): 316–17, 332.

38. Quotation from "Meeting of the Workers' Ex-Servicemen's League," July 18, 1932, file # 10110-2452; memorandum for the chief of staff, June 8, 1932, file # 10110-2452 (298h). Both in 65/165, NA.

39. Report of Bonus Marchers from Knoxville, Tenn., June 9, 1932, file # 10110-2452 (316b); 65/165, NA.

40. Memorandum for the chief of staff, July 12, 1932, file # 10110-2452 (414); 65/165, NA.

41. Pelham D. Glassford to the commissioners, District of Columbia, June 3, 1932, "World War Veterans Bonus—Reports, 1931–32, July 25," box 376, SF-HHPL.

42. For contradictory accounts over who deserves credit for the supplies, see Irving Bernstein, "The Bonus Army," in *The Underside of American History*, vol. 2, ed. Thomas R. Frazier and John Morton Blum (New York: Harcourt Brace Jovanovich, 1974), pp. 204–5. Daniels, *Bonus March*, pp. 97–105. Lisio, *President and Protest*, pp. 73–75.

43. Memo to Major Paschal, July 12, 1932, file # 10110-2452; 65/165, NA.

44. Memorandum for the chief of staff, May 31, 1932, file # 10110-2452 (292a); 65/165, NA.

45. Workers' Ex-Servicemen's League meeting, July 6, 1932, and Report by Capt. J. A. Sullivan, June 9, 1932, "World War Veterans Bonus—Reports: Army, 1932." Both in box 375, SF-HHPL. Hines to Joslin, July 26, 1932, "World War Veterans Bonus—Reports, 1931–32, July 26–31," box 376, SF-HHPL; memorandum for Maj. Paschal, July 5, 1932, file # 10110-2452; 65/165, NA.

46. Quotation from Hines to Hoover, June 24, 1932, "World War Veterans Bonus—Reports, 1931–32, July 25," box 376, SF-HHPL. For reports from intelligence officers that veterans exhibited little interest and sometimes outright hostility toward commu-

nism, see daily reports compiled by Col. Alfred T. Smith, assistant chief of staff, for May 31, 1932; June 3, 11, 20, and 22, 1932. All in file # 10110-2452; 65/165, NA.

47. George Van Horn Moseley, "One Soldier's Journey" (unpublished memoir, 1938), pp. 142–43. George Van Horn Moseley Papers, Library of Congress.

48. Daniels, *Bonus March,* contends that Hoover was worried about the communist presence all along; Lisio, *President and Protest,* feels that Hoover only accepted this explanation after the rout. Both explanations are speculations based on fragmentary evidence indicating both fear and restraint from Hoover during the march.

49. Joslin, diary entry, June 10, 1932, box 10, Joslin Papers, HHPL.

50. In addition to documents cited throughout, see also Edgar Richard Rickard diary, George Drescher Oral History, and James Henderson Douglas, Jr., Oral History in Herbert Hoover Presidential Library, West Branch, Iowa.

51. Requests from California Contingent, July 19, 1932, and Oregon Contingent, July 21, 1932, "World War Veterans Bonus—Veto of Bonus Bill, Disapproval," SF-HHPL.

52. John O. Le Gorce, Aug. 2, 1932, "World War Veterans—Bonus Correspondence, 1932," box 373. Robert Cottrell, executive secretary, Washington Board of Trade, to Hoover, Aug. 8, 1932, "World War Veterans—Bonus—Public Comment Commending, 1932, Aug. 6–15," box 374. Both in SF-HHPL.

53. *New York Times,* June 20, 1932, clipping in "World War Veterans—Bonus Press Comment, 1932, Jan.-June," box 373, SF-HHPL.

54. *B.E.F. News,* July 9 and 16, 1932, "World War Veterans—Bonus Press Comment, 1932," box 373, SF-HHPL.

55. Memorandum for the chief of staff, June 10, 1932, file # 10110-2452 (306); June 14, 1932, file # 10110-2452 (319); and July 1, 1932, file # 10110-2452 (390). All in 65/165, NA. Lisio, *President and Protest,* p. 80.

56. Joslin, diary entry, June 17, 1932, box 10, Joslin Papers, HHPL.

57. *New York Times,* June 18, 1932, clipping in "World War Veterans—Bonus, Press Comment," box 373, SF-HHPL.

58. Memorandum for the chief of staff, June 18, 1932, file # 10110-2452 (343); 65/165, NA.

59. Daniels, *Bonus March,* p. 121.

60. *New York Times,* June 18, 1932.

61. Memorandum for the chief of staff, June 20, 1932 (cited n. 36 above).

62. Memorandum to Major Paschal, July 12, 1932 (cited n. 43 above).

63. Memorandum for the chief of staff, July 14, 1932, file # 10110-2452 (416); 65/165, NA. Daniels, *Bonus March,* pp. 129–31.

64. Memorandum for the chief of staff, July 15, 1932, file # 10110-2452 (419); 65/165, NA.

65. Memorandum for the chief of staff, July 29, 1932, file # 10110-2452 (444); 65/165, NA. Chief of Staff Douglas MacArthur to Senator Duncan U. Fletcher, Aug. 16, 1932, file 240 Bonus; RG 407. Lt. Col. L. A. Kunzig, 12th Infantry, to commanding general, 16th Brigade, Aug. 6, 1932, in "Report of Operations Against the Bonus March-

ers," Aug. 4, 1932; III Corps Area—District of Columbia, Records of the U.S. Army Continental Commands, 1920–40, Record Group 394 (hereafter III Corps/394, NA); National Archives, College Park, Md.

66. Lisio, *President and Protest,* pp. 160–62.

67. Irving Bernstein, *The Lean Years: A History of the American Worker, 1920–1933* (Boston: Houghton Mifflin, 1961), pp. 437–55.

68. Lou Henry Hoover to Herbert Hoover, Aug. 1932, Lou Henry Hoover Collection, Herbert Hoover Presidential Library, West Branch, Iowa. Whether or not the commissioners called for troops before or after the mêlée is a source of disagreement between Daniels, *Bonus March,* pp. 154–55, and Lisio, *President and Protest,* pp. 185–87, 268–70.

69. L. H. Reichelderfer, president, Board of Commissioners of the District of Columbia, to Hoover, July 28, 1932, file # 10110-2452 (444d); 65/165, NA.

70. For a complete official description of the day's events, see "Report of Operations Against Bonus Marchers," Aug. 4, 1932; III Corps/394, NA.

71. Van Horn Moseley, "One Soldier's Journey," p. 139. Memorandum for the chief of staff, June 4, 1932, and memorandum report on Bonus Riot, Aug. 5, 1932, in "Report of Operations Against Bonus Marchers."

72. Dwight D. Eisenhower, Oral History, pp. 2–3, in Herbert Hoover Presidential Library, West Branch, Iowa.

73. *New York Herald Tribune,* July 29, 1932, "World War Veterans—Bonus Press Comment," box 373, SF-HHPL.

74. Brig. Gen. P. L. Miles to Gen. Van Horn Moseley, Sept. 23, 1932; file 240 Bonus, RG 407, NA. Lt. Col. James M. Lockett, 16th Brigade to commanding officer, 3rd Battalion, 12th Infantry, Aug. 4, 1932, and Lt. Col. L. A. Kunzig to commanding general, 16th Brigade, Aug. 8, 1932, in "Report of Operations Against Bonus Marchers."

75. Lt. Col. L. A. Kunzig to commanding general, 16th Brigade, Aug. 6, 1932, in "Report of Operations Against Bonus Marchers."

76. Summary of participation in the evacuation of Bonus Army, July 28 and 29, 1932, 3rd Battalion, 12th Infantry, July 30, 1932. Second Squadron, 3rd Cavalry to commanding general, 16th Brigade, July 30, 1932. Both in III Corps/394, NA. "Report of Operations Against the Bonus Marchers," pp. 4–5.

77. "Report of Operations Against the Bonus Marchers," pp. 6–7.

78. Capt. A. R. Bolling to commanding general, 16th Brigade, Aug. 1, 1932, in "Report of Operations Against the Bonus Marchers."

79. Memorandum for the chief of staff, Sept. 23, 1932, in "Report of Operations Against the Bonus Marchers."

80. Secretary of War Patrick Hurley to MacArthur, July 28, 1932; file 240 Bonus, RG 407, NA. Lisio, *President and Protest,* pp. 199–200. Lisio suggests that the appearance of Hurley and MacArthur in Hoover's office to urge him to use troops indicates that the request from the District of Columbia commissioners did not alone prompt Hoover to take this step.

81. Van Horn Moseley, "One Soldier's Journey," pp. 144–45.

82. Eisenhower, Oral History (cited n. 72 above), p. 3.

83. Lou Henry Hoover to Herbert Hoover, Aug. 1932 (cited n. 68 above).

84. Herbert Hoover, *The Memoirs of Herbert Hoover,* vol. 3: *The Great Depression, 1929–1941* (New York: Macmillan, 1952), pp. 226–27. Donald J. Lisio, "A Blunder Becomes Catastrophe: Hoover, the Legion, and the Bonus Army," *Wisconsin Magazine of History* 51 (Autumn 1967): 37–50.

85. Hoover to Lawrence Richey, Oct. 23, 1934, "World War Veterans Bonus, Mar., 1932–59," box 355, Subject File—Post-Presidential Papers, Herbert Hoover Papers, Herbert Hoover Presidential Library, West Branch, Iowa (hereafter SF-PP-HHPL).

86. MacArthur's statements in interview with secretary of war by the press at 11 P.M., July 28, 1932; file 240 Bonus, RG 407, NA. D. Clayton James, *The Years of MacArthur,* vol. 1: *1880–1941* (Boston: Houghton Mifflin, 1970), pp. 403–4.

87. R. B. Davis, Indianapolis, to Hoover, Aug. 1, 1932, "Public Comment on Presidential Action, Protesting, 1932, Aug. 1," box 375, SF-HHPL.

88. Unsigned letter, Pittsburgh, Pa., to Hoover, July 31, 1932, "World War Veterans Bonus—Public Comment—Opposed, 1932," box 375, SF-HHPL.

89. Percy Hocking to Henry L. Stevens, national commander, American Legion, Aug. 3, 1932, "Veteran Welfare—Adjusted Compensation—Federal—Immediate Cash Payment, 1931-32, BEF," ALNH.

90. Henry L. Stimson and McGeorge Bundy, *On Active Service in Peace and War* (New York: Harper & Brothers, 1948), pp. 200–219.

91. Mrs. W. D. Clemons, Oklahoma City, to Hoover, July 29, 1932, "World War Veterans Bonus—Public Comment Opposed, July 29," box 375, SF-HHPL.

92. H. L. Caldwell to Hoover, Aug. 5, 1932, "World War Veterans Bonus—Public Comment—Protesting, 1932, Aug. 5," box 375, SF-HHPL.

93. Joslin, diary entry, July 29, 1932, box 10, Joslin Papers, HHPL. Letters protesting and commending Hoover were sent to the White House and the War Department. For the latter, see file 240 Bonus, RG 407.

94. Congressman Royal C. Johnson (R-S.D.) to Richey, Sept. 7, 1932, "World War Veterans Bonus Correspondence, 1932, Sept.," box 373, SF-HHPL. *New York Times,* Aug. 28, 1932, clipping in "Veteran Welfare, Adjusted Compensation—Immediate Cash Payment, 1932," ALNH.

95. *New York Times,* July 29, 1932, clipping in "World War Veterans—Bonus Press Comment, 1932, July 30," box 373, SF-HHPL.

96. Victor B. Galloway, commander, VFW Post, Dearborn, Mich., to Joslin, Aug. 22, 1932, "World War Veterans—Bonus Public Comment on Public Action, Protesting, 1932 Aug. 11–Sept.," box 375, SF-HHPL. A. H. Kirchhofer, *Buffalo Evening News,* to Newton, Sept. 13, 1932, "Republican National Committee, New York, 1932, Sept.," box 265A, SF-HHPL. For the administration's success in killing censuring resolutions at the Legion convention, see S. H. Connor to Hines, Aug. 20, 1932, "Veterans' Bureau Corresp. 1932, Aug.," box 357, SF-HHPL.

97. John C. Mullen to Hoover, July 31, 1932, "World War Veterans Bonus—Public Comment, Opposed, 1932, July 31," box 375, SF-HHPL.

98. Gen. George E. Leach to Walter Newton, secretary to the president, Sept. 11, 1932, "World War Veterans—Bonus Correspondence, 1932, Sept.," box 373, SF-HHPL.

99. Lisio, *President and Protest*, pp. 85–86, 283–85. Richard Norton Smith, *An Uncommon Man: The Triumph of Herbert Hoover* (New York: Simon & Schuster, 1984), p. 140. David Burner, *Herbert Hoover: A Public Life* (New York: Knopf, 1978), pp. 311–12. John Tebbel and Sarah Miles Watts, *The Press and the Presidency: From George Washington to Ronald Reagan* (New York: Oxford University Press, 1985), pp. 430–32. Liebovich, "Press Reaction to the Bonus March of 1932," unconvincingly questions the conclusion that the Bonus March affected Hoover's reelection.

100. Peter Guldbrandsen, Berkeley, Calif., to Hoover, Aug. 27, 1932, "World War Veterans Bonus—Public Comment on Public Action, Protesting, 1932, Aug. 11–Sept.," box 375, SF-HHPL.

101. S. R. Ross, Narberth, Pa., to Hoover, July 30, 1932, "World War Veterans Bonus—Public Comment Opposed, 1932, July 30." Victor Galloway, Dearborn, Mich., to Hoover, Aug. 12, 1932, "World War Veterans—Bonus Public Comment on Public Action Protesting, 1932, Aug. 11–Sept." Chas. P. Smith, Henderson, Tex., to Hoover, Aug. 1, 1932, "World War Veterans Bonus—Public Comment Protesting, 1932, Aug. 1." All in box 375, SF-HHPL.

102. Louis Kirchheiner, Baltimore, Md., to Hoover, Aug. 3, 1932, "World War Veterans—Bonus—Public Comment on Presidential Action, Opposed, 1932, July 29," box 375, SF-HHPL.

103. Frank Murray, South Bend, Ind., to Hoover, Aug. 1, 1932, "World War Veterans Bonus—Public Comment, Protesting, 1932, Aug. 1," box 375, SF-HHPL.

104. Frederick Gambrill, White Marsh, Md., to Hoover, July 30, 1932, "World War Veterans—Bonus—Public Comment on Presidential Action, Commending, 1932, July 30," box 374, SF-HHPL.

105. Joslin, diary entry, June 2, 1932, box 10, Joslin Papers, HHPL. For Washington Board of Trade letter, see Cottrell to Hoover, Aug. 8, 1932 (cited n. 52 above).

106. Alan Dawley, *Struggles for Justice: Social Responsibility and the Liberal State* (Cambridge, Mass.: Harvard University Press, 1991), pp. 360–70.

107. Executive Order No. 5398, July 21, 1930.

108. Theda Skocpol, *Protecting Soldiers and Mothers: The Political Origins of Social Policy in the United States* (Cambridge, Mass.: Harvard University Press, 1992), p. 129.

109. Unsigned memo, Oct. 1929, "Coordination of Veterans Affairs, 1929, October," box 166, SF-HHPL.

110. Data re Veterans Matters, June 1929, "Coordination of Veterans Affairs, 1929, October," box 166, SF-HHPL. Hoover and FDR differed on disabled pensions. Hoover's 1930 Disability Act, for instance, added 407,584 veterans with non-service-related disabilities to pension rolls. FDR intended to reverse this trend. Lisio, *President and Protest*, p. 23.

111. Office Report to Roy Roberts, sent to FDR, May 9, 1933, "World War I Veterans, Jan.–June 1933," box 1, OF 95, FDRL.

112. Undated memo, "American Legion, July–Dec. 1933," box 1, OF 64, FDRL.

113. John C. Fischer, Board of Veterans' Appeals, to Stephen F. Early, Sept. 15, 1933, "American Legion, July–Dec. 1933," box 1, OF 64, FDRL.

114. Address of President Hoover to the 13th Annual Convention of the American Legion, Sept. 21, 1931 (cited n. 25 above).

115. Blanche Martin, Ashkum, Ill., to FDR, June 13, 1933, "World War I Veterans—June 1933." Hal A. Lloyd, San Diego, Calif., to FDR, June 15, 1933, and Mary I. Seely, Detroit, Mich., to FDR, June 14, 1933, "World War I Veterans—June–Dec. 1933." All in box 1, OF 95, FDRL.

116. President Franklin D. Roosevelt, address to American Legion Convention, Oct. 2, 1933, President's Personal File, Speeches, # 651, FDRL.

117. H. D. Derrick, Lawrenceburg, Tenn., to FDR, Oct. 3, 1933, file # 200, PPF, FDRL.

118. Thomas Rumer, *The American Legion: An Official History, 1919–1989* (New York: M. Evans, 1990), pp. 212–17. The legislators' only modification was limiting presumptive cases to 75 percent of their prior allowance.

119. Memorandum for the chief of staff, May 20, 1933, file # 10110-2452 (556); 65/165, NA. "White House Statement Promising Review of Veterans' Regulations and Schedules," in *The Public Papers and Addresses of Franklin Delano Roosevelt*, vol. 2: *The Year of Crisis, 1933*, ed. Samuel I. Rosenman (New York: Random House, 1938), pp. 168–69.

120. Hines to FDR, May 6, 1933. Memorandum for the president, May 8, 1933, from L. Douglas. Col. Duncan K. Major, Jr., War Department representative on the Advisory Council, Emergency Conservation Work, to Louis Howe, secretary to the president, May 6, 1933. All in "May 1–15, 1933," OF 268-CCC, FDRL.

121. Hines to FDR, May 25, 1933, "World War I Veterans, Jan. to June 1933," box 1, OF 95, FDRL.

122. Undated White House statement, "Marches on Washington, 1934–36," box 1, OF 391, FDRL.

123. *Vet Rank and File* (Fort Hunt, Va.), final issue, May 27, 1934, p. 2. Henkelmen Papers, Wayne State. *Annual Report of the Administrator of Veterans' Affairs for the Fiscal Year Ended June 30, 1934* (Washington, D.C.: GPO, 1935), p. 6. Memorandums for the chief of staff, May 19, 1933, file # 10110-2452 (555), and May 20, 1933, file # 10110-2452 (556); 65/165, NA.

124. See, e.g., Hines to Marvin H. McIntyre, assistant secretary to the president, Aug. 31, 1935, "VA-1935," box 1, OF 8, FDRL. Memorandum for Mr. McIntyre, Aug. 1, 1933, "June–Aug. 1933," box 6, OF 268mis., FDRL. Robert Fechner, director, Emergency Conservation Work, to Howe, July 7, 1934, Mar.–July 1934, box 2, OF 268, FDRL.

125. Hines to Fechner, Sept. 12, 1935. Fechner to FDR, Sept. 13, 1935. Memorandum for White House Files, Sept. 17, 1935 (quoted). All in "July–Sept. 1935," box 3, OF 268, FDRL.

126. Hines to McIntyre, Dec. 10, 1935, "VA-1935," box 1, OF 8, FDRL.

127. Lawrence Westbrook to McIntyre, Nov. 14, 1935, box 3, OF 268, FDRL.

128. *Annual Report of the Administrator of Veterans' Affairs for the Fiscal Year Ended June 30, 1941* (Washington, D.C.: GPO, 1942), p. 6.

129. U.S. War Department, *War Department Regulations: Relief of Unemployment, Civilian Conservation Corps* (Washington, D.C.: GPO, 1935), pp. 16–25. "Physical Examinations of Veterans," June 9, 1933, file 370.19, CCC, unnumbered letter orders, 1933–39, IV Corps Area, RG 394.

130. "Civilian Conservation Corps (Veterans)," June 6, 1933, file 370.19, CCC, unnumbered letter orders, 1933–39, IV Corps Area, RG 394.

131. *Annual Report of the Director of the Civilian Conservation Corps for the Fiscal Year Ended June 30, 1939* (Washington, D.C.: GPO, 1939), pp. 7–8.

132. Ibid., pp. 6–9.

133. Concern that CCC veteran camps were providing a place for veterans to organize another march on Washington arose in 1934 when veterans realized that their one-year terms were about to expire. The decision to allow veterans to reenlist and thus keep their CCC jobs indefinitely served the administration's purpose of using CCC camps to contain veteran activism. Robert Fechner, director, CCC, to Maj. Gen. James F. McKinley, adj. gen., June 15 and 29, 1934, file 240, Bonus, RG 407.

134. Turner to FDR, May 16, 1935 (cited n. 7 above).

135. M. V. Birney to FDR, May 16, 1935, "Bonus Bill Veto, 1935, Against," box 169, file # 200L, PPF, FDRL.

136. "The President Vetoes the Bonus Bill, May 22, 1935," in *The Public Papers and Addresses of Franklin D. Roosevelt*, vol. 4: *The Court Disapproves, 1935*, ed. Samuel I. Rosenman (New York: Random House, 1938), pp. 182–93.

137. "Veterans Bonus, Interviews Conducted Nov. 4–9, 1935," in *The Gallup Poll: Public Opinion, 1935–1971*, vol. 1 (New York: Random House, 1975), p. 4. *New York Herald Tribune*, Dec. 8, 1935, p. 1.

138. Herman H. Glasser to FDR, May 6, 1935, "Soldier's Bonus—In favor of, D–G," box 4, OF 95, FDRL.

139. "The President Vetoes for a Second Time the Soldiers' Bonus, January 24, 1936," in *The Public Papers and Addresses of Franklin D. Roosevelt*, vol. 5: *The People Approve, 1936*, ed. Samuel I. Rosenman (New York: Random House, 1938), p. 67.

140. *Annual Report of the Administrator of Veterans' Affairs for the Fiscal Year Ended June 30, 1936* (Washington, D.C.: GPO, 1936), p. 1.

141. Fechner to FDR, May 13, 1936, Mar.–June 1936, box 4, OF 268, FDRL. *Annual Report of the Administrator of Veterans' Affairs for the Fiscal Year Ended June 30, 1937* (Washington, D.C.: GPO, 1937), p. 4.

142. *Annual Report of the Administrator of Veterans' Affairs for the Fiscal Year Ended June 30, 1938* (Washington, D.C.: GPO, 1938), pp. 8–9.

Epilogue   The GI Bill

1. These reports are all part of the Thomas File; 310/165, NA.

2. Eli Ginzberg, *The Ineffective Soldier: Lessons for Management and the Nation,*

3 vols. (New York: Columbia University Press, 1959). Eric Dean, *Shook over Hell: Post-Traumatic Stress, Vietnam, and the Civil War* (Cambridge, Mass.: Harvard University Press, 1997), pp. 35–36.

3. For examples of the Research Division's work, see Samuel A. Stouffer et al., *The American Soldier,* vol. 1: *Adjustment During Army Life,* and vol. 2: *Combat and Its Aftermath,* Studies in Social Psychology in World War II (Princeton, N.J.: Princeton University Press, 1949; reprint, New York: John Wiley & Sons, 1965).

4. Stouffer, *American Soldier,* 1: 589.

5. Ibid., 1: 592.

6. It took another combat emergency in the spring of 1951 during the Korean War to get the army to abandon segregated forces. The minimal racial friction observed between black and white soldiers "supported the racial contact hypothesis developed during World War II: the more contact white soldiers had with black troops, the more favorable their attitude towards racial integration was," according to Martin Binkin and Mark J. Eitelberg, *Blacks and the Military* (Washington, D.C.: Brookings Institution, 1982), p. 29.

7. Michael Sherry, *Preparing for the Next War: America Plans for Postwar Defense, 1941–45* (New Haven, Conn.: Yale University Press, 1977), pp. 1–15, 34–39, 58–83.

8. On the troop survey, see Stouffer, *American Soldier,* 1: 309; on demobilization point system, see ibid., 2: 520–48, with FDR quoted p. 525.

9. R. Alton Lee, "The Army 'Mutiny' of 1946," *Journal of American History* 53 (Dec. 1996): 555–71.

10. Stouffer, *American Soldier,* 1: 369–82. The Doolittle Board also considered the problem of reforming the military justice system, as did the Vanderbilt Committee (1946) and the Roberts Board on Clemency (1945–47).

11. FDR, Fireside Chat, July 28, 1943, in *Ah That Voice: The Fireside Chats of Franklin Delano Roosevelt,* ed. Kenneth D. Yeilding and Paul H. Carlson (Odessa, Tex.: John Ben Shepperd, Jr., Library of the Presidents, Presidential Museum, 1974), pp. 214–15.

12. "Mustering Out" Pay for Veterans, Jan. 24, 1944, in *The Gallup Poll: Public Opinion, 1935–1971,* vol. 1 (New York: Random House, 1975), p. 428.

13. Hines to FDR, Aug. 6, 1943, "Vets—Bonus, 1943," box 28, OF 4675m, FDRL.

14. H. L. Chaillaux, director, National Americanism Commission, to F. W. Ames, adjutant, Fifth District American Legion, Dec. 19, 1944, "Great War—US Manpower—Benefits—Legion Bill," folder # 5, ALNH.

15. Education proposals also came from administration planning agencies such as the National Resources Planning Board's Post-War Manpower Conference and the Armed Forces Committee on Post-War Educational Opportunities, and education lobbying groups. The legislative history of the GI Bill is well told in a number of works, including Michael J. Bennett, *When Dreams Came True: The GI Bill and the Making of Modern America* (Washington, D.C.: Brassey's, 1996); Davis R. B. Ross, *Preparing for Ulysses: Politics and Veterans During World War II* (New York: Columbia University Press, 1969); and Keith Osborn, *The GI Bill, the Veterans, and the Colleges* (Louisville: University Press of Kentucky, 1974).

16. U.S. House, 78th Cong., 2d sess., *World War Veterans' Legislation* (Washington, D.C.: GPO, 1944), p. 392 (hereafter House hearings).

17. U.S. Senate, Committee on Finance, Subcommittee on Veterans' Legislation, 78th Cong., 2d sess., *Hearings on Veterans' Omnibus Bill* (Washington, D.C.: GPO, 1944), p. 2.

18. Bennett, *When Dreams Came True,* p. 129.

19. House hearings, p. 449.

20. House hearings, p. 263.

21. "The Veterans Adjustment Pay Act of 1944" was based on the 1924 model and sponsored by the VFW, DAV, Military Order of the Purple Heart, Regular Veterans Association, and Army and Navy Union. Bennett, *When Dreams Came True,* p. 146.

22. James McMillan, "Father of the GI Bill: Ernest W. McFarland and Veterans' Legislation," *Journal of Arizona History* 35, no. 4 (Winter 1994): 367.

23. Examples of this promotional material is in the "Great War—US Manpower Benefits—Legion Bill" folders, ALNH.

24. Bennett, *When Dreams Came True,* pp. 76–81.

25. Telegram from Jack Cejnar, American Legion publicity director, to Boyd Stutler, May 10, 1944, "Great War—US Manpower Benefits—Legion Bill," folder # 6, ALNH.

26. House hearings, p. 392.

27. Donald G. Glascoff, national adjutant, to Roy McMillian, national vice-commander, Apr. 7, 1944, "Great War—US Manpower-Benefits—Legion Bill," folder # 5, ALNH.

28. Ross, *Preparing for Ulysses,* pp. 110–16.

29. Ibid., pp. 118–19. Bennett, *When Dreams Came True,* pp. 184–86.

30. Thomas Rumer, *The American Legion: An Official History, 1919–1989* (New York: M. Evans, 1990), pp. 247–48.

31. Ross, *Preparing for Ulysses,* p. 117.

32. Dixon Wecter, *When Johnny Comes Marching Home* (Cambridge, Mass.: Houghton Mifflin, 1944), pp. 522–23.

33. Ibid., p. 523.

34. John Thomas Taylor, director, National Legislative Committee, to General Omar N. Bradley, VA director, Sept. 27, 1945, "Great War—US Manpower Benefits—Legion Bill," folder # 5, ALNH.

35. House Hearings, pp. 260–63.

36. Bennett, *When Dreams Came True,* p. 149.

37. Army Orientation Branch, *The GI Bill of Rights and How It Works* (Washington, D.C.: War Department, 1945), p. 7.

38. Robert J. Sampson and John H. Laub, "Socioeconomic Achievement in the Life Course of Disadvantaged Men: Military Service as a Turning Point, circa 1940–1965," *American Sociological Review* 61 (1996): 347–67.

39. U.S. Public Law 346, 78th Cong., 2d sess., June 1944. A year's worth of education and training was available to any veteran who had served at least ninety days. Veterans with service-connected injuries with less than ninety days' service were also

eligible. A veteran's length of service, age, and previous schooling determined if he was eligible for additional years of tuition and livings benefits. Public Law 268, 79th Cong., 1st sess., Dec. 1945, gave all veterans, regardless of age or previous school enrollment, the same educational benefits for the same period of service.

40. Glen H. Elder, Jr., "War Mobilization and the Life Course: A Cohort of World War II Veterans," *Sociological Forum* 2 (1987): 449–72.

41. House hearings, p. 398.

42. The law after 1955 technically provided free care to veterans with service-connected disabilities, those over 65, on pensions, or unable to pay. The liberal interpretation of this latter provision essentially opened up VA health care to all. Sar A. Levitan and Karen A. Cleary, *Old Wars Remain Unfinished: The Veteran Benefits System* (Baltimore: Johns Hopkins University Press, 1973), pp. 73–76.

43. Glen H. Elder, Jr., Michael Shanahan, and Elizabeth Clipp, "When War Comes to Men's Lives: Life Course Patterns in Family, Work, and Health," *Psychology of Aging* 9 (1994): 5–16.

44. Theodore R. Mosch, *The GI Bill: A Breakthrough in Educational and Social Policy in the United States* (New York: Exposition Press, 1975), p. 23.

45. Bennett, *When Dreams Came True*, pp. 242–43.

46. Jere Cohen, David R. Segal, and Lloyd V. Temme, "The Impact of Education on Vietnam-Era Veterans' Occupational Attainment," *Social Science Quarterly* 73 (1992): 397–409. Although he fails to take into consideration the diminished significance of GI Bill–type benefits for Vietnam veterans in the economic climate of the 1970s, Eric Dean otherwise makes a convincing case refuting the notion of Vietnam veterans as a uniquely disadvantaged veteran generation in American history. Dean, *Shook over Hell*, pp. 180–225.

47. Bennett, *When Dreams Came True*, pp. 140–47.

48. U.S. Public Law 225, 78th Cong., 2d sess., Feb. 1944.

49. Ross, *Preparing for Ulysses*, p. 218.

50. In *Gallup Poll* (cited n. 12 above), 1: 600 (Veterans, Sept. 1946), 71 percent of ex-servicemen replied "Yes" to the question "Has the Government given you, as a veteran, all the help you think it should?" Those whose response was "No" listed a bonus, more veteran living quarters, and cutting red tape as additional help the government could provide.

SOURCES

Primary Sources

Beginning in 1975, the U.S. Army Military History Institute, Carlisle Barracks, Carlisle, Pennsylvania, launched the World War I Survey project and sent retrospective questionnaires out to approximately 94,000 surviving veterans of the war. Given the advanced age of most of the respondents, few were able to complete the questionnaire in much detail. Alerted to the institute's interest, however, veterans and their families responded by sending letters, personal memoirs written in earlier periods, memorabilia, unit histories, photographs, and information on veterans' activities. These materials provide extensive insight into American citizen-soldiers' military experience, and I consulted thousands of individual soldiers' files, which are arranged by unit. Another collection of letters and diaries, assembled by the Virginia War History Commission, is to be found in the Virginia State Archives, Richmond, Virginia.

W. E. B. Du Bois collected extensive documentation on African-American soldiers' experience for a planned book, but it was never published. Inasmuch as the Emmett Scott Papers at Morgan State University remain closed to researchers, Du Bois's papers are indispensable to the historian of black U.S. soldiers in World War I. Du Bois papers held by the University of Massachusetts–Amherst, Amherst, Massachusetts, are available on microfilm at many major research libraries, but the World War I Du Bois materials at Fisk University, Nashville, Tennessee, have to be consulted there.

Manuscript collections critical in tracing citizen-soldiers' evolving relationship with the army include the Johnson Hagood Papers, Charles Gerhardt Papers, Guy V. Henry Papers, Hugh Drum Papers, Karl B. Bretzfelder Papers, Charles E. N. Howard Papers, Oswald Moore Papers, and Horace Hobbs Papers at the

U.S. Army Military History Institute. In the Library of Congress, Washington, D.C., I found these manuscript collections especially useful for the wartime experience: National Association for the Advancement of Colored People Papers, John J. Pershing Papers, Newton E. Baker Papers, Charles P. Summerall Papers, James Harbord Papers, Robert Lee Bullard Papers, Henry T. Allen Papers, Henry B. Dillard Papers, Woodrow Wilson Papers, Tasker Bliss Papers, and Peyton March Papers.

To trace the army's policymaking process both in Washington and in France, I consulted a wide range of records in the National Archives (cited in notes as NA), then located at the Washington, D.C., facility, but now housed in College Park, Maryland. Key records detailing problems training and commanding citizen-soldiers are found in the Textual Records of the War Department General & Special Staffs, Record Group 165, including the Office of the Chief of Staff: General Correspondence, 1917–21 (entry 8), the War College Division and War Plans Division, 1900–1942: General Correspondence, July 1919–October 1920 (entry 279), General Correspondence, 1903–19 (entry 296), Records of the Historical Section (entry 310), Correspondence Relating to Morale at Army Installations (entry 377), and Correspondence of the Athletic Division, 1917–19, Commission on Training Camp Activities (entry 398). Equally important are records in the Adjutant General's Office, found in the General Records of the Adjutant General's Office, Record Group 407, Decimal Correspondence File, 1917–25 (entry 37) and the Records of the AEF 1917–23, Record Group 120, especially Office of the Commander in Chief, 1917–20: General Correspondence, 1917–19 (entry 6), Reports of the Commander-in-Chief . . . World War I (entry 22), Reports, Studies, Monographs . . . of the First Army in France During World War I, Historical File, 1917–19 (entry 24), the General Staff, 1917–19: Reports Relating to the Morale of American Troops, 1917–18 (entry 195), and from the Administrative Staff, 1917–19: Inspector General, General Correspondence, 1917–19 (entry 588). The records of the Intelligence Department yielded an unexpected bonanza of information on the varied adaptations of citizen-soldiers to the army, because this agency developed full-fledged internal surveillance programs during World War I. These records are found in Office of the Director of Intelligence (G-2), 1906–49, Security Classified Correspondence and Reports, 1917–41 (entry 65), Record Group 165.

Unnoticed in their wartime work by most American officials, French liaison officers reported weekly on the everyday workings of the U.S. Army to their superiors. Interested primarily in the fighting abilities of American troops, French liaison officers analyzed their training, leadership, performance, progress, and failures. Besides commenting on morale in the U.S. Army, intelligence officials analyzed the letters of French soldiers to learn their views about their new American allies. Their reports are filed in série 6N: Fonds Clemenceau; série 7N: Bureau spécial franco-américain; série 16N: 2ᵉ bureau, Section de renseignements aux armées (SRA), Grand quartier général; and série 17N: Mission militaire française près l'armée américaine, all located at the Service historique de l'Armée de terre, Château de Vincennes, Paris. American reactions to the French are filed throughout the above-mentioned official papers, but the letters sent to General Pershing by Lieutenant Colonel Paul H. Clark, chief, American Military Mission, French General Headquarters, offers key insight into the American view of the French Army. These letters are found in the Private Papers of General of the Armies John J. Pershing (entry 18), Record Group 200, National Archives. I consulted the Directorate of Military Operations and Intelligence: Papers, WO 106 in the Public Records Office, London, but found little in them.

Records for the North Russian Expedition are scattered throughout these collections, but two key sets of documents are in Record Group 120: AEF, North Russia, 1918–19, General Correspondence, 1918–19 (entry 1537) and Historical File, 1918–19 (entry 1540) in the National Archives. The personal papers of nearly fifty participants are located in the Michigan Historical Collections, Bentley Historical Library, University of Michigan, Ann Arbor. The Army War College Curriculum Files located at the U.S. Army Military History Institute proved key to studying the impact of the Great War on the army. During the interwar period, numerous classes of regular army officers attending the Army War College undertook a series of studies of the army's experience during World War I. Copies of those studies, many of which addressed problems of managing and disciplining a mass, conscripted army, and lectures delivered by visiting generals to the College are in these files. The Thomas file, a series of studies commissioned at the beginning of World War II, provided an equally important source for lessons learned by the army. Colonel C. H. Goddard's report "A Study of Anglo-American and Franco-American Relations During World War I" was particularly useful. The Thomas file is located in Record Group 165: Records of the Historical Section (entry 310) in the National Archives.

The Records of the American Commission to Negotiate Peace, Record Group 256, General Records of the American Commission to Negotiate Peace, 1918–31 (entry 27), reveal the general worries of policymakers concerning American soldiers' quick reconciliation with the Germans. Civilian reactions to returning soldiers' complaints against the military and growing political activism are located in the following Library of Congress manuscript collections: Thomas Connally Papers, James Wadsworth, Jr., Papers, Wallace H. White Papers, Henry D. L. Flood Papers, George William Norris Papers, Everett Sanders Papers, William E. Borah Papers, Thomas James Walsh Papers, Theodore Roosevelt, Jr., Papers, and George Van Horn Moseley Papers. The Archives of Labor History and Urban Affairs, Wayne State University, Detroit, Michigan, contains some limited information on radical veteran politics in the William Henkelmen Papers, Ben H. Williams Papers, *The New Solidarity,* and *One Big Union Monthly.*

American Legion records are essential for all aspects of veteran political activism, but especially the adjusted compensation and GI Bill campaigns. At the American Legion National Headquarters Archives in Indianapolis, Indiana, I found valuable material under the rubrics of the Records of Military Policy Committee, Administration and Organization Records, Records of Americanism Committee, Universal Draft, and Veterans Welfare—Adjusted Compensation Great War—US Manpower—Benefits—Legion Bill.

For the Bonus March, the essential records are held by the Herbert Hoover Presidential Library, West Branch, Iowa. I found important material in these Presidential Period files: Subject File, President's Personal File, Secretary's File, Individual Name File, and Press Relations. In the Post-Presidential Period files, the General Correspondence File, Individual Correspondence File, and Subject File proved useful. Researchers should not overlook the Special Collections, which contain Hoover Scrapbooks, Articles, Addresses, and Public Statements, 1915-64, and Clippings Files, 1920-64. Other useful manuscript collections in the Hoover Library include the Theodore G. Joslin Papers, Hanford MacNider Papers (especially for the Republican Service League), Edgar Richard Rickard Papers, and Lou Henry Hoover Papers. The library also has an extensive oral history collection. I found interesting, if not always reliable, reminiscences in the interviews with Senator Clarence Dill, George Drescher, James Henderson Douglas, Jr., Dwight D. Eisenhower, and F. Trubee Davidson.

The Records of the U.S. Army Continental Commands, 1920–40, Record Group 394, III Corps Area—District of Columbia and IV Corps Area in the National Archives contain key policy statements and reports of the army's actions the night of the Bonus Army eviction. The Franklin D. Roosevelt Presidential Library in Hyde Park, New York, houses extensive correspondence from average Americans and official reports on the adjusted compensation issue and the GI Bill in the President's Official Files, President's Personal File, Speeches, and President's Secretary's File.

Selected Secondary Sources

This study builds on a wide range of secondary sources from history, psychology, and sociology. I particularly relied on military histories of the making of the modern army, studies of state building in America, work on combat and motivation, life-course research tracing veterans' postwar lives, and literature on entitlements and the fledgling welfare state.

A substantial literature explores the impact of World War I on state building in America, including Valerie Jean Conner, *The National War Labor Board: Stability, Social Justice, and the Voluntary State in World War I* (Chapel Hill: University of North Carolina Press, 1983); Ellis Hawley, *The Great War and the Search for a Modern Order: A History of the American People and Their Institutions, 1917–1933* (New York: St. Martin's Press, 1979); Barry D. Karl, *The Uneasy State: The United States from 1915 to 1945* (Chicago: University of Chicago Press, 1983); and

Ronald Schaffer, *America in the Great War: The Rise of the War Welfare State* (New York: Oxford University Press, 1991). These works describe the wartime federal government as an uneasy state, an associative state, a fledgling welfare state, and a voluntary state. These labels characterize the types of wartime partnerships that the state constructed with various segments of society to mobilize the nation's resources. The government's dependence on business elites (who either temporarily headed governmental bureaus or controlled critical economic resources), Progressive social welfare reformers, and labor gave these groups influence over governmental policies and within wartime state agencies.

Procuring adequate supplies for the wartime army was an important civil-military relationship. Paul A. C. Koistinen, whose works include *The Military-Industrial Complex: A Historical Perspective* (New York: Praeger, 1980) and *Mobilizing for Modern War: The Political Economy of American Warfare, 1865–1919* (Lawrence: University Press of Kansas, 1997), and Robert D. Cuff, *The War Industries Board: Business-Government Relations During World War I* (Baltimore: Johns Hopkins University Press, 1973) debate whether the twentieth-century military-industrial complex originated from the partial integration of manufacturing abilities and military needs during World War I. For works that explore how the government-business relationship affected labor, see James Weinstein, *The Corporate Ideal in the Liberal State* (Boston: Beacon Press, 1968), and David Montgomery, *The Fall of the House of Labor: The Workplace, the State, and American Labor Activism, 1865–1925* (New York: Cambridge University Press, 1987). David M. Kennedy, *Over Here: The First World War and American Society* (New York: Oxford University Press, 1980), and Stephen Skowronek, *Building a New American State: The Expansion of National Administrative Capacities, 1877–1920* (New York: Cambridge University Press, 1982), conclude that conservative influences gained the upper hand and contaminated the Progressive ideal of an independent, caretaker state during the war. Others challenge the view that only capitalist or government-instigated excesses led to the demise of Progressive regulatory reform. Nancy Bristow, *Making Men Moral: Social Engineering During the Great War* (New York: New York University Press, 1996), and Alan Dawley, *Struggles for Justice: Social Responsibility and the Liberal State* (Cambridge, Mass.: Harvard University Press, 1991), argue that the moral zeal employed by wartime federal reformers often created a backlash in communities intent on preserving local control and traditions. Hawley, *The Great War and the Search for a Modern Order*, exposes how the government drew on the war experience in the 1920s to foster a partnership with business. William E. Leuchtenburg, "The New Deal and the Analogue of War," in *Change and Continuity in Twentieth-Century America*, ed. John Braeman, Robert H. Bremner, and Everett Walters (Columbus: Ohio State University Press, 1965), pp. 81–143, notes how reformers in the 1930s modeled New Deal symbolism, rhetoric, and relief agencies on measures that had worked successfully in 1917–18. In a more theoretical work on state building, *Statemaking and*

Social Movements: Essays in History and Theory (Ann Arbor: University of Michigan Press, 1984), the editors, Charles Bright and Susan Harding, urge scholars to consider how the state reflects the character of the society it governs, yet at the same time remains distinct from it. This perspective applies particularly well to the military, which shared some civilian values without losing its institutional distinctiveness.

Works calling for a reevaluation of the role of the state by a historiography dominated by social history have also greatly influenced this study, among them *Bringing the State Back In,* ed. Peter B. Evans, Dietrich Rueschemeyer, and Theda Skocpol (New York: Cambridge University Press, 1985); *Reliving the Past: The Worlds of Social History,* ed. Olivier Zunz and David W. Cohen (Chapel Hill: University of North Carolina Press, 1985); and William E. Leuchtenburg, "The Pertinence of Political History: Reflections on the Significance of the State in American History," *Journal of American History* 73, no. 3 (December 1986): 585–600.

The power available to the enlisted man within the military altered significantly in the twentieth century in response to the demands of modern warfare. Morris Janowitz argued in his classic *The Professional Soldier: A Social and Political Portrait* (Glencoe, Ill.: Free Press, 1960) that the scale of modern warfare made it impossible for commanders to supervise troops in the field directly. Charles Moskos, however, disagreed in *The American Enlisted Man: The Rank and File in Today's Military* (New York: Russell Sage Foundation, 1970), claiming that the army's rigid and authoritarian traditions remained intact for those who served in combat. Leonard V. Smith, *Between Mutiny and Obedience: The Case of the French Fifth Infantry Division During World War I* (Princeton, N.J.: Princeton University Press, 1994), has recast combat and mutiny in the French Fifth Division as a negotiation between soldiers and officers over the degree of belligerence acceptable to those going over the top. Eric J. Leed, *No Man's Land: Combat and Identity in World War I* (New York: Cambridge University Press, 1979), and Tony Ashworth, *Trench Warfare, 1914–1918: The Live and Let Live System* (New York: Holmes & Meier, 1980) reveal that European soldiers established unofficial "live-and-let-live" truces along the Western Front to control the way they fought the war in quiet sectors.

Other important works that evaluate the tensions between citizen-soldiers and the state include Eliot A. Cohen, *Citizens and Soldiers: The Dilemmas of Military Service* (Ithaca, N.Y.: Cornell University Press, 1985); Cynthia Enloe, *Ethnic Soldiers: State Security in Divided Societies* (Athens: University of Georgia Press, 1980); Samuel P. Huntington, *The Soldier and the State: The Theory and Politics of Civil-Military Relations* (Cambridge, Mass.: Harvard University Press, 1957); Walter Millis, *Arms and Men: A Study in American Military History* (New York: G. P. Putnam, 1956); and David R. Segal, *Recruiting For Uncle Sam: Citizenship and Military Manpower Policy* (Lawrence: University Press of Kansas, 1989).

Detailed studies of soldiers' experiences in the Great War that proved par-
ticularly useful include Fred Baldwin, "The Enlisted Man During World War I"
(Ph.D. diss., Princeton University, 1964); Arthur Barbeau and Florette Henri, *The
Unknown Soldiers: Black American Troops in World War I* (Philadelphia: Temple
University Press, 1974); Hal S. Chase, "Struggle for Equality: Fort Des Moines
Training Camp for Colored Officers, 1917," *Phylon* 39, no. 4 (December 1978):
297–310; Russell Lawrence Barsh, "American Indians in the Great War," *Ethno-
history* 38, no. 3 (1991): 276–303; Thomas Anthony Britten, "American Indians in
World War I: Military Service as Catalyst for Reform" (Ph.D. diss., Texas Tech
University, 1994); Alfred Crosby, Jr., *Epidemic and Peace, 1918* (Westport, Conn.:
Greenwood Press, 1976); Nancy Gentile Ford, " 'Mindful of the Traditions of His
Race': Dual Identity and Foreign-Born Soldiers in the First World War Ameri-
can Army," *Journal of American Ethnic History* 16, no. 2 (1997): 35–57; Paul Fussell,
The Great War and Modern Memory (New York: Oxford University Press, 1975);
Jennifer D. Keene, "Intelligence and Morale in the Army of a Democracy: The
Genesis of Military Psychology During the First World War," *Military Psychology*
6, no. 4 (1994): 235–54; Daniel J. Kevles, "Testing the Army's Intelligence: Psy-
chologists and the Military in World War I," *Journal of American History* 55, no. 3
(December 1968): 565–81; Mark Meigs, *Optimism at Armageddon: Voices of Ameri-
can Participants in the First World War* (New York: New York University Press,
1997); John J. Pershing, *My Experiences in the World War* (New York: Frederick A.
Stokes, 1931); Bruce W. White, "The American Indian as a Soldier, 1890–1919,"
Canadian Review of American Studies 7 (1976): 15–25; and Charles Williams, *Sidelights on Negro Soldiers* (Boston: B. J. Brimmer, 1923).

I also relied heavily on these classic historical and sociological studies of con-
scription, army policymaking, military institutional life, problems of command,
and morale: Thomas M. Camfield, " 'Will to Win,'—The U.S. Army Troop
Morale Program of World War I," *Military Affairs* 41 (October 1977): 125–28;
John Carson, "Army Alpha, Army Brass, and the Search for Army Intelligence,"
Isis 84, no. 2 (1993): 278–309; John W. Chambers, *To Raise An Army: The Draft
Comes to Modern America* (New York: Free Press, 1987); Edward Coffman, *The
War to End All Wars: The American Military Experience in World War I* (New
York: Oxford University Press, 1968); Theodore J. Conway, "The Great Demobi-
lization: Personnel Demobilization of the AEF and the Emergency Army, 1918–
19: A Study in Civil-Military Relations" (Ph.D. diss., Duke University, 1986);
Alfred E. Cornebise, *The Stars and Stripes: Doughboy Journalism in World War I*
(Westport, Conn.: Greenwood Press, 1984); John Dickinson, *The Building of an
Army: A Detailed Account of Legislation, Administration and Opinion in the United
States, 1915–1920* (New York: Century, 1922); William T. Generous, Jr., *Swords
and Scales: The Development of the Uniform Code of Military Justice* (Port Washing-
ton, N.Y.: Kennikat Press, 1973); Eli Ginzberg, *The Ineffective Soldier: Lessons for
Management and the Nation*, 3 vols. (New York: Columbia University Press, 1959);

Kenneth E. Hamburger, *Learning Lessons in the American Expeditionary Forces* (Washington, D.C.: U.S. Army Center of Military History, 1997); Marvin A. Kreidburg and Merton G. Henry, *History of Military Mobilization in the U.S. Army, 1775–1945*, Dept. of the Army Pamphlet no. 20-212 (Washington, D.C.: Dept. of the Army, 1955); Thomas C. Leonard, *Above the Battle: War-Making in America from Appomattox to Versailles* (New York: Oxford University Press, 1978); Leonard Lerwill, *The Personnel Replacement System in the United States Army*, Dept. of the Army Pamphlet no. 20-211 (Washington, D.C.: Dept. of the Army, 1954); John M. Lindley, "A Soldier's Also a Citizen: The Controversy over Military Justice in the U.S. Army, 1917–1920" (Ph.D. diss., Duke University, 1974); *The Military in America: From the Colonial Era to the Present*, ed. Peter Karsten (New York: Free Press, 1980); Allan R. Millett, "Over Where? The AEF and the American Strategy for Victory, 1917–1918," in *Against All Enemies: Interpretations of American Military History from Colonial Times to the Present*, ed. Kenneth J. Hagen and William R. Roberts (Westport, Conn.: Greenwood Press, 1986), pp. 235–56; Bernard C. Nalty, *Strength for the Fight: A History of Black Americans in the Military* (New York: Free Press, 1986); Timothy K. Nenninger, "American Military Effectiveness in the First World War," in *Military Effectiveness*, vol. 1: *The First World War*, ed. Allan R. Millett and Williamson Murray (Boston: Allen & Unwin, 1988), pp. 116–56; Michael Sherry, *Preparing for the Next War: America Plans for Postwar Defense, 1941–45* (New Haven, Conn.: Yale University Press, 1977); Tamotsu Shibutani, *The Derelicts of Company K: A Sociological Study of Demoralization* (Berkeley: University of California Press, 1978); Samuel A. Stouffer et al., *The American Soldier*, vol. 1: *Adjustment During Army Life*, and vol. 2: *Combat and Its Aftermath*, Studies in Social Psychology in World War II (Princeton, N.J.: Princeton University Press, 1949; reprint, New York: John Wiley & Sons, 1965); David F. Trask, *The AEF and Coalition Warmaking, 1917–1918* (Lawrence: University Press of Kansas, 1993); Russell Weigley, *History of the United States Army* (New York: Macmillan, 1967), and *Towards an American Army: Military Thought from Washington to Marshall* (New York: Columbia University Press, 1962); Harold Wool, *The Military Specialist: Skilled Manpower for the Armed Forces* (Baltimore: Johns Hopkins Press, 1968); and Stephen D. Wesbrook, "Historical Notes," in *The Political Education of Soldiers*, ed. Morris Janowitz and Stephen Wesbrook (Beverly Hills, Calif.: Sage Publications, 1983), pp. 251–84.

Key political battles of the era were examined in John P. Finnegan, *Against the Specter of a Dragon: The Campaign for American Military Preparedness, 1914–1917* (Westport, Conn.: Greenwood Press, 1974); George Flynn, *The Mess in Washington: Manpower Mobilization in World War II* (Westport, Conn.: Greenwood Press, 1979); David S. Foglesong, *America's Secret War Against Bolshevism* (Chapel Hill: University of North Carolina Press, 1995); Theodore Kornweibel, Jr., *Seeing Red: The Federal Campaign Against Black Militancy, 1919–1925* (Bloomington: Indiana University Press, 1998); John W. Long, "American Intervention in Russia: The North Russian Expedition, 1918–19," *Diplomatic History* 6, no. 1 (Winter 1982): 45–67; Eugene P. Trani, "Woodrow Wilson and the Decision to Intervene in Russia: A Reconsideration," *Journal of Modern History* 48, no. 3 (September 1976): 440–61; Robert J. Maddox, *The Unknown War with Russia: Wilson's Siberian Intervention* (San Rafael, Calif.: Presidio Press, 1977); and Betty Miller Unterberger, *America's Siberian Expedition, 1918–1920: A Study of National Policy* (Durham, N.C.: Duke University Press, 1956).

The Americans' tumultuous relationship with the French is traced by André Kaspi, *Le temps des Américains: Le concours américain à la France en 1917–1919* (Paris: Université de Paris I, 1976); Jennifer D. Keene, "Uneasy Alliances: French Military Intelligence and the American Army During the First World War," *Intelligence and National Security* 13, no. 1 (Spring 1998): 18–36; and William R. Keylor, " 'How They Advertised France': The French Propaganda Campaign in the United States During the Breakup of the Franco-American Entente, 1918–1923," *Diplomatic History* 17 (Summer 1993): 351–73.

Most scholars examine the World War I soldier and veteran separately. Key works on World War I veterans include Michael J. Bennett, *When Dreams Came True: The GI Bill and the Making of Modern America* (Washington, D.C.: Brassey's, 1996); Irving Bernstein, "The Bonus Army," in *The Underside of American History*, vol. 2, ed. Thomas R. Frazier and John Morton Blum (New York: Harcourt Brace Jovanovich, 1974), pp. 197–212; Roger Daniels, *The Bonus March: An Episode of the Great Depression* (Westport, Conn.: Greenwood Press, 1971); Donald J. Lisio, *The President and Protest: Hoover, Conspiracy, and the Bonus Riot* (Columbia: University of Missouri Press, 1974); William Pencak, *For God and Country: The American Legion, 1919–1941* (Boston: Northeastern University Press, 1989); Davis Ross, *Preparing for Ulysses: Politics and Veterans During World War II* (New York: Columbia University Press, 1969); Theodore R. Mosch, *The GI Bill: A Breakthrough in Educational and Social Policy in the United States* (New York: Exposition Press, 1975); Thomas A. Rumer, *The American Legion: An Official History, 1919–1989* (New York: M. Evans, 1990); and Richard Severo and Lewis Milford, *The Wages of War: When American Soldiers Come Home—From Valley Forge to Vietnam* (New York: Simon & Schuster, 1989).

Traditionally, social scientists have minimized the importance of military service as a politicizing experience. Influential writings such as Samuel A. Stouffer et al., "The Soldier Becomes a Veteran," in *The American Soldier*, 2: 596–644; Robert Havighurst et al., *The American Veterans Back Home: A Study of Veterans' Readjustment* (New York: Longmans, Green, 1951); Dixon Wecter, *When Johnny Comes Marching Home* (Cambridge, Mass.: Houghton Mifflin, 1944); and David R. Segal and Madi Wechsler Segal, "The Impact of Military Service on Trust in Government, International Attitudes, and Social Status," in *The Social Psychology of Military Service*, ed. Nancy Goldman and David R. Segal (Beverly Hills, Calif.: Sage Publications, 1976), pp. 201–11, depict twentieth-century American soldiers as concerned primarily with personal issues, relatively close to their civilian peers in political sentiment, and uninterested in reforming American society or the world. Life-course researchers found more significant differences when they focused on how military service affected veterans' marriage stability, mental health, or occupational status. For these findings, see Glen H. Elder, Jr., and Eliza K. Pavalko, "World War II and Divorce: A Life Course Perspective," *American Journal of Sociology* 95 (March 1990): 1213–33; Paul A. Gade, "Military Service and the Life Course Perspective: A Turning Point for Military Personnel Research," *Military Psychology* 3, no. 4 (1991): 187–99; John Modell and Timothy Haggerty, "The Social Impact of War," *Annual Review of Sociology* (1991): 205–24; and John Modell, Marc Goulden, and Sigurdur Magnusson, "World War II in the Lives of Black Americans: Some Findings and an Interpretation," *Journal of American History* 76, no. 3 (December 1989): 838–48.

Other scholars have challenged the prevailing view that military service only affects veterans' personal lives. The Vietnam war, for example, clearly affected how many veterans manifested their political views in the 1970s, according to M. Kent Jennings and Gregory B. Markus in "Political Participation and Vietnam War Veterans: A Longitudinal Study," in *The Social Psychology of Military Service,* ed. Nancy Goldman and David R. Segal (Beverly Hills, Calif.: Sage Publications, 1976), pp. 175–200; Fred Milano, "The Politicization of the 'Deer Hunters': Power and Authority Perspectives of the Vietnam Veterans," in *Strangers at Home: Vietnam Veterans since the War,* ed. Charles R. Figley and Seymour Leventman (New York: Praeger, 1980), pp. 229–47; and Christopher G. Ellison, "Military Background, Racial Orientations, and Political Participation Among Black Adult Males," *Social Science Quarterly* 73, no. 2 (June 1992): 360–78. Wilbur J. Scott, *The Politics of Readjustment: Vietnam Veterans since the War* (Hawthorne, N.J.: Aldine de Gruyter, 1993), traces how Vietnam veterans obtained recognition of post-traumatic stress syndrome as a legitimate war-related illness and construction of the Vietnam Veterans' Memorial, which recognized their courage and sacrifice.

Besides building on studies that illustrate how soldiers influenced policy within the military, and how military service politicized citizen-soldiers, I have also drawn on the growing literature on veterans' entitlements and the early history of the American welfare state. It is not surprising, given the pervasiveness of contractual language in American public life, that each generation of citizens that performs wartime military service believes itself to have entered into a binding contract with the government. But the terms of the contracts vary. Stuart McConnell, *Glorious Contentment: The Grand Army of the Republic, 1865–1900* (Chapel Hill: University of North Carolina Press, 1992), illustrates that Union veterans believed they deserved pensions for having saved the nation, and Theda Skocpol, *Protecting Soldiers and Mothers: The Political Origins of Social Policy in the United States* (Cambridge, Mass.: Harvard University Press, 1992), traces how their recruitment into the Republican Party made them the most entitled group of their day. Skocpol's work is the fountainhead of recent scholarship on the early history of entitlements and the welfare state, but other important works on this topic include Laura S. Jensen, "The Early American Origins of Entitlements," *Studies in American Political Development* 10 (Fall 1996): 360–404, a fascinating account of how Revolutionary War veterans' service pensions made American democracy one in which the government developed special interest, rather than universal, relationships with its citizens, and the debate between Linda Gordon, "Gender, State and Society: A Debate with Theda Skocpol," and Theda Skocpol, "Soldiers, Workers, and Mothers: Gendered Identities in Early U.S. Social Policy," *Contention* 2, no. 3 (Spring 1993): 139–83, over which segments of society helped mold nonuniversal social welfare policies such as Civil War veteran pensions.

INDEX

Absent without leave. *See* AWOL

Adjusted compensation, veteran, 6–7, 170–79, 182–85, 190, 197, 208, 211, 214, 262–63n. 1; American Legion and, 170–78, 184–85, 202; details of, 176, 262n. 83. *See also* Bonds; Bonuses; Pensions

AEF (American Expeditionary Forces), 42–61, 105–50; and alcohol, 72–73; demobilization of (*see* Demobilization); discipline in, 62–69, 72–75; and French army contrasted, 110–11; French soldiers and, 106–10, 239n. 1; manpower problems of, 47, 225n. 43; as melting pot, 109; on-job training for, 44–50, 225–26n. 52; postwar, 117–50; racism (*see* Racism; Segregation); religious comfort for, 49; in Russia, 142–50. *See also* Pershing, John J.

Alcohol: army focus on, 72–73; CTCA vs., 24, 41, 75; deserter resort to, 68, 69; doughboy/German barter for, 114, 116; French-based noncombatants and, 53; and soldier crime, 72, 231n. 29; as training-camp peril, 24, 41, 75. *See also* Prohibition

Aliens. *See* Immigrants / Immigration

Alsace-Lorraine, 119, 123

American Commission to Negotiate Peace, 118, 124, 125, 134

American Expeditionary Forces. *See* AEF

American Federation of Labor (AFL), 16, 169–70, 176

American Legion / Legionnaires, 155–58; and AFL, 170, 176; and Americanism, 177; anticommunism of, 166; as anti-union, 169; army efforts to manipulate, 167; birth of, 126, 155; and blacks, 157, 177, 255nn. 109 & 110; and Bonus March, 186, 196; vs. Chamber of Commerce, 173–74, 261n. 72; deputization in Omaha, 166; FDR before, 200; and GI Bill, 208–10; Hoover and, 185, 196, 200; vs. IWW, 168–69; and jobs for veterans, 163; police alliances of, 167; regular army members of, 157, 255n. 112; as veteran lobby, 6–7, 170–71, 177, 179–80, 184–85, 196, 199, 200, 202, 209–10, 262–63n. 1, 264n. 18; WWI honored by, 263n. 16

Ansell, Samuel, 151–54, 253n. 86

Archangel, Russia, 142, 144, 145, 146

Armaments industry, U.S., 203
Armistice Day, 263n. 16
Army: British (*see* British Army); Canadian, 50, 144; Chinese, 144; French (*see* French Army); German (*see* German Army); Italian, 144; Japanese, 143; U.S. (*see* U.S. Army)
Army and Navy Union, 273n. 21
Army War College, 159–60, 256n. 124
Articles of War, overhaul of, 153–54
AWOL (absent without leave), 69–72, 134

Baker, Newton E., 10, 14, 16; Ansell and, 151; and black "problem," 23; and conscientious objectors, 29; as embarkation camp visitor, 141; empathy of, 29; and Paris prison abuses, 152; and peacetime army, 136, 159, 256n. 22; and Rowan affair, 86; and "Sam Browne's death," 137; and soldiers' execution, 65; and universal military training, 158; Wilson and, 250n. 43
Beatings, in AEF prison, 152–54
Benefits, veteran: FDR and, 199–203, 208, 269n. 110. *See also* Adjusted compensation; Bonuses; Disability benefits; Education; Health care; Hospitalization; Loans, housing; Pensions; Unemployment benefits
Bethel, W. A., 65–66, 80, 154–55
Black-advancement organizations, 84, 86, 91, 94, 129, 142, 163, 235n. 9, 238n. 65
Blacks: in army (*see* Soldiers, black); conscription of, 20, 23–24; government lobbied by, 23; and northward migration of U.S., 164
Bliss, Tasker H., 16–17, 22–23, 125, 147
Bonds, adjusted-compensation, 7, 174, 179, 180, 182, 184, 191, 203, 262n. 83
Bonuses, veteran, 171–74, 176, 190, 203, 213
Bonus March, x, 7, 178, 179–204, 209, 211, 214; army vs., 7, 193–97, 267n. 80;

end of, 191–96, 268n. 48; successors to 1932, 201; support for, 186, 188, 190; wives accompanying, 183. *See also* Camps, bonus marchers'
Boxing matches, 40–41, 187
Brest, France, 56, 125
British Army, 47, 50, 108, 144–45, 225n. 52
Brownsville, Texas, 91

Camp Funston, Kansas, 98, 237n. 46
Camp Marks, 188–92, 194–95
Camp Merritt, New Jersey, 70, 91, 94–98
Camps: bonus marchers', 187–96; CCC, 202, 271n. 133; training (*see* Training camps)
Camp Upton, New York, 70–71, 96–97
Censorship, 77, 78, 80, 133, 137, 145, 149, 234n. 59, 248n. 15
Centralia, Washington, 168–69
Chamber of Commerce, U.S., 173–74
Charleston, South Carolina, 91–93
Chevrons, 58–59, 229nn. 100 & 101
Chicago, 164
Children, aid to orphans, 200
Christine, Carl H., 148, 149, 252n. 62
Civilian Conservation Corps (CCC), 201–2
Civil War, ix–x, 2, 3, 5, 8, 10, 63–64, 99, 162, 163, 171, 233n. 53
Coast Guard, 215n. 2
Coblenz, Germany, 120
College: as conscription alternative, 217n. 18; for veterans (*see* GI Bill)
Colmery, Harry, 208, 209, 213
Commission on the Classification of Personnel, 25, 29
Commission on Training Camp Activities (CTCA), 24–25, 40–41, 75, 207, 220n. 49
Committee on Public Information, 75
Communists, 161–62, 187–89, 195, 201, 266n. 48
"Comrades in Service," 155, 156

Congress, U.S.: as army critic, 133, 140–42, 151–53; and GAR, 254n. 98; legion members in, 210; vs. Russian campaign, 147, 150; and training camps, 31; and veterans, 6, 7, 140–42, 174, 185, 188, 190, 191, 199–200, 203, 208–10, 254n. 98, 270n. 118; and war profiteering, 203
Conscientious objectors, 28, 29
Conscription, x, 1–5, 8–12; acceptance of, 14; of blacks, 20, 23–24; in Civil War, 2, 3, 10; deferment from, 18–19, 26, 215n. 1; end of, 6; evasion of, 8, 11 (*see also* College); Southern encouragement of black, 23–24. *See also* Draft boards; Draft riots; Universal military training
Coolidge, Calvin, 171, 177
Court(s)-martial: citizen-officers on, 74; criticism of, 131; for malingerers, 68; overseas, 66, 230n. 10; reform of, 151, 153, 154, 207; of Rowan, 85–86; WWII-era review of, 205
Crisis, The, 246n. 117
Czech Legion, 143–44, 148

Demobilization, 132–42, 160, 164, 205, 207, 258n. 19
Depression, Great, 179–204
Deserters/Desertion, 53, 66–72; army study of, 159, 216n. 8, 256n. 120; and AWOL contrasted, 70; CCC, 202; Civil War, 3, 63–64; education as factor, 28–29; at embarkation points, 70–72; punishment of, 12, 64–66, 68, 70, 71, 229n. 3; WWII, 205. *See also* AWOL; Malingerers
Disability benefits, 175, 181, 199, 200, 269n. 110
Disabled American Veterans (DAV), 209, 273n. 21
Discharges, military, 12, 142, 172
Disease, 54–55, 190, 227n. 82. *See also* Influenza; Venereal disease
Doctors: and Bonus March, 190; ex-amining recruits, 26–27; in France, 50–51, 55–56; in training camps, 54, 227n. 82
Doughboy (term), 3
Draft. *See* Conscription
Draft boards, 8–11, 17–19, 26, 132, 172
Draft riots, Civil War, 3, 10
Du Bois, W. E. B., 22, 128–30, 136, 142, 246n. 117

Economy Act (1933), 199, 201, 209
Education: army policy re, 20, 28–29, 218n. 33; as veteran benefit, 174, 205, 208–10, 212–14, 272n. 15, 273–74n. 39
Enlistees, army, 9, 12, 14–15, 20, 216nn. 1 & 2

Facts and Questions Concerning the N.R.E.F. (Christine), 148, 252n. 62
Farm / Farmers, 19, 172, 202–3, 210
Federal Housing Administration, 212
Fiske, H. B., 106, 109, 134, 138–39
Foch, Ferdinand, 120, 123, 226n. 63
Ford Motor Company, veterans at, 165
Fort Des Moines Colored Officers' Training Camp, 22, 23, 219n. 37
Fort Hunt, 201
Fosdick, Raymond, 24, 138–39, 207
France, 72–73, 107–9, 118–19, 122, 125–30. *See also* French, doughboy disdain for; French Army; Paris
Fraternization, AEF/German, 113–17, 120–21, 125, 242n. 50, 243n. 66, 245n. 88
French, doughboy disdain for, 108–9, 118–19, 121, 122, 124, 130, 240n. 22
French Army: AEF and, 106–11, 118, 240n. 20; AEF command evaluation of, 38, 110–11; American volunteers in, 15; apathy of, 108 (*see also* Warfare, "live-and-let-live"); doughboy influence on, 106–8; mutinies in, 106, 232n. 40, 239n. 1; in Russia, 144; U.S. black soldiers with, 23
Furlough days, unused, 214

GAR (Grand Army of the Republic), 154, 254n. 98, 255n. 109, 264n. 18
Gas, 67, 76, 193, 195
German Army, 47, 49–50, 111–17, 125, 134, 241n. 34
Germany, 119–25, 143, 243n. 61
GI Bill (1944), x, 7, 175, 176, 205–14; scope of, 212. *See also* Education; Loans, housing; Unemployment benefits
Glassford, Pelham D., 188, 191, 192, 196
Great Britain, 143. *See also* British Army
Grenades, German tricks with, 47

Haan, William, 137, 157, 167
Harbord, James, 51, 53, 57, 58, 138
Harding, Warren G., 171, 173, 177
Health care, government-funded, 177, 200, 211, 262n. 87. *See also* Hospitalization
Hines, Frank, 182, 184, 208, 262n. 87
Home Owners Loan Corporation, 211
Hoover, Herbert, 198, 199; and bonus issue, 185; and Bonus March, 186–92, 194–98, 266n. 48, 267n. 80, 268n. 93, 269n. 99; Depression policy of, 7, 179–80; and disability pensions, 269n. 110; at legion convention, 184–85; after stock-market crash, 179; and universal draft, 177
Hospitalization, as veteran benefit, 177, 199, 200–201, 213, 262n. 87, 274n. 4
Hospitals, VA, 201, 213
Housing, veteran. *See* Loans, housing
Houston, 23, 91, 236n. 27
Hurley, Patrick, 192, 194, 267n. 80

Illiteracy, as conscript problem, 28–29
Immigrants / Immigration, 19–21, 33, 112, 162
Indians, American. *See* Native Americans
Industrial Workers of the World (IWW), 168–69
Industry, draft exemptions for, 19

Influenza, 54–55, 132, 134–35, 227nn. 81 & 82
Insurance, serviceman life, 171
Intelligence, doughboy, 27–28

Japan, 143, 207
Jewish Welfare League, 25, 94
Johnson, Royal, 152, 253nn. 85 & 86
Johnstown, Pennsylvania, 195–96
Joslin, Theodore, 185, 189, 195

Khaki Shirts, 196
Knights of Columbus, 25, 94

League of Nations, 158
Literacy. *See* Illiteracy
Loans, housing, 205, 211, 212
Lorraine, France, 108, 240n. 22. *See also* Alsace-Lorraine
Loving, William H., 86, 87, 97, 103, 138
Lumber camps, Northwest, 52, 168
Lynching, of IWW member, 169

MacArthur, Douglas, 158–59, 191, 193–95, 241n. 38, 267n. 80
MacNider, Hanford, 177–78, 185–86, 196
Malingerers, 64–69, 206
March, Peyton, 158, 256n. 122
Marines, U.S., 215n. 2
Marne River, second battle of, 108
Medals, 57–58, 160, 228n. 96; French, 125
Medical care, for WWII veterans, 208, 213. *See also* Disability benefits; Health care; Hospitalization
Mellon, Andrew, 173, 174
Meuse-Argonne offensive, ix–x, 42, 44, 50–51, 66–67, 118, 152
Military justice, reform of, 272n. 10. *See also* Court(s)-martial
Military Order of the Purple Heart, 273n. 21
Military police, 66, 68, 72, 88–89, 92, 101, 152, 235n. 19
Morale Division, U.S. Army, 14, 76, 138,

206; dissolution of, 159. *See also* U.S. Army, creating morale in

Mothers, pensions for, 175, 176

Murder: of black veterans, 164; soldiers executed for, 65

Mustering-out pay, 208, 214

Mutiny, doughboy, 148–49. *See also* French Army, mutinies in

NAACP (National Association for the Advancement of Colored People), 142, 235n. 9

National Guard, 2, 9; army absorption of, 16, 215n. 1; black units of, 22, 23; bonus army assisted by, 186; GAR and, 154; political aspects of, 17; regionalism essential to, 30; regular army vs., 17, 35, 79, 153; reserve training pushed by, 158. *See also* Officers, National Guard

Native Americans, 21, 218–19n. 36

Navy, U.S., 215n. 2

Newspapers: bonus-marcher, 187, 190; training-camp, 28. *See also* Press

Noncombatants, 39; alienation of, 51–57, 60; blacks as, 23, 69, 83–84, 85, 87, 102; combat veteran contempt for, 55, 60; and demobilization, 133–34; dilemma of, 36, 51, 68; to front lines, 69; medals denied to, 57, 58; souvenir scrounging by, 59–60; training of, 39; as U.S. itinerant workers, 52; vagaries of French-based, 53

Obedience, 5, 13, 37, 62–81, 90

Officers, 16–17, 217n. 21; American Legion dominated by, 156; black, 5, 22, 89–90, 96, 160, 219n. 37, 235n. 14; criteria for, 16; and demobilization, 135–39; furlough pay for, 214; leniency of citizen, 74; morale, 139; National Guard, 16–17; as privileged class, 74, 131, 135–37, 207 (*see also* Sam Browne belt); racist, 82, 85–88, 128–29; reform-minded, 74–78, 81, 138–39; resentment

toward, 133, 159 (*see also* Saluting); veteran abuse of, 135; workmen as, 16–17

Omaha, 166

Pacifism, 75, 76, 232n. 40

Palmer, A. Mitchell, 161–62

Paris, 134, 152–53

Pensions, veteran, 162, 171, 199, 257n. 6, 269n. 110; Civil War, 175, 176, 199, 264n. 18; Revolutionary War, 175, 176; Supreme Court on, 257n. 6. *See also* Mothers

Pershing, John J., 14, 109; AEF exalted by, 112; and AEF/French animosity, 124; on alcohol, 72; Allied criticism of, 226n. 63; discipline as paramount to, 63–65, 79; as final authority, 36; and fraternization, 115, 245n. 88; French influence resisted by, 110; at Lafayette's tomb, 108; on malingerers, 65, 138; noncombatants recognized by, 57; and peacetime promotions, 136; and recruit training, 37, 38; as reformist, 138–39; and (Theodore) Roosevelt, Jr., 155; on Russian situation, 147; and soldier suffrage, 80; and *Stars and Stripes*, 77; strategies of, 38, 42–44, 52, 106, 225n. 43; and universal military training, 158, vs. venereal disease, 25, 70; and veterans, 155–56; victorious doughboys stroked by, 133; Wilson and, 65, 124

Pétain, Henri Philippe, 109–10, 232n. 40

Pioneer infantry units, 24, 219–20n. 48

"Polar Bear" Association, 150

Press: black, 86, 237n. 46 (*see also* Black-advancement organizations); and Bonus March, 192, 194–96; vs. Camp Funston decision, 237n. 46; dough-boy complaints in, 140 (see also *Stars and Stripes*); legion use of, 209; Russian campaign lambasted in, 150; vs. training camp discrimination, 86

Prisoners of war, 20, 78, 109, 113

Prisons, abuses in military, 152–54
Private Soldiers and Sailors' Legion,
169, 171–72
Profiteering, 5, 59, 162–63, 165, 173, 174,
203, 262n. 1
Progressives, 21, 24–25, 75, 220n. 49
Prohibition, 166, 231n. 29, 259n. 28
Prostitution, 24–25, 75, 102, 129
Psychology, army and, 27–28

Quarantines, training camp, 100,
227n. 82

Race riots, 90–91, 94–98, 102, 127, 164,
166, 236n. 27
Racism, in army, 5, 32–33, 82–104, 126–
30, 160, 206–7. See also Segregation;
Soldiers, black
Rape, 65, 101, 127, 238nn. 64 & 65
Reconstruction Finance Corporation
(RFC), 179, 197, 198
Recruit Educational Centers, 218n. 33
Red Scare, U.S., 161–62, 165, 166
Regular Veterans Association, 273n. 21
Reparations, German, 195
Republican Service League (RSL),
177–78, 185, 264n. 29
Rhineland, 120–21, 125, 130
Rhine River, demilitarization of, 120
Roosevelt, Franklin D. (FDR), 7, 197–
203, 207–8, 209, 211, 233n. 53, 269n.
110
Roosevelt, Theodore, 4
Roosevelt, Theodore, Jr., 126, 139, 155,
162, 185, 255n. 112, 257n. 8
Rowan, C., 85–86
Russia, 6, 142–50, 165, 250n. 43. See also
Archangel; White Russians
Russian Revolution, 142
Russo-Japanese War, 143

Saint-Mihiel offensive, 44, 54, 118
Saluting: aversion to, 68, 73–74,
248n. 12; of black officers, 88

Sam Browne belt, mystique of, 136–37
Scott, Emmett J., 86–87, 142, 237n. 46
Segregation, racial: in American
Legion, 157; army commitment to, 5,
21–24, 81–102, 160, 187, 219nn. 37 &
44; black soldiers vs., 219n. 39; among
bonus marchers, 187–88; end of mili-
tary, 91, 206–7, 272n. 6; in France,
127; as law, 21
Selective Service Act, on alcohol, 72
Selective Service System, 215–16n. 1
Service of Supply (SOS), 52–53, 56, 58,
227n. 69
Servicemen's Readjustment Act. See GI
Bill
Sex education, training camp, 25, 75
Shell shock, 50–51, 206, 229n. 101
Siberia, AEF in, 143–44
Slowdowns, noncombatant work, 134
Socialism, in postwar Germany, 123
Social Security Act (1935), 211
Soldiers, black, 21–24, 54, 56–57, 82–104,
126–30; as cooks, 83–84; demobilization of, 142; in England, 102; fighting
record of, 22, 99, 160; in France,
85, 89–90, 102–3, 119, 126–30; and
Frenchwomen, 102–3; and German
propaganda focusing, 99–100; morale
of, 40, 56, 87, 102, 223n. 14, 235n.
9; persecution resisted by, 89, 235–
36n. 19 (see also Race riots); regional
differences among, 32; segregation of
(see Segregation); as sentries, 87–88;
and southern white soldiers, 32, 94–
97; training of (see Training camps);
and venereal disease, 53, 90; white
civilian fear of, 22–23, 219n. 39; with
white riflemen, 206; white violence
against, 88–89, 92–97 (see also Race
riots); in WWII, 205–7. See also
National Guard; Noncombatants;
Officers; Training camps; Veterans
Soldiers' homes (institutions), 199
Souvenirs, battle, 59–60, 113, 139

Stars and Stripes, 77–78, 135, 137, 156, 201

Stock market, crash of (1929), 179, 186

Strike (breaker)s, 52, 140, 161, 164, 168, 169, 197, 212

Submarines, German, 105

Suffrage, soldier, 79–81, 165–66, 205, 233n. 53, 234nn. 56 & 57, 59, 259n. 28. *See also* Women's suffrage

Tanks, U.S., 42

Terrorism, in postwar America, 161

Torture, AEF prison guard use of, 152

Training camps, 5, 9, 12–14, 31–33; blacks in, 22–23, 32–33, 40, 56–57, 100–102, bootlegging near, 72; boxing matches in, 41–42; congressional focus on, 31; deserters from, 12, 64, 69–70, 229n. 3; disease in, 227n. 82; dismantling of, 132, 133; drilling emphasized in, 37–38, 40; in France, 222n. 8; hazing in, 40; horrors of, 40; integrated recreational facilities of, 94; intelligence monitoring of, 14 (*see also* Morale Division, U.S. Army); marksmanship emphasized in, 37, 38; officer, 16, 22, 31, 88, 235n. 14; racial tensions in, 32–33; regimen of, 36–42, 44, 222n. 8, 224n. 32; and regionalism, 30–32, 85; skills assessment in, 29–30; transient nature of, 37; as traumatic, 13. *See also* Commission on Training Camp Activities

Trans-Siberian Railway, 143, 144

Truman, Harry, 91, 207

Unemployment, veterans and, 170, 172, 181, 197, 198, 203–4

Unemployment benefits, veteran, 205, 208, 210–12, 214

Uniform, doughboy pride in, 91–92

Unions, labor, 168–70

U.S. Army: abroad (*see* AEF); Americanization programs of, 20–21, 256 n. 122; blacks in (*see* Soldiers, black);

and Bonus March (*see* Bonus March); bureaucratic invasion of, 30–31; and conscripts, 8–15, 215n. 1; criminals in, 12 (*see also* Deserters / Desertion); creating morale in, 75–79, 81, 139, 159, 256n. 124 (*see also* Soldiers, black); desegregation of, 91, 206; domestic political objectives of, 6, 17, 79, 133, 134, 154–55, 158; earnings patterns in, 73, 231–32n. 33 (*see also* Mustering-out pay); ethnic barriers in, 33–34; foreign-born element of, 19–21, 218n. 33; German Americans in, 33–34, 108, 121; and labor unrest, 159; legacy of war for, 132–60; "limited service" units of, 27; and modern management theory, 5–6, 14, 31; racism in (*see* Race riots; Racism; Segregation); recruitment standards of, 25–29; postwar reforms within, 151–54, 158–60, 256nn. 122 & 123; skills makeup of, 29–30, 223n. 12. *See also* AEF; Baker, Newton E.; Bliss, Tasker H.; Conscription; Demobilization; Enlistees; MacArthur, Douglas; Military justice; Military police; National Guard; Noncombatants; Officers; Pershing, John J.; Pioneer infantry units; Soldiers, black; Training camps; Veterans

Universal military training, 10, 16–17, 112, 155, 157, 158

Upton, Emory, 17, 158, 241n. 35

Venereal disease, 25, 53, 70, 90

Versailles, Treaty of, 125

Veterans, 4; adjustment of, 160–78; agendas of, 5–7; army courting of, 133, 154–56, 158, 254n. 99; black, 157, 173, 177, 187–88; as civil servants, 177, 262n. 86; Depression woes of, 180–204; emotionally wounded, 182, 183, 208–9 (*see also* Shell shock); female, 212; 1929 Russian mission of, 150–51;

Veterans (*continued*)
Pershing bow to, 139; as policemen, 165; unemployment among, 163–64, 181, 203–4. *See also* American Legion / Legionnaires; Benefits; Bonus March
Veterans Adjustment Pay Act (1944), 273n. 21
Veterans Administration, 199, 201, 210–11
Veterans' Bureau, 262n. 87
Veterans of Foreign Wars (VFW), 196, 209, 273n. 21
Veterans' organizations, 154–58, 167–72, 177. *See also* American Legion / Legionnaires; "Comrades in Service"; GAR; Veterans of Foreign Wars
Vietnam War, 213, 274n. 46

War Camp Community Service, 25
Wards, interracial hospital, 90
Warfare: combat experiences in France, 42–55, 107, 108, 111, 113; in Russia, 144–45; "live-and-let-live," 46–47, 94, 108, 113–17, 224n. 36 (*see also* Fraternization); psychological costs of, 50, 226n. 57
War Plans Division, 12, 216n. 4
War Plan White, 167
War Policies Commission, 177
Washington, D.C., 186–87. *See also* Bonus March; Congress, U.S.; *and under individual presidents*
White, George A., 155, 254n. 103
White Russians, 144
Widows, aid to war, 200
Wilhelm II, kaiser, 123
Wilson, Woodrow: as conscription author, 4, 8; and peace negotiations, 105, 132, 137, 147; and Pershing, 65, 124; Russian policy of, 142–47, 250n. 43; soldier-convicts pardoned by, 65; vs. training camp temptations, 24; on U.S. entry into war, 3–4, 105; and veteran compensation, 162, 171, 177
Winchester, England, 102
Women's suffrage, 142, 163
Workers' Ex-Servicemen's League, 189